The BALKAN
COOKBOOK

THE BALKAN COOKBOOK

Published by
JUGOSLOVENSKA KNJIGA
Belgrade, Yugoslavia

Prepared by
Mladinska knjiga, TOZD Koprodukcija
Ljubljana

Editors
Snežana Pejaković and
Jelka Venišnik-Eror

Texts by
Jelena Katičić,
Suzana Djurić and
Slobodan Jović

Translated into English by
Zorka Mitrović

Art Editor and Covers by
Tomislav Bogdanović

Illustration on and paper
Dragica Gajić

Graphic design
Gradimir Avramov

Photographs in colour
Zoran Dimić

Illustrations and photo design
Mario Ivanišević

Printed by
Mladinska knjiga, TOZD Tiskarna,
Ljubljana 1987

Printed in Yugoslavia

First run
10.000 copies

YU ISBN 86-7411-002-9

YUGOSLAVIA · RUMANIA · BULGARIA · ALBANIA · GREECE · TURKEY

Contents

BON APPETITE!

Diet is the oldest of human "habits". This fact may offer an answer to the question why people have paid more attention to other phenomena of their existence in the long history of mankind and less to food and diet. Nevertheless, in spite of being more concerned with other activities and vital problems of existence, people have from time immemorial created imaginative and most enjoyable varieties of food and drinks, most often spontaneously, inspired by the happy events in life, by customs, tradition or ritual motives.

Consequently, from everyday occasions to the most festive ones the appearance and contents of the dining table have been the precious crown, the inevitable spice of all human joys and sorrows. For the first time a unique book is being presented to the readers — the book about culinary attractions of the Balkan cuisine (from Yugoslavia, Roumania, Bulgaria, Albania, Greece and Turkey). It may easily be the case that the first recipes in Europe had originated in these parts, as here was the locality of the oldest, Greek, civilization and because there are indications that even in the 2nd millennium BC there existed some books on culinary skills in ancient Greece. It would, of course, be going too far to claim that some of the dishes presented here date back to the glorious times of ancient Trojan heroes...

The Balkan peninsula, as a unique geographical and natural region, offers to its inhabitants plenty of sun and a great variety of inland, freshwater and sea fruits. It may be the reason why in its long history many invaders crossed its paths and stayed here for shorter of longer periods of time, bringing along with them their customs and their eating habits. Aromas of the dishes both from the East and the West have been mingling here.

Oriental influence has been very pronounced in the course of the last few centuries, and yet tradition and specific living conditions have helped preserve national characteristics of individual styles of cooking, depending on religious customs, natural conditions and habits of certain regions, nations and states.

The Balkan dishes are therefore greatly similar and at the same time greatly different. Each nation kept to its own customs, traditions and local traits, as well as to its own dishes or ways of preparing them. Just as each member of a family has a favourite dish, each nation has a choice of favourite dishes, which are most frequently offered to the guests.

A specific feature of the Balkan cuisine is the use of a great many spices, mostly stronger ones. Onion and garlic, tomato, parsley, dill and particularly small hot pepper are to be found as inevitable folklore touches in each of these cuisines. In some parts sweet tastes are predominant, in some salty or strong (hot) ones, so that the dishes differ from one stove to another, from one frying pan to another, from one habit to another...

No matter how fancifully arranged, no table can be imagined without a careful choice of good aperitives and wines. And that is something the Balkans do not lack, not only beacuse of the long tradition (vine was grown in ancient Greece 3000 years ago), but because today this region is the greatest exporter of high quality wines in the world. For this reason the book contains a separate chapter on wines and strong drinks.

This book offers a choice of the best dishes of the Balkan countries and nations, in other words of all those dishes which have a "national identity" and are known and appreciated as Balkan specialties. Because of their originality and variety we trust they will satisfy most different tastes,

desires and needs, from everyday ones to those which special or festive occasions call for.
To promote easier usage of the book, it has been divided into chapters according to the type and purpose of the dish, each recipe stating what country it comes from. This arrangement makes it possible to combine complete menus (from hors d'oeuvre to sweets), either according to the country they come from, or to individual taste. The recipe always states how many persons it is intended for and if there is no such specification, it means that it is to serve four persons.

The disches, the pictures of which are presented in colour for the first time, have been prepared, according to the original recipes from this book, by the master of culinary skills Dušan Štulić, in the renowned Bohemian quarter "Skadarlija" in Belgrade, in the resturant "Dva bela goluba" (The Two White Doves).
In addition to the index according to the country of origin, and within this classification to the type and purpose of the dish, the book contains an index of terms which frequently occur in certain recipes, so that the reader may study these explanations beforehand and act accordingly.

To conclude, instead of describing the dishes any further, we suggest that you take up an apron and start preparing and tasting some of the Balkan specialties.

We hope you will enjoy them and bon appetite!

RADOJKO MRLJEŠ, dipl. ing.

1

APPETISERS

An appetiser, or hors d'oeuvre, is an "overture" to the main course. Gourmets are aware of this and for that reason pay much attention to appetisers, as their aim is to stimulate the appetite. They are mostly piquant dishes attractive to look at, which means that they require special efforts in garnishing and serving. Some appetisers are quite light, while others are filling and aromatic, that is why it has been noted in the recipes that they can also be served as the main course.
Appetisers of the Balkan cuisine are most varied, starting from cornbread and a variety of pies and "bureks" to delicious egg, ham or spinach rolls, or marinaded fish and shellfish. Not to mention a great many characteristic Balkan grilled specialties (presented in a separate chapter among meat dishes), most of which can also be served as appetisers.
A typical Balkan specialty, for which there are no recipes, is the so-called "meze", which in Persian means approximately "snack". It is, and at the same time is not an hors d'oeuvre in the true sense of the word, because it is served before the meal, but usually not at the table, but in the room where the quests are received on arrival. "Meze" is served mostly to have something to drink with and generally contains various kinds of salt smoked meat, smoked sausages, different kinds of cheese, hard boiled eggs, salt fish, tomato, paprikas, small hot peppers, spring onions and garlic, olives etc.
Instead of fresh vegetables, the ones from "turshiya", in other words home-made pickles, can also be served.
All these delicacies are cut into morsels and arranged on trays and are most often served with toothpicks. As a rule national aperitives are served with them.

HINTS TO HELP YOU

WEIGHT VERSUS VOLUME

Flour (more coarsely ground)

1 level teaspoon	3 grams
1 teaspoonful	8 grams
1 level tablespoon	8 grams
1 tablespoonful	25 grams
2,5 dcl pitcher	130—150 grams

Flour (finely ground)

1 level teaspoon	3 grams
1 teaspoonful	7 grams
1 level tablespoon	12 grams
1 tablespoonful	20 grams
2,5 dcl pitcher	160—180 grams

Semolina

1 level teaspoon	3 grams
1 teaspoonful	7 grams
1 level tablespoon	10 grams
1 tablespoonful	20 grams
2,5 dcl pitcher	170 grams

Rice

1 tablespoonful	30 grams

Edible starch

1 level teaspoon	3 grams
1 teaspoonful	10 grams
1 level tablespoon	12 grams
1 tablespoonful	25 grams

Sugar

1 level teaspoon	4 grams
1 teaspoonful	10 grams
1 level tablespoon	12,5 grams
1 tablespoonful	25 grams

Powdered sugar

1 level teaspoon	3 grams
1 teaspoonful	8 grams
1 level tablespoon	12,5 grams
1 tablespoonful	25 grams

Poppy seed

1 level tablespoon	17 grams
2,5 dcl pitcher	250 grams

Lard or butter

1 level tablespoon (solid)	14 grams

Lard or butter

1 level tablespoon (liquid)	12 grams

Vegetable fat

1 level tablespoon	20 grams
1 level tablespoon (melted)	14 grams

Milk or water

1 tablespoon	17 grams
1 wine glass	100 grams
1 water glass	200 grams
1 cup	250 grams
2,5 dcl pitcher	250 grams
1 soup plate	350 grams

Roumania

CHEESE AND SOUR CREAM CAKES

(for 4—6 persons)

500 gr the so-called German cheese (unripened, unsalted cheese in crumbs)
100 gr butter or margarine
4 egg yolks
1 egg
200 gr sour cream (1 carton)
150 gr flour
salt
some sugar
200—300 gr sour cream to serve with the cakes
butter or oil for frying

Pass cheese through a sieve or crush well. Beat butter well, add egg yolks, cheese, sour cream, the egg and flour. Mix well. Form smaller, flat cakes with some flour, fry in heated butter or oil until nicely brown.

Serve warm with sour cream.

Yugoslavia

CORNBREAD WITH CHEESE AND KAYMAK

450 gr maize flour
50 gr wheat semolina
300 gr cheese
100 gr kaymak or 1 carton (2 dl) sour cream
3—4 eggs
1 dl oil
2 dl mineral water
lard or oil for greasing

Mix maize flour and semolina. Crush cheese well, add kaymak, or sour cream, egg yolks, oil and mineral water. Mix all well, then add mixed corn flour and semolina. Whisk egg whites stiffly and blend them in carefully. Grease baking pan well with oil, pour the mixture into it. Bake in the oven preheated to 175°C about 50 minutes.

Cool cornbread a little, then cut into squares. Serve with sheep or cow cheese, cheese spread or with drinking or thick yoghurt.

Albania

CORNBREAD WITH GREEN VEGETABLES

(for 8—10 persons)

750—1000 gr maize flour
3/4 l milk
some lukewarm water
salt

For filling:
1 kg sorrel or spinach
500 gr ripened cheese
150 gr kaymak
3 eggs
oil for greasing the tepsiya or baking pan
salt
1 l sheep thick yoghurt to pour over

Put maize flour into a deeper dish, pour over hot milk and water and leave to stand about 30 minutes.

In the meantime prepare the filling: clean sorrel or spinach (remove thicker leaf ribs), wash, drain and cut into thicker strips, add salt and leave for a while to get soft. Crush cheese a little, add to it kaymak, egg yolks and soft spinach or sorrel, mix all well. Whisk egg whites stiffly and add carefully into the cheese and vegetable mixture.

Grease a tepsiya or a baking pan well with oil, pour into it half of the maize flour, turn the mixture over it and then the rest of the mixed maize flour. Level with a wet tablespoon. Bake in the oven preheated to 200 °C. When it is done cut into smaller squares, pour thick yoghurt over it and leave in the pan until the yoghurt is absorbed.

Serve with thick yoghurt and with pickled paprikas or unripe tomatoes from turshiya.

Yugoslavia

CORNBREAD FROM UŽICE

(for 8—10 persons)

1,5 kg maize flour
500 gr ripened Serbian cheese
250 gr kaymak
500 gr cracklings
4—6 eggs
salt
lard for greasing and pouring over
warm water as needed

Sift maize flour and add to it crushed cheese, kaymak, ground cracklings, beaten eggs and salt. Pour in water bit by bit until the batter is soft (slightly watery). Grease the baking pan well, turn the prepared mixture into it, level. Cut into squares right away and pour heated lard over it. Preheat oven to 200 °C, bake about 45 minutes, until nicely brown. Serve warm with sauerkraut salad or pickled paprikas from turshiya.

Albania

"FILIYAS"

(for 6 persons)

2 eggs
500 gr fine wheat flour
2 dl milk
1 dl water
salt
300 gr kaymak or butter

Heat the tepsiya and in the meantime prepare the dough for filiyas: beat eggs well, adding in turn flour, milk and water, add salt in the end. The dough

should be smooth and slightly thicker than the pancake mixture. When the pan is heated, grease it with kaymak or butter, pour in a thinner layer of dough, bake in the oven preheated to 200°C. When the layer is done, brush with kaymak or butter, again pour in a layer of dough and bake again. Repeat until all the dough is used. When done, cover the filiyas with a clean cloth and leave to cool.

"Filiyas" are always served with thick yoghurt or pickled paprikas from turshiya.

In the traditional Albanian cuisine the filiyas are baked under the iron pan placed in the fire cinders.

Yugoslavia

HOME MADE BREAD — "POGATCHA" WITH EGGS

750 gr — 1 kg flour
salt
2 tablespoons lukewarm milk or water
20 gr fresh yeast
1 teaspoon sugar
1/2 dl oil
lukewarm water as needed
2—3 eggs
salt
lard or oil for greasing
flour for dusting

Sift flour. Crumble yeast, add some sugar, some flour and lukewarm milk or water, mix well until smooth and leave to stand in a warm place to rise.

Make a well in the centre of flour, add oil, egg yolks and one whole egg, salt and creamed yeast. Pour in some lukewarm water and mix all. Knead into a smooth dough until bubbles appear on it. Dust the dough with some flour and leave it to stand in a warm place for about 45 minutes. Grease a tepsiya with oil or lard. Toss the risen dough on to a board dredged with flour, knead it shortly, put into the tepsiya and spread to the size and shape of the tepsiya, cover and leave to stand like that for about 10—15 minutes. Before baking, prick with a fork in several places. Bake in the oven preheated to 200°C for about 30—35 minutes. When the crust is brown, it can be covered with clean paper or tin foil. When done, sprinkle the pogatcha with some water and wrap it up with a clean cloth.

Serve warm, preferably with kaymak, some cheese spread or the like, as an appetiser.

Plain pogatcha is part of everyday diet of village population in Serbia, Kosovo, Macedonia and Bosnia and is used instead of bread. This pogatcha with eggs is prepared on more festive occasions.

Yugoslavia

"OCVIROVKA"

(for 8—10 persons)

For dough:
1 kg flour
50 gr yeast (1 small packet)
1/2 l milk
2 eggs
3 tablespoons oil
salt

For filling:
50 gr lard or oil
4 eggs
500 gr cracklings
1—2 dl sour cream
1 bunch of parsley
2 cloves
1 egg yolk

Sift flour. Crush yeast, add some lukewarm milk and some flour, leave in a warm place to rise. Make a well in the center of the flour, pour in oil, eggs and salt, yeast and lukewarm milk. Work into a smooth batter and leave in a warm place about 40 minutes, i.e. until it rises.

For the filling beat lard well, add egg yolks, sour cream, minced cracklings, chopped parsley and crushed cloves. Whisk egg whites stiffly and mix them in carefully.

Roll out the risen dough until about 1 cm thick, brush it with some oil or lard, put the filling over it evenly and roll together. Place into a greased baking pan, and leave in a warm place to rise. Before baking, brush with beaten egg yolk. Bake about 30—40 minutes in the oven preheated to 200°C.

When done leave to cool and then cut into rounds.

In Slovenia "ocvirovka" is usually prepared in winter, at the time when pigs are slaughtered and fat rendered, so that there are a lot of cracklings.

Bulgaria

FESTIVE POLENTA

(for 6 persons)

For polenta:
500 gr maize flour
3/4 l water
100 gr margarine (butter)
salt

For filling:
250 gr young beef or lamb liver
250 gr fresh mushrooms (button mushrooms or similar)
1 onion
1/2 glass white wine
salt
pepper
80 gr butter or margarine
50 gr grated kachkaval or similar cheese
1 egg
150 gr smoked ham in thin slices

Heat water and add salt. When it boils pour flour in slowly, stirring all the time to get a smooth batter. Continue cooking at medium heat for 45 minutes. Towards the end add margarine or butter. When polenta is cooked turn it into a deep dish (pot) well greased with margarine, level and leave to cool.

For the stuffing cut liver into strips and roll in flour. Trim mushrooms, wash and slice. Chop onion finely. Heat butter or margarine, add onion, cook slowly to get soft, add liver and cook together until slightly tender, pour in wine, stir, add mushrooms, continue to cook slowly until all is tender. Add salt and pepper. When polenta is quite cold turn it out of the pot, make a circle in the middle with a knife, making sure that the bottom remains intact. Cut the cut-out part carefully into thin slices and take out. The mould obtained this way should have walls about 2 cm thick. Grease well the pot in which the polenta cooled with butter, line with slices of ham dipped into beaten egg and then return the "mould" of polenta into the pot. Turn in a layer of filling at the bottom of polenta, then a layer of sliced polenta, pouring over it melted butter every time and sprinkling it with grated cheese, then repeat. Finish with slices of polenta crumpling slices of ham over them. Put the polenta prepared this way into the oven preheated to 200 °C and bake about 40—45 minutes. When done, turn it carefully on to a bigger plate and cut into slices. Serve warm with grated cheese (kachkaval, Permesan or the like).

Albania

MEAT PIE — "BUREK" WITH MEAT

(for 8—10 persons)

1 bigger onion
40 gr oil
400—500 gr ground young beef
salt
pepper
500 gr layers of dough for the pie (to be bought in shops or at markets)
1 dl oil to sprinkle the dough and to pour over the pie
2—3 eggs
1 glass of drinking yoghurt
1,5 dl mineral water

Cook finely chopped onion slowly in heated oil until slightly tender, then cool. When cooled, add meat, salt and pepper. Mix all well.

Grease a baking pan or tepsiya. Place 2—3 layers of dough, sprinkle with some oil, then put a layer of meat over, repeat until all the dough and meat are used. Finish with 2—3 layers of dough and srinkle with oil. Cut into squares and pour over with the following:

Beat eggs well with yoghurt, add mineral water and the rest of oil, mix all well.

Leave "burek" to stand about 15 minutes. Bake for about 40 minutes in the oven preheated to 200 °C.

Serve warm.

Greece

GREEK MEAT PIE — "BUREK" WITH MEAT

(for 8—10 persons)

40 gr butter
2 smaller onions
450 gr ground mutton or young beef
1 dl white wine
1 riper tomato
salt
pepper
50 gr grated kachkaval (or Parmesan)
1 egg
2 hard boiled eggs
1/2 bunch of parsley
3 tablespoons breadcrumbs
450—500 gr thin layers of dough for the pie
2 dl melted butter

Cook slowly finely chopped onion in heated butter until soft and beginning to colour, add ground meat, stir while cooking, pour in wine, peeled and chopped tomato, salt and pepper. Cover and cook about 30 minutes. When meat is tender, set aside, add grated cheese, beaten egg, chopped parsley, 2 snipped hard boiled eggs and breadcrumbs. Mix all well and add more salt and pepper if needed.

Thin layers of dough should be cut into strips about 15 × 30 cm big. Brush each strip with melted butter. Put one tablespoon of meat filling on the narrow end of the dough so that at least 2 cm at

each side should be without filling. Fold the sides of the dough into the center and roll up. Grease the baking pan with butter, then place the rolls on it so that the end of the dough is turned downwards. Repeat until all the dough strips and filling are used. Sprinkle little "bureks" with melted butter, bake for about 20—30 minutes in the oven preheated to 175 °C. Serve warm. Wine, tomato and breadcrumbs can be replaced by one cupful of thick béchamel sauce.

Turkey

"TCHIL BUREK"

(for 8—10 persons)

For dough:
500 gr flour
2 eggs
2 tablespoons thick yoghurt
or 500—700 gr ready-made thin layers of dough for the pie
1/2 l bone stock or soup from cube
1 onion
40 gr oil
500 gr ground mutton
salt
red paprika pepper
100 gr margarine or butter or 1 dl oil to sprinkle dough
1/2 l thick yoghurt
1—2 cloves of garlic

Prepare bone stock or soup from cube.

Prepare layers of dough from flour and other ingredients or separate ready-made thin layers of dough for the pie and dry a little.

Cook slowly finely chopped onion in heated oil until slightly tender, then add ground meat and cook until it is tender and the juice evaporates. Add salt, red paprika pepper and mix.

Grease the baking pan, a deeper one, with heated oil. Place 1—2 dough layers at the bottom, sprinkle with oil, pour over some soup. Continue with the dough layers, abundantly sprinkling them with oil and soup, until all are used.

Beat thick yoghurt, add finely chopped or crushed garlic and pour half of it over the arranged dough layers. Turn the meat mixture over and pour in the rest of the yoghurt.

Bake in the oven preheated to 200 °C about 40—60 minutes. When done, cool and cut into squares.

This "burek" can be served as the main dish with a thick vegetable soup and mixed salad.

Bulgaria

BEANS PURÉE — "PAPULA"

(for 7—8 persons)

500 gr white beans
2—3 cloves of garlic
1—2 dl oil
salt
pepper
red paprika pepper to taste
bunch of parsley

Pick over beans, wash and leave in cold water to stand overnight. Then cook in the same water, and add salt when half cooked. Drain cooked beans and pass through a sieve or a meat grinder. Heat oil a little, add snipped garlic and red paprika pepper. Fry shortly together, stir into the puréed beans and mix well. Form a cone of beans on the serving plate, sprinkle it with red paprika pepper and garnish with parsley leaves.

This dish is served as an accompaniment to fried fish. Pickled paprikas, sauerkraut and pickled unripe tomatoes are also served with it, as well as hot cornbread instead of bread.

Yugoslavia

CHICKEN PIE FROM SARAJEVO — "BUREK"

1 smaller chicken or hen
salt
pepper
150 gr flour
1 egg
1 dl milk
40 gr butterfat (oil or margarine)
300 — 350 gr dough layers for the pie
butterfat or oil for greasing and sprinkling
1/2 l thick yoghurt or sour cream

Wash chicken or hen well, put up to cook in warm water, bring to the boil, salt and simmer.

Sift flour, mix well egg and milk, pour the mixture over flour and knead well with fingers to get small crumbs, the so-called "tirit". Fry tirit quickly in heated butter or oil.

Remove cooked chicken meat from bones, mince it and add salt and pepper as needed.

Grease a tepsiya with oil or butterfat, place a dough layer in it and sprinkle it with oil or melted butterfat. Place a few more dough layers over in the same manner and cover the last with half of the tirit and chicken meat. Then place some more dough layers over, sprinkling them with fat every time, add the rest of tirit and meat, pour over with butterfat or oil, cover with two dough layers and sprinkle with butterfat or oil. Bake in the oven preheated to 175—200 °C

for about 35—40 minutes, until nicely brown. When "burek" is nearly done, cut it into squares, pour chicken soup over it and finish baking. While still warm, pour over it whipped thick yoghurt or sour cream, put back into the oven (leave it slightly open) and let it stand like that for a while.

The well-known Turkish 17th century chronicler, Evliya Tchelebiya, mentions this chicken "burek" as a "renowned dish" — a specialty of Sarajevo. That is why it is called the Sarajevo "burek".

Greece

CHEESE PIE — "BUREK" WITH CHEESE

(for 8—10 persons)

225—250 g sheep cheese (slices)
225 g cheese for grating
4 tablespoons melted butter (40 gr)
4 tablespoons flour (40 g)
1 cup of milk
2 eggs
some chopped parsley
ground nutmeg
450 gr thin layers of dough for the pie
150 gr butter (margarine or oil)

Crush or pass through a sieve sheep cheese, add grated cheese. Heat butter, add flour, fry it quickly so that it does not change colour. Pour in milk gradually stirring all the time and cook at medium heat about 10 minutes. Take off heat, add well beaten egg yolks, chopped parsley and nutmeg. Mix all with cheese.

Cut each layer of dough into three rectangles, brush each piece with melted butter, fold and brush again. Put a spoonful of filling at the far end, fold the long sides inwards about 3 cm and roll up. Grease the baking pan with butter, arrange little "bureks" in it with the ends of the dough downwards. Preheat the oven to 175°C and bake about 20 minutes until nicely brown. Serve warm.

The given quantities give about 48 small pieces of "burek".

Bulgaria

COURGETTE PIE — "BUREK" WITH COURGETTES

1 kg courgettes
30 gr flour
1 dl oil
4 eggs
200 g cheese
30 gr flour
1/2 bunch of dill or parsley
salt
pepper
2 dl sour cream or milk

Peel courgettes, wash, cut into rounds and salt. Leave them to stand for a while, then roll in flour and fry in heated oil to get brown.

Mix two egg yolks and cheese, add salt, pepper, chopped dill and two stiffly whisked egg whites. Mix all slowly. Grease a fireproof dish, or tepsiya, with oil, then put layers of courgettes and cheese in turn, finishing with courgettes. Pour over with some oil and bake in the oven preheated to 200°C about 20 minutes. Beat well the other two eggs, flour and sour cream or milk, pour over the "burek" and return into the oven to brown. Serve warm.

Yugoslavia

BAKED BEANS WITH ONION — "PREBRANATS"

(for 6—8 persons)

450—500 gr white beans (big seeds, like the well-known beans from Tetovo, Macedonia)
3 dl oil
1—1,5 kg onions

salt
pepper
red paprika pepper
1 bayleaf
small dried hot pepper (optional)

Pick over beans, wash and put up to cook in cold water. Cook until tender (do not overcook, as the seeds must remain whole). Slice onion finely and cook slowly in heated oil until tender and slightly brown, add salt, pepper, red paprika pepper, bayleaf and hot paprika if desired.

Grease a deeper enamelled or fireproof pan with oil. Turn into it layers of beans and onion in turn. The last layer should be of beans. Pour over with oil in which onion was fried and some water in which beans were cooked. Bake in the oven preheated to 175 °C until water evaporates and the beans remain in oil. Do not mix while baking.

In Macedonia this dish is called "tavtche" the diminutive of "tava" — the pan in which the dish is prepared.

Serve warm or cold, not only as an appetiser, but also as an accopmaniment to some egg, offal, cheese or other dishes.

Albania

RISOTTO WITH MUSHROOMS

1—2 onions
1 dl oil (olive or other)
1 dl white wine
150—200 gr fresh mushrooms (ceps, button mushrooms and the like)
300 gr rice
0,75—1 l bone stock or soup from cube
salt
pepper
100—150 gr cheese (kachkaval, Trappist or harder sheep cheese)
1/2 bunch of parsley

Peel onion and chop finely. Heat oil a little, add onion, cook until nearly tender, pour in wine, then cook together until it boils. Trim mushrooms, wash and slice finely, add to the onion and cook together for a short while. Pick over rice, wash and drain well, add to the mushrooms, fry together for a while, then pour in soup (or lukewarm water), add salt and pepper and stir slowly. Simmer until rice is tender. When the

risotto is cooked, stir in grated cheese and chopped parsley.

With fresh vegetables (tomatoes, paprikas, cucumbers) this dish can also be served as light supper.

Roumania

ARTICHOKES MOLDAVIAN WAY

4 young artichokes
1 lemon
2 onions
50 gr sunflower oil
500—750 gr tomatoes
2 cloves of garlic
1/2 bunch of dill
2 dl white wine

Remove outer leaves, stalks and tops from artichokes, quarter them, remove the so-called "hay" from the inside. Wash them in water to which lemon juice was added. Heat oil, add finely chopped onion, cook slowly until tender and slightly brown. Add artichokes, peeled and chopped tomatoes, crushed or chopped garlic, some grated lemon rind, chopped dill and white wine. Simmer covered until all is tender. Serve cold with toast and mayonnaise.

To preserve the colour of artichokes, they should be washed in water with lemon juice added, or rubbed with lemon juice. They must not be cooked in aluminium pots, in which they get a very dark colour.

Turkey

"YOSHIRLUK" WITH MEAT

(for 4—6 persons)

400 gr spring onions
60 gr oil or butter
250 gr ground young beef or lamb
1,500 gr spinach
2 cloves of garlic
80 gr rice
1 tablespoon tomato purée
1 tablespoon oil
red paprika pepper
pepper
salt
2 dl thick yoghurt

Trim onion, wash, drain and chop finely. Heat oil or butter, add onion, cook it a little, then add meat, salt and cook until meat is half cooked.

Clean spinach (remove stems and thicker leaf ribs), wash, drain, cut into strips and add to the meat. Also add bigger pieces (or half cloves) of garlic. Blanch rice shortly (cook about 5 minutes in boiling, slightly salted water), drain, add to meat and spinach, stir in tomato, add some water if necessary and simmer until all is tender. Mix oil and red paprika pepper and add to the "yoshirluk" when it is cooked.

Serve with thick yoghurt.

Roumania

COURGETTES WITH CHEESE

(for 6 persons)

1 kg young courgettes
salt
butter for greasing
breadcrumbs for sprinkling the baking pan
150 gr kachkaval or similar cheese
50 gr butter
1 bunch of parsley
salt
pepper
breadcrumbs for sprinkling over the dish
1 carton (2 dl) sour cream

Wash courgettes, cook about 15 minutes in slightly salted water to get soft, but not overcooked. Cool and cut lengthways. Grease the baking pan or a fireproof dish with butter or oil, sprinkle with breadcrumbs. Arrange the courgettes. Grate cheese, mix it with chopped parsley and fill with it the courgette halves, add salt and pepper, cover with thin slices of butter or margarine and sprinkle with breadcrumbs.

Preheat the oven to 180—200°C and

bake about 30 minutes, until the cheese melts and gets slightly brown.

With courgettes stuffed this way serve sour cream mixed with some sugar to taste, as well as the freshly baked pogatcha.

Greece

STUFFED GRAPEVINE LEAVES

250 gr (2—3) onion
1 dl oil
50—70 gr rice
1—2 dl warm water
50 gr pistachios
2 tablespoons chopped parsley
2 tablespoons chopped dill
several leaves of fresh mint
salt, pepper
some sugar
200—250 gr fresh, young grapevine leaves not sprayed with insecticide (or canned)
2—3 tablespoons lemon juice
30—40 gr melted butter (about 3—4 spoons)

Cook slowly finely chopped onion in heated oil, when tender add picked over and washed rice, fry it shortly, add warm water, pistachios, chopped herbs, salt, pepper and some sugar. Mix well, add some more warm water as needed and cook slowly for 10—15 minutes. Then cool.

Pour boiling water over grapevine leaves, leave them to stand for a while, then rinse with cold water and drain well. Line the bottom of the pan in which the dolmas will cook with several leaves. Place the rest of the leaves on the board with bottom sides up. Put a spoonful of filling on each leaf, fold leaf corners over it, roll up and place into the dish in which they are to be cooked (best a fireproof one). Over the dolmas pour lemon juice, melted butter (margarine or oil) and warm water. Simmer for about 40—45 minutes. Cool and serve with lemon and eggs souce ("avgholemono") /see recipe on page 234/.

Greece

SHEEP CHEESE PIE

(for 6—8 persons)

600 gr frozen puff pastry (2 packages)
500 gr sheep cheese (slices)
5 tablespoons butter
6 tablespoons flour
2 dl milk
salt
white pepper
6 eggs
about 100 gr butter (or margarine) for brushing and greasing

Let puff pastry thaw out to room temperature. Crush cheese well. Melt butter and heat it a little, add flour, fry shortly, but it must not change colour. Add milk slowly and cook about 5 minutes stirring all the time. Add salt and pepper and cool, stirring occasionally to prevent the skin forming on top. Add eggs one by one to the cooled sauce and mix well. Add cheese in the end.

Divide puff pastry into 6 parts, then roll out 6 rounds about 24 cm in diameter. Grease a deep cake tin with butter and line with one piece of pastry brushed with some butter. Turn in some cheese filling and cover it with another piece of pastry. Arrange cheese filling and pastry in turn, brushing the pastry every time. Brush the last piece of pastry with butter.

Bake in the oven preheated to 200 °C about 45 minutes. Cut the pie into slices and serve warm.

With lettuce or tomato salad this pie can also be served as light supper.

Bulgaria

STUFFED DRIED PAPRIKAS

(for 10 persons)

10—15 bigger red dried paprikas (long ones!)
1—1,5 dl oil
2 onions
150 gr rice
700 gr mixed ground meat (pork and young beef)
salt
pepper
ground hot paprika
some lukewarm water

Scoop out seed from paprikas, dip them in warm water and leave to get soft. Heat oil, add finely chopped onion, cook it slowly until slightly brown. Pick over rice, wash and cook in salted water, rinse, drain and add to soft onion, then stir in meat. Cook slowly together, add salt, pepper and ground paprika. Cool a little.

Drain the softened paprikas, stuff with the prepared mixture and place in a well greased baking pan or fireproof dish, add some lukewarm water and bake for about 30 minutes in the oven preheated to 175°C. Serve warm or cold.

Yugoslavia

PAPRIKAS STUFFED WITH CHEESE

(for 8—10 persons)

8—10 paprikas (red, fleshy, long ones)
500 gr unripened cow cheese, in crumbs or in slices
250 gr riper kaymak
salt
bunch of parsley
bunch of dill

Wash paprikas, wipe, cut tops off and scoop out seed. Pass cheese through a sieve, add kaymak, mix well, add salt as necessary, add chopped parsley and dill. Stuff paprikas well with this mixture so that there is a firm stuffing inside, without hollows. Leave paprikas in the refrigerator for about 1—2 hours.

Cut cooled paprikas into rounds with a sharp knife, arrange then on a nice wooden board or earthenware plate and garnish with dill and parsley leaves.

These paprikas can be served with cornbread or pogatcha, garnished with ham, prosciutto or finely sliced smoked neck of pork.

Bulgaria

PAPRIKAS STUFFED WITH SWEETCORN

4 red paprikas (big ones or tomato-shaped bigger paprikas)
salt
sweet red paprika pepper
250—300 gr cooked sweetcorn (or canned)
40 gr butter or margarine
1/2 bunch of parsley
1 teaspoon sugar
1 tablespoon wine vinegar
margarine for greasing
30 gr butter
50 gr grated kachkaval or similar cheese

Wash paprikas, cut tops off and scoop out seed, rinse out, drain and then rub the insides well with salt and paprika pepper. Cook shortly in slightly salted boiling water, take out and drain. Drain cooked sweetcorn, turn into heated butter, cook slowly for a while, add salt, sugar, wine vinegar, chopped parsley. Mix. Stuff drained paprikas with sweetcorn. Arrange them in a greased fireproof dish, pour over melted butter, sprinkle with grated kachkaval, add some warm water and cook in the oven preset at 200 °C about 20 minutes.

Paprikas prepared this way, but without cheese, can be served as an accompaniment to roast or stewed lamb.

Bulgaria

PAPRIKAS STUFFED WITH BEANS

(for 8—10 persons)

500 gr young ripe beans
1 dl olive (or sunflower) oil
500—700 gr onion
2 dl olive (or sunflower) oil
1 tablespoon flour
red paprika pepper
salt
pepper
1 bunch of parsley
1/2 bunch of celery leaf
2—3 cloves of garlic
oil for greasing
8—10 paprikas

Pick over beans, pour in cold water, bring to the boil, take off the heat, leave to cool in the same water, then drain well. Heat olive (or other) oil, add drained beans, cook them a little, add just enough water to cover them and simmer.

Peel onion and slice finely, cook slowly in oil, stirring often until nicely brown. Add a spoonful of flour, mix and fry together shortly, blend in red paprika pepper, salt, pepper, chopped parsley and celery, crushed or chopped garlic and add beans in the end, when they are cooked. Mix all well.

Wash paprikas, remove stems and core them, then fill with beans. Grease a deeper enamelled baking pan or fireproof dish with oil and arrange the stuffed paprikas. Add the remaining beans in between the paprikas, adding some water they were cooked in, as necessary. Bake in the oven preheated to 175°C about 35—40 minutes. Serve warm or cold.

This dish is most often prepared in early autumn when there are young ripe beans to be found and big paprikas of good quality.

Yugoslavia

BUTTON MUSHROOMS WITH CHEESE

500—750 gr ripened cheese in slices
1/4 l milk
3—4 eggs
2 big red paprikas
1 dl sour cream
1 tablespoon red paprika pepper
butter for greasing
300 gr fresh button mushrooms or 2 cups canned ones

Grate cheese, add milk, well beaten egg yolks, then washed, cored and dices paprikas, sour cream and red paprika pepper. Whisk egg whites stiffly and stir them in slowly.

Grease a flameproof dish (not so deep) with butter (or oil) and turn in the prepared mixture. Arrange button mushrooms over it, drained if they are canned, and trimmed, washed, blanched and drained if fresh. They may also be cooked for a while first. Bake in the oven preheated to 175°C until nicely brown. Serve with toast or freshly baked pogatcha. Other kinds of edible mushrooms can be used for this dish instead of button mushrooms.

Turkey

"TIRIT" PIE

(for 8—10 persons)

750 gr flour
2—2,5 dl lukewarm water
1 egg
salt
1 chicken or a smaller hen
root vegetables (carrot, parsley root, some celery, parsnip)
salt
pepper
2—3 tablespoons oil for greasing and sprinkling
1/2 l sour cream or thick yoghurt
2 cloves of garlic

Sift flour, make a well in the center, add some salt, the egg and lukewarm water as needed. Knead into a smooth dough for the pie, divide it into 8—10 small balls, cover and leave to stand. Roll out the dough into rounds, not too thin. Bake them on top the stove or in a dry baking pan in the well heated oven, until brown and brittle.

Cook the chicken in slightly salted water with roots. When cooked, take the chicken out, strain soup into a bigger pan. Remove bones, chop meat, add salt and pepper.

Dip baked dough layers one by one into the soup, arrange in the greased tepsiya, covering each with minced meat, repeat until all the dough layers and meat are used.

Pour the pie over with heated oil and bake in the oven preheated to 200°C about 40 minutes or until nicely brown. In the meantime crush garlic and mix with beaten sour cream and pour over the tepid (not hot) pie, cover with a clean cloth or another tepsiya and leave to stand for a while.

Albania

LEEK PIE

(for 8—10 persons)

500—750 gr leeks
750 gr ready-made layers of dough for the pie
2—3 dl oil
500 gr riper white cheese
4 eggs
salt

Trim leeks, wash and cut into rounds, cook slowly for a while in heated oil, then cool. Crush cheese, add egg yolks, cooled leeks, salt and then mix well. Whisk egg whites stiffly and stir slowly into the prepared mixture.

Grease a tepsiya or a baking pan well with oil, place two to three dough layers at the bottom, sprinkle them with oil, then put in the layer of cheese and leeks. Place dough layers again and sprinkle with oil. Repeat until all is used. Press the dough ends overflowing the pan with fingers like a "wreath". Before baking sprinkle with oil. Preset the oven at 200°C and bake about 40 minutes.

Serve warm, cut into squares.

Yugoslavia

CHEESE PIE — "GIBANITSA"

(for 6 persons)

500 gr thinner layers of dough for the pie
700 gr white cow cheese (in crumbs or in slices)
3—4 eggs
1/4 l milk
1—1,5 dl oil
salt

Choose 6 nice dough layers. Grease well a tepsiya or a pan with oil and put in 3 dough layers.

Crush cheese, add egg yolks, milk, then put in the rest of the dough layers, except the 3 set aside, and mix well. Add stiffly whisked egg whites. Turn this filling in, pour over some oil and cover with the remaining 3 dough layers. Sprinkle with oil and water.

Bake in the oven preheated to 200°C about 40—45 minutes.

When done, cut the "gibanitsa" into slices and serve warm.

Turkey

STUFFED SAUERKRAUT WITH WALNUTS

1 bigger head of pickled cabbage (about 1,5—2 kg)
3—4 onions
50 gr oil
80 gr rice
1 teaspoon red paprika pepper
2—2,5 dl lukewarm water
100 finely chopped or ground walnuts
20 gr oil
15 gr flour
1 dl warm water
salt

Cut good leaves off the cabbage, remove thick parts of the leaf ribs, wash in cold water and drain.

Peel onion and chop finely. Heat oil, add onion, cook slowly until soft and beginning to colour, add picked over and washed rice, 1/2 teaspoon of red paprika pepper, mix, add lukewarm water, cook slowly until rice is tender, then stir in walnuts.

Put a certain quantity of filling on each prepared leaf, roll up and place the dolmas in the pan, barely cover with cold water, cover and simmer until cabbage is soft.

Heat oil, add flour, fry it until slightly brown, add the rest of red paprika pepper, pour in about 1/2 dl of cold, then 1 dl of warm water, cook shortly and pour over the cooked dolmas, shake well and leave to simmer for another 10—15 minutes.

Greece

SPINACH PIE

(for 6 persons)

1 package frozen puff pastry
750—1000 gr fresh spinach
1 bunch of spring onions
1—2 cloves of garlic
50 gr butter
salt
white pepper
nutmeg
4 eggs
2 dl sour cream
4—5 tablespoons breadcrumbs
1 egg yolk

Let the puff pastry thaw out. Remove spinach stems, wash it and drain. Peel onion and garlic, chop and cook slowly in heated butter until soft and "glassy". Cut spinach into bigger strips and cook it together with onion about 10 minutes. Season with salt, pepper and nutmeg. Beat eggs well, add sour cream, mix into them the prepared spinach and add breadcrumbs in the end. Divide the pastry into two parts and roll out thinly. Rinse the baking pan with cold water. The bottom part of the dough should be bigger to go over the pan edges. Turn in the filling and fold the dough ends over it, inwards. Cover with the other dough layer. Cut strips from the left over dough (with a pattern cutter) and arrange them over the dough like crossed bars. Brush with beaten egg yolk, prick with a toothpick and bake about 50 minutes, until gold. Cut into squares and serve warm.

Yugoslavia

MEAT PIE

(for 6—8 persons)

400 gr ground young beef (or mixed ground meat)
40 gr oil
salt
pepper
1 bunch of parsley
500 gr thinner layers of dough for the pie
1—2 dl oil for greasing and sprinkling the dough layers
2 dl mineral water
3 eggs

Cook ground meat slowly in heated oil. When soft, add salt, pepper and chopped parsley. Divide dough layers into three parts. Place them in the greased baking pan one by one, sprinkling each with oil. Put half of the filling over the first part of the arranged dough layers, then the second part of the dough layers, sprinkled with oil, the other half of the filling, and then the thrid part of the dough layers. Cut the pie into squares. Mix mineral water with eggs, beat well and pour over the pie. Leave to stand 5—

10 minutes. Bake for about 40 minutes in the preheated oven to 150—175 °C.

Serve warm.

Greece

TUNNY-FISH PIE

(for 6—8 persons)

1 package of puff pastry (frozen)
300 gr canned tunny-fish
4 hard boiled eggs
2 eggs
1 dl sour cream
salt
pepper

Let the pastry thaw out and divide it into two parts. Drain oil from the fish and crush it well. Shell and chop hard boiled eggs, mix them with tunny-fish, add egg yolks and sour cream. Whisk egg whites stiffly, stir them slowly into the mixture, add salt and pepper.

Line a cake tin with one part of puff pastry, turn in the filling, level and cover with the other part of the pastry. Prick with a fork in several places. Bake in the oven preheated to 200 °C about 30—35 minutes. When done, cool a little, then cut into slices. Serve warm. With some salad or fresh vegetables like radishes, spring onions, cucumbers, this pie can be served as the main dish in the evening.

Greece

"TOURTA" — LAMB PIE FROM CRETE

(for 8 persons)

1 lamb shoulder of about 1,5 kg
2—2,5 dl water
2 teaspoons salt
pepper
600—700 gr flour
1 teaspoon salt
150 gr butter
a few fresh mint leaves
1 tablespoon butter for greasing
1 dl sour cream
250 gr white cow cheese in slices
1 egg
2 spoonfuls of sesame seeds

Wash meat, cut into pieces, put into a pan with water, add 2 teaspoons of salt and some pepper. Cover and cook at medium heat about 30 minutes. Cool and remove bones.

Put flour into a bowl (put some aside for dusting), add softened butter, 1 teaspoon of salt and mix with a fork. While mixing gradually add some lamb soup to get a thick dough. Toss it on to a board dusted with flour and knead it for a few more minutes. Divide it onto two parts, of which one should be a bit bigger. Roll out the bigger part into a round about 5 mm thick, and big enough to cover the bottom and the wall of the tepsiya. Grease the pan with butter and line with the rolled out dough. Place pieces of cooked meat over it. Cut cheese into small pieces and put them in between the pieces of meat and over them. Srinkle with chopped mint and pour over with sour cream. Roll out the other part of the dough about 5 mm thick and cover meat and cheese with it. Join firmly together the ends of the lower and the upper layer of dough and crumple them into a "wreath". Brush the pie with the beaten egg, sprinkle with sesame seeds and bake in the oven preheated to 175 °C about 45 minutes or until nicely browned.

Serve warm.

Yugoslavia

SAUERKRAUT PIE

(for 10—12 persons)

800—1000 gr ready-made layers of dough for the pie
1—1,5 kg pickled cabbage
50 gr oil
2 onions
salt
pepper
red paprika pepper
oil for greasing

Chop pickled cabbage finely, pour over with warm water and simmer until tender. In the meantime cook slowly finely chopped onion in oil until soft and beginning to colour, add salt and pepper, cooked and drained cabbage, some red paprika pepper and mix well.

Grease a tepsiya or a baking pan with oil, place 2—3 dough layers at the bottom, sprinkle them with oil, put over some cabbage filling, then dough layers again. Repeat until all the filling and dough layers are used. Finish with dough layers. Sprinkle with oil. Bake in the oven preheated to 200 °C about 45—60 minutes. When done, sprinkle with water, cover with a clean cloth, leave for a while to soften, then cut into squares. Serve warm or cold.

Yugoslavia

BOSNIAN "TIRIT"

(for 10 persons)

1 hen of about 2 kg
1 bunch of root vegetables (2 carrots, 1 parsley root, parsnip)
200 gr lard or 2 dl oil
200 gr onion or 2 bunches of spring onions
1 bunch of parsley

salt
pepper
5—6 dl sour cream
0,5—1 dl milk
750—1000 gr layers of dough for the pie

Clean hen wash and put into warm water. Bring to the boil and add scraped roots, pepper and salt. Simmer until tender. Heat half of the lard or oil, add finely chopped onion, cook slowly to soften. Cool cooked meat a little, remove bones, taking care that pieces of meat remain whole. Add onion to the meat, add salt, a bit more pepper and chopped parsley. Grease a tepsiya with oil or lard, place 10 dough layers one by one, sprinkling each with lard or oil. Put the prepared meat over them, level and then cover with the other 10 layers, also sprinkling them with oil or lard. Pour sour cream dissolved in milk over the pie. Bake in the oven for 45—50 minutes at 175°C.

When done, sprinkle with water, cover and leave to stand for a while, then cut into slices and serve warm.

"Tirit" can also be the main dish at lunch or supper.

Albania

YEAST DOUGH PIE

(for 10 persons)

1 kg flour
2 tablespoons lukewarm milk
salt
50 gr fresh yeast (1 small package)
50 gr oil (5 tablespoons)
lukewarm water as needed
500 gr sheep cheese (slices)
4—6 eggs
1 dl oil for greasing and pouring over the dough

Sift flour. Crumble yeast, add lukewarm milk and 1 tablespoon of flour, stir and set in a warm place to rise.

Make a well in the center of the flour, add oil, salt, yeast and enough lukewarm water to get a softer dough. Work up well with a mixing spoon (or mixer) until smooth and no longer sticky. Cover and set in a warm place to rise.

Grease well a tepsiya with oil, toss in the risen dough, spread it with the hand so that a thicker layer of dough is round the wall of the pan, slightly overflowing the edge. Crumple this surplus of dough into a "wreath". Put the pan into the oven preheated to 175°C and bake just long enough for a thin skin to form. Take the pie out of the oven, remove the skin carefully and pour heated oil over the dough.

Beat egg yolks and add well crushed cheese. Whisk egg whites stiffly and stir them in slowly. Turn this mixture over the half-baked dough, return to the oven to bake on at 175—200°C.

When done, cool and cut into slices.

Yugoslavia

SORREL PIE — "PITA ZELJANITSA"

250—300 gr sorrel
250 gr riper soft white cheese
2—3 eggs
2—3 tablespoons sour cream or kaymak
1/2 cup of milk
3—4 tablespoons lard or oil
250—300 gr thinner layers of dough for the pie

Wash sorrel, remove stems and thick leaf ribs, drain, cut into strips, cook slowly in oil or lard, then cool.

Crush cheese well, add egg yolks, sour cream or kaymak, sorrel and milk. Mix all well. Carefully stir in stiffly whisked egg whites.

Grease well a tepsiya or a fireproof dish with lard or oil. Place two or three dough layers at the bottom, sprinkle them with oil or melted lard, add several spoonfuls of filling, then place some more dough layers over. Repeat until the dough and the filling are used. The last dough layer should be a nice one. Press it a little and sprinkle with oil or lard.

Bake in the oven preheated to 250°C

about 40 minutes or until it rises and gets nicely brown. Then turn off the oven and leave the pie in the oven for 10 more minutes. After that cool a little and cut into squares or rectangles and serve warm.

Sorrel can be replaced by spinach, Swiss chard or tips of young nettles. Nettle should first be blanched in slightly salted water, drained and chopped.

Yugoslavia

RICE PIE

(for 6—8 persons)

250 gr rice
1 dl oil
2 onions
3 eggs
salt
pepper
50 gr kaymak
500 gr readymade dough layers for the pie
oil for greasing

Pick over rice, wash, cook in slightly salted water, rinse with cold water and drain well. Cook slowly finely chopped onion in half of the oil until soft and beginning to colour, add cooled rice, mix, add egg yolks, salt, pepper and kaymak. Whisk egg whites stiffly and stir carefully into the rice.

Grease tepsiya with oil, put 2—3 dough layers at the bottom, sprinkle with oil, then a layer of rice filling. Repeat until all is used. Pour the rest of oil over the last layer of dough. Bake in the oven preheated to 175—200 °C about 40 minutes, until nicely brown. When done, sprinkle with water, cover and leave to stand for a while. Cut into squares and serve warm, with kaymak or unripened cheese if desired.

The rice pie has a long tradition in Serbia. It was mostly prepared at the times of fasting.

Roumania

ROUMANIAN PIE

(for 8—10 persons)

750 gr—1 kg maize flour
1,2—2 l water
salt
350 gr kaymak
350 gr smoked meat or smoked homemade sausages
50 gr oil for pouring over and greasing

Sift flour, put it into a baking pan and bake in the heated oven for a while to change colour. Heat water in a deeper pot, add salt. Bring it to the boil, then add gradually the baked flour, stirring constantly, to get a smooth batter, without lumps. Cover and simmer, stirring occasionally.

Put kaymak into a fireproof dish, melt it a little, put a layer of cooked polenta over it, sprinkle with oil (or lard), arrange over it cubed smoked meat or sausages cut into rounds. Put layers of polenta and meat until all is used. The

last layer should be polenta, levelled with a spoon dipped in hot oil (or lard) and sprinkled with some oil. Bake in the oven preheated to 200 °C about 30—40 minutes, until the pie is brown.

Serve warm. Slices of pickled cabbage or paprikas from turshiya are most often served with this pie.

Turkey

"ATCHAK" PIE

(for 6—8 persons)

For dough:
500 gr flour
1 dl (or more if needed) lukewarm water
1 egg
1—2 tablespoons oil
salt

For filling:
40 gr oil
1 onion
500 gr sheep thick yoghurt
4 eggs
salt, pepper
1/2 bunch of dill
oil for greasing and sprinkling over

Sift flour, mixed with some salt. Make a well in the center, add the egg, some oil and lukewarm water as necessary to make a smooth, softer dough, knead it into a ball and leave to stand for a while. Roll out into a round bigger than the baking pan for about 10 cm all around.

Prepare the filling in the following way: cook slowly finely chopped onion in heated oil until soft and beginning to colour, cool, add egg yolks, thick yoghurt, salt, pepper and chopped dill. Slowly stir in stiffly whisked egg whites. Turn into the baking pan lined with the dough, sprinkled with oil. Carefully fold over the filling the ends of the dough which go over the edges, making tiny folds. Only the middle of the pie remains uncovered with the dough. Sprinkle with oil and bake in the oven preheated to 175 °C about 40—50 minutes. When done, sprinkle with some water, cover with a clean cloth and leave for a while, then cut into slices.

"Atchak" pie means an open pie. It is prepared mostly in the mountainous parts where sheep thick yoghurt of exceptional quality is produced ("so thick that it can be cut with a knife").

Bulgaria

NETTLE PIE

(for 10 persons)

1 kg young nettles (only the young tops)
350—400 gr cheese in slices
150 gr kaymak
4 eggs, salt
some milk (as needed)
1 dl oil for sprinkling the dough layers
600 gr thinner dough layers

Wash nettles, blanch in slightly salted water, drain well, add to them crushed cheese, kaymak, egg yolks, mix all, add salt and some milk if necessary. Whisk egg whites stiffly and stir them in.

Spread dough layers on a clean cloth, sprinkle with oil, three at a time. Put the filling along the longer side, roll up and place into the greased baking pan. When all the rolls are arranged, sprinkle each with oil and some water. Bake in the oven preheated to 175 °C for 40—45 minutes. When done, cut diagonally into nice slices. Serve warm.

The rolled pie with young nettles is most often prepared in the parts where nettle replaces spinach or sorrel. It is a very useful habit, as the young leaves of nettle are a true treasury of mineral substances, chlorophyll, vitamin C, provitamin A and a number of other preventive food factors. Growing on the soil without chemical fertilizers, it represents a truly natural food.

Greece

MEAT PIE FROM CEPHALONIA

(for 10 persons)

1 kg leaner lamb
40 gr butter (margarine or oil)
1/2 to 1 cup warm water
salt
pepper
2 cloves of garlic
1 bunch of parsley
1 dl white wine
40—50 gr rice
3 ripe tomatoes of medium size
2 hard boiled eggs
350 gr sheep cheese (slices)
2—3 layers of dough for the pie (slightly thicker)
1/2 dl stock or milk
butter for greasing

Wash meat, wipe and cut into pieces the size of a walnut. Heat butter, add meat, fry it for a while, add salt, pepper, snipped or crushed garlic, pour in water, cover and simmer about 30—40 minutes, stirring occasionally. Then pour in wine and continue cooking half covered with the lid. Wash tomatoes, peel and cut into pieces. Pick over rice, wash and cook in slightly salted water (about 5 minutes), then drain. Chop hard boiled eggs. When meat is tender, add tomatoes, rice and crushed cheese. Mix all well and add more salt and pepper as needed.

Grease a tepsiya of 50 cm in diameter with butter, line it with a layer of dough so that 5—6 cm of dough overflow on all sides. Sprinkle it with butter, add the prepared mixture, cover with other layers of dough. Moisten the ends of the dough a little, press and form folds with the fingers. Brush the surface with butter, prick with a fork here and there and make a hole in the middle with a wooden mixing spoon. Bake for about 1 hour in the oven preheated to 175—200 °C. While baking pour some stock or milk into the hole in the middle.

Serve warm, cut into slices.

Bulgaria

ONION AND PAPRIKA PIE

(for 6—8 persons)

For dough:
400 gr flour
1 dl milk
1 egg
40 gr butter
1 tablespoon oil
20 gr yeast
salt
oil for greasing

For filling:
1 kg onion
250—300 gr paprikas
1 dl oil
2 eggs
100 gr sheep cheese in slices
2 bayleaves
salt
pepper
black olives for garnishing

Peel onion, cut into thin slices, wash and core paprikas, cut into strips or rounds. Heat oil, add onion, paprikas, bayleaf, salt and pepper. Cook slowly until onion is soft and brown, then cool.

Sift flour, make a well in the center, add yeast dissolved in lukewarm milk, oil, salt and butter. Work into a smooth batter, divide it into two parts, roll them into balls, cover and set in a warm place for about 40 minutes. Then roll out the dough into two round layers. Grease a cake tin or a tepsiya with oil, spread one layer of dough slightly over the edge of the pan, then turn in the filling prepared as follows: add beaten eggs to cooked onion and paprikas, mixed with crushed cheese, salt and pepper. Over it place the other dough layer to cover the filling well, and press the ends of the two dough layers. Brush with oil and prick with a fork here and there. Bake in the oven preheated to 150 °C about 45 minutes.

When done, garnish with olives, cool and cut into slices.

Yugoslavia

MEAT AND VEGETABLE PIE

(for 6 persons)

For filling:
1—2 onions
40 gr lard or oil
250—300 gr ground pork
2 carrots
1 parsley root
1/2 celery root
1 cup shelled peas (fresh or frozen)
1 small head of cooked cauliflower
2 smaller potatoes

For dough:
40 gr margarine (butter)
3 eggs
1 dl sour cream
3 tablespoons flour
1/2 bunch of parsley
50 gr grated kachkaval or similar cheese
butter or margarine for greasing
breadcrumbs to sprinkle over

Cook finely chopped onion slowly in heated oil or lard until slightly soft, add ground meat. Cook slowly together until meat is nearly soft. Scrape and dice carrot, parsley and celery. Break cauliflower into sprigs. Peel potatoes, wash and also dice. Add the prepared vegetables to the meat, mix, add salt, pepper and some water, cover and simmer until all is tender, then cool. In the meantime beat well butter or margarine, add egg yolks and sour cream. Whisk egg whites stiffly. Add flour and egg whites to the egg yolks and sour cream in turn, mix slowly. Also add chopped parsley.

Grease a fireproof dish with butter or margarine, sprinkle with breadcrumbs. Turn in half of the dough, then the cooled vegetables and meat, then the other half of the dough, shake lightly, sprinkle with cheese and bake in the oven preset at 175—200 °C. When done, cut the pie into slices, cool a little and serve in the dish in which it was baked.

Yugoslavia

"MANTLES"

(for 10—12 persons)

For dough:
550—750 gr flour
100 gr oil (or lard)
1/2 dl lukewarm water
salt

For filling:
750 gr ground pork
40 gr oil
200 gr onion
salt
pepper
red paprika pepper
oil or lard for greasing

Prepare the dough for the pie from flour, salt, lukewarm water and oil. Roll it out to be about 2—3 mm thick, then cut into squares, the size of 10 × 10 cm.

Prepare the filling as follows: cook

slowly finely chopped onion in heated oil until soft. Add meat, continue cooking until the meat is soft and the juice evaporates, add salt, pepper and red paprika pepper. Mix all well. Put a spoonful of filling in the middle of every square of dough, then join the ends of the square over the filling. This way, the filling is wrapped in a "mantle". Grease a tepsiya with oil or lard, arrange the mantles so that the joined ends are turned downwards. Bake in the oven preset at 200°C until nicely brown. When done, sprinkle them with water, cover with a clean cloth and leave for a while to soften.

The "mantles" are more tasty when warm but can also be served cold. As making this delicious Serbian specialty takes a lot of time, it represents special honour to the guest for whom they are prepared.

Albania

TWICE-BAKED PIE

(for 8—10 persons)

For dough (layers of it):
500—600 gr plain wheat flour
50—70 gr oil or lard
about 1/2 dl water (depending on the quality of flour)
salt

For filling:
300—400 gr cow or sheep cheese in slices
3—4 eggs
oil for greasing

Prepare the dough as explained in the basic recipe for the layers of dough for the pie (see page). Grease a tepsiya with oil, line with one thicker layer of dough, or several thinner ones, sprinkle with oil or lard. From the left-over dough make an edge "wreath". Bake the dough prepared this way in the oven preheated to 200°C. When done, turn in the prepared filling and return to the oven for the filling to bake. Hence the name of the pie.

Prepare the filling as follows: crush cheese, add egg yolks, carefully stir in whisked egg whites.

This pie is usually prepared for unexpected guests or in other situations when the pie is to be made quickly.

Bulgaria

YOGHURT SOUFFLÉ

(for 3—4 persons)

3,5 dl drinking yoghurt
3—4 eggs
2,5 dl milk
250 gr young cow or sheep cheese in crumbs
4 tablespoons breadcrumbs
salt, pepper
1 spoonful chopped parsley
butter for greasing

Beat well yoghurt with eggs to make a smooth mixture. Add milk and crushed cheese and mix well (preferably with a mixer) until quite smooth. Add breadcrumbs, salt, pepper and parsley and turn into a baking pan greased with butter. Bake in the oven preheated to 200°C for 35—40 minutes. Serve at once.

Yugoslavia

FRIED STUFFED HAM

(for 6 persons)

500—600 gr homemade ham
1/4 l milk
150—200 gr kachkaval or similar cheese
salt, pepper
hot red paprika pepper
2—3 tablespoons flour
2 eggs
breadcrumbs
1/4 l oil for frying
1 lemon
1/2 bunch of parsley

For sauce:
2—3 dl sour cream
2—3 tablespoons ketch-up or ayvar
1—2 tablespoons fresh or canned horseradish
salt
1/2 bunch of parsley

Cut ham into thin rashers, pour cold milk over them and leave to stand for several hours. Then take out and drain well. Sprinkle each rasher with grated cheese, add salt (as needed), pepper and red paprika pepper, roll up, stick with a toothpick, roll in flour, beaten egg and breadcrumbs. Fry in heated oil until nicely brown.

Arrange on a serving dish or plate, garnish with lemon rounds and parsley leaves.

For the sauce beat sour cream, add ketch-up or ayvar, grated horseradish and salt to taste. Serve in a separate little bowl. Fried stuffed ham is a specialty from Vojvodina (the city of Subotica and the vicinity) where it is also served as the main dish with potatoes or rice and with some warm sauce (with dill or mushrooms etc.).

Bulgaria

OMELET WITH COURGETTES

1 onion
40 gr butter or margarine
300—400 gr young courgettes
salt
pepper
3 bigger ripe tomatoes
8 eggs
50 gr grated kachkaval or similar cheese

Cook slowly finely chopped onion in heated butter until soft and beginning to colour. Add washed courgettes, cut into rounds, then add salt and pepper. Wash tomatoes, peel, remove seed, cut into pieces and add to the courgettes. Cook slowly together about 45 minutes. Beat eggs well, add salt and pepper, pour over the vegetables, mix and fry at medium heat, shaking the dish occasionally. When the omelet is done, sprinkle with grated cheese. Serve warm.

Omelet like this can be prepared with other vegetables (cauliflower, asparagus, young carrots and the like).

Roumania

BAKED EGGS

4 eggs
1 onion
40 gr lard or oil
300 gr mixed ground meat
salt
pepper
bunch of parsley
30 gr butter or margarine
30 gr flour
3 dl milk
50 gr grated kachkaval or similar cheese

Hard boil eggs, shell and cut in halves lengthways. Chop onion finely and cook in heated oil until tender, add ground meat, salt and pepper and continue cooking slowly. When the meat is done, add chopped parsley.

Arrange egg halves at the bottom of a fireproof dish. Heat butter or margarine in a pot, add flour and fry it a little (it must not change colour) and pour in warm milk, stirring all the time. Simmer for 10 minutes, then cool and add salt to taste. Cover egg halves with meat, pour in the milk sauce (béchamel), sprinkle with grated cheese and bake for 25—30 minutes in the oven preheated to 200°C.

Serve warm.

Roumania

EGG ROLL

For roll:
8 eggs
1 l water
1 tablespoon lemon juice or vinegar
peppercorns
1 teaspoon salt
1 bayleaf
oil or lard for greasing the pan
breadcrumbs for sprinkling over
For filling:
100—150 gr ground ham
1 dl sour cream
salt, pepper
pressed egg yolks
1 bunch of parsley
For pouring over:
2 dl sour cream
2—3 tablespoons breadcrumbs

Separate eggs. Plunge egg yolks carefully into hot water to which peppercorns, lemon juice or vinegar and bayleaf have been added. Hard boil egg yolks, drain and pass through a sieve.

Mix ground ham, sour cream, salt, pepper and pressed egg yolks to get a mixture easy to spread. Mix in chopped parsley at the end.

Grease a baking pan with butter or oil. Whisk egg whites slowly and pour into the prepared pan, bake in the oven preset at 175°C just long enough to get stiff. Turn them carefully on to a board sprinkled with breadcrumbs, spread over it the prepared mixture, roll up, place in a greased fireproof dish, cut into 4—5 pieces, pour over with sour cream, sprinkle with fried breadcrumbs, and bake shortly in the oven preset at 200°C.

Yugoslavia

SMOKED TONGUE WITH EGGS

40 gr butter
8 eggs
salt
pepper
200 gr smoked tongue
50 gr grated kachkaval
1 bunch of shallots (or spring onion leaves)

Melt and heat butter in a frying pan, then brake eggs carefully one by one and fry, sunny side up, slowly about 4 minutes. After 2 minutes of frying, cover the pan with a lid. Sprinkle salt and pepper over the egg whites.

Grease a shallow fireproof dish with butter, cut the tongue into rounds and arrange at the bottom of the dish. Put eggs over the tongue and sprinkle with grated cheese. Bake in the oven preheated to 250°C for 5—10 minutes. When done, sprinkle with chopped shallots or chopped spring onion leaves.

Serve warm in the dish in which it was prepared.

Yugoslavia

EGGS IN BRINE

(for 5—6 persons)

10—12 eggs
1 l water
3—4 tablespoons salt
2 small hot peppers
a pinch of thyme
2 bayleaves
2 onions
a few rosemary leaves

Dip eggs into cold water, heat and boil about 10 minutes. Put salt into one liter of water, add small hot pepper, thyme, bayleaf, peeled and halved onions to which the last skin had not been removed and rosemary leaves. Cook the brine for 10 minutes and then cool.

Break egg shells slightly, arrange eggs in a bigger jar and pour the brine over. Leave to stand in a cool place for at least 2 days.

Serve as appetiser with mustard sause or horseradish sauce with sour cream and with warm cornbread, pogatcha or brown bread. Butter or kaymak spread can also be served with the eggs.

Greece

"FROUTALIA" — OMELET WITH POTATOES AND SAUSAGES

500 gr potatoes
250 gr sausages
120 gr ham
40—50 gr butter
1 tablespoon chopped fresh mint
6—8 eggs
salt
pepper

Peel potatoes, wash and cut into rounds. Cut sausages also into rounds. Melt butter in a bigger frying pan, add sausages and ham cut into strips. Fry together for a while, then take out sausages and ham, put on a plate and set in a warm place. Put potatoes into the same fat, cover and cook slowly until tender. Shake or stir occasionally. When potatoes are cooked, add sausages and ham. Scramble eggs well, add mint and pepper, pour over the potatoes and sausages. Fry at medium heat until the lower part is nicely brown. Carefully turn on to a bigger plate, return to the frying pan and fry the other side to get evenly brown.

This omelet is called "froutalia" at the island of Andros and is prepared from smoked pork sausages and smoked ham, kept in big earthen pots, covered with melted lard.

The quantities given are enough for 4—5 persons.

Yugoslavia

SPINACH ROLL

(for 6 persons)

1 kg spinach
5 buns (or 5—6 slices white bread)
2—3 dl milk
150 gr butter or margarine
5 eggs
70 gr breadcrumbs
lard for greasing the baking pan
breadcrumbs for sprinkling over
salt
pepper

For filling:
4 eggs
50—100 gr ham
butter for pouring over
50 gr kachkaval or Parmesan

Wash spinach, remove stems and leaf ribs, cook it in salted water, drain and grind or pass through a sieve. Soak buns or bread in milk, drain when soft, mix with spinach. Beat well butter or margarine, add egg yolks and then spinach with buns. Whisk egg whites until foamy and stir into the spinach in turn with breadcrumbs.

Grease well the baking pan, sprinkle with breadcrumbs and turn in the prepared mixture. Bake for 30—35 minutes in the oven preset at 175°C. When done, carefully turn out, on to a cloth sprinkled with breadcrumbs. Spread with the following filling: beat eggs well, add chopped ham. Fry in heated oil or lard. Arrange over baked spinach, roll up slowly, pour over with melted butter and sprinkle with grated cheese. Serve warm. In spring spinach can be replaced with young nettle.

Yugoslavia

"SHTRUKLI" FROM ZAGORJE

(for 4—6 persons)

350 gr flour
some salt
1 dl oil
some lukewarm water
350 gr riper white cow cheese in crumbs
3 dl sour cream
2 eggs
80 gr butter
20—30 gr breadcrumbs
1,5—2 l salted water

Sift flour, make a well in the center, add salt, oil and lukewarm waters as needed. Knead into a smooth, softer dough. Divide into two parts, cover and leave to stand about 20 minutes. Then dust with flour and carefully roll out into bigger rectangular layers, leaving them for a while to dry.

In the meantime prepare the filling: pass cheese through a sieve or crush well, add half of the sour cream, eggs and salt as needed. Mix well.

Arrange the filling on both dough layers, then roll them up. Cut the rolls into pieces about 10—12 cm long with the blunt side of the knife or the edge of a saucer. Heat a lot of salted water. When it begins to boil slowly, plunge "shtruk-

li'' into the pan and cook for 10 minutes. When cooked, take out and drain, arrange in an enamelled or fireproof dish in which butter had been melted, pour over with butter and the rest of sour cream, sprinkle with breadcrumbs. Bake in the oven preheated to 175°C until browned. Serve straight away.

Roumania

HAM OMELET

For omelet:
6—8 eggs
2 tablespoons flour
1 tablespoon grated cheese (kachkaval or similar)
1/2 dl milk
salt
oil for frying
For filling:
50—70 gr butter
some mustard
5—6 gherkins
1/2 dl sour cream
100—150 gr ham (cook or pressed)
For garnishing and serving with omelet:
parsley, radishes, spring onions

Beat eggs, add flour, grated cheese, milk and salt. Heal oil in a bigger frying pan, add prepared eggs and fry omelet on both sides. Turn it out slowly on to a bigger plate or board and leave to cool.

Beat butter until foamy, add mustard and finely chopped gherkins, salt and sour cream. Mix well until easy to spread. Cut ham into thin, bigger rashers. Arrange them over the cooled omelet, spread the butter mixture over evenly, roll up and leave in a cool place for 1—2 hours. Cut into nice rounds before

serving, garnish with radishes and parsley leaves.

With this omelet serve spring vegetables, such as radishes and spring onions.

Bulgaria

AUBERGINE PIE

(for 6 persons)

For dough:
250 gr flour
75 gr land or margarine
1 egg
1/2 glass of water
salt

For filling:
1 kg aubergines
1 dl olive oil
salt
pepper
500 gr tomatoes
100 gr older kachkaval cheese
100 gr olives

Sift flour. Make a well in the center, add lard or thin slices of margarine, egg, salt and water. Knead the dough quickly and leave to stand in a cool place for about 15—20 minutes.

In the meantime wash aubergines, peel, cut into bigger cubes, salt, leave to stand for about 15—20 minutes, rinse with cold water, drain and add into one half of heated oil, season with salt and pepper and cook slowly until half tender.

Roll out the dough to a round big enough to cover a greased tepsiya. Bake in the oven preset at 200°C about 15 minutes. Then arrange cooked aubergines over the dough, the peeled tomatoes cut into rounds, fine slices of cheese and olives.

Pour over with the rest of olive oil. Bake for another 20 minutes, until all is brown and the cheese melts.

When the pie is done, cool a little and then cut into slices.

Greece

BAKED AUBERGINES

(for 4—6 persons)

1 kg ripe tomatoes
20 dl oil
1 onion
2 cloves of garlic
1 bayleaf
a pinch of thyme
6 aubergines of medium size
some flour for aubergines
2 dl olive oil
4—5 small grill sausages
40 gr butter
parsley
salt
pepper

Heat oil, add finely chopped onion, cook slowly to soften, add chopped garlic, bayleaf, thyme and sliced tomatoes. Cook at medium heat until all is tender and the water evaporates. Pass through a sieve, bring to the boil (if the sauce is not thick enough), add salt and pepper.

Peel aubergines, cut into rounds, salt and leave to stand for about 30 minutes, rinse with cold water, drain and wipe, then roll in flour and fry in olive oil until slightly brown. Prick each suasage with a needle here and there and bake (preferably grill). Place aubergines in a fireproof dish, sprinkle with pepper, then place sausages over. Pour over with tomato sauce. Put fine slices of butter on top. Preheat oven to 250°C, and bake about 20—25 minutes.

Serve warm.

Turkey

AUBERGINES WITH CHICK-PEAS

(for 8 persons)

1 kg aubergines
1/4 l olive (or plain) oil
3 onions
salt
pepper
400 gr cooked chick-peas
1,5 kg tomatoes

Wash aubergines, remove stalks, peel and cut into bigger cubes and drain. Heat oil, add cubed aubergines, cook slowly about 5—10 minutes, then take them out and spread in a fireproof dish. Peel onion, slice finely and cook slowly in oil until brown, then spread over the aubergines, pour in oil in which onion was fried, add salt and pepper. Add cooked chick-peas, level and pour in the rest of the oil. Wash tomatoes, cut into rounds and place over the chick-peas. Add salt and pepper once again, pour in 3—4 dl of water, bring slowly to the boil, then put in the oven, preheated to 200°C. Bake about 40 minutes. Serve warm with cornbread or pogatcha. In addition to Turkey, this dish is often prepared in Bulgaria and in Greece.

Bulgaria

AUBERGINES WITH CHEESE

(for 6 persons)

6 aubergines
1 l salted water
250—300 gr sheep cheese
200 gr kaymak
1 onion
1 bunch of parsley
1 egg
oil or butter for greasing

Peel aubergines and cook in salted water. When tender, take out, drain and cool. Cut into halves and carefully take out the meat, chop it and fry in some oil. Crush cheese well, add 150 gr kaymak, finely chopped onion, chopped parsley, cooled aubergine meat, egg and salt. Mix well. Fill the aubergine halves with this filling and place in greased baking pan or fireproof dish. Put some leftover kaymak over each aubergine.

Preheat the oven to 200 °C and bake the aubergines about 30—40 minutes or until slightly brown.

In the traditional Bulgarian cuisine, aubergines prepared this way can also be served as the main dish for the evening meal.

Turkey

STUFFED AUBERGINES – "IMAM BAYILDI"

600 gr (4) aubergines
2 tablespoons oil
100 gr onion
500 gr tomatoes
20 gr butter
2 cloves of garlic
salt
1 bayleaf
1 cinnamon bark
pepper
2 bunches of parsley
butter or oil for greasing
6 black olives
6 fillets or rolls anchovies

Cut off the stalks and "caps" of aubergines. Heat oil in a bigger frying pan, put in aubergines, fry them on all sides about 5 minutes, then cool and peel. Cut them lengthways, taking care that they do not split at their ends, then scoop out the meat carefully.

Peel onion and slice finely. Blanch and peel tomatoes, then cut into rounds. Heat butter, add onion, cook slowly until slightly brown, add tomatoes, cook for another 10 minutes, then add crushed garlic, bayleaf, cinnamon bark, salt and pepper. Cook slowly together for a short while. Add chopped parsley in the end. Remove bayleaf and cinnamon bark and fill the aubergines with the mixture. Grease a fireproof dish with oil or butter, arrange aubergines in it and bake in the oven preset at 180 °C about 15 minutes.

Take out of the oven and garnish with olives and fillets or rolls of anchovies. Serve warm or cold.

"Imam bayildi" literally translated from Turkish means the "fainted imam". Namely, there is a story that an imam from Istanbul was so delighted with the taste of that dish that he fainted.

Greece

CALF'S HEAD WITH MARINADE

1—1,5 kg calf's head
juice of 1/2 lemon
2 smaller onions
2 leeks
2 carrots
1 sage leaf
1/2 bunch of parsley
salt

For marinade:
10—12 fresh mint leaves
2 dl oil
1/2—1 dl vinegar
1—2 cloves of garlic
1 teaspoon mustard
salt
pepper to taste

Clean calf's head well, leave it to stand in cold water for a while, then rub well with lemon juice, place in a corresponding pot with enough cold water to cover it, add peeled and sliced onion, leeks, carrots, add sage, parsley and salt. Simmer until tender (about 2 hours). Take the head out, drain and cut into pieces. While the meat is still warm, put it on a clean wet cloth, form a "loaf", tie up with string and leave in the refrigerator overnight to harden. (The parcel can be pressed with a heavier object.)

Prepare the marinade in the following way: in a deeper bowl mix well vinegar, oil, salt and pepper, add crushed garlic and finely chopped mint leaves. Leave to stand for 10—15 minutes.

Take the meat out of the cloth, cut into rounds and arrange on a plate. Serve with marinade, with fresh pogatcha or with any kind of homemade bread.

Bulgaria

CALF'S HEAD IN TRIPE

(for 10 persons)

1 calf's head
1 calf's liver
1 calf's lights (lungs)
1 calf's tripe
50 gr lard
1 lemon
3 onions
salt
peppercorns
ground pepper
red paprika pepper
1 bunch parsley
3 tablespoons lard or oil for greasing and pouring over

Clean calf's head well, wash and put into enough salted water to cover it, then half cook it. Leave in the soup to cool. Cook liver and lights, cool and chop finely. Wash well calf's tripe, leave to stand in water to which several slices of lemon, rounds of onion and a few peppercorns have been added.

Cook slowly 2 chopped onions in heated lard, until tender and brown, add chopped liver and lights, cook together, add salt, pepper, red paprika pepper and chopped parsley. Drain tripe, wipe a little and spread out. Place cooled head on the tripe. Arrange liver evenly round the head and truss the tripe. Grease well a bigger baking pan with oil or lard, place the head with the tripe round it and pour over with melted lard or oil. Bake in the oven preheated to 175 °C until the tripe is brown and tender. When done, leave to cool and then serve. The whole head can be brought to the table, or else meat can be separated and arranged nicely with the filling.

This dish, also a traditional Serbian specialty, is usually served with ayvar, fresh young vegetables etc.

Turkey

CROQUETTES FILLED WITH CHEESE

For dough:
120—150 gr flour
1 egg
some water
salt
For filling:
50 gr butter or margarine
30 gr flour
1/4 l milk
250 gr kachkaval (or similar cheese)
salt
cayenne pepper or small hot peppers
1 egg
about 3 dl oil for frying

Sift flour, add egg, salt and very little water. Work into a smooth, harder dough, leave to stand for a while, then roll out thinly.

Melt butter, warm a little, add flour, fry stirring until brown, pour in warm milk slowly, mix well and simmer about 5—10 minutes, add salt, cayenne pepper or diced small hot peppers. Mix and roll into cork shapes (croquettes).

Cut dough into rectangles the size of the croquettes. Fold each croquette into the dough on all sides. Roll in well beaten egg and fry in heated oil until nicely brown.

Serve warm with some savoury sauce.

Roumania

CROQUETTES WITH COOKED BEEF

(for 4—6 persons)

400 gr cooked beef
150 gr leaner pork
salt
red paprika pepper
pepper
marjoram
3 eggs
several tablespoons flour
150 gr breadcrumbs
2—3 dl oil for frying

Grind cooked beef and pork, add salt, pepper, red paprika pepper, marjoram and 1 egg. Mix all well and leave to stand for a while. Roll into cork shapes (croquettes) about 10 cm long. Roll them in flour, beaten eggs and breadcrumbs. Fry in heated oil on all sides until nicely brown.

In Romania tomato sause (see page 229) is usually served with these croquettes. Other sauces, warm or cold, can also be served with them.

Turkey

FRITTERS WITH THICK YOGHURT

(for 8—10 persons)

500 gr flour
2—3 dl milk
30 gr yeast
2 eggs
2 whole eggs
120 gr butter or margarine
1 small glass of rum
salt
about 400 gr oil for frying
1—1,5 thick yoghurt or sour cream
5—6 cloves of garlic

Sift flour and warm it a little. Crumble yeast, add 2—3 tablespoons of lukewarm water and some flour, mix well and leave in a warm place to rise. In the meantime mix egg yolks, whole eggs, warm milk in which butter or margarine has melted, salt and rum. Turn all into the well made in flour, mix, add creamed yeast. With a wooden spoon or a mixer, make a smooth batter which does not stick and has a lot of bubbles in it. Set in a warm place to rise. When it has risen, heat oil, take up bits of batter with a spoon, drop into hot oil and fry until evenly brown.

Arrange warm fried fritters in a baking pan or a fireproof dish and pour thick yoghurt or sour cream, to which finely chopped or crushed garlic has been added, over each row of fritters. In the end pour over some melted butter and bake shortly in the oven preheated to 250°C. Serve warm.

Yugoslavia

DOUGHNUTS WITH HAM FROM VOJVODINA

(for 8—10 persons)

For dough:
500 gr flour
30 gr yeast
1/4 l lukewarm milk
50 gr butter or margarine
salt
1 egg
3—4 dl oil for frying
cheese for sprinkling over

For filling:
200 gr cooked or smoked ham
2—3 tablespoons sour cream
salt
pepper

Warm flour a bit, then sift. Make a well in the center, add crumbled yeast, pour over 2—3 tablespoons of lukewarm milk, mix and dust with some flour. Set in a warm place to rise. Mix the creamed yeast with flour, add the rest of the lukewarm milk in which butter or margarine has melted, then add beaten egg and salt. Knead into a smooth, fairly soft dough. Leave in a warm place to rise.

In the meantime grind ham, mix with sour cream, add pepper and salt as needed.

Toss the risen dough on board dredged with flour and roll out a slightly thinner layer. Cover half of the dough with spoonfuls of ham filling, rather close to each other. Cover with the other half of the dough. Take out the rounds of dough with a cutter so that the ham filling is always in the middle. Fry in heated oil or lard, drain on brown paper, arrange on a serving plate and sprinkle with grated kachkaval. Serve warm.

Yugoslavia

HAM "BREAD" FROM SREM

(for 6 persons)

400—500 gr lean cooked ham
30 gr butter or margarine
30 gr flour
1/4 l warm milk
salt
pepper
allspice
1 tablespoon lemon juice
6 gelatin sheets
1/4 l double cream
2 dl warm water

For garnishing:
100 gr (1/2 head) lettuce
juice of 1/2 lemon
250 gr sprigged cauliflower
1 lemon
40 gr horseradish (from jar or tube)

Chop ham finely. Heat butter or margarine, add flour and fry shortly stirring all the time (so that it does not change colour), pour in milk slowly and simmer about 10 minutes, stirring occasionally. Add salt, pepper, allspice, lemon juice and the chopped ham in the end. Soak gelatin in lukewarm water, drain, add 3 tablespoons of lukewarm water, mix until completely dissolved, stir into the ham and leave in a cool place to stand for about 30 minutes.

Beat cream, mix into the cooled ham. Line a longer, deeper baking pan with tin foil, turn in the prepared mixture,level, cover with foil and leave in the refrigerator for 2—3 hours. Before serving, dip the pan shortly into hot water and turn the "bread" out carefully. Cut into slices about 1,5—2 cm thick. Wash lettuce, wipe, pour over with lemon juice. Place on a serving dish and arrange ham "bread" slices over. Garnish with lemon rounds, cooked cauliflower springs and horseradish.

It can also be served with the horseradish and cream sauce (see page 234).

Yugoslavia

HAM BAKED IN DOUGH

(to serve several times)

1 kg flour
30 gr yeast
1 teaspoon sugar
salt
2—4 dl lukewarm water (depending on the quality of flour)
1 ham of medium size

Sift flour and add salt. Crumble yeast, mix with some flour, 2 tablespoons of lukewarm water and sugar, then set in a warm place to rise. Mix creamed yeast with flour, gradually pour in lukewarm water and knead into a softer dough. Leave in a warm place about 30 minutes to rise a little.

Wipe the ham well with warm water and a clean cloth. Roll out the dough into a bigger layer, put the ham in the middle, wrap it on all sides with the dough to be covered completely. Grease a baking pan with lard, put the ham in it, prick with a fork in several places. Heat the oven to 175°C and bake about 3—4 hours until the crust is nicely brown.

Take the ham out of the oven, cool a little and take off the dough carefully. Cut the ham into nice slices, and the dough into pieces. Serve with pickled cabbage, pickled paprikas, gherkins, spring onions and the like.

The ham prepared this way is very tasty, as it preserves its own flavour and remains juicy.

Yugoslavia

SHORTBREAD WITH HAM

(for 6 persons)

For dough:
200 gr flour
200 gr white cow cheese (the so-called German cheese)
200 gr butter or margarine

For filling:
80—100 gr butter or margarine
4 eggs
1/2 bun or as much white bread
1/2 dl lukewarm milk
1/2—1 dl sour cream
200—250 gr ground ham
salt
pepper
1 egg for brushing over
75 gr grated kachkaval or similar cheese

Sift flour, add crumbled cheese, thinly sliced butter or margarine. Knead quickly into a smooth dough, form into a ball and leave in a cool place to stand about 60 minutes.

In the meantime prepare the filling: beat butter until fluffy, add egg yolks, salt, pepper, bun or bread soaked in milk and drained, sour cream and ground ham, mix well. Whisk whites of egg stiffly. Stir slowly half of the grated cheese and whisked egg whites in turn into the ham.

Roll out half of the dough to cover the greased bottom of the baking pan, turn in the filling over it, cover with the other half of the rolled out dough, press it a little to stick to the filling. Brush the pie with a well beaten egg and sprinkle with the rest of cheese. Bake in the oven preset at 175°C about 40—45 minutes. When done, cool and cut into squares. Serve warm.

Yugoslavia

OFFAL SERBIAN WAY — "KAVURMA"

(to serve several times)

1 pig's liver
1 pig's lights (lungs)
1 kg pig's entrails
1 kg young bull's tripes
1 pig's heart
1 pig's stomach
1 kg cracklings
1 kg onion
1 tablespoon lard
salt
pepper
1—2 bayleaves
red paprika pepper
2—3 cloves of garlic

Wash offal thoroughly, cook in water to which salt has been added, 1 onion, 2 cloves of garlic, a few peppercorns and bayleaf. When tender, take out, drain, cool and cut into cubes.

Cook finely chopped onion slowly in heated lard until quite soft, add cubed offal, cook together for 40 more minutes, stirring constantly, then add cracklings, salt, pepper and continue cooking slowly for 15—20 minutes. Stir in red paprika pepper in the end. Pour the mixture into a tepsiya or an enamelled baking pan, level and leave to cool and harden.

"Kavurma" can be poured over with melted lard and preserved that way, if it is not all used up.

Serve warm or cold. When cold, cut into bigger squares. It is usually served with sauerkraut and pickled paprikas from the turshiya.

Greece

SALAD WITH TUNNY-FISH

500 gr tomatoes
2 paprikas (red and green)
1 lettuce
1 tin of tunny-fish
vinegar
mustard
salt
3 gherkins
100 gr olives (black and green)
2 hard boiled eggs
2—3 small gherkins to garnish

Cut paprikas into halves, remove seeds and cut into strips. Wash tomatoes, drain, slice, remove seeds and juice. Wash lettuce, drain and arrange at the bottom of the salad bowl. Take tunny-fish from can, crumble, add oil from the can, mustard, vinegar, some salt and gherkins cut into rounds. Add papri-

kas and tomatoes, to which some oil has been added, and olives. Mix all slowly and arrange over the lettuce leaves. Garnish with rounds or slices of hard boiled eggs, decoratively cut small gherkins and with olives.

Serve with warm lepinyas or with homemade brown bread.

Greece

COLD FISH APPETISER

1 kg sea-bream or other white sea fish
2 carrots
1 parsley root
1 onion
1 bayleaf
2 slices of lemon
salt
peppercorns
100—150 gr mayonnaise (or mayonnaise made of 2 eggs)
1 green and 1 red paprika
1 lemon
1/2 bunch parsley

Clean and wash fish well, sprinkle with lemon juice. Pour water in a deeper pan, add scraped root vegetables, sliced onion, bayleaf, salt, pepper and lemon slices, cook at medium heat for 15—20 minutes, then plunge into it the prepared fish. Simmer. When tender, cool, take out of water, drain, remove skin and bones. Arrange on an oval plate, taking care that pieces of fish remain whole. Cover the whole fish with mayonnaise.

Garnish with rounds of lemon, green and red paprikas and with parsley leaves.

Greece

MARINADED MACKERELS

(for 10 persons)

10 mackerels
juice of 1 lemon
100—200 gr flour
salt
1—1,5 dl olive (or sunflower) oil

For marinade:
3 onions
2 carrots
1 parsley root
1/2 celery root
2 fresh green paprikas
1 bayleaf
4 cloves of garlic
salt
pepper
juice of 1 lemon
1 dl white wine
1 dl water
1 bunch of parsley

Clean mackerels, wash, drain, wipe, sprinkle with lemon juice and salt. Roll in flour and fry in heated oil. Arrange fried mackerels in a corresponding, slightly deeper dish (preferably a fireproof one).

Peel onion, scrape carrots, parsley and celery, wash and core paprikas. Cut all into rouns and strips, add water, wine, chopped garlic, bayleaf, salt, pepper and lemon juice. Cook, covered, about 40 minutes. When vegetables are soft, pour in oil in which fish was fried (or new one) and add chopped parsley.

Pour hot marinade over the fish, leave to cool and then put into refrigerator for at least 1 hour.

Roumania

MARINADED STUFFED STERLETS

4 young sterlets (not longer than 25 cm)
1 carrot
1 celery root
1 parsley root
2 onions
1 tablespoon chopped parsley
1/2 tablespoon chopped dill
salt
pepper
1 dl olive oil
1,5 dl white wine

Clean fish well and rub outsides and insides with salt and pepper. Scrape carrot, celery and parsley, cut into small cubes. Peel onion and chop finely. Cook onion slowly in one spoonful of oil, then add vegetables and cook until tender. Towards the end stir in parsley and dill. Add some water as needed, because vegetables should not get dark. Fill fish with this filling and then truss or stick the opening with toothpicks. Leave some filling aside, and place it at the bottom of the baking pan. Arrange stuffed fish over it. Mix the rest of oil with wine and pour over the fish. Bake in the oven preheated to 170°C for 30—40 minutes, or until fish soften. Take them out of the pan, remove thread or toothpicks, arrange on a serving plate and keep in a cool, dry place, but not in the refrigerator!

Vegetables can be eaten separately or with fish.

Greece

CODFISH CROQUETTES

(for 6 persons)

450—500 gr salt fillets of cod
500 gr cooked potatoes
1 tablespoon butter
1/2 cup milk
pepper
powdered nutmeg
2 eggs
some chopped parsley
1 cup grated cheese (kachkaval or similar)
2—3 tablespoons flour
1 cup breadcrumbs
2—3 dl oil for frying

Soak salt fillets of cod in lukewarm water and leave them to stand for 24 hours. Drain, crumble with a fork, add peeled and sieved or pressed potatoes, butter, milk, pepper and nutmeg. Warm at low heat until the mixture is thick. Take off the heat, cool a little, mix in one egg and one egg yolk, chopped parsley and grated cheese. Mix, cover and leave in the refrigerator for 2—3 hours. When cool, roll into square croquettes, roll in flour. Mix well oil and white of egg (preferably with a mixer). Roll croquettes in whisked egg white, then in breadcrumbs and fry in heated oil until nicely brown. Drain and place on absorbent paper. Serve sprinkled with chopped parsley.

Egg and lemon sauce can be served with croquettes: beat well 3 eggs, gradually pouring in hot bone or meat stock, or soup from cube, then juice of one bigger lemon. Add salt and mix over steam until thick. Cool stirring constantly. Serve sauce in a separate bowl. Garnish with lemon rounds and a sprig of parsley.

Yugoslavia

ASPIC — "PIHTIYE"

(for 6—8 persons)

1 kg pork for meat jelly (legs, ears, skins, part of the head)
2—2,5 l water
2 bayleaves
peppercorns
1 parsley root
1 parsnip
1 carrot, 1 onion
2—3 cloves of garlic
salt
1—2 hard boiled eggs

Put well cleaned and washed pig's legs, ears, skins and parts of head into cold water, bring to the boil and simmer. When the scum on the surface settles down, add the prepared root vegetables, bayleaf, pepper, peeled and halved onion, garlic and salt. Simmer until the liquid half evaporates and becomes sticky, and the bones begin to separate from the meat. Take off the heat and leave to cool a little. Remove the surplus of fat from the surface, take out meat and strain the soup through a strainer and a clean white cloth. Remove bones from meat. Cut carrot and hard boiled eggs into rounds.

Arrange pieces of meat into a deeper bowl (or several smaller ones), add carrot and egg rounds and pour the strained soup over. Leave in a cool place or in the refrigerator.

Before serving, shake carefully out, on to a big, shallow plate. Aspic can be poured over with oil mixed with lemon juice or vinegar, or it can be served with grated horseradish mixed with wine vinegar, or with mayonnaise.

Yugoslavia

ROLL WITH BRAINS FROM VOJVODINA

(for 6 persons)

1/2 l milk
80 gr flour
6 eggs
oil for greasing
flour for dusting
50 gr grated kachkaval (or Parmesan)

For filling:
20 gr oil or lard
2 onions
300—350 gr young bull's brains
salt
pepper
1 bunch of parsley

Heat milk, bring to the boil and pour in flour all at once, mix until thick and sticking to the wall of the pot. Cool and add egg yolks one by one, stirring well every time. Whisk egg whites stiffly and stir in slowly.

Pour the prepared batter into a greased baking pan, dusted with flour. Bake about 25 minutes in the oven preset at 175°C.

In the meantime prepare the filling: slowly cook chopped onion in heated oil or lard, add chopped brains from which veins and blood were first removed in warm water. Cook slowly about 10—15 minutes, add salt and pepper, crumble the brains slightly with a fork, add chopped parsley and mix.

Turn the baked dough on to a clean cloth or board, sprinkle with grated cheese, spread the filling over, roll up, pour over with heated butter and sprinkle with cheese again. Serve warm.

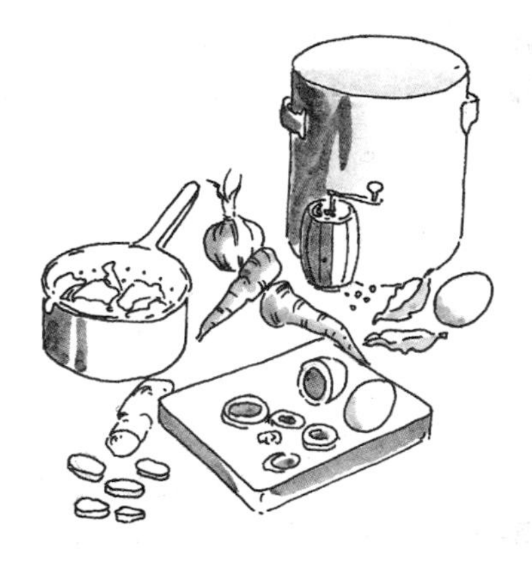

Turkey

COATED BRAINS

1 calf's brains
1 tablespoon salt
1 egg
100 gr flour
50 gr grated kachkaval
1—2 dl oil for frying
egg and lemon sauce

Soak brains in cold water and leave to stand about 1 hour, then pour out water. In the meantime bring to the boil about 1 liter water with salt, pour it over brains, cover and leave for about 10 minutes. Remove membrane and veins from the brains. Wipe and cut into small pieces. Roll them in flour, then in beaten egg and finally in grated cheese. Fry in hot oil at medium heat until golden brown. Drain on brown paper. Serve warm with egg and lemon sauce (see page 234).

Bulgaria

CHICKEN WITH SPINACH

(for 6 persons)

750 gr spinach
100 gr butter or margarine
400 gr white bread without crust
2 dl milk
600—700 gr chicken breast without bones
1 smaller onion
salt, pepper
nutmeg
3 egg yolks
2 dl sour cream
100 gr kachkaval or similar cheese
breadcrumbs for sprinkling over

For sauce:
2 dl sour cream
1—2 red paprikas
2 tablespoons horseradish (freshly grated or from the jar)
2 smaller carrots for garnishing

Wash spinach, remove stems, cook in salted water, drain well, chop and cook slowly in some heated butter or margarine. Pour lukewarm milk over bread, leave to soften, drain and press. Wash chicken meat, cut into smaller pieces, remove bones. Chop onion finely, cook shortly in some butter or margarine, add meat, cook slowly together until tender. When cooked, grind the meat, add spinach, egg yolks, softened bread, sour cream, grated cheese, salt, pepper, nutmeg and in the end stiffly whisked whites of eggs. Mix all slowly.

Grease a baking pan or a fireproof dish, sprinkle with breadcrumbs, turn in the prepared mixture, level. Bake for about 60 minutes in the oven preheated to 175 °C. Pierce with a knife to check whether it is done. If the knife remains clean, the dish is ready. Leave it in the pan for a while, then turn out. Garnish with cooked carrot rounds.

Separately serve cream sause with finely chopped paprikas and freshly grated horseradish.

Yugoslavia

LUMPY PIE FROM KOZARA

1 chicken
salt
4—5 eggs, 200 g flour
2 dl sour cream (or young kaymak)
1 dl milk
1 dl mineral water
red paprika pepper
oil, lard or margarine for greasing

Wash chicken, cut into smaller pieces (neck, wings and back can be used for soup or broth), salt and leave for a while to stand. Beat egg yolks well, add flour, 1 dl of sour cream, milk and mineral water. Mix all well. Then add stiffly whisked whites of eggs.

Grease a tepsiya or a tin pan well, heat and pour in the prepared dough. Arrange pieces of chicken meat over the dough, sprinkle with red paprika pepper. Preheat the oven to 200 °C and bake the pie about 35—40 minutes, take out, brush with the remaining sour cream and bake on for 20 minutes until it is evenly brown and the meat soft.

Cool the "lumpy pie" a little, then cut into pieces and serve warm.

2

SOUPS AND THICK SOUPS

Soup should have a magic quality: it should stimulate the appetite, stir up desire for the following course, satisfy hunger a little, but not fill up. If it does not answer to all these requirements, it has not fulfilled its task. That is why soup or broth must be very tasty but not heavy, it must be warm enough but not hot, it should have enough spices to stimulate digestion but only up to a certain point.

All these things have been taken into consideration in the choice of recipes. One of the characteristics of the Balkan soups is that meat is cooked with rather a lot of different vegetables. They are sometimes served on a separate plate with strained, clear soup and eaten straight after the soup with pickled horseradish or horseradish sauce. Thick soups are made with a great variety of vegetables, from potatoes to nettles and young sweetcorn. In addition to warm thick soups, there are some cold ones, served in a warmer season. They come from the coastal parts of the Balkans where summers are hot.

Fish thick soups are a special delicacy, particularly in Yugoslavia and Roumania, where they are prepared by the banks of the Danube in pots hanging over open fires. They are the so-called fishermen's thick soups well-known in these parts, which can be a culinary sensation even when prepared on the kitchen stove.

Greece

SOUP WITH LEMON — SOUP "AVGHOLEMONO"

(for 6 persons)

1,5 l clear chicken soup
50 gr rice (the longish grains)
4 eggs
juice of 1 bigger lemon
salt, pepper

Prepare chicken soup in the usual way. Wash rice, drain. Heat the soup, bring it to the boil, add rice and simmer for 15—20 minutes, then remove from heat.

Beat eggs well (with a wire whip preferably), slowly adding lemon juice.

Take out 1/4 to 1/2 l of chicken soup. When it boils remove from heat and slowly stir in the beaten eggs with lemon, and then pour the mixture very slowly into the soup. Heat soup but do not boil. When ready, add salt and peper.

In Greece, many dishes like thick soups, ragouts and the like are seasoned with the mixture of lemon and eggs ("avgholemono").

Yugoslavia

BEY'S THICK SOUP

400—500 gr chicken meat
1—1,5 l water
100 gr carrots
50 gr parsley root
50 gr celery
salt, pepper
50 gr rice
50 gr okras
2 egg yolks
1,5 dl sour cream
2 tablespoons chopped parsley

Wash meat and put it into cold water, heat slowly. Clean and wash vegetables and add them to the soup when it starts to boil, add salt and simmer meat and vegetables until tender. Take everything out when cooked and strain soup. Remove bones, cut meat and vegetables into smaller cubes, return to strained soup, add separately cooked rice and okras. Simmer together for a short while, add salt and pepper to taste.

Mix egg yolks and sour cream and add to the soup constantly stirring, just before serving.

In the traditional Bosnian cuisine parsley was not added to this thick soup, but now it is added before serving — for better taste and more vitamins.

Turkey

THICK BEEF SOUP

(for 6—8 persons)

1,5 l strong beef soup
40 gr flour
500 gr cooked beef
40 gr melted butter
red paprika pepper

Prepare beef soup in the usual way and strain it. Blend flour with cold water into a smooth, not very thick mixture. Pour it into the simmering soup, then cook for 10—15 minutes. Cut cooked beef into smaller cubes.

Mix melted butter with red paprika pepper. Pour into the soup just before serving it. Beef cubes can be added to the soup or served separately.

Greece

THICK LAMB SOUP — "MAYIRITSA"

(for 6 persons)

lamb offal (liver and lights, heart and entrails)
salt
juice of 1/2 lemon
5 spring onions
1 dl melted butter (margarine or oil)
1/2 bunch of fresh dill
pepper
90—100 gr rice
3 eggs
juice of 1 bigger lemon
2 dl hot soup

Wash liver, lights and heart. Clean entrails separatley, wash and turn inside out with the help of a wooden spoon handle, rub with salt and lemon juice, leave to stand and then wash well. Heat 1,5 l water, add washed offal and simmer. Bring to the boil, remove part of the scum, add salt and cook until tender. Drain cooked offal, cut into cubes or strips. Clean and cut spring onions. Heat butter, add onions, cook slowly until tender, add chopped dill, meat and pepper and cook slowly together about 5 minutes. Stirring all the time, add strained soup in which offal was cooked, simmer for another 20—25 minutes.

Pick over rice, wash, cook about 20 minutes in slightly salted water, drain and add to the soup.

Beat eggs, add to them slowly and in turn lemon juice and some hot soup and stir all the time. Pour this mixture slowly into the hot soup, which must not boil any more. Serve very warm.

Greece

THICK SOUP WITH MEAT BALLS

(for 6 persons)

40 gr oil or lard
1 onion
2 smaller carrots
1 smaller celery root
20 gr flour
200—250 gr ground young beef or mixed ground meat
20 gr rice
1 egg
salt
pepper
1 egg yolk
juice of 1/2 of lemon

Heat oil or lard, add finely chopped onion and carrots and celery peeled and cut into rounds. Cook together until slightly tender, then add about 1—1,5 l of water. Cook at medium heat until tender. Blend flour with some cold water, pour slowly into simmering soup, cook shortly and strain.

Pick over rice, cook in slightly salted water, drain, mix with ground meat, add the egg, salt and a bit more pepper, then mix well. From this mixture shape small balls and cook them in simmering soup about 20 minutes.

Dice cooked celery and carrots and add them to the soup. Mix well egg yolk and lemon juice adding some hot soup slowly. Then add it to the soup which must not boil any more.

Yugoslavia

CHICKEN SOUP FROM VOJVODINA

1 bigger hen (of about 1,5 kg)
root vegetables (2—3 carrots, 2 parsley roots, 1 parsnip, 1/2 celery root, 1/2 kohlrabi, 1 cabbage or kale leaf, 1/2 leek)
1 onion
1 clove garlic
1 small horseradish root
1—2 potatoes
salt
peppercorns

Wash chicken, cut into bigger pieces, pour over it 2—3 l cold water, bring to the boil and simmer. After some time add cleaned vegetables, unpeeled onion baked on top the stove, unpeeled clove of garlic, scraped horseraddish root, peeled potatoes, salt and peppercorns. Simmer until meat and vegetables are tender. Then pour into the soup a glass of cold water, draw aside, leave to stand for a while and strain. The usual thing to add to the strained soup are home-made noodles, semolina dumplings, chicken liver dumplings or the like.

The scum that rises to the surface should not be removed, as it contains important meat substances (albumen) and it dissolves while cooking and partly settles down to the bottom. For a "mighty" soup, people in Vojvodina often cook beef and chicken together.

With this soup, here is the recipe for chicken liver dumplings:

1 small spoon butter or lard
1 bigger chicken liver, 2 eggs
1 tablespoon breadcrumbs
parsley leaves
salt, pepper

Mix butter or lard well, add finely chopped (or scraped) liver, 1 egg, breadcrumbs, salt, pepper, chopped parsley and 1 whipped egg white. Mix all well and leave to stand for a while.

Bring soup to the boil, turn the heat down, take up bit by bit of the prepared mixture with a teaspoon and dip into the simmering soup. When the dumplings emerge to the surface, let them simmer for a further 5—7 minutes. Chopped parsley can also be added to the soup.

Albania

THICK LAMB LIVER SOUP

(for 8—10 persons)

1 lamb liver and 1 lights (lungs)
2 l water
1 bunch of root vegetables
1 bayleaf
1 onion
2 cloves of garlic
2 eggs
40 gr oil
20 gr flour
2 egg yolks
juice of 1 lemon
1 dl sour cream
salt
pepper

Wash liver and lights, put them into a bigger pot, add water and cook at medium heat. When the water boils, add peeled roots and unpeeled onion broiled shortly of the stove on both sides, bayleaf, salt, pepper and a few peppercorns. Hard boil both eggs. When the liver and lights are cooked, cool them and grind together with the hard boiled eggs.

Heat lard or oil, add flour, fry a little until nearly brown, pour in some cold water, then the strained liver soup and in the end the ground livers. Mix well and cook together for a short while.

Mix well egg yolks, sour cream and lemon juice in the soup dish, slowly pouring in the soup and stirring all the time.

Croûtons can be served with this thick soup.

Yugoslavia

THICK CHICKEN SOUP WITH KAYMAK

(for 6 persons)

1 chicken
1—1,5 l lukewarm water
40 gr lard
200—250 gr kaymak
2 onions
20 gr flour
2 tablespoons of kaymak
red paprika pepper
pepper
salt
1/2 bunch of parsley

Clean the chicken, cut into pieces, wash and wipe a little. Heat lard, add pieces of chicken, fry to brown on all sides and then take out. To the leftover lard add finely chopped onion, cook slowly until tender, then add the kaymak and continue frying. Blend flour with some kaymak, add red paprika pepper, mix and add to stewed kaymak, stir, add lukewarm water, meat, more water if necessary, salt and pepper. Simmer all until meat is tender. Sprinkle with chopped parsley before serving.

This broth is most often prepared in Serbia, where the best kaymak is produced.

Turkey

"TUTMATCH" OR "UVALACI" THICK SOUP

(for 6 persons)

1,5 l bone stock (or soup from cube)
150 gr ground lamb or young beef
2 eggs
salt, pepper
flour
2 dl oil for frying
1 smaller thin layer of dough usually used to make "pita" (a type of pie)
1—2 cloves of garlic

Strain soup or prepare soup from cube. Add salt, pepper and 1 egg to the meat, mix, form small balls ("uvalaci"), roll them in flour and fry in heated oil on all sides.

Bring soup to the boil, put in the small meat balls and simmer about 15—20 minutes. Cut the dough layer into tiny squares, add to the soup and cook together for another 10 minutes. Add salt if necessary. Snip garlic and add it to the soup. Beat the egg and pour it in, stirring the simmering soup. Add pepper to taste. This thick soup is mentioned by the poet and chronicler from Sarajevo, Basheskiya, in his chronicle from the middle of the 18th century.

Yugoslavia

SOUR THICK SOUP FROM SHTAYERSKA

750 gr—1 kg pigs' feet and tails
1 bigger carrot
1 bigger parsley root
2 sprigs of celery leaf
1 smaller onion
1—2 cloves of garlic
salt
pepper
500 gr potatoes
30 gr oil or lard
15 gr flour (1 tablespoonful)
1—2 tablespoons wine vinegar

Clean pigs' feet and tails well, wash and cut into smaller pieces, pour in 1,5—2 l of cold water and cook at medium heat. Peel and halve onion, clean garlic and leave the thin skin on.

Bring legs and tails to the boil, leave to simmer about 5—10 minutes, then add prepared vegetables, celery leaf, salt and pepper. Simmer until meat and vegetables are tender.

Peel potatoes, cut into cubes and cook in salted water.

Take cooked meat and vegetables out, strain soup, remove bones, cut meat and vegetables into smaller pieces, return to the soup, add cooked potatoes and some water in which they were cooked (as necessary).

Heat oil, add flour, fry until slightly brown, add some cold water, pour into the soup, mix and leave to simmer about 5—10 minutes. Salt to taste, add vinegar. If desired add chopped parsley to the soup.

Greece

THICK SOUP WITH UNRIPENED BEANS

(for 6—8 persons)

500 gr young (unripened) beans
1,5 l water
30 gr oil
5—6 paprikas
5—6 tomatoes
30 gr flour
30 gr oil
4 cloves of garlic
1 teaspoon red paprika pepper
salt
a few mint leaves
parsley
2 tablespoons oil

Pick over beans, wash, put into cold water, add 1—2 spoons of oil and simmer. Clean paprikas and tomatoes, add to the beans, cook until soft, then take out 3—4 paprikas and the same number of tomatoes.

Heat oil, add flour, fry it a little, add 2 cloves of chopped garlic and red paprika pepper. Fry very shortly, pour in some cold water, then some water in which beans are being cooked, mix and pour into the beans. Simmer for another 10—15 minutes. In the end add chopped mint leaves and parsley.

Skin cooked paprikas and tomatoes, chop and mix with 2 cloves of snipped garlic. Mix well (a mixer may be used), add some heated oil and serve with the soup.

This soup is a bit thicker than the usual thick soups.

Yugoslavia

THICK SOUP WITH SMOKED MEAT

(for 6 persons)

300—350 gr smoked pork
1 onion
1 bunch of root vegetables (carrot, parsley, parsnip, celery)
2 tablespoons tomato purée (from tube)
2 cloves of garlic
1 dl sour cream
1 teaspoon red paprika pepper
1 tablespoon vinegar
1 egg yolk
1 dl sour cream

Wash smoked meat in lukewarm water, add 1—1,5 l cold water and simmer. When meat is half cooked, add chopped onion and roots. Continue simmering until meat and vegetables are tender. Take meat and vegetables out of the soup, add to the soup snipped or crushed garlic and tomato and cook for another 5—10 minutes, then strain. Mix well half of the sour cream, flour, red paprika pepper and vinegar, pour into the strained soup which is only simmering and stir all the time. Simmer for another 10—15 minutes. Remove from heat. Cut meat and greens into cubes and add to the soup. Beat well the egg yolk and the rest of sour cream in the soup dish and then pour in the soup slowly.

This thick soup is prepared mostly in winter months or in early spring, and is considered to be the specialty of Srem (the part of Vojvodina, north-west of Belgrade), although with some small variations (e.g. smoked sausages instead of smoked meat) it is also prepared in other parts of Yugoslavia.

Bulgaria

THICK SOUP WITH YOUNG NETTLES

500 gr young nettles (only the top parts)
40 gr oil
30 gr flour
1—2 cloves of garlic
1/2 l milk and 1/2 l warm water
1 egg
1 dl sour cream
salt
pepper

Clean young nettles, wash and cook in slightly salted water. Drain, rinse, drain again and then chop or pass through a sieve. Heat oil, add flour, fry it a little until slightly brown, add snipped garlic, pour in cold and then warm water, add nettles, milk, salt and pepper, then simmer for another 10 minutes. Beat egg yolk with sour cream, add to the soup stirring it all the time just before serving.

Croûtons can be served with this thick soup.

Thick soups with spinach, Swiss chard or sorrel can be prepared in the same way.

Yugoslavia

THICK SOUP WITH SAUERKRAUT BRINE

(for 5—6 persons)

1 bunch of root vegetables
30 gr oil (3—4 tablespoons)
30 gr flour
1 onion

1 bayleaf
salt
pepper
1 small hot pepper
1 l brine (in which cabbage has fermented for 4—6 weeks)
1—2 dl lukewarm water

Clean soup greens (carrot, parsley root, parsnip, 1/2 celery root), wash and cut into rounds. Heat oil, add prepared roots, fry them a little, dust with flour, stir for a short while, add chopped onion, bayleaf and hot pepper. Cook slowly together for a while, add some lukewarm water. When the vegetables are tender pour in the brine, heat at medium fire and cook for another 15—20 minutes. Separately cooked rice or some chopped sauerkraut can be added to the soup.

If a richer brine soup is desired, thicker slices of sausage from Kranj (Slovenia), of frankfurter or of thin Serbian sausage poached in boiling water, can be placed in the soup dish.

This thick soup is usually prepared after some festivity at which there has been too much eating and drinking, as customary in the Balkans, so that some "fasting" as a rest for the stomach is essential.

Bulgaria

THICK SOUP WITH LEEKS AND CHEESE

500 gr leeks
50 gr butter or margarine
40 gr flour
2 dl cold and 8 dl warm water
80 gr kachkaval or ripened cheese in slices
2 eggs
1 dl thick yoghurt
salt
1 tablespoon chopped celery leaf

Trim leeks, wash, cut into thinner rounds, wash again and drain. Heat butter, add leeks, cook slowly until slightly soft, add flour, fry together until brown, pour in cold and then warm water. Simmer for about 15—20 minutes. Towards the end of cooking add grated or crushed

cheese. Beat egg yolks well with thick yoghurt, add some soup, mix and add to the ready soup. Before serving add celery and salt to taste.

Bulgaria

THICK SOUP WITH ENTRAILS

(for 6 persons)

500 gr intestines of young lamb or suckling pig
salt
juice of 1/2 lemon
1—1,5 l water
1 onion
1—2 cloves of garlic
peppercorns
40 gr oil or lard
1 bunch of spring onions
20 gr flour
1 teaspoon red paprika pepper
1/2 bunch of parsley
1 egg yolk
1 dl thick yoghurt (or sour cream)
vinegar to taste (1—2 spoons)

Clean well the entrails of young lamb or suckling pig, wash and turn inside out with a wooden spoon handle or a thin stick. Rub with some salt and lemon juice, leave them to stand for a while, then wash again well, drain and cut into smaller pieces, add water and cook at medium heat. When it boils, add crudely chopped onion, garlic, salt and peppercorns, then cook until the entrails are tender. When cooked, take them out and drain. Heat oil, add chopped spring onions, fry them until soft, dust with flour, fry until it gets slightly brown, add red paprika pepper, pour in some cold water and then the strained soup in which the guts were cooked. Cook for another 10—15 minutes, add the entrails and chopped parsley.

Beat eggs well with thick yoghurt, add some soup, mix, pour everything into the soup, add vinegar to taste as well as salt and pepper.

With small variations this thick soup is prepared in all the Balkan countries, especially in spring.

Bulgaria

THICK SOUP WITH TRIPES

(for 6—8 persons)

500—700 gr cooked tripes
1,5 l soup of cooked tripes
40 gr oil or melted butter
1 bigger onion
2—3 fresh paprikas
20 gr flour
1 tablespoon tomato purée (from the tube)
2 cloves of garlic
salt
marjoram
bayleaf
thyme
pepper
40 gr grated kachkaval cheese
1/2 bunch of parsley

Heat oil or butter, add chopped onion, cook it slowly, add cored paprikas cut into strips, fry until all is tender. Dust with flour, fry it a little, add slightly diluted tomato and tripes cut into strips. Pour over with the soup in which tripes were cooked (or soup from cube), add salt and pepper, a bit of each spice and chopped or crushed garlic. Simmer shortly. Before serving add chopped parsley and kachkaval.

Kachkaval can be served separately.

Bulgaria

THICK SOUP WITH HERBS

100 gr parsley
100 gr dill
40 gr mint leaves
40 gr celery leaves
50 gr butter or oil
40 gr flour
3/4—1 l water
2 eggs
2 dl thick yoghurt (or slightly diluted sour cream)
juice of 1 lemon
salt

Wash spice herbs, remove stalks and snip all. Heat butter or oil, add prepared herbs, cook slowly in a covered pot. When tender, add flour, fry a little and add water. Simmer for about 10—15 minutes.

Mix separately egg yolks, thick yoghurt or sour cream and lemon juice. Add soup slowly, then stir all well. The soup must not boil any more.

Croûtons can be served with this thick soup.

Bulgaria

THICK MILK SOUP WITH COURGETTES

4—5 dl milk
3 dl water
450 gr courgettes
40 gr semolina
40 gr butter
1—2 eggs
1 dl thick yoghurt or sour cream
salt
1/2 bunch parsley or dill

Mix milk and water, add salt and heat. When it boils add cleaned courgettes cut into cubes and simmer. When courgettes are tender, add semolina to which water or milk had first been added, then add butter. Simmer together and if necessary add some more warm water. When the soup is ready beat egg yolk with milk or sour cream and pour into it, then sprinkle with chopped parsley or dill.

This delicious, light and nutritious thick soup is particularly good for summer days.

Roumania

THICK POTATO SOUP

(for 8 persons)

2 l cold water
6—8 big potatoes
3 bigger onions
2 big ripe tomatoes
1 carrot
1 tablespoon chopped shallots (or leeks or spring onion leaves)
1 tablespoonful chopped parsley
1 clove of garlic
salt
pepper
2—3 rashers streaky smoked bacon
1 small finely chopped onion
1—2 tablespoons flour
1 teaspoon red paprika pepper
1 egg yolk
1,5 dl sour cream
1 tablespoon chopped dill
2 dl sour cream for serving

Peel potatoes, wash and dice. Put into cold water and heat. Peel onion and cut into slices, peel tomatoes and cut into smaller pieces, scrape carrot and cut into small rounds. When the water boils put in all the vegetables, together with chopped shallot (or leek or spring onion leaves) parsley and chopped garlic and simmer until potatoes are half cooked. Add salt and pepper.

Fry bacon cut into cubes in the frying pan. When it lets out fat, add chopped onion, fry a little, add flour, stir a couple of times, add salt, pepper and red paprika pepper, mix well, add some cold water, stir and mix into the soup. Simmer further until all the vegetables are tender.

Beat egg yolk with sour cream, add chopped dill and mix into the cooked soup.

Serve in small deep table soup dishes, and put a spoonful of sour cream into each dishful of soup just before serving.

Turkey

COLD POTATO SOUP

(for 6 persons)

1—1,5 l water
500 gr potatoes (the floury variety)
salt
1—1,5 dl milk
2 tablespoons oil
salt
pepper
juice of 1/2 lemon
1 tablespoon chopped parsley

Peel potatoes, cook in salted water. When soft, drain, mash, add heated milk, oil, salt and pepper to taste, mix well, add water in which potatoes were cooked. Mix all well to make a smooth, slightly thicker soup. In the end add lemon juice and chopped parsley and cool. This refreshing and nourishing thick soup is popular, particularly in summer months.

Bulgaria

COLD THICK SOUP WITH STRING BEANS

250 gr string beans
40 gr oil
1 onion
1 bigger carrot
1 parsley root
1 smaller celery root
salt
pepper
1 teaspoon red paprika pepper
1 l warm water
1 bigger ripe tomato (or 1 levelled tablespoon tomato from tube)
20 gr rice
20 gr flour
1/2 bunch of parsley or dill
2 dl thick yoghurt

Clean string beans, wash and cut into smaller pieces. Chop onion finely, scrape carrot, parsley and celery, wash and cut into rounds or strips. Heat oil, add onion, cook it slowly until soft, then add string beans, carrot, parsley, celery and red paprika pepper. Cook on for a while, then add warm water, cover and simmer. When vegetables are tender, add peeled and chopped tomatoes, salt, pepper and the picked over and washed rice. Simmer on until rice is tender. Mix flour with some cold water into a smooth, not very thick paste and pour it into the soup. Cook for 10 minutes, remove from stove, add chopped parsley. Serve cold and seasoned with thick yoghurt.

This thick soup is often prepared in the traditional Bulgarian cooking, especially in summer and autumn.

Bulgaria

CREAM SOUP WITH COURGETTES

500 gr courgettes
1 onion
40 gr butter or margarine
1/2 l warm water
40 gr flour
4 dl milk
1 hard boiled egg
1/2 bunch of dill
salt

Wash courgettes, peel and cut into cubes. Chop onion finely. Heat butter, add chopped onion and cook slowly until tender, add courgettes, cook shortly together, then add warm water. Simmer at medium heat. When courgettes are tender, pass everything through a sieve. Mix flour with some cold milk, add purée of courgettes and add the rest of milk. Cook together about 10—15 minutes. Before serving add chopped hard boiled egg and snipped dill.

Croûtons can be served with this thick soup.

Turkey

THICK MUTTON SOUP

(for 6—8 persons)

1,5 l mutton soup
30 gr flour
2—3 eggs
juice of 1 bigger lemon
salt
2 tablespoons lukewarm water

Prepare soup with about 500 gr somewhat more fatty mutton. When the meat is tender, take it out and strain soup. Mix flour, eggs, lemon juice and water into a smooth mixture, add hot soup slowly bit by bit, then pour it slowly into the remaining soup. Simmer it for 10—15 minutes. Salt to taste. In the end add cooked mutton cut into cubes. Serve very warm.

Roumania

THICK SOUP WITH SWEETCORN

3 young corncobs
250 gr smoked pork ribs
1—2 tablespoons vinegar
1 tearspoon salt
peppercorns
caraway seeds
marjoram
1 bayleaf
1 onion
2 cloves of garlic
200 gr new potatoes
1 dl milk
1 onion
2 tablespoons lard
pepper
salt

Put the following into 1 liter of cold water: 1 teaspoon of salt, a few peppercorns, a bayleaf, a pinch of caraway seeds and of marjoram, a peeled and halved onion, peeled cloves of garlic. Water with spices should be cooked 10—15 minutes, then cooled.

Wash pork ribs well, cut into pieces and put into the cold marinade to stand overnight.

Fry chopped onion in lard the following day, add ribs from the marinade. Peel and dice potatoes, husk and crush sweetcorn, add everything to onion and ribs and cook slowly for a while. Pour in milk and the strained marinade and simmer until all is tender. If necessary add some more salt and pepper.

Turkey

THICK SOUP WITH SQUASH

(for 6 persons)

700 gr pared squash
40 gr butter (or margarine)
15 gr flour
1—1,5 l milk
50 gr young kaymak or 1/2 dl sour cream
salt
20 gr butter or margarine
1/2 teaspoon red paprika pepper

Cut pared squash into small cubes, cook in mildly salted water. When cooked, drain.

Heat butter, add flour, fry it a little, slowly pouring in warm milk, cook, add kaymak or sour cream, simmer about 10 minutes, add cooked squash, then cook together for a short while (about 5 minutes).

Before serving, pour over the soup heated butter with some red paprika pepper added to it.

Bulgaria

COLD SOUP WITH THICK YOGHURT

1 l thick yoghurt
2 fresh cucumbers
350—400 gr cooked young beetroot
2 eggs
salt
1/2 bunch of dill

Beat thick yoghurt, add peeled and diced cucumber, cooked and also diced beetroot, salt, then mix. Hard boil both eggs and dice. Wash dill and wipe, remove stems and snip. Add eggs and dill to the soup and mix. Keep in a cool place until serving.

In summer months this thick soup is a delicious and nutritious refreshment.

If beetroot is cooked together with leaves, they can be passed through a sieve and added to the soup.

Roumania

THICK ROE SOUP

400 gr roe (of sturgeon, perch etc.)
juice of 1 lemon or 2 tablespoons wine vinegar
1 bunch of root vegetables
several peppercorns
salt
1 bayleaf
1—2 cloves of garlic
40 gr oil
30 gr flour
2 eggs
1 dl sour cream
1/2 bunch of parsley

Wash roe, remove thin skin, put into a deeper pot, cover with water to which some vinegar or lemon had been added, leave to stand for a while. In the meantime clean root vegetables, pour over with 1 liter of water, add peppercorns, salt, bayleaf and garlic. Simmer until vegetables are tender, then take them out and cut into smaller cubes.

Heat oil a little, add flour, fry it for a short while, add water in which the greens were cooked, put in the prepared roe and the cubed greens. Simmer about 20—25 minutes, stirring frequently. Beat the egg yolks in the soup dish, add sour cream, lemon juice and chopped parsley. Pour the ready soup into the dish, stir and serve.

This thick soup is prepared in places by the Danube, but also by other rivers where bigger fish of good quality are caught.

Roumania

THICK FISH SOUP

(for 6 persons)

2—3 onions
1—1,5 l water
2—3 carrots
1 parsley root
1 parsnip
1 smaller celery root
1—2 bayleaves
peppercorns
salt
1—1,5 kg freshwater fish
30 gr oil
30 gr flour
1 teaspoon red paprika pepper
salt
pepper
1 dl sour cream
1 egg yolk
juice of 1 lemon

Pour water into a deeper pot. Peel onion, cut into slices. Scrape carrot, parsley, parsnip and celery, cut lengthways and put into cold water together with bayleaf, some salt and a few peppercorns. Heat and simmer until vegetables are tender. Then strain soup and heat it again. Cut cleaned fish into bigger pieces and simmer in strained soup until tender.

Heat oil, add flour, fry until slightly brown, add red paprika pepper, pour some cold water and then some soup, mix all and pour into the soup with cooked fish. If necessary add more salt and pepper and simmer for a short while. Add cooked and chopped roots to the soup.

Before serving, beat egg yolk with sour cream in the soup dish, add lemon juice and stirring all the time pour into the soup. Croûtons or fried bun rounds can be served with this thick fish soup.

Yugoslavia

FISHERMAN'S SOUP

(for 2 persons)

500 gr small freshwater fish (tench, perch)
1/2—3/4 l water
2 onions
1 bigger paprika
1 clove of garlic
1 bunch of parsley
200—300 gr sterlet or catfish
1 tablespoon tomato purée
1 dl white wine
salt
pepper

Clean small fish, wash, cut into halves, add chopped onion and garlic, paprikas cut into bigger strips, sprigs of parsley. Pour in cold water and simmer until all is tender. Pass through a sieve, add tomato, salt, pepper, bring to the boil again and then add pieces of sterlet or catfish, pour in white wine and simmer for another 20—25 minutes.

Greece

GREEK FISH SOUP — "KHAKHAVIA"

(for 6—8 persons)

1 kg mixed sea fish (smaller and larger)
2 l water
450 gr onion
450 gr peeled ripe tomatoes
1 bunch of parsley
1 dl olive (or sunflower) oil
salt
pepper

Clean and wash fish. Pour water into a bigger pan, and sliced onion, tomatoes cut into smaller pieces, chopped parsley, oil, salt and pepper. Bring to the boil and add smaller fish. Simmer until vegetables and fish are tender, then pass through a sieve. Put pieces of larger fish into this thick soup. Simmer for 20—25 minutes until tender.

3

MAIN DISHES

VEGETABLE DISHES

In the Balkan cuisine vegetables have been used abundantly since ancient times when there was no knowledge of vitamins, minerals and chlorophyl. A great many different kinds of vegetables are grown in the Balkans, so that preparing vegetables both as accompaniment to the main dishes, or as the main course without meat has in the course of time greatly improved and become richer.
Numerous kinds of pod vegetables, cabbages, root vegetables and squashes have been used by the inhabitants of the Balkan countries since times long past. It is interesting, however, that the kinds brought over from the New World, such as tomato and paprika, are not used anywhere else in so many different ways and in such quantities as in the Balkan cuisine. Potato came to these parts much later, but was quickly accepted. In the true Balkan cuisine there are less dishes with potatoes than in the cuisines of western Europe, but they are added to other vegetables quite a lot, or frequently served as accompaniment, just boiled and poured over with some fat, or mashed. Vegetable dishes, however, most often contain several different kinds of vegetables.

Bulgaria

ORIENTAL "YANIYA"

500—700 gr aubergines
250 gr courgettes
1 dl oil
2—3 paprikas
2 onions
250 gr tomatoes
salt
3—4 cloves of garlic
2 bayleaves
1/2—1 dl white wine
1 tablespoon flour
1—1,5 dl warm water
1/2 bunch of parsley
peppercorns

Cut aubergines into slices, add salt and leave them to stand for about 30 minutes, then rinse with cold water and drain well. Peel courgettes and also slice them. Wash paprikas, dry and bake them, then skin and cut into strips. Wash tomatoes, peel and cut into slices.

Cook aubergines and courgettes quickly in heated oil. Put vegetables into a flameproof casserole one after the other. Each layer should be sprinkled with a pinch of salt, chopped garlic and crushed bayleaf. In the oil left over after frying aubergines cook finely chopped onion at low heat. When tender and slightly brown, add flour, fry it quickly, add some cold and then some warm water, add wine and cook. Pour this sauce over the vegetables. Bake in the oven preheated to 175—200°C until everything is soft and the sauce thick.

Before serving sprinkle the "yaniya" with chopped parsley and some freshly ground pepper.

Greece

SUMMER VEGETABLES POT

(for 6—8 persons)

450 gr string beans
450 gr aubergines
450 gr courgettes
2 big paprikas
450 gr potatoes
600 gr tomatoes
2 onions
salt, pepper
2 teaspoons sugar
2,5 dl olive (or plain) oil
1 bunch of parsley
2—3 dl warm water

Wash string beans, remove tops and strings and cut into 2—3 cm long pieces.

Wash aubergines, cut into cubes, salt and leave to stand for about 30 minutes, then rinse with cold water. Peel courgettes, wash, cut in halves, seed and cut into 2 cm thick cubes. Wash paprikas, core and cut into strips. Peel potatoes, wash and cut into bigger cubes. Wash tomatoes, peel and slice. Peel onions and cut into fine slices.

Put some oil into a deeper pan and arrange vegetables in layers. Sprinkle each layer with salt and pepper, add sugar, chopped parsley and olive oil. Pour in warm water, cover and simmer for about 2 hours. It could also be covered with tin foil and baked in the oven preheated to 175 °C. Bake until all the vegetables are tender and the juice evaporates. The ready pot should not contain too much juice. Serve warm.

Yugoslavia

BAKED PEAS PURÉE

100 gr butter or margarine
1 smaller onion
1 kg shelled peas
2 dl lukewarm water
salt
2 dl milk
2 eggs
70 gr grated kachkaval, Trappist or similar cheese
2 dl sour cream
1/2 bunch of parsley

Heat butter or margarine (50 gr), add finely chopped onion, cook it a little, add peas, pour in lukewarm water and simmer until peas are tender. Towards the end add salt. Three quarters of the peas cool a little and then strain through sieve. Add 30 gr of butter to the strained peas, slowly pour in hot milk and mix well to get a fluffy purée. Separate egg yolks and whites. Mix egg yolks, the rest of peas in seed and half of the grated cheese into the purée. Mix well, slowly mix in the whisked egg whites, add more salt if necessary.

Beat the sour cream and add chopped parsley to it.

Grease a fireproof casserole with butter, turn peas into it, level with a knife, pour sour cream over it, add the rest of grated cheese and bake in the oven heated to 200 °C until brown.

Peas prepared this way can be served as the main dish at lunch or dinner with lettuce, mixed salad of paprikas and tomato, cucumber salad with yoghurt etc.

Albania

COURGETTES WITH TOMATO

(for 6 persons)

1,5 kg young courgettes
500 gr tomatoes
1/2 bunch of parsley
2—3 cloves of garlic
salt
pepper
1,5 dl oil
1—1,5 dl warm water

Peel courgettes and cut into cubes of medium size. Pour a tablespoon of oil into a flameproof casserole and put the courgettes into it. Peel the tomatoes, cut into slices and place over the courgettes, add salt and pepper, sprinkle with chopped garlic and parsley, pour in warm water and oil, shake, cover and simmer.

This dish can be served warm or cold, as an addition to meat or egg dishes, roast or fried.

Bulgaria

AUBERGINE "YANIYA"

1 kg aubergines
1 dl oil
2 onions
20 gr flour
1 teaspoon red paprika pepper
250 gr tomatoes
2—3 cloves of garlic
1 lemon
2 bayleaves
salt
1/2 bunch of parsley
2—3 dl hot water

Peel aubergines and cut into cubes, add salt and leave to stand for about 30—45 minutes, then rinse with cold water, drain and wipe a little, fry quickly in heated oil and take out. In the same oil cook finely chopped onion slowly. When it is tender and slightly brown, add red paprika pepper, peeled and finely chopped tomatoes, crushed garlic, thin slices of lemon, bayleaf and fried aubergines, mixing it all. Pour in hot water, cover and bake in the oven preheated to 175—200°C until all is tender, the juice evaporates and the dish becomes slightly brown. Before serving sprinkle with chopped parsley.

Greece

STUFFED COURGETTES

(for 4—6 persons)

1 kg—1,5 kg courgettes
salt
40 gr olive oil
250 gr fresh mushrooms
60 gr rice
1 tablespoon tomato purée
1/2 teaspoon red paprika-pepper
pepper

Wash courgettes but do not peel, blanch in slightly salted water. When tender (but not too soft!), drain and cool. Cut them in halves, lengthways. Scoop out the thick parts. Heat oil (30 gr), add finely sliced mushrooms and cook them slowly about 30 minutes, add cooked rice, tomato and red paprika pepper, salt and pepper to taste. Mix well. Fill the courgettes with the mixture and drop some oil over each. Serve cold with egg dishes, fish, offal and the like.

Turkey

"YANIYA" WITH SWISS CHARD

500 gr Swiss chard
1 bigger onion
2 cloves of garlic
500 gr tomatoes
1/2 bunch of parsley
250 gr potatoes
1 dl oil
salt
pepper

Wash Swiss chard, drain and boil in salted water for about 5 minutes. Peel potatoes, dice and boil in salted water for about 15 minutes. Peel onion and chop finely; crush or chop garlic. Peel tomatoes, seed and cut into small pieces. Heat oil, add onion and cook until tender, add garlic, tomato and chopped parsley. Cover and simmer for about 30 minutes, then add drained, half-cooked Swiss chard and potato cubes. Add salt and pepper and simmer about 30 minutes. Shake occasionally, add water in which potatoes were cooked, as needed.

Water in which potatoes and chard were cooked could be used for making broth.

Chard "yaniya" is most often served with boiled or roast fish, with egg dishes, meat balls or offal stews.

Turkey

CHICK-PEAS WITH TOMATOES

400 gr chick-peas
1 dl oil
30 gr butter
1 slice of white bread
100 gr onion
200 gr tomatoes
2 cloves of garlic
1 hard boiled egg
salt
pepper

Pick over chick-peas, soak overnight, then cook in about 2 l of water, add salt when nearly cooked. Heat oil and butter, fry bread to brown, take it out and cook finely chopped onion slowly in the same fat until tender and brown. Peel tomatoes, crush, add to the fried onion, cook together until tomatoes are soft. Then add drained chick-peas and a few spoonfuls of water in which peas were cooked. Crush garlic, add fried bread, crush it too, add yolk of the hard boiled egg, add a few spoons of water left over from cooking, add everything to the chick-peas. Dice white of the hard boiled egg, stir it in, add some more water if necessary, cover and simmer for about 30—40 minutes.

(Chick-peas never become soft and overcooked. Even when quite cooked they remain firm.)

Chick-peas prepared this way are good as an accompaniment to offal or egg dishes, breaded cheese, various kinds of meat balls. Fresh vegetables should be served with this dish (tomatoes, spring onions, radishes and others) or some fresh salad (lettuce, cucumber, paprikas etc.).

Greece

MIXED VEGETABLES WITH WINE

200 gr smaller onions
4 artichokes
1 smaller cauliflower
2 carrots
2 tomatoes
1 lemon
1/2 teaspoon thyme
2—3 tablespoons chopped parsley
2 crushed bayleaves
1—1,5 dl olive oil
1/4 l white wine
salt
pepper
butter for greasing

Peel onions and chop finely. Clean artichokes (remove stems, tops and "hay", and the harder scales if necessary), cut into smaller pieces. Wash cauliflower and break into sprigs. Scrape carrots, wash and cut into rounds or cubes. Wash tomatoes, peel, seed and slice.

Grease a flameproof casserole or a corresponding pan with butter, arrange vegetables sprinkling them at the same time with salt, pepper and aromatic spices. Pour over oil, wine and some water if necessary. Cover and simmer at medium heat until tender, then cool. Serve cold.

Bulgaria

AUBERGINES STUFFED WITH RICE

800 gr—1 kg aubergines
salt
100 gr oil
1 bigger onion
1 bigger carrot
1/2 celery root
2—3 tomatoes
100 gr rice
1/2 bunch of parsley
pepper

Wash aubergines, drain, remove stalks, scoop them out carefully, add salt and leave to stand for about 30 minutes, then rinse with cold water and wipe. Fry them slightly on all sides in heated oil. Fry finely chopped onion and carrot and celery cut into small cubes in the same oil, until rather tender. Wash rice, cook in slightly salted water for about 5 minutes, then drain, add to the vegetables, fry quickly, add peeled and chopped tomato (one), and some water (1 dl) if necessary, cook together until rice and vegetables are soft. Then remove from the fire and add chopped parsley and pepper. Mix well. Carefully fill the fried aubergines with this mixture. Grease a fireproof dish or a casserole (djuvetch) a little, place the stuffed aubergines, cover with the rest of chopped tomatoes and bake in the oven preheated to 175°C until all is tender.

Turkey

STEWED AUBERGINES AND TOMATOES

(for 2—3 persons)

250 gr aubergines
500 gr tomatoes
50 gr butter or margarine
2 onions
salt, pepper
150 gr kaymak or sour cream

Wash aubergines, remove the stalks, cut into 1/2 cm thick slices, salt and leave to stand for about 30 minutes, then rinse and drain well. Wash tomatoes, blanch quickly in hot water, pour cold water over them, peel and cut into slices.

Heat butter or margarine preferably in a flameproof casserole, add finely chopped parsley, cook slowly until tender and glassy, add tomato slices, salt them a little, then add aubergine slices, salt, pepper and pour beaten kaymak or sour cream over. Cover well with tin foil and stew at medium heat for about 30 minutes. Shake occasionally.

Serve as an accompaniment to roast or breaded meat (lamb, chicken) to various omelets and the like.

Bulgaria

AUBERGINES WITH WINE — "BAYALDO"

3—4 aubergines
salt
juice of 2 lemons
3 tablespoons flour
oil or lard for frying and greasing
3 bigger onions
1 bunch of parsley
2—2,5 dl white wine

Wipe aubergines, bake in the heated oven or grill for about 15 minutes, then cool a little, peel, cut into thicker slices, add salt and lemon juice and leave to stand for about 30 minutes. Then drain and wipe the slices, roll in flour and fry both sides in heated oil for about 5 minutes.

Grease a tepsiya or a flameproof casserole with oil or lard and place in the fried aubergines. Sprinkle them with finely chopped onion and parsley, add wine and cook in the oven preheated to 175°C for about 30 minutes, that is until there is no liquid.

In the Balkan cuisine aubergines are used for many dishes. To intensify their taste in a way, it is necessary to put them into the heated oven or grill them for 15—20 minutes. After that it is also easier to peel them.

Yugoslavia

KALE WITH BACON

1 kg kale
2 onions
2 cloves of garlic
150 gr streaky smoked bacon
pepper, salt
caraway seeds
1/2 l beef soup from cube, 40 gr lard

Trim kale, wash, cut into thicker strips, boil in salted water about 10 minutes, then drain.

Chop onion finely. Cut bacon into cubes.

Grease a fireproof dish, arrange kale and then onion and bacon. Sprinkle with salt to taste, pepper, caraway seeds and chopped garlic. Repeat. The last layer should be kale.

Pour in beef cube soup, then melted lard and bake in the oven preheated to 200°C about 40—45 minutes.

Serve with meat loaf, meat balls, stewed liver or kidneys, cheese omelet, fried eggs and the like.

Bulgaria

AUBERGINE MOUSSAKA

750 gr aubergines
salt
1—1,5 dl oil
1 bigger onion
80 gr rice
1 bunch of parsley
2 dl warm water
40 gr flour, 2 eggs
2 dl milk or sour cream

Wash aubergines, peel and cut into slices lengthways, salt and leave to stand for about 30—60 minutes. Then

rinse and drain. Heat oil, fry drained aubergines quickly on both sides to brown a little. Add finely chopped onion to the same oil and cook until tender. Wash rice, drain it well and add to the fried onion, cook until it becomes glassy, add about 100 gr tomatoes, peeled and cut into smaller pieces, add salt, 1 tablespoon of chopped parsley and warm water. Stew until rice is tender.

Arrange peeled and sliced tomatoes in a casserole, then over them fried aubergines, then rice. Repeat until all is used. The last layer should be sliced tomatoes. Heat the oven to 200°C and bake the moussaka for about 30 minutes and then mix well fried flour, milk or sour cream and eggs, pour over the moussaka, put back into the oven and bake until brown.

Instead of rice the moussaka can be prepared with potatoes or cheese.

Albania

AUBERGINE STEW WITHOUT MEAT — "DJUVETCH"

2—3 aubergines
salt, 1 dl oil
2 onions
3 bigger paprikas
4—5 tomatoes
2 smaller courgettes
pepper
1/2 teaspoon red paprika pepper
50—70 gr rice
1/2 bunch of parsley
2—3 tablespoons oil to pour over
1—3 dl warm water

Peel aubergines, cut into cubes, salt and leave to stand for 30—60 minutes, then wash with cold water and drain. Heat oil, add finely chopped onion and cook until tender. Add aubergines, cored paprikas cut into strips, peeled tomatoes cut into cubes and courgettes cut into cubes. Add salt, pepper, red paprika pepper and simmer until all the vegetables are tender. Stir at times and if necessary add some warm water.

Wash rice and cook it shortly in slightly salted water, drain, add to the vegetables, mix and add chopped parsley. Grease a fireproof dish or a casserole a little, put in the mixture, add 2 dl of warm water and pour over some oil.

Bake in the oven preheated to 175°C until rice and vegetables are quite tender.

With this "djuvetch" without meat serve egg or cheese dishes and the like.

Bulgaria

TOMATOES STUFFED WITH MUSHROOMS

1 kg firmer medium-sized tomatoes
2 onions
250—300 gr fresh mushrooms (button mushrooms, ceps or similar)
1 dl oil
50 gr rice
salt
pepper
1/2 bunch of parsley
2 eggs
1 tablespoon flour
2 dl milk or sour cream

Wash tomatoes, drain, cut a slice from the top of each (not stalk end), then scoop out the seeds and core with a teaspoon. Peel onion and chop finely;

trim mushrooms, wash and cut into thin slices. Heat oil, add onion and cook a little, then add mushrooms and cook for a short while until all is tender. Wash rice, cook in slightly salted water about 5 minutes, then drain and add to the mushrooms. Also add half of the scooped out tomato meat, season with salt and pepper. Simmer together until rice is quite soft. Cool a little and add chopped parsley. Fill the tomatoes with this mixture.

Grease a fireproof casserole, turn into it the rest of the tomato meat and arrange stuffed tomatoes over it. Bake in the oven preheated to 175°C until tender. Towards the end of baking, pour over a mixture of beaten eggs, flour and milk (or sour cream), then bake until nicely brown.

Stuffed tomatoes can be served as an accompaniment to offal, egg or potato dishes, but also as an appetiser.

Bulgaria

OKRA "PLAKA" WITH MUSHROOMS

750 gr fresh, young okras
1 dl oil
250 gr fresh mushrooms
200 gr small onions
2—3 cloves of garlic
1—1,5 dl white wine
3 tablespoons wine vinegar
2 bigger tomatoes, salt
peppercorns
1 bunch of parsley

Clean and wash okras. Clean mushrooms, wash and slice finely. Peel small onions, wash and leave whole. Clean garlic and chop it finely. Mix all vegetables, salt, add peppercorns, oil, wine and diluted vinegar (3 spoons vinegar, 3 spoons water), turn into a greased casserole. Wash tomatoes, peel, slice and arrage over the vegetables. Cover well and simmer until everything is tender. When the "plaka" is ready, sprinkle it with chopped parsley. Serve cold.

Roumania

MIXED VEGETABLES MONASTERY WAY

2—3 dl oil
2 onions
2 carrots
100 gr string beans
100 gr peas
100 gr cauliflower
100 gr courgettes
200 gr big paprikas
100 gr aubergines
150 gr fresh tomatoes
100 gr okras
250 gr potatoes
4—5 cloves of garlic
1 bunch of parsley
2—3 tablespoons vinegar
pepper
salt
3/4 l warm water

Heat oil, add finely chopped onion and cook until brown. Clean carrots and cut into small cubes, cut string beans into small pieces, shell peas, sprig cauliflower, peel courgettes and aubergines and dice, add salt to aubergines and leave them for about 20 minutes, then rinse and drain. Peel tomatoes and cut into smaller pieces. Clean fresh okras, wash and leave for a while in water with vinegar. Peel potatoes, wash and dice. Chop or crush garlic.

Add prepared vegetables to fried onion, add salt, pepper, mix well and put into a fireproof dish or a deeper djuvetch, add warm water to cover the whole mixture, cover well or put tin foil over. Put into the oven preheated to 175°C and bake until everything is tender. Serve warm with unripened cheese.

Greece

BAKED VEGETABLES — "TURLU FURNO"

3—4 aubergines
500 gr potatoes
500 gr courgettes
1 onion
2 cloves of garlic
1 bunch of dill
1/2 bunch of parsley
2 dl olive or plain oil
salt
pepper
3—4 dl bone stock (or soup from cube)
2—3 tomatoes
1—2 tablespoons breadcrumbs
100 gr grated Parmesan or similar cheese

Aubergines should be peeled, cut into slices about 1/2 cm thick, salted and left to stand for about 40—60 minutes. Peel the potatoes, wash and cut into thicker strips. Wash the courgettes and cut into slices about 1/2 cm thick.

Rinse aubergines with cold water, drain well, then mix with potatoes and courgettes, add dill and parsley. Heat oil, add chopped onion and garlic, cook until tender, then add other vegetables, salt, pepper, peeled tomatoes cut into cubes, breadcrumbs and half of the cheese. Grease well an enamelled baking pan, a tepsiya or a flameproof casserole, put in vegetables, pour in the soup and cook in the oven preheated to 175°C until everything is tender. Before baking is over, sprinkle with the rest of cheese. Serve with corn bread or pogatcha.

Bulgaria

SPINACH WITH RICE

1 onion
1 dl oil
1 kg young spinach
150 gr rice
20 gr tomato purée
2 dl thick yoghurt
1/2 bunch of parsley
pepper
salt
2—3 dl warm water

Peel onion, chop and cook slowly in heated oil until tender. Clean spinach (remove stems and thicker leaf ribs), wash, drain and cut into smaller strips, add to the fried onion, cover and simmer until tender.

Clean and wash rice, cook it shortly in slightly salted water, drain.

Grease a flameproof casserole a little, add the spinach mixture, rice, tomato purée, salt, pepper, chopped parsley, then add warm water. Bake in the oven preheated to 175—200°C until rice is tender and the juice evaporates. Then pour over thick yoghurt and leave it in the oven for a short while. Swiss chard, young sorrel and nettle can be prepared in the same way.

Yugoslavia

CAULIFLOWER WITH CHEESE SAUCE

1 cauliflower of about 1 kg
200—250 gr fresh cow cheese in crumbs
1/2 dl milk or 1—2 tablespoons lemon juice
2 eggs
1 dl milk
50 gr butter or margarine
1 bunch of shallots (or spring onion leaves)
1 bunch of dill
2 dl sour cream
salt
pepper

Trim cauliflower of outer leaves and damaged sprigs, if any, and wash well. Cook in salted water to which either 1—2 spoons of lemon juice or some milk can be added so that the nice white colour of the cauliflower is preserved.

Crush cheese well or strain, add yolks and milk, melted butter, chopped shallots and dill, salt and pepper. Beat sour cream and mix it with cheese.

Drain boiled cauliflower, put it on the serving dish and pour over it the prepared sauce. Whites of egg can be cooked, finely chopped and sprinkled over the cauliflower.

This dish can be served with roast and breaded meats, quickly fried liver, various omelets, fried eggs sunny-side up, poached eggs and the like.

If the cauliflower is tightly packed and there is a possibility that there is an insect, a tiny snail etc. in between the sprigs, before cooking it should be left for a while in salted or sugared water which will "draw out" the uninvited guests.

Roumania

ROUMANIAN CABBAGE

1 head of cabbage (about 1,5 kg)
salt
1 teaspoon sugar
10 gr lard or oil
2—3 dl lukewarm water
100 gr rice
pepper
150 gr smoked bacon
100 gr hard sheep or cow cheese in slices or kachkaval

Trim discoloured outer leaves, wash cabbage and cut it into 4—6 parts. Heat about 2 l of water, add salt and sugar and when boiling add the cabbage and cook until tender.

Heat lard (or oil), add cleaned, washed and drained rice, fry it to become glassy, add lukewarm water and simmer until tender. Grease a fireproof casserole with some lard or oil, turn in rice and then cabbage over it, add salt and pepper to taste. Cut bacon into thinner strips, fry and then arrange over the cabbage. Bake in the heated oven (200°C). Before serving sprinkle with grated cheese.

Serve with egg dishes, grilled liver, stewed kidneys etc.

Roumania

BUTTON MUSHROOMS "YANIYA"

3—4 onions
1 dl olive or sunflower oil
300—350 gr fresh button mushrooms or ceps
salt
pepper
500 gr fresh tomatoes
1 bunch of dill

Peel onion and chop finely. Heat oil, add onion and cook slowly until tender and slightly brown. Trim button mushrooms, wash, drain and cut into slightly thicker slices. Fry together with onion slowly until tender. Wash tomatoes, cut into pieces and strain through a sieve, pour over the mushrooms, add salt, pepper and chopped dill. Simmer for another 20 minutes.

Bulgaria

PAPRIKAS STUFFED WITH VEGETABLES

500—750 gr paprikas (big or pointed ones)
salt
2 smaller onions
2 smaller carrots
1 smaller celery root
1 dl oil
2 medium-sized potatoes
2 tomatoes
1—2 cloves of garlic
1—2 tablespoons chopped parsley
100 gr cow cheese crumbs or cheese in slices
1—2 eggs
2 dl milk or sour cream

Wash paprikas, core, seed and slightly salt the insides. Prepare the filling in the following way: peel onions, carrots and celery, wash and cut into fine cubes. Heat half of the oil, add the prepared vegetables and simmer, adding water occasionally. When the vegetables are tender, add potatoes, also cut into small cubes, then 1 tomato peeled and cut into pieces, chopped garlic, crushed cheese and chopped parsley. Mix well and add salt. Stuff paprikas with this mixture and place them in a greased pan (preferably flameproof). Put the remaining chopped tomatoes among the paprikas, add some water and the remaining oil. Bake in the oven preheated to 175°C until all is tender. Towards the end pour over the paprikas milk beaten with eggs, put back into the oven and leave to brown.

Greece

STEWED RED CABBAGE

1 onion
50 gr butter or margarine
1 kg red cabbage
2 big paprikas
250 gr shelled peas
2 dl mutton or beef soup (or from meat cube)
salt, pepper, caraway seeds

Peel onion and chop finely. Heat butter, add onion, cook until tender and brown. Trim cabbage of damaged leaves, cut it into thin strips (or shred it), add to fried onion. Clean paprikas, cut into cubes and add to cabbage together with peas. Pour in soup, add salt, pepper, caraway seeds, cover and simmer until all vegetables are tender.

Cabbage prepared this way is most often served with fried smoked sausages.

Albania

VEGETABLES WITH SWEETCORN

2 onions
2—3 paprikas (green and red)
500 gr tomatoes
1 dl olive or plain oil
300 gr boiled sweetcorn (or canned)
salt
1/2 teaspoon hot red paprika pepper
pepper
4—6 eggs
2 tablespoons ketchup or chilli sauce
75 gr grated hard cheese (kachkaval, Trappist or similar)
1/2 bunch of parsley

Peel onion and slice into thin rounds or slices. Wash paprikas, core and cut into strips. Dip tomatoes in hot water, then in cold, peel, seed and cut into slices.

Heat oil, add onion and paprikas, cook slowly. Boil sweetcorn (if canned, just drain). Add it to fried onion and paprika, then add tomato, salt, red paprika pepper, pepper. Mix. Grease a flameproof casserole and pour into it the prepared vegetables. Beat eggs well, add ketchup or chilli sauce, salt if necessary. Pour it over the vegetables, sprinkle with grated cheese and bake in the oven preheated to 175—200°C about 30 minutes, until tender and brown. Before serving sprinkle with chopped parsley.

Serve with various kinds of meat balls, with quickly baked, fatty meat or offal dishes, egg dishes and the like.

Bulgaria

BEANS WITH SORREL

500—700 gr sorrel (garden or meadow variety)
300 gr beans
1 dl oil
1 onion
1 carrot
1 parsley root
150 gr fresh tomatoes or 15 gr tomato paste (from tube)
2 eggs
2 dl thick yoghurt
20 gr flour
a few mint leaves
1 tablespoon chopped dill
1 tablespoon chopped parsley
salt, pepper
1 teaspoon red paprika pepper

Pick over beans, wash and leave in cold water several hours, then boil and drain. Clean sorrel, remove stalks and thicker leaf ribs, wash, drain and cut into thinner strips.

Heat 1/2 dl oil, add coarsely grated carrot and parsley root, cook slowly to become tender, add beans, pour in some water in which they were boiled and simmer. In the other pan, in the other half of oil, cook slowly sorrel, chopped onion, chopped tomatoes and red paprika pepper until nearly tender. Pour in beans, add mint, dill, parsley and simmer together, adding water left over after boiling beans, as necessary.

Towards the end add well beaten eggs with thick yoghurt and flour. Mix carefully or shake well and cook for another 10 minutes. Serve warm or cold, richly peppered, as a delicious accompaniment to offal dishes, egg and cheese dishes or grilled meat.

Roumania

WHITE BEANS "YANIYA"

250—300 gr white beans
3 onions
1 dl olive or sunflower oil

salt, pepper
juice of 1 lemon
1 bunch of dill

Pick over beans, wash, soak in cold water and leave to stand for several hours, then boil.

Peel onion, slice thinly and fry in heated oil until tender and brown, add salt and pepper. Drain cooked beans and while still warm mix with onion. Season with some more salt and pepper if necessary. Pour in some water left over after boiling beans and simmer together for a short while. Add chopped dill.

Serve cold as an accompaniment to egg, cheese, offal and other dishes.

Roumania

BEANS WITH STRING BEANS

100 gr brown beans
100 gr white beans
1 bigger onion
2 cloves of garlic, salt
100 gr streaky smoked bacon
1 teaspoon thyme
200 gr fresh green string beans
200 gr yellow string beans
3 sprigs of fresh savory or 1/2 teaspoon of dried one
1 teaspoon lemon juice

Pick over and wash beans, then soak in cold water (preferably overnight).

Chop onion finely, crush garlic well with salt. Cut bacon into cubes, fry in a deeper pan until it is glassy, add onion and garlic, cook together about 3 minutes, until all is slightly tender. Add beans, thyme, about 1,1/4 l water, cover and simmer until beans are tender, add salt.

In the meantime wash string beans, remove tops, tails and strings, if any, cut into smaller pieces and add to the beans. Add savory, go on cooking together until all is tender. When cooked, add lemon juice.

It is served as an accompaniment to grilled pork, meat balls or fried homemade sausages.

Instead of two kinds of beans and string beans, one kind of each can be used, but the dish will be more tasty and attractive if more kinds are mixed into this "beans-fête".

Bulgaria

BEANS WITH THICK YOGHURT

300 gr beans, white or brown
1—1,5 dl oil, salt
1/2 teaspoon red paprika pepper
2—3 cloves of garlic
2—3 dl thick yoghurt

Pick over beans, wash, leave in cold water (preferably overnight) and then boil. When cooked, drain.

Put oil in a fireproof casserole, heat, add paprika pepper, fry it very shortly, turn in drained beans, fry a little and mix. Beat thick yoghurt, add finely chopped garlic and mix. Pour over the beans and bake in the oven heated to 200°C until brown.

With the beans prepared this way serve various egg dishes (omelet, eggs sunny-side up, scrambled eggs), stewed offal, meat balls etc., as well as different kinds of salads (lettuce, cucumber, mixed salad, sauerkraut, shredded cabbage, paprikas etc.).

Yugoslavia

BEANS MOUSSAKA

500 gr beans
6 eggs
1 dl oil or 100 gr lard
250 gr harder cow cheese in slices or kachkaval
2 dl sour cream
salt, pepper

Pick over beans, wash and boil. When nearly tender, add salt and when cooked, drain and strain through a sieve.

Hard boil 4 eggs, cool, shell and cut

into rounds. Grate cheese crudely. Heat oil or lard a little.

Grease a fireproof casserole, put strained beans in, pour in some oil or lard, season with salt and pepper (as necessary), arrange egg rounds on top, sprinkle them with cheese, spoon with some oil, then repeat until all the ingredients are used. Add pepper and some oil every time. The last layer should be beans.

Beat well two eggs with sour cream and pour over the beans. Bake in the oven preheated to 200°C for about 30—40 minutes or until brown. With the moussaka serve sauerkraut salad, pickled paprikas, chopped paprika and aubergine salad "ayvar", etc.

Bulgaria

POTATO MOUSSAKA WITH CHEESE

1 kg potatoes
1/2 dl oil
350 gr ripened cow cheese in slices (or kachkaval)
2 eggs, 2 dl sour cream
salt, pepper

Peel potatoes and boil in slightly salted water. When soft, drain (use water to add to the broth), cool a little, then slice into rounds.

Grate or crush cheese well, mix in egg yolks, salt to taste. Whisk egg whites stiffly. Add half of the sour cream to mixed cheese and egg yolks, then carefully mix in egg whites.

In a greased fireproof casserole put layers of potatoes and filling one after the other, sprinkling salt and pepper over each. The last layer should be potatoes. Sprinkle with oil and pour in the rest of sour cream. Bake in the oven preheated to 200°C for 35—40 minutes, or until brown.

With the moussaka serve a fresh salad (lettuce, shredded cabbage, mixed salad and the like).

Bulgaria

POTATO AND SPINACH MOUSSAKA

1 kg potatoes
750 gr spinach
100 gr butter or margarine
1 bunch of parsley
100 gr cheese (cow cheese in slices, kachkaval or other)
salt
pepper
2 eggs
2—3 dl milk

Scrub potatoes and boil in their skins. When soft, drain, peel and cool, then grate coarsely. Wash spinach, remove stems and thicker leaf ribs, cut finely and fry slowly in 40 gr of butter. Grease a casserole with some butter, put a layer of potatoes, sprinkle with parsley, then a layer of cheese, then of spinach. Put some salt and pepper every time. The last layer should be potatoes, salted and peppered.

Melt the rest of butter, add eggs and milk. Beat well and pour over the mous-

saka. Heat the oven to 175—200°C and bake for about 40 minutes, namely until brown.

Instead of milk, sour cream or thick yoghurt can be used with beaten eggs.

With the moussaka serve a salad of fresh vegetables.

Yugoslavia

"BAKERY" POTATOES

1 kg potatoes
200 gr home-made ham or streaky smoked bacon
250 gr onion
2—3 dl warm water or soup from meat cube
salt
pepper
1 dl oil (or 50 gr lard)

Peel potatoes, wash and slice in rounds. Peel onion and slice or shop finely. Cut ham or bacon into thin strips.

Put some oil or lard into a fireproof dish or a corresponding djuvetch. Salt potatoes and mix well. Put in potatoes, sprinkle with onion, then arrange ham or bacon over. Pour in some oil or lard every time. Repeat. The last layer should be potatoes. Pour in warm water or soup. Bake in the oven preheated to 175°C about 60—70 minutes. Potatoes should get nicely brown.

This dish is most often served with shredded cabbage salad, beetroot salad, various pickles and other winter salads, as the "bakery" potatoes are a true "winter dish".

Roumania

BAKED POTATOES

1 kg potatoes
50—75 gr butter (or margarine)
2 onions
salt
150 gr kachkaval or cow cheese in slices
1—2 cloves of garlic (optional)
pepper
nutmeg
5—6 dl milk
1 egg

Peel potatoes, wash and cut into thinner rounds. Grease a fireproof dish (or a corresponding djuvetch) with butter, put in a layer of chopped onion, salt slightly, then a layer of potatoes, sprinkle with grated cheese and with some pepper. Repeat until all the ingredients are used. Heat one half of milk (about 3 dl) and pour over the potatoes. Bake in the oven heated to 175—200°C until potatoes absorb all the liquid.

Add nutmeg, pepper and the beaten egg into the remaining milk. Mix well and pour over the half-baked potatoes, sprinkle with grated cheese, add thin slices of butter and continue baking. If potatoes are to have the taste of garlic, rub the baking dish with the split clove of garlic.

Baked potatoes are served with some fresh salad as the main dish in meatless days. Cheese, egg and milk with their nutritious value are an excellent substitute for meat.

VEGETABLE AND MEAT DISHES

Dolmas, kapamas, yaniyas, moussakas, djuvetches, pilafs... the very names of these dishes excite a gourmet's imagination. And then there are various "pots", since nearly every region has its own "pot" or its own variation of stuffed paprikas, tomatoes, courgettes and aubergines.
The choice is really great and the ingredients are as varied as the ways of preparing these dishes, which look nice and stimulate the appetite and are therefore favourite and always present both as parts of everyday meals or of those on festive occasions.
Various kinds of vegetables used in the Balkan cuisine have been dealt with in the section about vegetable dishes. Something should be said, however, about rice. In fact, rice is not a vegetable but a type of wheat, but it is often used instead of vegetables as an independent accompaniment and particularly in combination with meat (in pilafs), or in meat and vegetable dishes discussed here. In the Balkans it had certainly been used earlier than in other parts of Europe (except Spain, where it was brought by the Arabs as early as the 8th century), because the customs of the East and with them the cooking of the Asiatic countries have reached these parts earlier. And while it began to be used in the central and northern parts of Italy as late as the 16th century (it was mentioned as medicine at the time of Julius Caesar in the 1st century B. C.), its use in the Balkans, as chronicles testify, had at that time already been wide-spread. In many parts of the peninsula, especially in those where it is grown, rice has priority over potato, both as a separate dish, or in combination with other foods.

Turkey

TURKISH DOLMAS IN GRAPEVINE LEAVES —"JALANCI DOLMASI"

2 onions
30 gr (3 tablespoons) oil
300 gr ground mutton
40—50 gr rice
salt
pepper
1/2 bunch of dill
15—20 grapevine leaves
3—5 dl sheep bone stock

Chop one onion finely, cook slowly a little in heated oil (2 tablespoons), add half-cooked rice, meat, salt, pepper and chopped dill. Mix all well.

Pour hot water over young grapevine leaves (not yet sprayed), leave them to stand for a while to soften, then drain. Put a spoonful of stuffing on each leaf, fold sides towards the middle, then roll up into dolmas.

Line the bottom of a pan or fireproof dish with thinly sliced onion, pour some of the remained oil over, arrange dolmas tightly side by side. Pour over stock made of sheep bones. Cover and simmer until stock is nearly quite reduced, then cool.

Serve dolmas cold.

Roumania

DOLMAS ROUMANIAN WAY

1 bigger head of pickled cabbage (about 1,5—2 kg)
350 gr ground pork
250 gr ground young beef or beef
50 gr rice
1 smaller onion

1—2 cloves of garlic
salt
pepper
For stewing:
2 onions
40—50 gr lard
1—2 dl sauerkraut brine
2 dl tomato juice
2 dl sour cream

Separate nicer sauerkraut leaves and remove part of thick leaf ribs. Mix ground meat, add picked over and half-cooked rice, finely chopped onion and garlic, salt and pepper. Mix all well and leave to stand for a while.

Wash sauerkraut leaves with cold water and drain. Put some stuffing in the middle of each leaf, fold sides over the stuffing and then roll up into dolmas.

Heat lard in a bigger pan, add finely chopped onion and cook slowly until soft and beginning to colour, then add the rest of sauerkraut cut into strips, arrange dolmas over, cover with sauerkraut leaves, pour in the brine and tomato juice, cover and stew in the oven preheated to 175—200°C until tender. Shake the pan now and then and pour in some warm water as needed. With dolmas serve sour cream.

Yugoslavia

SERBIAN GRAPEVINE DOLMAS

30—40 bigger young not sprayed grapevine leaves
1 l warm salted water
50 gr lard or oil
1 onion
50 gr rice
400—450 gr ground mixed meat
1/2 bunch of dill
pepper
salt
1 egg
30 gr oil or lard
15 gr flour
1/2 teaspoon red paprika pepper
1 dl warm water
2 dl white wine
2 dl thick yoghurt

Cover young grapevine leaves with warm salted water, leave to stand until soft, then drain.

Heat lard or oil, add finely chopped onion, cook slowly to soften. Then add picked over and half-cooked rice, meat, chopped dill, pepper and salt. Mix all, cook shortly together, cool a little, add egg and mix well.

Put a small spoonful of stuffing on each leaf, fold sides over the stuffing and roll up into dolmas. Arrange them tightly in a pan, pour over 1/2 l cold water, cover and simmer for about 30—45 minutes.

Heat oil or lard, add flour, fry a little until light brown, add red paprika pepper, pour in 2—3 spoons of cold, then warm water, cook shortly, then add to dolmas. Shake pan, pour in white wine and simmer for 15—20 more minutes.

Serve dolmas with thick yoghurt.

Roumania

DOLMAS IN SPINACH LEAVES

(for 8 persons)

1 kg spinach (with big leaves)
350 gr ground pork
250 gr ground beef
50 gr rice
1 smaller onion
2 cloves of garlic
1 egg
salt
pepper

For stewing:
2—3 chopped bigger onions
50 gr lard or oil
2 dl tomato juice
20 gr flour
1—2 dl warm water
2 dl sour cream

Clean spinach, wash, drain, remove thick leaf ribs, blanch shortly (pour over with hot water or plunge shortly into hot water and rinse with cold water at once), then drain. Mix meat, add half-cooked rice, finely chopped onion and garlic, egg, salt and pepper. Mix all well.

Fill spinach leaves with this stuffing, roll them up and press both ends tightly, so that the stuffing does not come out in cooking. Heat lard in a bigger pan or enamelled djuvetch, add one half of chopped onion, cook shortly until slightly soft, arrange dolmas over, cover with the rest of chopped onion, pour in tomato juice, cover and stew in the oven preheated to 175—200°C. While stewing, shake the pan several times and add some more warm water as needed. Towards the end add flour mixed with 2—3 tablespoons of cold water, add some more warm water and put back into the oven.

Serve sour cream with the dolmas.

Roumanian dolmas in grapevine leaves are prepared in the same way.

Yugoslavia

SERBIAN DOLMAS IN SAUERKRAUT

(for 8—10 persons)

350 gr ground pork
350 gr ground beef or young beef
30 gr lard
1 onion
50 gr rice, 1 egg
1/2 bunch of parsley
salt, pepper
200 gr smoked pork (smoked ribs and similar)
100—150 gr smoked bacon
2 kg pickled cabbage (a bigger head)
20 gr flour
1 teaspoon red paprika pepper
1 dl warm water
1 dried small hot pepper (optional)

Heat lard, add finely chopped onion, cook slowly to soften, then add mixed meat, cook shortly together, mix in washed rice. Cool a little, add egg, chopped parsley, salt and pepper. Mix well. Wash smoked meat and bacon in warm water and cut into smaller pieces. Cut nice, whole sauerkraut leaves off the head, remove part of the thick leaf ribs, wash in cold water if necessary. Put a spoonful of meat stuffing on each leaf. Fold leaves over the stuffing and roll up into small firm dolmas, press tightly both ends, so that they do not fall apart when cooking. Put some chopped sauerkraut into the pan bottom, arrange dolmas over. In between dolmas put pieces of smoked meat and bacon. Cover with chopped sauerkraut and barely cover with lukewarm or cold water. Cover and simmer. When dolmas are tender, mix flour with some cold water and red paprika pepper, pour in some warm water and pour over the dolmas, shake the pan well, and simmer on for 20—30 minutes, shaking the pan at times.

With dolmas cornbread is usually served.

Dolmas in sauerkraut are usually prepared in greater quantity, as they are equally good when warmed up.

Turkey

DOLMAS WITH PARSLEY

0,75—1 kg leaner lamb
50—75 gr rice
1—2 eggs
pepper
salt
2 bunches of parsley
30 gr oil
15 gr flour
a pinch of red paprika pepper
1/2 l thick yoghurt

Wash meat, wipe and grind. Pick over rice, wash and cook, drain, mix meat and rice, add eggs, salt, pepper, mix well and work into a smooth meat mixture. Leave to stand in a cool place for a while, then shape with moistened hands into cork-shaped rissols, the size of dolmas.

Wash parsley, remove stalks, wipe and chop finely. Roll prepared dolmas in parsley, put on a plate or board and put into the refrigerator to stand about 30—40 minutes.

Pour 1—1,5 liter of water into a pan, add salt, bring to the boil, dip prepared dolmas in carefully and simmer for about 30 minutes. Turn dolmas while cooking. When they are cooked, mix flour with oil, some red paprika pepper and 2 tablespoons of cold water and add to the water in which the dolmas were cooked. Simmer on until the sauce thickens.

Serve dolmas with thick yoghurt.

Roumania

FRITTERED DOLMAS IN KALE (OR CABBAGE)

(for 4—6 persons)

1 bigger head of kale
500 gr mixed ground meat (pork and young beef)
30 gr oil
1 onion
50 gr rice
salt, pepper
1 egg

For fritter batter:
1 egg
150 gr flour
2 dl milk
salt
1—2 dl oil for frying
10 gr flour
1/2 l tomato juice
2 dl sour cream

Trim kale, pour hot water over, leave to stand for 10—15 minutes, then separate leaves, remove part of thick leaf ribs.

Heat oil, add finely chopped onion, cook slowly for a while, add half-cooked rice, meat, salt, pepper and egg. Mix all well. Put a spoonful of stuffing on each leaf, fold inwards over the stuffing and roll up into dolmas. Put dolmas in a cool place.

In the meantime prepare batter: beat egg well, add flour and milk in turn, work into a smooth thick batter (mixer can also be used), add salt. Dip each dolma in batter and fry in heated oil until nicely brown, Arrange frittered dolmas in a fireproof dish. Mix tomato juice with some left-over batter, pour over dolmas. Bake at medium heat (175—200°C) in the oven until the juice reduces. When done, pour sour cream over and bake on for a short while.

Greece

DOLMAS WITH LIVER

1 head of fresh cabbage
700—750 gr liver (young bulls' or pigs')
40 gr oil
2 finely chopped onions
40 50 gr rice
salt
pepper
1 egg
1/2—3/4 l tomato juice
150 gr smoked bacon

Trim cabbage, wash, separate leaves, remove part of the thick leaf ribs, cook for about 5 minutes in slightly salted water, take out and drain.

Wash liver, wipe and cut into smaller pieces. Heat oil, add half of the chopped onion, cook slowly until nearly soft, then add liver, cook slowly together about 15—20 minutes. Pick over rice, half-cook, drain and rinse. Cool softened liver a bit, then grind. Add to it rice, salt, pepper and egg. Mix all well. Put the rest of chopped onion into the bottom of the pan, pour the juice from cooking liver over. Put a small spoonful of stuffing on each cabbage leaf and roll up into dolmas. Arrange them in the pan over onion, pour in tomato juice (and some water if needed), season with salt and pepper to taste. Cover dolmas with rashers of smoked bacon. Bake in the oven preheated to 175—200°C about 40 minutes, that is until bacon is nicely brown.

With dolmas mashed potatoes can be served, or potatoes boiled and mixed with fried onion.

Yugoslavia

DOLMAS IN SORREL

(for 4—6 persons)

200—250 gr nice leaves of meadow (or garden) sorrel
For stuffing:
50—75 gr lard or oil
1 onion
50 gr rice
150 gr fresh tomatoes or 25 gr purée (from tube)
salt
1/2 teaspoon red paprika pepper
2—2,5 dl warm water (or bone stock)
500 gr fatter ground lamb
pepper
1/2 bunch of parsley
1/2 bunch of dill (or a few mint leaves)
0,5 l warm water
2 eggs
2 dl thick yoghurt
20 gr flour
40 gr butter
1 teaspoon red paprika pepper
1/2 l thick yoghurt

Wash sorrel leaves, pour over with hot water and leave to stand for 15—20 minutes to soften. Drain and remove thick leaf ribs. Heat lard or oil, add finely chopped onion, cook it slowly a little, then add picked over and washed rice, cook shortly together until rather soft. Wash tomatoes, peel and cut into smaller pieces, add to rice, sprinkle with salt and red paprika pepper, pour in lukewarm water, mix and cook for a while, then add ground meat, pepper, chopped parsley and dill. Mix and cook shortly together. Cool and add eggs.

Put a spoonful of stuffing on each sorrel leaf, fold sides inwards over the stuffing, then roll up into dolmas. Arrange dolmas in a bigger, but not very deep pan, pour in warm water and simmer until tender.

Add flour browned in butter, with some red paprika pepper added, then simmer shortly together.

Serve dolmas with thick yoghurt.

Greece

MIXED STEW — "PAPAZYANIYA" I

(for 5—6 persons)

1—1,25 kg beef or young beef from shoulder
150 gr smoked bacon
1 onion
1 garlic
2 carrots
1 parsley root
1 parsnip
1/2 celery root
1/2 bunch of parsley
1 sprig of celery
750 gr potatoes
salt
peppercorns
1/2 l white wine
1 tablespoon wine vinegar
1 tablespoon flour

Wash meat and cut it into bigger cubes; cut bacon into cubes; scrape carrots, parsley, parsnip and celery and cut into rounds; chop parsley and celery leaves; peel potatoes, wash and cut into slices; leave garlic whole, (remove only dried outer skin); peel onion and slice thinly.

Melt bacon in a frying pan, take out cracklings, then fry meat quickly to brown. Turn meat and fat into a pot or a deep pan, add vegetables, mix, add salt and peppercorns, pour in wine and barely cover with water.

Mix flour with some water and wine vinegar, add to meat and vegetables and stir. Cover pot with tin foil tightly pressing it to pot edges. Simmer or stew in the oven preheated to 175—200°C, until meat and vegetables are tender and the sauce thickened.

The word "papazyaniya" is of Greek origin and means the "priest's yaniya", namely the priest's dish in which meat is cooked with various vegetables, while popularly the word means "a bit of everything". This way of preparing meat and vegetables is recommended as healthy, as their nutritious and aromatic substances are preserved to the full.

Bulgaria

MIXED STEW — "PAPAZYANIYA" II

600—750 gr somewhat fatter meat (beef, veal, lamb or pork)
1 dl oil
1 onion
100 gr carrots
50 gr celery root
1 teaspoon red paprika pepper
2 bayleaves
1 dl wine
250 gr fresh tomatoes
1/2 l hot water
750 gr button onions
70—100 gr garlic
20 gr flour
salt
pepper

Wash meat, wipe and cut into bigger chunks. Heat oil, add meat and fry quickly on all sides until brown. Add finely chopped onion, scraped carrots and celery cut into rounds, then cook slowly together for a while until slightly tender, add red paprika pepper, bayleaf, wine, peeled tomatoes cut into smaller pieces, add salt and pepper, pour in hot water, cover well and simmer. When meat is half cooked, add peeled button onions and slivered garlic, then flour mixed in cold water. Stir, add more warm water as needed, cover (it is best to cover the pot tightly with tin foil), simmer until all is tender. When cooked, sprinkle with chopped parsley.

With slight variations "papazyaniya" is prepared in other Balkan countries, too.

Turkey

MIXED MEAT AND VEGETABLES — "TÜRLÜ TAVA"

(for 8—10 persons)

750 gr — 1 kg meat (lamb, veal)
1 dl oil
salt
pepper
4—5 onions
3 paprikas
1 aubergine
500 gr potatoes
500 gr okras
250 gr string beans
200 gr young courgettes
500 gr tomatoes
1 tablespoon vinegar
2—3 dl warm water

Wash meat, wipe, cut into cubes. Heat oil, add meat, fry it quickly to brown, add salt. Peel onion, chop it finely and cook together with meat until slightly soft. Add paprikas cored and cut into strips.

Peel aubergine, cut into cubes, salt, leave to stand about 30 minutes, then rinse with cold water and add to meat. Peel courgettes and potatoes, cut into cubes. Wash okras, trim and cook shortly in salted water with vinegar, then drain. Add to meat together with courgettes, potatoes and peeled tomatoes cut into pieces. Add salt and pepper to taste, pour in warm water. Simmer. When all is tender enough, turn into a fireproof dish or djuvetch and bake in the oven preheated to 175°C until brown and the liquid evaporates. Pour a few tablespoons of oil over, as needed.

The name of this dish in the original means "a deep pan", such as it used to be prepared in. The characteristic of this dish is that all the ingrediants should, as a rule, be young (meat, vegetables).

Yugoslavia

BALKAN POT

(for 6 persons)

800 gr mutton
4 paprikas
450 gr onion
5 cloves of garlic
750 gr potatoes
750 gr fresh cabbage
2 bayleaves
20 gr flour
2 dl drinking yoghurt
1/2 bunch of parsley
caraway seeds
pepper
salt
50 gr oil

Wash meat, wipe and cut into cubes. Wash paprikas, core and cut into longer strips. Peel potatoes, wash and cut into bigger cubes. Wash cabbage and cut into broad strips. Chop onion and garlic finely. Put some oil into a deeper pan or a pot, then put in meat and vegetables in turn. Sprinkle each layer with chopped parsley, caraway seeds, salt and pepper. Pour in enough water to cover all. Put tin foil over the pot and simmer until everything is tender. Towards the end add mixed flour and yoghurt, simmer together for 10—15 more minutes.

While cooking, shake the pot from time to time. It is done when the contents have diminished to half the original quantity and there is very little juice left.

Yugoslavia

BOSNIAN POT

(for 8—10 persons)

1 kg mixed meat (beef or young beef, mutton and pork)
100 gr lard or 1,5 dl oil
200 gr onion
2 carrots
1 kohlrabi
2 parsley roots
1 smaller celery root
100 gr string beans
2 paprikas

300 gr tomatoes
500 gr potatoes
2 leeks
1 small garlic
250 gr fresh cabbage
1 teaspoon red paprika pepper (hot to taste)
2—3 bayleaves
1 bunch of parsley
2 sprigs of celery
0,5—1 l lukewarm water
pepper
salt
5—6 dl white wine
2 tablespoons wine vinegar

Wash meat, wipe and cut into bigger chunks. Chop onion and garlic finely, as well as parsley and celery leaves. Mix all, add salt, pepper and bayleaves. Clean all other vegetables, wash and cut into rounds, slices or cubes. Put some oil or melted lard into a bigger pot. Put in vegetables and meat in turn. Sprinkle each layer with mixed spice vegetables (onion, parsley, celery etc.). Add more salt and pepper to taste. Mix wine, vinegar and red paprika pepper, pour over vegetables and meat and pour in enough lukewarm water to reach 1/3 of the ingredients in the pot. Cover with tin foil, put into the oven preheated to 175—200°C, stew until all is tender (about 3 hours).

Albania

SHEPHERDS' POT

(for 5—6 persons)

750 gr — 1 kg fattier mutton
4—5 onions
1 smaller garlic
500 gr potatoes
3 paprikas
3 tomatoes
1 bunch of parsley
1 small hot pepper
caraway seeds
0,5—1 dl lukewarm water
30 gr flour
1/2 l sheep thick yoghurt
pepper, salt

Wash meat, drain, wipe and cut into bigger chunks. Peel onion and chop finely, peel garlic, crush and chop. Peel potatoes and cut into cubes or slices. Core paprikas and cut into strips. Peel tomatoes and cut into cubes.

Grease a bigger pot with oil, place in meat and mixed vegetables in turn. Sprinkle each layer with salt, pepper, chopped parsley, chopped small hot pepper and caraway seeds. Barely cover with lukewarm water. Cover well with a lid, or even better, with tin foil. Simmer until all is tender. While cooking, shake the pot at times and pour in some more lukewarm water if needed. Towards the end, add flour blended into thick yoghurt and simmer together for another 10—15 minutes. The ready "pot" should have some juice, as pots of this kind are complete meals (containing thick soup, meat and vegetables).

Roumania

ROUMANIAN POT

(for 5 persons)

350 gr beef
350 gr mutton
250—300 gr fresh paprikas
500 gr tomatoes
250 gr potatoes
20 button onions (slightly bigger)
4 cloves of garlic
1/2 bunch of parsley
1 sprig of celery
2 bayleaves
150 gr peas
1 dl oil
salt
pepper

Wash meat, wipe and cut into bigger cubes. Wash paprikas, core and cut into strips; peel tomatoes and cut into rounds; peel potatoes and cut into cubes or slices. Remove only the outer skin from button onions; peel garlic and crush, then chop. Chop parsley and celery leaves finely.

Pour some oil into the pot, then put in meat and vegetables. Sprinkle each layer with chopped parsley and celery, add salt and pepper and crushed bayleaf. When all is in, pour in enough warm water to reach half the ingredients arranged. Cover with lid or tin foil and simmer. Shake occasionally while cooking.

The pot is ready when everything is tender and the juice nearly completely reduced.

Turkey

TURKISH POT

400 gr aubergines
salt
600 gr mutton from leg
20 gr olive oil (2 tablespoons)
150 gr onion
150 gr tomatoes (2)
200 gr string beans
300 gr paprikas
200 gr courgettes
1/2 l soup from meat cube
1 teaspoon crushed dried basil
1 teaspoon thyme
1 teaspoon marjoram
pepper (white if possible)
1—2 cloves of garlic

Wash aubergines, wipe and cut into cubes of about 2 cm, sprinkle with salt, leave to stand for 30 minutes, then rinse with cold water and drain. Wash meat, wipe and cut into cubes (2—3 cm). Heat olive (or other) oil, add meat, fry it on all sides to brown.

Chop onion finely or cut into thin slices, add to meat, cook slowly until soft and glassy.

Wash tomatoes, remove stalk ends and cut into slices. Wash string beans, remove tops and tails, cut into pieces about 3 cm long. Wash paprikas, core and cut into cubes. Wash courgettes, peel thinly and cut into bigger cubes.

Add prepared vegetables to meat, pour in soup, add spice herbs, salt, pepper, chopped or crushed garlic. Cover well, simmer until meat and vegetables are tender.

As accompaniment cooked rice mixed with raisins is most often served.

This "pot" was originally the dish of the shepherds, but in time, from a modest meal from the mountains it became the piquant and favourite dish in the Turkish cuisine.

Yugoslavia

SMOKED MUTTON WITH GREENS

(for 10 persons)

2 kg smoked mutton
300 gr onion
250 gr smoked bacon
2,5 kg some kind of cabbage or beet greens (or fresh cabbage)
1 kg potatoes
100 gr lard or oil
4—5 cloves of garlic
1 teaspoon red paprika pepper
salt
pepper

Wash meat in warm water, leave it to stand in warm water for several hours, to draw out extra salt. Then drain and cut into bigger pieces, pour in clean warm water and put up to cook. When it boils, add peeled and sliced onion and bacon in one piece. Cook at medium heat until meat is half cooked. Remove any discoloured leaves from cabbage greens, wash and cut into broad strips, add to meat, cook together until it is half cooked, then add peeled potatoes, cut into bigger slices (or leave whole if smaller). Heat lard or oil, add red paprika pepper, chopped garlic, fry quickly, add to meat and greens. Add salt and pepper and simmer until meat and vegetables are tender.

When cooked, the dish should have little juice. Cut bacon into nice rashers and arrange over the dish.

Cabbage greens used, "rashtan" in the original, is a special kind of cabbage, which does not form a head. The leaves used are of vivid green colour and with a slightly bitter taste. It grows and is cultivated along the Croatian coast, in Dalmatia and Montenegro, but less in other parts of Yugoslavia.

Turkey

LAMB "KALJA"

(for 5—6 persons)

1,5 dl oil
200 gr onion
800 gr lamb
15 gr flour
1 teaspoon red paprika pepper
1 tablespoon tomato purée (from tube)
salt
2—3 dl warm water
2 kg cabbage

Heat oil, add finely chopped onion, cook slowly until tender. Wash meat, wipe and cut into bigger cubes, add it to onion, cover and stew. When meat juice has evaporated, add flour, fry it a little, add red paprika pepper, diluted tomato purée and salt. Mix all, pour in warm water and stew on.

Trim cabbage, wash, cut into 8 slices, pour slightly salted hot water over. Bring to the boil, then drain, add to half--cooked meat, pour in warm water as needed, cook on together until cabbage and meat are quite tender.

When cooked, "kalja" should have plenty of its own juice. The word "kalja" is of Arabic origin, so it is to be presumed that the dish originated in the Arabic cuisine. It is similar to the "pot", the difference being that for kalja only one kind of vegetable is usually used. Meat can be mixed (beef, mutton, lamb), while offal such as liver can also be used, or else game (wild duck and others).

Yugoslavia

SERBIAN LAMB "KAPAMA"

1 kg lamb
30 gr flour
1—2 dl oil or 100 gr lard
300—350 gr onion
2 bunches of spring anions, salt
1 teaspoon red paprika pepper
pepper
0,5—1 l warm water
1/2 l thick yoghurt

Wash meat, wipe and cut into bigger pieces, roll in flour and fry on all sides in heated oil (or lard) until brown. When meat is fried, take it out. Put peeled and finely chopped onion into the same fat, cook it slowly until half soft, then add trimmed and chopped spring onions together with green leaves. Cook together until soft and slightly brown, then add fried meat, salt, pepper and red paprika pepper. Barely cover with warm water (or soup from meat cube). Cover well and simmer until all is tender. Shake the pan occasionally and take care that juice does not reduce completely.

With "kapama" serve thick yoghurt.

Roumania

BAKED "KAPAMA"

(for 5 persons)

250 gr onion
1—1,5 dl oil
1 kg lamb
1 dl warm water
250 gr aubergines
250 gr courgettes
250 gr red paprikas
250 gr string beans
salt
pepper
some ground red paprika

Peel onion and chop finely. Wash meat, wipe and cut into bigger cubes. Heat oil, add onion, cook slowly to soften, then add meat. Cook together adding warm water at times.

Peel aubergines, cut into cubes, salt and leave to stand for 30 minutes, then rinse. Peel courgettes and cut into cubes; wash paprikas, core and cut into thicker strips; cut trimmed and washed string beans into smaller pieces. When meat is tender, add the prepared vegetables, salt and pepper, pour in some warm water as needed, cover and simmer. When all is tender, add some ground paprika (hot if desired), turn into a fireproof dish and bake in the oven preheated to 200°C.

Greece

"YANIYA" WITH CUCUMBERS

(for 5—6 persons)

900 gr — 1 kg mutton
2 onions
60—100 gr olive (or sunflower) oil
250 gr tomatoes
1/2 l hot soup from meat cube
salt
pepper
600—750 gr cucumbers
several tablespoons vinegar
1/2 teaspoon sugar
1/2 bunch of dill

Wash meat, drain and wipe a little, remove bones, cut into cubes about 2 cm big. Peel onion and chop finely. Heat oil (40 gr), add meat, fry it on all sides, add onion, cook slowly together until onion is glassy.

In the meantime wash tomatoes, peel, remove stalk ends and chop rather finely. Pour the rest of oil into a frying pan, heat, add tomatoes, cook for a while, then add to meat, pour in soup from meat cube (or bone stock), add salt, pepper and simmer together for about 30 minutes to reduce a little.

Wash cucumbers, peel, halve, remove seed, cut into cubes, add to meat and tomatoes, simmer together, add sugar and vinegar, shake well and cook until tender.

Wash dill, wipe and snip (with kitchen scissors preferably), add to "yaniya" before serving.

With "yaniya" serve boiled potatoes poured over with butter and sprinkled with chopped parsley.

Greece

CHICKEN "KAPAMA"

(for 5—6 persons)

1 chicken of about 1,5 kg
50 gr butter
1 onion

500 gr riper tomatoes
1 dl white wine
salt
pepper

Wash chicken, wipe and joint into 4—6 parts, fry in heated butter until nicely brown, take out and put into a pan. Cook slowly finely chopped onion in the same butter until soft. Wash tomatoes, peel and cut into smaller cubes, add to onion, pour in wine, add salt and pepper, cook shortly and pour over pieces of chicken, cover and simmer until chicken and vegetables are tender and the juice thick enough.

With this "kapama" serve mashed potatoes, pasta or rice.

CHICKEN "KAPAMA" WITH NOODLES

Prepare "kapama" as in the above recipe.

For noodles:

450 gr noodles
100—150 gr grated cheese (kachkval or similar)
40—50 gr butter

Cook noodles in slightly salted water, drain and turn over pieces of chicken. Pour juice from stewing over noodles, sprinkle with grated cheese and melted butter, bake in the oven preheated to 175°C about 35—40 minutes, that is until all is nicely brown.

CHICKEN "KAPAMA" WITH PEAS

Prepare "kapama" as in the above recipe. When chicken is nearly tender, add 900 gr cooked peas, pour in about 1—2 dl warm water in which peas were cooked. Cover and simmer together for 10—15 more minutes.

Turkey

LAMB "YANIYA" WITH SPINACH

(for 5—6 persons)

1 kg lamb (without bones)
1 kg spinach
2 smaller onions
1 bunch of spring onions
1—2 dl oil
10—15 gr flour (1 spoonful)
7—8 dl soup from cooking meat
salt
pepper
1 teaspoon red paprika pepper
1/2 l thick yoghurt

Wash meat, put up into lukewarm water to cook. When half cooked, take it out, cool and cut into bigger cubes.

Clean spinach (remove stalks and thick leaf ribs), wash, drain and cut into broad strips. Peel onion and chop finely. Heat oil, add chopped onion, cook it slowly a little, add chopped spring onions and spinach, add meat, salt, pepper, red paprika pepper, mix, pour in soup in which meat was cooked, shake well and simmer until all is tender. Towards the end blend in flour mixed in some cold water. Shake the pan well, add more soup as needed and simmer on until the juice is thick, for there should not be too much juice in "yaniya". Serve with thick yoghurt.

Greece

LAMB OR YOUNG BEEF "KAPAMA"

(for 5 persons)

1—1,25 kg lamb or young beef (from leg or shoulder)
2 smaller onions
1—2 cloves of garlic (optional)
50—100 gr butter or margarine or olive oil
2 dl hot water
salt
pepper
1/2 bunch of parsley
3 ripe tomatoes
1 teaspoon sugar

Wash meat, wipe and cut into bigger pieces. Heat butter, add meat, fry on both sides until brown, then take out. Add finely chopped onion into the same fat, chopped garlic, salt and pepper. Cook for a few minutes to soften, then add peeled tomatoes cut into smaller pieces, sugar and hot water. Dip meat into it, cover and simmer until the sauce is thick. With "kapama" serve baked potatoes, mashed potatoes, cooked rice or cooked pasta.

Greece

LAMB OR YOUNG BEEF "KAPAMA" WITH STRING BEANS

(for 6 persons)

1—1,25 kg lamb or young beef (from leg or shoulder)
2 smaller onions
1—2 cloves of garlic (optional)
50—100 gr butter or margarine or 1—1,5 dl olive oil
salt, pepper
1/2 bunch of parsley
3 ripe tomatoes
2 dl hot water
1 teaspoon sugar
1 kg young string beans

Wash meat, wipe and cut into bigger chunks. Heat butter, add meat, fry it to brown nicely, then take out. Add finely chopped onion and garlic to the same fat, add salt and pepper. Cook for a few minutes to soften a little, then add peeled tomatoes cut into small pieces, sugar and hot water. Put meat into it, cover and simmer until all is tender and the juice thick.

Trim string beans, wash and cut into pieces about 2 cm long. Cook in slightly salted water until half-cooked. Drain and add to meat, then simmer covered until quite tender and the juice thick enough.

LAMB OR YOUNG BEEF "KAPAMA" WITH POTATOES

Prepare "kapama" as in the above recipe.

Peel and wash 1 kg new potatoes, fry in 50 gr heated butter, put them over meat, pour in about 2—2,5 dl warm water, then simmer covered until potatoes and meat are quite tender and the juice thick enough.

Lamb "kapama" with courgettes is prepared in the same way. Courgettes are first fried in butter, then arranged over meat and simmered together until tender and the juice thick.

LAMB "KAPAMA" WITH BEANS

Prepare "kapama" as in the basic recipe. Pick over beans (500 gr), wash and cook. When tender, drain, add to meat, add warm water (2—2,5 dl) in which beans were cooked, cover and simmer until all is quite tender and the juice thick enough.

Bulgaria

"KAPAMA" WITH AUBERGINES

600 gr mutton (young beef or veal)
1—1,5 dl oil
1 bigger onion, salt
1 teaspoon red paprika pepper
pepper
2—3 dl warm water
750 gr aubergines
20—30 gr flour
2 dl oil for frying

Wash meat, wipe and cut into bigger chunks. Heat oil, add finely chopped onion, cook slowly for a while to soften, then add meat, salt, red paprika pepper, pour in some warm water, cover and simmer until tender.

Peel aubergines, cut into rounds, salt and leave to stand for at least 30 minutes. Rinse with cold water, wipe, roll in flour and fry in heated oil. When fried, arrange over nearly tender meat, pour in more water as needed and simmer until all is tender. Sprinkle with pepper before serving.

This "kapama" can be prepared in a different way. Aubergines are not fried, but cut into bigger cubes, salted, left to stand for a while, rinsed and added to nearly quite tender meat. Towards the end 2 peeled tomatoes cut into smaller cubes are added to meat and aubergines. To thicken the sauce, take 30 gr browned flour, mix with cold water, blend into "kapama" and simmer for another 10—15 minutes. In the end sprinkle with chopped parsley.

Yugoslavia

PLAIN "YANIYA"

(for 5 persons)

1 kg lamb from fore-quarter
750 gr — 1 kg spring onions
1 bunch of parsley
salt, pepper
1 dl oil
1 paprika (dried and hot if desired)
2—2,5 dl warm water

Wash meat, wipe and cut into bigger chunks. Trim onions and cut into smaller pieces. Heat oil, add onions, fry a little, then add chopped parsley.

Take a bigger, preferably fireproof dish, put a layer of spring onions, sprinkle with chopped paprika, then put several pieces of meat, repeat until all is used. Sprinkle each layer with salt and pepper. When all is put in, pour over with warm water, cover and simmer until meat is tender.

This kind of "yaniya" is prepared in Serbia, Macedonia, Bosnia and Kosovo, especially in sheep-breeding regions, as one of the first refreshing dishes in the spring time.

Albania

LAMB "KAPAMA" WITH EGGS

(for 5 persons)

1 kg lamb from leg
salt
20 gr flour
2 dl oil
500 gr onion
250—300 gr spring onions
pepper
1/2—1 l water (bone stock or soup from cube)
4 eggs
1/4—1/2 l thick yoghurt

Wash meat, wipe and cut into bigger pieces, salt, roll in flour and fry in heated oil on all sides. Take meat out and put thinly sliced onion into the same fat. When onion is half soft, add chopped spring onions. Cook slowly together until soft.

Arrange pieces of meat in a fireproof dish, add onion, pour in water (or soup), add salt and pepper. Stew in the oven preheated to 175—200°C until the juice is half reduced and the meat tender.

Beat eggs well, salt a little, pour over "kapama", then put back into the oven to brown.

Serve with thick yoghurt.

Turkey

"YANIYA" WITH STRING BEANS

600 gr mutton
salt
pepper
a pinch of powdered saffron
1—1,5 dl olive or other oil
3 onions
200 gr tomatoes
1 tablespoon tomato purée
1—1,5 dl lukewarm water
250—300 gr string beans
250 gr aubergines
100 gr olives

Wash meat, wipe, cut into cubes, sprinkle with salt and pepper, add a pinch of saffron in powder. Heat oil, add prepeared meat, fry it on all sides to brown, add finely chopped onion, peeled tomatoes cut into small pieces and tomato purée. Pour in lukewarm water, cover and simmer until half cooked.

Trim string beans and cut into smaller pieces. Peel aubergines, cut into rounds, salt, leave to stand about 30 minutes, then rinse. Add string beans and aubergines to meat, pour in more water as needed, then simmer covered until all is tender. Shake the pan while cooking at times and pour in more water. When cooked, "yaniya" must not have too much juice. Before serving sprinkle with chopped olives.

Turkey

"YANIYA" WITH OKRAS

(for 5—6 persons)

750 gr lamb from leg
1,5 dl oil
2 onions
3 cloves of garlic
ground red paprika or some crushed small hot pepper
250 gr fresh tomatoes of 2 tablespoons tomato purée (from tube)
500 gr fresh okras
1 tablespoon vinegar
salt
1 lemon
20 gr flour
1—2 dl warm water
1/2 bunch of parsley
3/4 l thick yoghurt

Wash meat, wipe and cut into bigger cubs. Heat oil, add meat, fry it on all sides until nicely brown, then add chopped onion. Cook slowly until slightly soft, add chopped or crushed garlic, fry shortly, add ground or crushed paprika, washed tomatoes peeled and cut into smaller pieces. Simmer all for a while.

Trim okras (make a gash in the upper part of pod) wash and cook in water to which some salt and vinegar have been added, then drain. Add okras prepared this way to meat, which is already half cooked. Add more warm water as needed. While simmering only shake the pan well.

Brown flour without fat, pour in cold water, then some warm water, boil shortly and add to "yaniya". Shake pan and add more water as needed. Simmer about 10—15 minutes.

With "yaniya" serve thick yoghurt.

Yugoslavia

"YANIYA" WITH SMOKED MEAT

300 gr smoked mutton
300 gr smoked beef
3 onions
40 gr oil
200 gr fresh tomatoes (or canned)
500 gr potatoes
pepper
salt
1/2 teaspoon red paprika pepper

Wash smoked meat, leave to stand in cold water (to draw out extra salt), then wash in cold water, cut into bigger pieces, pour in cold water and cook. Chop onion finely and cook slowly in heated oil until soft and beginning to colour. Add peeled tomatoes cut into smaller pieces, cook on until tomato is tender. Take meat out of water in which it was cooked, add it to onion and tomato, pour in abour 2—3 dl of water in which it was cooked. Simmer together. Towards the end, when meat is nearly cooked, add peeled potatoes, cut into slices, sprinkle with pepper and red paprika pepper, add more salt and water as needed. Simmer until all is tender and the juice reduced.

The Turkish author of travel books Evliya Tchelebiya mentions this "yaniya" as a specialty from Sarajevo. What was used in it was most probably mutton and beef smoked in the mountains, over the juniper sprigs fire.

Greece

GREEK MOUSSAKA

6 aubergines
1,5 dl oil
1 bigger onion
300 gr ground young beef or mutton
salt
pepper
some cinnamon or nutmeg
100 gr grated cheese (kachkaval or similar)
2 eggs

Peel aubergines and cut into slices lengthways, cook them in boiling water for 2 minutes (some oil can be added to water). Drain, rinse and wipe. Heat 1 dl oil, fry aubergines in it. Cook slowly finely chopped onion in the rest of oil. When soft, add ground meat, cook slowly for the meat to soften, then draw aside, add salt, pepper and cinnamon or nutmeg, mix and blend in the grated cheese. Grease a fireproof dish, put layers of aubergines and of meat in turn, finish with aubergines. Beat eggs well, pour over the moussaka. Bake in the oven preheated to 175°C about 45 minutes. With moussaka serve lettuce, mixed salad or thick yoghurt.

Roumania

MOUSSAKA WITH CAULIFLOWER

1 bigger head of cauliflower
salt
50 gr oil or lard
1 onion
300 gr ground young beef or lamb
pepper
2 eggs
150 gr flour
2 dl milk
1—2 dl oil for frying
2 dl sour cream

Trim cauliflower, wash, cook in slightly salted water, until half tender, then drain, cool and break into bigger sprigs. In the meantime heat oil, add finely chopped onion, cook slowly until soft, add meat, cook together about 25 minutes, add salt and pepper and mix.

Beat 1 egg, add to it flour and milk in turn, work up into a batter thicker than the pancake batter. Dip cooled cauliflower sprigs in batter and fry in heated oil until brown.

Arrange layers of cauliflower and meat in turn in a fireproof dish, finish with cauliflower. Beat egg with sour cream, pour over the moussaka. Bake in the oven preheated to 200°C for about 35 minutes, until tender and brown.

Turkey

MOUSSAKA WITH KALE

1 kg kale
salt, 2 eggs
150 gr flour
2 dl milk
2—3 dl oil
500—600 gr ground young beef or mutton
2 onions
1—2 cloves of garlic
pepper
1/2 bunch of parsley
2 eggs
2 dl sour cream
1 dl milk

Trim kale, wash and cut head into 8 slices. Remove thicker leaf ribs and cook shortly (blanch) in salted water, then drain and cool.

In the meantime beat eggs, add to them flour and milk in turn, work up into a smooth thick batter.

Heat 50 gr oil, add finely chopped onion, cook slowly until soft, add meat. Cook together for a while, then add chopped or crushed garlic, chopped parsley, salt and pepper.

Dip cooled slices of kale in batter and fry in heated oil until brown. Place layers of kale and meat in turn in a fireproof dish or djuvetch. The last layer should be kale. Beat eggs well with sour cream and milk. Pour this mixture over moussaka and bake in the oven preheated to 200°C until tender and brown. It usually takes about 30—40 minutes.

When done, cut into squares and serve warm.

Moussaka with fresh cabbage can be prepared in the same way.

Bulgaria

MOUSSAKA WITH KOHLRABI

600—700 gr veal
(lamb or young beef)
80 gr butter or margarine
2 smaller onions
1 egg
pepper
salt
1 bunch of parsley
1—1,5 dl lukewarm water or soup from cube
1 kg young kohlrabi
3 dl sour cream
1 dl milk
200 gr fresh tomatoes

Wash meat, wipe, cut into smaller pieces and grind. Heat one half of butter, add finely chopped onion (1), cook slowly until soft, add meat and cook together for a while. Draw aside, add salt, pepper, chopped parsey, then mix. Blend egg yolk and whisked white of egg into slightly cooled meat.

Wash peeled kohlrabi and cut into strips. Heat butter (30 gr), add finely chopped onion, cook to soften, add kohlrabi, cook together for kohlrabi to soften, pouring in some lukewarm water or soup from meat cube.

Grease a fireproof dish with butter, put in layers of kohlrabi and meat in turn, pour over each layer with some sour cream or soup. Cover with rounds of peeled tomatoes. Bake in the oven preset at 200°C for about 35 minutes. When tomato is soft and juicy, pour sour cream beaten with milk over the moussaka, put back into the oven for a short time until nicely brown.

With moussaka serve beetroot salad, lettuce or the like.

Turkey

MOUSSAKA I

1 kg tomatoes
500 gr aubergines
200 gr butterfat or 1—1,5 dl oil
1 onion
500 gr mutton or young beef
salt
pepper
1/2 l thick yoghurt

Wash tomatoes, peel and cut into rounds. Peel aubergines (optional), cut into cubes, salt and leave to stand for 30—60 minutes, then rinse with cold water, drain well and wipe. Heat half of butterfat, add aubergines and fry on all sides.

Peel onion, chop finely, cook slowly in heated oil to soften, add meat, cook together, add salt and pepper.

Grease a fireproof dish a little, put a layer of tomatoes at the bottom, salt a little, then arrange meat, then a layer of aubergines, sprinkle with salt and pepper, repeat until all is used, finish with tomatoes. Bake in the oven preheated to 175°C for about 40—45 minutes.

When serving pour moussaka with thick yoghurt or serve it separately.

Moussakas are a favourite dish in Turkey. They are prepared with various vegetables, this being one of the older ways of preparing this dish. Originally only aubergines and meat were used for moussakas, but now nearly all kinds of vegetables are, and the ways of preparing them differ. Now, vegetables are usually fried or frittered first, and moussakas poured over with a mixture of eggs and sour cream or milk, or with béchamel sauce.

Roumania

MOUSSAKA WITH POTATOES AND TOMATO

1 bigger onion
1,5—2 dl oil
300 gr ground mixed meat
salt, pepper
1 teaspoon red paprika pepper
1—1,5 kg potatoes
60 gr rice
2—2,5 dl warm water
2—3 tablespoons tomato purée
1 dl sour cream

Peel onion and chop finely, cook slowly in heated oil (50 gr) until slightly soft, add ground meat, salt, pepper and red paprika pepper, mix and cook together about 15—20 minutes. Then add picked over and cooked rice and mix all.

Wash potatoes, peel and cut into rounds. Grease a fireproof dish with oil, put in a layer of potatoes, sprinkle with salt and pepper, pour in some oil, then a layer of meat with rice, repeat, finish with potatoes. Pour warm water over moussaka. Bake in the oven preset at 175—200°C for about 45 minutes. When potatoes are tender and brown, pour sour cream beaten with tomato purée over them, put back into the oven and leave to brown.

With moussaka serve pickled paprikas, cabbage salad (fresh or pickled), beetroot salad and others.

Turkey

MOUSSAKA TURKISH WAY

750 gr — 1 kg aubergines
500—750 gr mutton
1 dl oil
2 leeks
250 gr tomatoes
salt
pepper
1/2 bunch of parsley
2—2,5 dl warm water

For tomato sauce:
30 gr oil
20 gr flour
500 gr fresh tomatoes or 2 spoons purée (from tube)
salt
1 teaspoon sugar

Wash aubergines, halve lengthways, make gashes here and there and bake in the heated oven (200°C). When done, scoop them out carefully. Chop scooped out "meat" finely. Heat oil, add trimmed and washed leeks cut into rounds, cook slowly to soften, add aubergine meat, minced mutton, peeled and chopped tomatoes. Add salt and pepper and simmer all to soften. When all is tender, blend in chopped garlic and parsley.

Grease a fireproof dish or a corresponding djuvetch, arrange scooped out aubergines, stuff them with the prepared filling, pour in some warm water and stew in the oven preheated to 200°C until all is tender.

When done, take out and pour over with tomato sauce prepared in the following way: heat oil, add flour, brown it a little, pour in some cold water, then cooked and puréed tomatoes (or purée diluted in lukewarm water), simmer for 10 minutes, add salt and some sugar.

Pour over moussaka and put back into the oven for 10—15 more minutes for the sauce to brown a little.

Greece

MOUSSAKA WITH TOMATOES

(for 6—7 persons)

1,5 kg tomatoes
salt
2 onions
1 dl oil
600—750 gr ground lamb
1/2 dl wine (with some wormwood added if desired)
pepper
some nutmeg
1 teaspoon oregano
60—75 gr breadcrumbs
500 gr riper tomatoes
0,5 dl oil
100 gr grated cheese (kachkaval, Trappist etc.)
50 gr butter or margarine
50 gr flour
3—4 dl milk
3 egg yolks

Peel aubergines, cut into rounds, salt, leave to stand about 60 minutes. Then rinse with cold water, wipe and fry in heated oil until brown. Chop onion finely and cook slowly in the rest of oil to soften a little. Add meat, wine, sugar and spices, cook together about 15 minutes, add some water as needed. Blend in breadcrumbs in the end.

Wash tomatoes, drain and cut into thicker rounds. Grease a fireproof dish, put a layer of aubergines, sprinkle with cheese, then a layer of meat mixture, then tomatoes, sprinkle with oil each time, repeat, finish with tomato rounds. Preheat oven to 175—200°C. Prepare béchamel sauce with butter, flour and milk, add to it egg yolks, salt and pepper, pour over moussaka and bake for about 60 minutes.

Yugoslavia

MOUSSAKA WITH HAM FROM BATCHKA

1 kg potatoes
200—250 gr minced or ground ham
1 dl oil or 50 gr lard
150 gr kachkaval or similar cheese cut into thin slices
salt
pepper

For béchamel sauce:
40 gr butter or margarine
20 gr flour
2—2,5 dl milk (half of it warm)
1/2 dl sour cream
1 egg yolk

Peel potatoes and cook in mildly salted water. When tender, drain and cut into rounds. Grease a fireproof dish with some oil or lard. Put in layers of potatoes, ham and cheese in turn. Sprinkle each layer of potatoes with salt and pepper and with some oil or melted lard. Repeat until all is used, finish with potatoes.

Pour béchamel sauce over moussaka: heat butter, add flour, fry a little but do not let it brown, slowly pour in cold, then warm milk. Simmer for 5—10 minutes. Beat well sour cream and egg, add to cooled béchamel, stirring all the time.

Bake in the oven preheated to 200°C about 30 minutes, until brown.

Serve with lettuce, beetroot salad with horseradish, cucumber salad or the like.

Roumania

MOUSSAKA WITH SAUERKRAUT FROM ERDELJ

100 gr rice (long grains if possible)
400 gr pork from neck
2 onions
2 cloves of garlic
150—200 gr smoked bacon
4 sausages (from Debrecen-thicker frankfurters)
salt
1 tablespoon red paprika pepper
1 kg pickled cabbage (shredded)
2 dl sour cream
1 teaspoon hot paprika pepper
2—2,5 dl hot water

Pick over rice, wash and cook in slightly salted water about 5 minutes, then drain and rinse with lukewarm water.

Wash meat, wipe and cut into cubes. Peel and chop finely onion and garlic; cut smoked bacon into bigger cubes, fry it to brown, take out cracklings. Put meat into the fat rendered and fry it on all sides to brown well. Then salt and put on a plate. Cook onion slowly in the same fat to soften, add garlic, Debrecen sausages cut into rounds, fry them a little, add fried bacon cubes (cracklings), meat, red paprika pepper. Mix all well and add more salt if needed.

Put a layer of sauerkraut into a fireproof dish or djuvetch, then a layer of meat mixture, then of rice. Repeat until all is used, finish with rice. Pour hot water over. Bake in the oven preset at 175—200°C. After 30—40 minutes pour whipped sour cream, with some red paprika pepper added, over the moussaka. Bake until all is tender and nicely brown.

With this sauerkraut dish serve mashed potatoes or potatoes boiled and mixed with fried onion.

Greece

MOUSSAKA WITH POTATOES GREEK WAY

50—75 gr butter
1 onion
2 cloves of garlic
450—500 gr ground mixed meat or ground young beef
500 gr peeled tomatoes
1 bayleaf
salt, pepper
1—1,25 kg potatoes
50 gr butter or 1/2 dl oil
2—2,5 dl warm water

Heat butter, add finely chopped onion and garlic, cook slowly until slightly soft, then add meat, mix with fork to crumble meat, cook until half tender, add tomatoes cut into pieces, bayleaf, salt and pepper. Cover and simmer about 30—45 minutes. Peel potatoes, wash, cut into slices or rounds, fry in butter or oil. Put a layer of potatoes in a fireproof dish, sprinkle with salt, then a layer of meat, repeat, finish with potatoes. Pour in enough warm water, cover and stew in the oven preheated to 200°C about 35—40 minutes. After about 30 minutes, take off lid and bake on until moussaka is nicely brown.

With moussaka serve lettuce, cucumber salad, mixed salad and others.

Greece

STUFFED VEGETABLES

6 even-size tomatoes
6 big paprikas
6 smaller aubergines
6 small courgettes
150 gr rice
500—600 gr mixed ground meat (beef, lamb, pork)
1/2—1 dl olive (or other) oil
2—2,5 dl warm water
50 gr grated cheese (kachkaval, Trappist etc.)
salt
pepper

Wash vegetables. Scoop out tomatoes carefully; core and deseed paprikas; scoop out aubergines, salt, leave to stand like that at least 30 minutes, then rinse with cold water and drain well; scoop out courgettes carefully and salt. Leave all the vegetables to drain.

Prepare the stuffing in the meantime: mix meat, add salt, pepper and half-cooked rice. Mix all well. Fill the prepared vegetables with this mixture. Pour olive oil into a bigger fireproof dish or djuvetch, arrange vegetables, pour in enough warm water, cover well (preferably with a tin foil) and simmer for about 90 minutes. When tender, uncover and sprinkle with grated cheese. Bake in the oven preheated to 200—250°C about 20 minutes.

Albania

MOUSSAKA WITH RICE

200 gr rice
1—1,5 dl oil
2 onions
200 gr fresh mushrooms
200 gr chicken livers
1/2 bunch of parsley
2 eggs
2 dl sour cream

Pick over rice, wash and cook in slightly salted water. When tender, rinse well and drain. Peel onion and chop finely. Heat oil, add onion, cook slowly to soften a little, then add trimmed mushrooms cut into thin slices, cook together about 10—15 minutes, then take out mushrooms with onion from oil. Wash parsley, wipe and chop finely. Wash chicken livers, cut into strips, drain and fry a little in the same oil, add salt and pepper.

Put a layer of rice into a greased fireproof dish, sprinkle with pepper and with salt if needed. Put a layer of mushrooms over and sprinkle with chopped parsley. Repeat until all is used. Cover with chicken livers and pour the rest of oil over. Heat oven to 200°C and bake about 20 minutes. Towards the end pour eggs beaten with sour cream over the moussaka, put back into the oven to brown.

With moussaka serve lettuce, cabbage salad, mixed salad and others.

Greece

STUFFED TOMATOES

(for 6 persons)

10—12 medium-size tomatoes
2 teaspoons of sugar
75—80 gr butter
1 onion
750 gr ground mixed meat or ground young beef
50 gr rice
1/2 bunch of parsley
salt
pepper
1/2 teaspoon cinnamon (optional)
some breadcrumbs for sprinkling

Wash tomatoes, drain, cut a slice from the top (not stalk end) of each tomato and scoop out carefully. Pass the tomato meat through a sieve and place scooped out tomatoes on a bigger plate, then put some sugar into each.

Cook finely chopped onion slowly in about 50 gr butter until slightly soft, then add ground meat. Mix with a fork to crumble it a bit, cook for a while, then add washed rice cooked shortly and drained, as well as chopped parsley, salt, pepper, cinnamon and 1 cup of puréed tomato. Cover and simmer about 10—15 minutes, draw aside and cool.

Fill the tomatoes with meat mixture, but not to the top, cover each with the cut-off lid. Melt the rest of butter, pour some over each tomato and sprinkle with breadcrumbs. Pour the rest of puréed tomato into a fireproof dish, then arrange stuffed tomatoes over and bake in the oven preheated to 175°C about 60 minutes, until tender and the juice thick enough.

Roumania

LAMB WITH AUBERGINES

1,5 kg lamb
salt
pepper
20 gr butter
30 gr oil (3 tablespoons)
3 aubergines
1 dl white wine
2,5 dl soup from meat cube or bone stock
2 tablespoons tomato purée (from tube)
1 tablespoon butter
1 tablespoon flour
1 tablespoon finely chopped parsley

Wash meat, wipe, cut into bigger cubes, sprinkle with salt and pepper. Mix butter and oil, heat, add meat, fry it on all sides to brown.

Peel aubergines, cut into cubes, salt. Leave to stand about 30 minutes, then rinse and wipe. Take fried meat out of fat on to a plate, put aubergines into the fat, fry a little and take out. Pour wine into the fat, boil shortly, add tomato diluted in water and butter mixed with flour. Cook together, add meat and aubergines, pour in soup. Simmer until all is tender, add salt and pepper as needed.

Serve with mashed potatoes, cooked noodles or rice.

Turkey

LAMB WITH OKRAS

750 gr—1 kg lamb
1 dl oil
2 onions
2—3 cloves of garlic
1 bunch of parsley
1/2 teaspoon red paprika pepper
750 gr okras
salt
1—2 dl warm water

Wash meat, wipe, cut into bigger cubes. Peel onion and chop finely. Heat oil, add onion, cook slowly until brown. Then add chopped garlic, chopped parsley and red paprika pepper. Cook shortly together, add meat, salt, pour in warm water, cover and simmer.

Trim okras, wash, cut into smaller pieces and cook in salted water about 10 minutes, drain, add to meat when it is half tender. Add more warm water (about 1 dl) as needed, simmer together until all is tender.

Serve with boiled potatoes, cooked rice and some salad.

Greece

STUFFED PAPRIKAS GREEK WAY

(for 5—6 persons)

10—12 bigger paprikas for stuffing
50 gr butter
1 onion
1—2 cloves of garlic
600 gr ground meat (young beef or mixed)
50—70 gr rice
1/2 bunch of parsley
2 ripe tomatoes
salt, pepper
50 gr breadcrumbs
50 gr butter

Wash paprikas, cut off stalk ends, remove stalks, core out seeds and thicker inner parts. Plunge them into boiling water and leave in it about 3 minutes, then quickly run cold water over them and drain.

Heat butter, add chopped onion, cook slowly to soften, then add meat and chopped garlic. Mix with fork to crumble the meat. Pick over rice, wash and cook shortly in slightly salted water, drain and add to meat. Add chopped parsley, peeled tomatoes cut into smaller pieces, salt and pepper, mix and stew on for about 5—10 minutes. Cool the mixture a little, stuff paprikas with it, cover with the cut-off lids and arrange in a greased fireproof dish or djuvetch. Mix bread-crumbs with melted butter and sprinkle each paprika with them. Pour the juice left over from stewing over the paprikas. Heat oven to 175°C and bake for about 60 minutes.

Roumania

STUFFED PAPRIKAS I

8—10 bigger paprikas
500 gr pork
250 gr young beef or beef
100 gr lard
1 onion
1 egg
salt, pepper
nutmeg (optional)
2 tablespoons chopped parsley
500 gr fresh, riper tomatoes
2—3 dl sour cream

Wash paprikas, remove stalks and core. Grind meat. Chop onion finely, heat lard (40—50 gr), add onion, cook it slowly until soft and slightly brown. Then cool, add meat, egg, salt, pepper, some nutmeg and parsley. Mix all well. Fill paprikas with this mixture. Heat the rest of lard, add paprikas and turn them in it to fry a little on all sides. Wash tomatoes, cut and pass through a sieve.

Grease a fireproof dish with lard left over from frying, pour in tomato, arrange stuffed paprikas. Bake in the oven preheated to 175°C until tender.

Serve sour cream with paprikas. Mashed potatoes or cooked rice with parsley are a very good accompaniment to paprikas prepared this way.

Turkey

STUFFED PAPRIKAS TURKISH WAY

(for 4—5 persons)

8—10 big paprikas
80 gr rice
350—400 gr cooked mutton
strained soup from cooking mutton
salt, pepper
1 egg
3 cloves of garlic
60 gr oil
2 onions
500 gr tomatoes

Core paprikas, boil shortly (about 5 minutes), run cold water over them, remove thin skin. Pick over rice and cook shortly in mutton soup. Grind or mince cooked meat, mix with rice, add salt, pepper, egg and finely chopped garlic. Mix all well. Fill paprikas with this mixture.

Heat oil, add finely chopped onion. cook slowly to soften and brown slightly, add peeled tomatoes passed through a sieve, add salt to taste. Arrange stuffed paprikas in this sauce, cover and stew in the oven preheated to 175°C about 35—40 minutes.

Greece

STUFFED AUBERGINES

(for 6 persons)

6 nice medium-size aubergines
salt
50 gr butter
1 smaller onion
500 gr ground meat
1/2 bunch of parsley
50 gr rice, pepper
2 bigger ripe tomatoes
1 teaspoon sugar

Wash aubergines, remove stalks, cut off tops about 2 cm thick. Scoop out aubergines with a teaspoon or a knife for peeling potatoes, taking out all the meat with seeds, then rub both the tops and aubergines with salt, leave to stand about 40—60 minutes, rinse carefully with cold water and drain well.

Heat butter in a bigger frying pan, cook slowly finely chopped onion in it, then the ground meat, add chopped parsley, salt and pepper. Pick over rice, wash, cook shortly and drain, add to meat, mix all, cook on together. Towards the end, add peeled tomatoes cut into smaller pieces (without juice), then cook all shortly. Cool a little and fill aubergines with this mixture, cover with the cut-off tops and arrange in a greased fireproof dish.

Mix the juice left over from cutting fresh tomatoes with 2 dl water and butter from cooking the ingredients, add salt, pepper and sugar and cook shortly, then pour over aubergines, cover and stew in the oven preheated to 175°C about 45 minutes. Towards the end take off lid and bake until aubergines are quite tender and the sauce thick enough.

Turkey

STUFFED ONIONS — "SAGAN DOLMA"

600—800 gr nice medium-size onions
2 dl vinegar
1 smaller onion (for stuffing)
400 gr beef or mixed mutton and young beef
60 gr rice
salt
pepper
1 egg
20 gr oil (2 spoons)
2 cloves of garlic (optional)
1/2 teaspoon red paprika pepper
2 tablespoons tomato purée
2 dl warm water
50 gr butter or margarine
4 dl sour cream or thick yoghurt

Peel onions, cook in slightly salted water to which vinegar has been added, then run cold water over. Press out inner parts with fingers, so that outer parts remain whole and about 1 cm thick (to put stuffing in).

Chop one onion finely, grind meat.

Cook rice, drain and add to meat, add salt, egg, red paprika pepper, finely chopped garlic. Mix all well. Fill onions with this mixture. Grease a fireproof dish with oil and arrange stuffed onions. Dilute tomato in warm water, add melted butter, pour over the onions, cover and simmer until all is tender.

With dolmas serve sour cream or thick yoghurt.

Yugoslavia

STUFFED KOHLRABI

1,5 kg young kohlrabi (about 8 medium-size kohlrabi)
salt
250 gr mixed ground meat
1 egg
pepper
20 gr breadcrumbs
30 gr fatter smoked bacon
1/4 l bone stock or soup from meat cube
1 smaller spoon of flour
1 dl sour cream
1 bunch of parsley

Peel kohlrabi (start with root end), wash, cook in slightly salted water about 10 minutes, then take out and drain. In the meantime mix meat with egg, add salt, pepper and breadcrumbs. Mix all well.

Cut of "lids" from cooled kohlrabi (the leaves' end) about 1—1,5 cm thick, scoop kohlrabi out carefully, so that they remain whole and with walls about 1 cm thick. Fill them with the prepared meat mixture, put lids on agains and fix them with toothpicks.

Cut bacon into smaller cubes, fry a little, add stuffed kohlrabi, fry them quickly, pour in soup from cube, cover and simmer until meat and kohlrabi are tender, but not overcooked. Take kohlrabi out and arrange in a warmed dish. Mix flour with some cold water, add to juice from cooking kohlrabi, add some more warm water or soup as needed, cook for about 5 minutes, draw aside, add sour cream mixed with chopped parsley and pour over kohlrabi.

Serve as the main dish with mashed potatoes.

Roumania

STUFFED PAPRIKAS II

10—12 bigger paprikas
500 gr pork
2 onions
40 gr margarine (lard or oil)
150 gr button mushrooms
250 gr tomatoes
1—2 dl warm water
salt, pepper
1 teaspoon mild red paprika pepper
1 teaspoon edible starch
2 tablespoons milk
ketchup to taste

Wash meat, wipe and cut into small cubes. Peel onion, chop finely and cook slowly in heated margarine or oil until soft, add to meat and cook together about 10 minutes.

Trim button mushrooms, cut into thin slices. Wash tomatoes, peel, cut into rounds and half of them (125 gr) add

to meat and onion. Add mushrooms, pour in water as needed, simmer for about 30 minutes until juice reduces, then add salt, pepper and red paprika pepper. Mix all well.

Wash paprikas, remove stalks and core. Fill them with the prepared mixture. Grease a fireproof dish a little, put in the rest of cut tomatoes, arrange paprikas, cover and simmer for about 30—40 minutes. When cooked, take paprikas out and put into a warmed dish.

Mix starch and cold milk, add it to tomato sauce in the fireproof dish, pour in some water (1—2 dl) as needed, cook shortly and then pass through a sieve. Pour it over arranged paprikas. Add some ketchup to taste.

With paprikas serve mashed potatoes or cooked rice seasoned with butter and chopped parsley.

Yugoslavia

STUFFED POTATOES

8—10 potatoes of medium size and smooth skin

For stuffing:
40 gr oil or lard
1 onion
150—200 gr fresh mushrooms (button mushrooms, ceps and the like)
200 gr mixed ground meat
salt
pepper
1/2 bunch of parsley

For pouring over:
60 gr butter or margarine
30 gr flour
1/4 l milk, half of which warm
50 gr cheese, kachkaval, Trappist or similar
1 dl sour cream

Wash potatoes, peel, halve lengthways, cook in slightly salted water about 5 minutes, then drain.

Heat oil or lard, add finely chopped onion, cook it slowly to soften, then add trimmed mushrooms cut into thin slices and ground meat. Cook slowly together at low heat until tender, add salt, pepper and chopped parsley. Mix all. Scoop out potato halves carefully (the scooped out parts can be used to make thick soup, together with water in which potatoes were cooked), then fill with the prepared mixture. Grease a fireproof dish with oil a little, arrange stuffed potatoes, pour in some warm water and bake in the oven preset at 175 °C about 30—40 minutes. Towards the end of baking pour over with the following: heat butter or margarine, add flour, fry it quickly so that it does not change colour, pour in some cold and then some warm milk, cook at low heat about 10 minutes, add grated cheese and sour cream and salt to taste. Turn heat to 200 °C and bake quickly to brown.

Serve stuffed potatoes with some salad.

Bulgaria

MEATBALLS WITH AUBERGINES

5 aubergines
5 cloves of garlic
salt
pepper
1 onion
20 gr oil
500 gr ground pork
1 slice of white bread
1/2 dl milk
1 egg
1 tablespoon chopped parsley
2 dl oil for frying
2 dl sour cream

Wash aubergines, bake in the oven, then peel and grind, add finely chopped garlic, salt and pepper. Mix all well. Chop onion finely, cook slowly in oil until slightly soft. Pour milk over bread to soften. Add cooled onion to meat, then add drained bread, egg, parsley, salt and pepper. Work into a meat mixture. Leave to stand in a cool place for 30—60 minutes. Shape into patties ("tchufte"), fry in heated oil to brown on both sides.

Pour oil from frying into a fireproof dish, put half of the aubergines, place meat patties over, cover with the rest of aubergines, level. Whip sour cream and pour over. Heat oven to 200°C and bake for about 30—40 minutes until nicely brown.

Serve with some fresh-tasting salad.

Greece

PILAF WITH CHICKEN MEAT

1 chicken
40 gr mutton suet or oil
2 onions
400 gr rice
250 gr paprikas
200 gr tomatoes
50 gr raisins
1—1,2 l bone stock
salt
pepper

Wash chicken, cut into pieces, remove bones and skin. Pour cold water over bones and skins, add some salt and cook at medium heat. Cut meat into smaller pieces. Heat suet or oil, add finely chopped onion, cook it gently to soften, add meat and cook at low heat. Pick over rice, blanch (cook in slightly salted water about 5 minutes), then rinse with warm water and drain. Wash paprikas, deseed and cut into cubes. Wash tomatoes, peel and cut into cubes.

Add rice, paprikas, tomatoes and raisins to half-cooked meat, pour in bone stock, add salt and pepper. Simmer until all is tender and the liquid absorbed.

While simmering, shake the pan occasionally and add a little more stock if necessary.

Turkey

COURGETTE DOLMAS

4—6 medium-size courgettes
250—300 gr ground young beef
salt
pepper
1 teaspoon red paprika pepper
2—3 cloves of garlic
40 gr oil
1 onion
1 egg
50 gr rice
5—8 dl soup from meat cube or warm water
50 gr. flour
2—3 dl sour cream or thick yoghurt

Add salt, pepper, red paprika pepper and finely chopped garlic to meat. Heat oil, add finely chopped onion, cook slowly to soften, add onion to meat, add egg, cooked and drained rice. Mix all well.

Wash young courgettes, peel thinly, halve if longer, then scoop out carefully with a teaspoon or the knife for peeling potatoes. Take care that they remain whole. Leave courgettes to stand for a while in cold water, then take out and drain well. Fill them with the prepared mixture.

Grease a fireproof dish with oil a little (left over from cooking onion), arrange courgettes with openings upwards, pour in enough warm water to cover them. Simmer until meat and courgettes are tender. Towards the end, add flour mixed with some cold water and red paprika pepper, cook on for another 5—10 minutes until the sauce becomes thick. Pour sour cream or thick yoghurt over courgettes when serving, or serve separately.

Turkey

CHICKEN PILAF

1 kg chicken meat (1 chicken)
1 bigger carrot
1/2 celery root
salt
6—8 peppercorns
1 onion
40 gr butter or oil
400 gr rice
2 bayleaves
pepper

Wash chicken, cut into pieces and put up to cook barely covered with cold water. When it boils, add scraped carrot and celery, salt, peppercorns, then simmer until meat is tender and strain. Peel onion and chop finely, add to heated oil or butter and cook gently until soft. Pick over rice, wash, wipe, add to onion, cook slowly together until rice is glassy, add bayleaves, pour in soup (8—10 dl), add chicken meat, pepper, some salt if necessary, cover and stew in the oven preheated to 175—200°C until rice is tender and the liquid absorbed. Serve warm.

Roumania

ROUMANIAN "DJUVETCH"

1 aubergine
2 onions
750 gr beef
salt
1/2—1 dl olive (or other) oil
5 big paprikas
1 cucumber
4 potatoes
5 tomatoes (riper)
2 eggs
1 lemon
1 tablespoon flour
2 dl milk
pepper

Peel aubergine, cut into cubes, salt and leave to stand for 40—60 minutes, then rinse with cold water and drain well. Chop onion finely. Cut beef into bigger cubes. Heat oil in a fireproof dish, add onion, cook it gently to soften a little, put in meat, salt, cook together for a while, then add aubergine, pour in some water and simmer covered.

Core paprikas and cut into cubes or strips, peel potatoes and cut into cubes, peel tomatoes and cut into bigger cubes, peel cucumber and also cut into cubes. Salt all the vegetables, mix, add to meat, pour in more water as needed, then cook slowly at low heat to soften.

Beat well eggs, lemon juice, flour and milk, add pepper. Pour this mixture over "djuvetch" when nearly done. Bake in the oven preset at 175—200°C until the liquid is reduced and the whole dish slightly brown. Serve in the same dish.

Yugoslavia

MEATBALLS ON SPINACH

For meatballs:
500 gr mixed ground meat
2 onions
1 bigger slice of white bread
2 dl lukewarm water or milk
1/2 bunch of parsley
1 egg
salt
pepper
2 dl oil for frying

For spinach:
1 kg spinach
2 onions
50 gr oil or lard
2 cloves of garlic
1 dl warm water
1 tablespoon flour
2 dl milk
salt
pepper
2 dl sour cream

Add finely chopped onion to ground meat, softened and drained bread, chopped parsley, egg, salt and pepper. Work well into a meat mixture and leave to stand in a cool place for 30—60 minutes.

Wash spinach, remove stalks and thick leaf ribs, cut into strips. Chop finely onion and garlic. Heat oil or lard, add chopped onion, cook slowly until soft, put in spinach, garlic, salt and pepper, cook together, pour in some warm water and simmer until spinach is tender. Then add flour mixed with cold milk. Simmer for 10 more minutes.

Shape meat into patties, fry them in heated oil. Put spinach into a greased fireproof dish. Place meat patties over. Bake in the oven preset at 200°C about 40 minutes. Towards the end, pour over with sour cream and put back into the oven to brown a little.

Serve with mashed potatoes or boiled potatoes sprinkled with parsley.

Yugoslavia

"DJUVETCH" MACEDONIAN WAY

1 medium-size chicken
2 l water
1 bunch root vegetables (2 carrots, 1 parsley root, 1 parsnip, 1/2 celery root, 1 leek)
1 paprika
salt

peppercorns
250 gr rice
40 gr oil or lard
1 onion
40 gr melted butter
pepper ground from mill

Wash chicken and put up to cook. When the water boils, add cleaned roots, paprika, salt and a few peppercorns. Simmer until chicken is tender.

Pick over rice, wash, pour lukewarm water over and leave to stand for 10—15 minutes, then drain.

Put oil or lard into a fireproof dish or enamelled djuvetch, add finely chopped onion, cook gently to soften. When chicken is cooked, take it out of soup and cut into nice pieces. Strain soup and cut root vegetables into cubes. Add rice to softened onion, pour in 3/4 l soup and cook until half soft. Mix cooked and cut root vegetables into rice, stir, add salt and pepper. Place chicken meat over rice, pour in more soup if needed. Bake in the oven preheated to 175—200°C until rice is tender and meat brown. Pour heated butter over and sprinkle with freshly ground pepper.

With "djuvetch" serve beetroot salad with horseradish, lettuce or cucumber salad with thick yoghurt or sour cream.

Turkey

WHITE PILAF

(for 5 persons)

500—600 gr meat (young beef, lamb)
1—1,5 l hot water
salt
40 gr butterfat (butter, margarine or oil)
1 onion
400 gr rice
1/2 bunch of parsley
pepper
4—5 dl thick yoghurt

Wash meat, cut it into bigger cubes and put up to cook in hot water. When it boils, add salt.

Heat butterfat, add onion cut into halves and fry it a little. Pick over rice, wipe, cook slowly together with onion until glassy, then pour in 8—10 dl strained soup, mix in meat, add chopped parsley, mix and simmer until rice is tender and the liquid completely absorbed, so that grains of rice remain whole.

As accompaniment serve thick voghurt.

Yellow pilaf is prepared in the same way, only some saffron is added to the soup to give the dish its vivid yellow colour.

Turkey

MEAT AND VEGETABLE STEW — "DJUVETCH"

(for 6—8 persons)

"Djuvetch" in Turkish (gügec, vulg, güvec) means an earthenware pan. Djuvetch as a dish is prepared with bigger chunks of meat mixed with onion, rice, potatoes and other vegetables and baked in an earthenware (fireproof) pan or dish.

2—3 onions
1 dl oil
1 kg young beef or lamb
300 gr potatoes
300 gr string beans
2 aubergines
5—6 tomatoes
80 gr rice
1 bunch of parsley
2 dl lukewarm water
2 eggs
1 dl sour cream
salt
pepper

Peel onion, chop finely, cook gently in heated oil to soften a bit, add washed and wiped meat cut into bigger chunks, cook slowly together. Peel potatoes, cut into slices or rounds; wash string beans, remove tops and tails and cut into smaller pieces; peel aubergines, cut into rounds, salt, leave to stand for 10 minutes, then rinse with cold water. Mix vegetables, put into a greased fireproof or enamelled dish, add salt, pepper, shortly cooked rice, finely chopped parsley, arrange half-cooked meat and onion over, pour in lukewarm water and bake in the oven preheated to 175—200°C until all is tender. When meat is done, arrange tomatoes over, peeled and cut into rounds, then put back into the oven to brown.

Beat well eggs with sour cream, pour over "djuvetch" and bake at high heat shortly to brown nicely. Serve in the same dish.

Bulgaria

MONASTERY "DJUVETCH"

600 gr meat (lamb, veal or pork)
1 dl oil or 80 gr lard
1 onion
200 gr tomatoes
salt
pepper
2—3 dl warm water or soup from cube
300 gr fresh mushrooms (or 100 gr dried)
150 gr paprikas
100 gr olives
100 gr rice
1 dl wine
1/2 bunch of parsley

Wash meat, wipe and cut into bigger pieces. Fry it quickly in heated oil, add finely chopped onion, cook gently until slightly soft, add half of the tomatoes (100 gr) peeled and cut into small pieces, add salt and pepper, pour in warm water or soup from cube (or bone stock), then simmer. When half tender turn into a fireproof or eathenware dish, add mushrooms trimmed washed and cut into thin slices and paprikas cut into strips. When mushrooms and paprikas are tender, add olives and rice picked over and half-cooked. Add more salt and pepper if necessary, pour in wine and some warm water as needed. Bake in the oven preheated to 175—200°C. After 10—15 minutes add the rest of tomatoes cut into

rounds and bake on until brown. When done, sprinkle "djuvetch" with chopped parsley and pepper.

Turkey

PILAF FROM ISTANBUL

(for 6 persons)

500 gr rice
salt
60 gr oil (6 tablespoons)
1—1,2 l chicken soup
1/2 teaspoon saffron
75 gr chicken livers
100—150 gr chicken breast meat
2 tablespoons peeled almonds
100 gr shelled peas

Pick over rice, pour over it lukewarm salted water, leave to cool, then drain and dry a little.

Heat oil, add rice, cook it gently, stirring all the time, until it is glassy. In the meantime heat soup with saffron. Mince liver and breast meat, add to soup. Also add peas and peeled almonds to soup. Cook all shortly, then add rice, simmer until tender.

Serve warm with some salad.

Yugoslavia

PILAF WITH PIGS' LIVER

500 gr pigs' liver
2 dl milk
1/2 teaspoon red paprika pepper
salt
bayleaf
1 onion
40 gr oil
400 gr rice
1—1,2 l soup from meat cube
pepper
1/2 bunch of parsley

Leave liver to stand in milk for at least 30 minutes, then drain, wipe and cut into cubes. Heat oil or lard, add liver, bayleaf and cook gently. Add salt and red paprika pepper in the end. Peel onion, chop finely, cook slowly in heated oil until slightly soft, add picked over and washed rice, cook it slowly, stirring all the time, until glassy, pour in soup from meat cube, add salt and pepper. Simmer covered for about 20 minutes. Then add liver, chopped parsley, level and bake shortly in the oven preset at 200°C

Serve pilaf with cucumber salad with thick yoghurt or sour cream, with lettuce or mixed salad.

Greece

"DJUVETCH" WITH MACARONI

(for 5 persons)

500 gr boneless lamb or young beef
1 dl melted butter
1 onion of medium size
1—2 cloves of garlic
4 dl tomato juice
20—25 gr tomato from tube
salt
pepper
250 gr macaroni
100 gr harder cheese (kachkaval, Trappist and similar)

Wash meat, wipe and cut into 5 bigger pieces. Heat butter, add meat and fry it quickly on all sides to brown nicely. Add finely chopped onion and garlic, cook slowly together until meat is tender. Pour in tomato juice, add tomato from tube, salt, pepper and barely cover with water. Cover and simmer until meat is quite tender and the sauce thick.

Cook macaroni in salted water, drain and rinse. Grease a fireproof dish or djuvetch with butter, put in half of the macaroni, place meat over, pour over with half of the juice from cooking meat, cover with the other half of macaroni, pour in the rest of juice, level and sprinkle with grated cheese.

Heat oven to 200°C, bake about 15—20 minutes, until nicely brown.

With this "djuvetch" serve lettuce, fresh cabbage salad, mixed salad and others.

Turkey

PILAF WITH MUTTON

500 gr rice
2 tablespoons salt
100 gr lamb or calf's kidneys
100 gr lamb or calf's liver
250 gr lean mutton
30 gr butter
2 onions
40 gr (4 tablespoons) olive oil
2 tablespoons pistachios
salt, pepper
ground cinnamon
4—5 allspice corns
1—1,2 l meat soup or soup from cube
2 tablespoons raisins
1 teaspoon sugar
1 tablespoon tomato from tube or can
3 tablespoons chopped dill

Pick over rice, wash and pour into it warm salted water. Leave to cool, then drain. Leave kidneys in cold water about 30 minutes. Drain, remove veins and extra suet, then cut into smaller pieces.

Wash liver and mutton, wipe and cut into smaller pieces. Heat butter, add kidneys and liver and cook gently.

Chop onion finely, cook in heated oil until soft, add meat and cook together until meat is slightly tender (about 15 minutes), add rice, cook slowly and stir until rice is glassy, add pistachios, spices, pour in soup, add washed raisins, sugar and tomato purée. Mix and simmer until rice and meat are nearly tender. Add liver and kidneys together with the fat they were cooked in to rice, add dill, pour in more soup if necessary and simmer together about 20 more minutes.

Greece

GREEK PILAF

(for 5 persons)

500 gr lamb
2 onions
40 gr mutton suet (or oil)
400—500 gr rice
250 gr tomatoes
50 gr cleaned okras
1 lemon
1—1,2 l meat soup or soup from meat cube
salt
pepper

Cut lamb into smaller cubes. Peel onion and chop finely. Heat suet or oil, add chopped onion, cook it gently to soften, then add meat, salt and simmer covered until tender. Pick over rice, wash and wipe. Wash tomatoes, peel and cut into small cubes. Wash okras and leave for a while to stand in water with lemon juice.

When meat is nearly cooked, add rice, tomatoes and okras, add salt and pepper as needed, pour in heated lamb or other soup, mix slowly and simmer until meat and rice are quite tender and the liquid absorbed.

Albania

PILAF WITH CHICKEN LIVERS

500 gr chicken livers
3 bigger onions
1 dl oil
2 tablespoons ground walnuts
200 gr rice
1 teaspoon sugar
salt
a few peppercorns
1/2 teaspoon cinnamon
1/2 teaspoon crushed cloves
150—200 gr raisins
3 tomatoes
1/2—3/4 l bone stock or soup from meat cube
a few sage leaves
1/2 bunch of parsley

Wash livers, wipe and cut into strips. Heat oil, add livers and fry at medium heat. When tender, take out. Add finely chopped onion to the same oil, cook gently until glassy, then add walnuts, cook together about 5 minutes. Add picked over and washed rice, some sugar, salt, raisins washed in warm water, washed tomatoes peeled and cut into small pieces. Mix all, pour in soup, cover and simmer until rice is tender. Shake at times, add a little more soup if necessary.

When rice is tender, add livers, chopped sage and chopped parsley. Mix slowly, cover and leave at very low heat for 10—15 minutes.

With pilaf serve lettuce, beetroot salad and the like.

Greece

RICE GREEK WAY

135 gr rice
20 gr butter or margarine
1 l chicken soup from cube
300 gr red paprikas
30 gr oil (3 taplespoons)
250 gr canned peas
200 gr (1 head) lettuce
salt
pepper
hot red paprika pepper
mild red paprika pepper
400 gr mixed ground meat
1 egg
1—1,5 dl oil for frying

Wash rice well, then drain. Heat butter or margarine, add rice, cook gently, stirring all the time, until glassy, pour in soup from cube, bring it to the boil, then simmer until tender. In the meantime core paprikas, wash and cut into cubes.

Heat oil, add paprikas, cover and cook about 10 minutes, add drained peas, cook slowly together about 5 minutes. Trim lettuce, wash and cut into strips about 1/2 cm broad, add to cooked vegetables, mix and cook together for a few minutes, draw aside, add salt, pepper, two kinds of red paprika pepper, keep covered in a warm place.

Mix ground meat with egg, add salt and pepper and shape into small balls (dumplings), then fry in heated oil on all sides until nicely brown.

Mix rice and vegetables, warm up

at low heat, add meatballs and mix. Arrange on a long heated plate and serve warm.

Turkey

"DJUVETCH" ISTANBUL WAY

500 gr boneless lamb
30 gr oil (3 tablespoons)
2 smaller onions
1—2 cloves of garlic
1/4 l hot soup from cube
120 gr apples
1 teaspoon curry
2 pineapple rounds (canned)
2 bananas
200 gr rice
salt
20—30 gr raisins

Wash meat, wipe and cut into bigger cubes. Heat oil, add meat, fry on all sides, then add finely chopped onion and garlic, cook genly about 5 minutes, pour in soup and simmer covered about 30 minutes. Then add peeled apples cut into cubes, curry, pineapple cut into small cubes, mix all and simmer on covered, until all is tender. A few minutes before the end add bananas cut into rounds.

Pick over rice, cook in about 1 liter of slightly salted water. When tender, rinse and drain well, blend into the "djuvetch" and cook together for about 5 minutes.

Wash raisins in warm water, drain. Before serving, sprinkle over the dish.

With this "djuvetch" serve lettuce, endive and the like.

Bulgaria

"DJUVETCH" WITH YOGHURT AND LAMB OR VEAL

600 gr meat
200 gr spring onions
1 dl oil
salt, pepper
1 teaspoon red paprika pepper
2—3 dl warm water (or soup from cube)
20 gr tomato from tube
1/2 l thick yoghurt
4 eggs
1 tablespoon flour (20 gr)
1/2 bunch of parsley

Wash meat, wipe and cut into bigger pieces. Trim onions and chop, put into heated oil, cook gently to soften a little, add meat, salt, pepper, red paprika pepper, cook together for a while, then turn into a fireproof or earthenware dish, pour in warm water (or soup) and bake in the oven preheated to 175—200°C about 40—50 minutes. When done, pour over with thick yoghurt beaten together with eggs, flour and tomato, sprinkle with chopped parsley, put back into the oven and bake on until nicely brown.

Yugoslavia

RED PILAF

(for 10—12 persons)

1—2 kg meat (lamb, veal)
2—3 l hot water
1 bunch of root vegetables
salt, 10—12 peppercorns

125 gr butterfat (butter or margarine)
750 gr fresh tomatoes of 50 gr tomato purée (from tube)
500 gr rice
ground pepper

Wash meat, cut into bigger cubes and put up to cook in hot water. When it boils, add scraped roots, salt, peppercorns. Cook at medium heat until tender. When meat is cooked, strain soup. Heat butterfat, add washed tomatoes peeled and cut into smaller pieces, cook gently until they turn into a mush. Pick over rice and add to tomato, cook together until rice is glassy, pour in one liter or more of soup, add salt. Add meat, cook together at low heat until rice is tender and all the liquid absorbed. Rice grains should remain whole. Sprinkle with ground pepper before serving. It can be served with thick yoghurt.

Pilaf is a Persian word for thickly cooked rice. It was taken over by the Turks, and from them by all the Balkan peoples for dishes with rice, meat and other ingredients.

In Bosnia the word also meant the evening feast on wedding-days, as well as the meal after taking the guild exams, as that dish was always served on such occasions. The chronicler from Sarajevo, Mula Mustafa Basheskiya, in his description of the "great pilaf" of the Sarajevo boot-makers in 1770, mentions three kinds of pilaf: red, yellow and white. The original recipe for the red pilaf has not been preserved, so it is not known what ingredient gave the pilaf its red colour. It most certainly was neither tomato nor red paprika pepper, as they were not used as food at that time.

Greece

GREEK "DJUVETCH"

(for 6 persons)

For stuffed chicken:
1 bigger chicken
2 slices white bread
1 dl milk
30 gr lard or oil
1 smaler onion
salt
pepper
1 egg
1 tablespoon chopped parsley
1 dl oil or lard for brushing the chicken

For vegetables:
1 dl oil
1 onion
1 kg potatoes
350—400 gr paprikas
500—700 gr tomatoes
salt
pepper
1 dl sour cream

Wash chicken, wipe and salt. Pour bread over with milk, leave to soften, drain and squeeze or crush well. Heat lard or oil, add finely chopped onion, cook gently until soft, add to bread. Add salt, pepper, parsley and mix well. With this stuffing fill the chicken. Truss with white thread if necessary. Brush with lard or oil.

Cook finely chopped onion a little in heated oil. Peel potatoes, cut into smaller slices, mix with onion, add paprikas cored and cut into strips or rounds, mix all.

Put potatoes and paprikas into a bigger djuvetch, leaving space in the middle for the chicken. Place rounds of washed and peeled tomatoes over potatoes and paprikas. Sprinkle with salt and pepper. Bake in the oven preheated to 175—200 °C. Pour in some warm water as needed. Baste chickin with vegetable juice while baking. When done, take it out, cool and cut into nice pieces. Arrange jointed chicken over the djuvetch, pour whipped sour cream over and put back into the oven to brown nicely. Serve "djuvetch" in the same dish.

As accompaniment serve some salad (lettuce, cabbage, beetroot.).

Greece

"DJUVETCH" FROM TRAKIYA

600 gr lamb, veal, mutton or pork
80 gr lard or oil
150 gr onion
60 gr carrots
100 gr celery
250 gr paprikas
200 gr tomatoes
1—2 dl warm water or soup
100 gr rice
1/2 bunch of parsley
savory
salt
pepper

Wash meat, wipe and cut into bigger pieces. Heat lard or oil, add meat, fry it on all sides to brown a little. Add finely chopped onion and diced carrots and celery. Cook all gently until tender, pour in some water if needed. When all is tender, add tomatoes (half of the given quantity) peeled and cut into smaller pieces, add salt and pepper, pour in water (or soup from cube). Simmer until water evaporates. Put vegetables and meat into a fireproof earthenware dish or djuvetch, mix in half-cooked rice, paprikas cut into slices and tomatoes cut into rounds. Pour in warm water as needed and bake in the oven preheated to 175—200 °C until all is tender.

When done, sprinkle with pepper ground from mill and finely chopped savory.

With "djuvetch" serve some salad.

Bulgaria

VEGETABLE AND MEAT "DJUVETCH" FROM VARNA

600 gr meat (lamb, young beef, pork)
1 bigger onion
1 dl oil, salt
1 teaspoon red paprika pepper
pepper
1 tablespoon vinegar
200 gr paprikas
200 gr tomatoes
200 gr aubergines
100 gr okras
50 gr unripe grapes
2—3 dl warm water
1/2 bunch of parsley
2 eggs

Wash meat, wipe and cut into medium-size pieces. Chop onion finely, cook gently in heated oil, add meat, salt, red paprika pepper and pepper, cook slowly until meat is tender.

In the meantime prepare the vegetables: core paprikas and cut into rounds or strips; peel aubergines, cut into rounds, salt and leave to stand about 10 minutes, then rinse with cold water; trim okras and leave in water with vinegar added for 30 minutes; wash and drain grapes; chop parsley finely, then mix all.

Put meat into a fireproof dish or tepsiya, cover with mixed vegetables, add salt and pepper as needed, pour in warm water and bake in the oven preheated to 200°C until all is tender and the juice quite reduced.

When done, pour beaten eggs over and put back into the oven to brown.

With "djuvetch" serve cabbage salad, beetroot salad or cucumber salad with drinking or thick yoghurt.

Roumania

"DJUVETCH" WITH GROUND MEAT

1 onion
1 dl oil
500 gr big paprikas
1 kg potatoes
500 gr tomatoes
80 gr rice
400—500 gr mixed ground meat (young beef, lamb, pork)
salt
pepper
2—4 dl lukewarm water
1 egg yolk
1 dl sour cream

Cook finely chopped onion in 2—3 tablespoons of heated oil to soften a little. Add paprikas cored and cut into strips, cook slowly together. Peel potatoes and cut into rounds (or cubes). Peel tomatoes and cut into rounds. Pick over rice, cook shortly and drain.

Put a layer of onion and paprika into a fireproof dish or djuvetch (or tepsiya), sprinkle with salt and pepper, then a layer of potatoes, then of ground meat (with salt and pepper added), of rice and of tomatoes. Repeat until all is used, sprinkle each layer with salt and pepper and finish with tomatoes.

Mix the rest of oil with lukewarm water, pour over "djuvetch" and bake in the oven preset at 175—200°C until all is tender, and the water reduced. While baking, pour in some warm water if necessary. Pour over with egg yolk beaten with sour cream and put back into the oven until nicely brown.

Serve with fresh cabbage salad, lettuce, cucumber salad, beetroot salad or the like.

Yugoslavia

CATFISH "DJUVETCH"

(for 5 persons)

700—750 gr onion
2 dl oil
1 teaspoon red paprika pepper
pepper
1 tablespoon chopped parsley
2—3 paprikas
1 aubergine
1 courgette
1 bigger potato
4 tomatoes
50—75 gr rice
1 kg catfish cut into pieces
2—3 dl warm water

Heat oil in a fireproof dish or djuvetch and cook gently thinly sliced onion in it. When tender and beginning to colour, add red paprika pepper, pepper, parsley and salt. Wash paprikas, core; peel aubergine, cut into cubes, salt and leave to stand for 10 minutes, then rinse with cold water and drain. Peel courgette, remove seed, cut into cubes and salt a little. Peel potatoes, wash and cut into cubes; wash tomatoes, peel and cut into rounds. Pick over rice, cook shortly until half cooked. Add the prepared vegetables to onion, add salt and pepper. In the end mix in rice and add pieces of fish. Barely cover with warm water. Heat oven to 175—200°C and bake until all is tender. When done, the dish should be juicy but not watery. Serve with some salad.

Bulgaria

KIDNEYS WITH MUSHROOMS

600 gr calf's kidneys
2 tablespoons flour
1 dl oil
200 gr fresh mushrooms
1—1,5 dl warm water
1 dl sour cream
1/2 bunch of parsley
salt

Wash kidneys well, leave them to stand in cold water for a while, then cut into thicker strips, roll in flour and fry in heated oil to brown nicely. Add trimmed mushrooms washed and cut into thin slices, cook gently adding warm water. When kidneys and mushrooms are tender, add salt, chopped parsley and sour cream. Simmer together for about 5 minutes.

Serve with cooked vegetables: potatoes, cauliflower or carrots.

Turkey

CHICKEN LIVERS WITH PEAS

600—750 gr chicken livers
5—6 cloves of garlic
40—50 gr almonds
500—750 gr tomatoes
50 gr (5 tabelspoons) olive or other oil
1 kg shelled young peas
2 onions
1 tablespoon butterfat or butter
2 tablespoons sugar
2—3 dl warm water
1 bunch of parsley
40 gr oil
a few basil or sage leaves
salt, pepper

Wash livers and drain well, cut into smaller pieces if necessary.

Peel garlic, pour hot water over almonds, skin, then chop both finely. Wash tomatoes, peel and cut into small pieces. Heat olive oil a little, add garlic, almonds and tomatoes and cook gently together.

Wash peas and drain. Chop onion finely. Heat oil, add sugar, brown it a little, add chopped onion, cook slowly to soften, then add peas, pour in warm water, cover and simmer.

Fry livers in some oil quickly, add tomato with almonds, then cooked peas, mix, add salt and pepper and pour in a little more warm water if needed, then cover and simmer for another 15—20 minutes.

Before serving sprinkle with chopped parsley and basil or sage. Serve with lettuce, radish salad and the like.

Bulgaria

TRIPES WITH VEGETABLES

(for 6 persons)

1,5 kg tripes
1 dl oil or 100 gr lard
50 gr streaky smoked bacon
2 onions
3—4 carrots
2 parsley roots
750 gr new (unripe) beans
2 dl warm water
750 gr tomatoes
2 cloves of garlic
salt
peppercorns
50 gr grated kachkaval or similar cheese

Wash tripes well, cook until tender (garlic, peppercorns and bayleaf can be added to water). When cooked, take them out of water, cool and cut into strips. Put bacon cut into cubes into heated oil, fry until brown, put in chopped onion, cook gently to soften a little, add carrots and parsley cut into cubes, washed new beans, pour in warm water and simmer. When vegetables are half cooked, add tomatoes peeled and cut into smaller cubes, chopped garlic, salt and pepper, cook shortly together, add tripes, pour in some more warm water as needed, then simmer until quite tender.

Sprinkle tripes with grated cheese or serve it separately.

Roumania

ROLL WITH PEAS PURÉE

500—600 gr mixed ground meat or ground young beef
1 onion
1 tablespoon chopped parsley
1—2 eggs
500 gr peas (canned or cooked)
20 gr butter
1/2 dl milk
salt
pepper
50 gr breadcrumbs
1 dl oil for baking
2 dl sour cream

Add finely chopped onion to ground meat, as well as parsley, salt, pepper and eggs. Work into a smooth meat mixture. Leave to stand in a cool place for 30—60 minutes.

Drain peas, pass through a sieve, add butter, some milk, salt. Work well into a homogenous mixture.

Sprinkle the board or a clean cloth with breadcrumbs, shape meat mixture into a bigger square, cover with peas purée, then roll up. Grease a baking pan or a fireproof dish with oil, put the roll in, pour heated oil over. Bake in the oven preheated to 175°C about 1 hour. Baste from time to time while baking. Add a little more hot water if necessary.

Pour sour cream over the roll when done, then leave in the oven for a short while. Serve warm with stewed vegetables and salad, or cold with sour cream and horseradish sauce.

Bulgaria

CALF'S LIVER WITH LEEKS AND PAPRIKAS

600 gr calf's liver
4 leeks
1 dl oil
3 paprikas
salt
pepper
3 dl sour cream
1—2 dl warm water

Wash liver, wipe and cut into bigger strips. Heat oil, fry liver and take out. Put trimmed and washed leeks cut into rounds into the same oil, cook gently until slightly soft. Add cored paprikas cut into strips, add salt and pepper and cook together for about 10 minutes, then add liver, pour in some warm water, cover and simmer until vegetables are tender. In the end add sour cream, shake and cook for a further 5 minutes.

With liver serve peeled and cooked potatoes with parsley, cooked rice and the like.

MEAT DISHES

The choice is rich and varied and the possible combinations innumerable. The characteristic Balkan way of preparing meat is spit roasting and grilling and every country or region has some specific way of its own. In some places it is the question of additional ingredients and spices and in others of special kinds of wood even, for the spit of for the gridiron charcoal. Meat is, of course, more tasty when prepared in the open and over real charcoal, but a properly heated oven can be an excellent substitute, since modern kitchen stoves are in most cases supplied with spits and grill racks. In all this the choice of meat is of special importance and it has to be first class and from the part indicated in the recipe.

Kebabs, mutchkalitsas, tchervishes, krzatmas, piryans are the well-known Balkan meat dishes in which natural taste is most often preserved thanks to the ways of preparing them.

The Balkan stewed dishes with chopped meat, most often known as goulashes and paprikashes, rather differ in the ways of preparing them, in ingredients and consequently in taste from the dishes of the same name in other countries. Abundant use of onion, tomato and other vegetables, together with various spices and wine, give them a special flavour because of which they have become widely used and popular.

Many specialties are prepared with ground meat, but various kinds of meatballs (tchufte) are best known. There is practically no region which does not have its own recipe for these small meat dumplings, with or without sauce.

Game is more difficult to acquire, but nevertheless it is prepared in many different ways. The recipes date from the times when there was more hunting and much more game. If someone is fond of a dish in the so-called hunters' way, a hare can be replaced with a rabbit or a nice piece of beef and a very tasty dish can be prepared with the help of recipes from this book.

Offal, or pluck, especially that of lamb, is used in preparing many dishes in the Balkan cuisine. Cleaning and preparing it takes a lot of time, but it is worth the effort, as those dishes are of excellent taste and the ones with liver are considered to be healthy. Offal has another advantage — it is cheaper than meat and no roast can compete in taste with the well prepared baked lamb offal.

Among roasts, the best known are undoubtedly the roast suckling pig or lamb. In almost all the countries slaughtering the suckling pigs is forbidden, but since a special festivity or wedding feast is hard to imagine without it, especially in Yugoslavia, there are always "secret channels" of "connections with the country" to be found, in order to get hold of the necessary pig. When baked in the oven of an electric or gas cooker (at home or at the baker's), as suggested in the recipe in this book, it does not lag behing the pig spit roasted in the open, either in taste or in appearance.

Poultry have always been abundantly used as food in the Balkans. There were not many big cities before, but there were a lot of small towns and villages, so that many people kept fowls in their "back yards". So there is a great variety of dishes with poultry meat, many of which are prepared with a lot of imagination and a choice of ingredients, so that it is sometimes hard to recognize that there is chicken, goose or turkey as the main component in the dish. There are less and less "back yards" today in which chicken or geese range freely, but there are more and more poultry farms, so that this meat is still very much in use. It is cheaper than other meat, there is always a great choice of it, it is quick and easy to prepare and its taste can be altered in countless ways, depending on additional ingredients and spices.

GRILLED MEAT

Yugoslavia

"TCHEVAPCHI-TCHI" FROM LESKOVAC

1 kg more crudely ground beef
50 gr onion
1 ground hot pepper
salt
oil for greasing

Work ground meat well into a meat mixture. Leave in a cool place to stand for 10—12 hours. Then grind again, but more finely, add finely chopped onion, crushed or ground hot pepper and salt. Mix well again and leave to stand in a cool place for 1—2 hours. Shape into tchevapchitchi, grill first on very hot gridiron, then turn down the heat a little. While grilling turn and brush with oil.

Serve very warm with spring onions, baked paprikas or radishes.

Albania

YOUNG BEEF "TCHEVAPCHI-TCHI"

600 gr young beef
salt, pepper
a few rosemary leaves
1—1,5 dl oil (or 50 gr suet)

Wash meat, wipe, cut into smaller pieces and grind, add salt, pepper, some rosemary. Work into a meat mixture for about 15—20 minutes. Leave in a cool place (refrigerator) to stand for several hours. By hand, or with the help of the utensil for making sausages fixed on the meat grinder, shape meat into small sausages about 2 cm thick and 5—7 cm long.

Brush gridiron with oil (or suet), grill tchevapchitchi about 5—7 minutes turning them all the time.

With tchevapchitchi serve chopped onion, fresh tomatoes, baked green paprikas.

Roumania

BEEF "TCHEVAPCHI-TCHI" — "MITITEI"

500 gr fresh (just slaughtered) beef
salt, pepper
thyme
allspice
3 cloves of garlic
2 dl warm soup (from meat cube or bone stock)
oil for grilling
bicarbonate of soda (optional)

Wash meat, wipe and grind, add salt, pepper, thyme, allspice and crushed garlic, pour in soup. Work into a smooth meat mixture. Leave in a cool place to stand for 1—2 hours.

Moisten the wooden board a bit and shape meat on it into small sausages (rissols) about 2 cm in diameter and about 7 cm long.

Heat gridiron, brush with oil, grill tchevapchitchi on all sides about 5—7 minutes

They are usually served with fresh or pickled paprikas.

This kind of tchevapchitchi is considered in Roumania as national "fresh sausages".

Yugoslavia

MACEDONIAN "TCHEVAPCHI-TCHI"

(for 5—6 persons)

800 gr ground young beef
200 gr ground mutton
100 gr onion
20 gr oil
5 cloves of garlic
pepper
salt
oil for brushing

Mix meat, work out properly and leave in a cool place to stand for several hours. Chop onion finely, heat oil, add onion and cook slowly until soft and beginning to colour. Peel garlic and chop finely. Add onion and garlic to meat, season with salt and pepper. Work all into a meat mixture, leave for a short while in a cool place, then shape into smaller tchevapchitchi. Grill at first on very hot gridiron greased with oil. Then grill slowly at medium heat and turn all the time.

These tchevapchitchi are served in lepinyas.

Bulgaria

BULGARIAN "TCHEVAPCHI-TCHI"

400 gr boneless beef (or young beef)
200 gr boneless mutton
1 onion
1—2 cloves of garlic
salt
pepper
1 dl oil

Wash meat, wipe and grind. Chop onion finely, cook a little in oil until soft, cool and add to ground meat. Crush garlic well and then chop, add salt and pepper. Work all into a smooth meat mixture. Leave in the refrigerator to stand for 2—3 hours. Shape into bigger tchevapchitchi. Grill on well heated gridiron. Brush with oil while grilling.

Serve with spring onions, tomatoes, small hot peppers.

Yugoslavia

"TCHEVAPCHITCHI" FROM THE TOWN OF UZICE

600 gr beef (or young beef)
30 gr onion
1 small hot pepper
1 bunch of parsley
salt
pepper
100 gr kaymak from Uzice
4—5 baked paprikas
4—5 tablespoons chopped onion
some oil for grilling

Wash meat, wipe and grind, add finely chopped onion, small hot pepper and parsley, salt and pepper. Work into a meat mixture. Leave to stand in the refrigerator for 2—3 hours. By hand or with the utensil for making sausages shape into somewhat longer tchevapchitchi. Grill on gridiron greased with oil. Turn constantly while grilling. They are done after 15 minutes.

Before serving pour over with melted kaymak, garnish with baked paprikas and chopped onion.

Yugoslavia

HUNTERS' "TCHEVAPCHITCHI"

400 gr venison (from leg or shoulder)
125 gr rabbit (from leg)
80 gr streaky smoked bacon
100 gr onion
1—2 cloves of garlic
salt
pepper
1 tablespoon chopped celery leaves
1 dl oil for brushing
1—2 dl red wine
1 tablespoon chopped parsley

Wash meat, wipe and grind together with bacon. Chop finely onion and garlic, or grind together with meat and bacon, add salt, pepper and finely chopped celery leaves. Work into a meat mixture and leave to stand in a cool place (refrigerator) for 2—3 hours.

Prepare the wine for pouring over in the meantime: cook wine shortly with some pepper, chopped parsley and, if desired, some garlic juice.

Shape meat into tchevapchitchi, grill at medium heated gridiron. Turn and pour oil over while grilling.

Before serving pour cooked wine over the tchevapchitchi.

Turkey

LAMB HAMBURGERS

600 gr lamb
120 gr (2) onions
2 cloves of garlic
salt
pepper
oil for grilling (1/2—1 dl)

Wash meat, wipe and grind. Chop onion finely, crush garlic well, then chop. Mix meat, onion, garlic, salt and pepper, work well into a mixture and leave in a cool place to stand about 15—20 minutes.

Shape into flat patties the size of the palm, preferably on the moistened wooden board. Brush gridiron with oil, grill patties, turning them, for 10—15 minutes. Pour oil over while grilling, as needed.

With hamburgers serve chopped onion, spring onions, tomatoes or baked small peppers.

Roumania

HAMBURGERS ROUMANIAN WAY

400 gr young beef
200 gr pork
salt
150 gr hot pepper (fresh or ground)
1 onion (80 gr)
50 gr oil for grilling

Wash meat, wipe, grind, add finely chopped onion, hot pepper and salt. Work into a meat mixture. Leave to stand in a cool place for 20—25 minutes. Then shape into flat patties the size of the palm.

Brush heated gridiron with oil, grill patties for 8—10 minutes and turn while grilling. Serve at once with spring onions, green paprikas, tomatoes and the like.

Yugoslavia

SERBIAN HAMBURGERS

400 gr beef from neck
200 gr pork from shoulder
100 gr fresh chopped paprikas (hot or mild)
100 gr chopped onion
2 cloves of garlic
salt
pepper
oil for grilling

Wash meat, wipe, cut into bigger cubes and grind. Add hot paprikas, finely chopped onion, crushed garlic, salt and pepper. Work into a meat mixture. Leave in a cool place to stand for 15—20 minutes. Shape meat into flat patties the size of the palm. Heat gridiron, brush with oil, grill patties, turning them, for about 10—12 minutes.

Chopped onion, fresh paprikas or tomatoes are usually served with hamburgers.

In the parts where kaymak of good quality is produced, grilled patties are poured over with melted kaymak.

Diced kachkaval and some more onion can be added to hamburgers. They are prepared that way in the vicinity of Pirot, the town in Serbia, so such patty is called "pirotska". If the grilled patty is sprinkled with chopped baked paprikas, finely chopped onion and garlic and finely cut tomatoes, then the patty has a richer, slightly different taste and is called "Vranjanka", as it is prepared that way in the Serbian town of Vranje and the vicinity.

Yugoslavia

HAMBURGERS FROM VOJVODINA

800 gr ground pork
6 onions
2—3 tablespoons hot red paprika pepper (or mild)
salt

pepper
oil (about 1,5 dl)
onion
small hot peppers

Add finely chopped onion, salt, pepper and red paprika pepper to ground meat. Work all well into a smooth meat mixture. Leave to stand in a cool place for several hours.

Before grilling shape into flat patties the size of the palm, grill on gridiron greased with oil. While grilling turn at times.

Serve with plenty of chopped onion and with small hot peppers cut into rounds.

Bulgaria

KEBABS I

500—700 gr lamb from shoulder or leg
1 onion
salt
pepper
1,5 dl oil

Wash meat, wipe, separate from bones and cut into smaller pieces. Chop onion finely. Put meat into a deeper pan, cover with onion, pour oil over and leave in a cool place to stand for 2—3 hours.

Before grilling take meat out without onion, thread on to skewers and grill on medium heated gridiron. While grilling brush with the oil in which the meat stood.

When done, sprinkle with pepper ground from mill and with salt.

With kebabs serve chopped onion.

Baked paprikas salad, lettuce and tomato salad are also very good accompaniment to kebabs.

Turkey

OSMANLI KEBAS

600 gr fatter mutton
juice of 1 lemon (or 2 tablespoons vinegar)
2 onions
200 gr rice
40 gr oil
4—5 dl warm water
salt
pepper
1 teaspoon saffron

Wash meat, wipe, cut into bigger cubes, put into a deeper pan, pour lemon juice (or vinegar) over, sprinkle with chopped onion. Leave to stand in a cool place for at least 1 hour. In the meantime pick over rice, wash and dry. Heat oil, add rice and cook slowly until glassy, pour in warm water in which saffron has been dissolved, add salt and pepper. Simmer until tender. Thread meat on to skewers without onion. Grill on medium heated gridiron. Turn while grilling and brush with oil, as needed.

Put rice on a serving plate and arrange kebabs over it. Serve with some fresh vegetables (spring onions, tomatoes, paprikas or lettuce, with tomato salad and the like).

Yugoslavia

HAMBURGERS FROM SJENICA

800 gr ground mutton
1 onion
250—300 gr kachkaval or hard cheese from Sjenica
salt
pepper
oil for the grill
1/2—3/4 l sheep thick yoghurt

Mix ground meat with finely chopped onion, salt and pepper. Work into a smooth meat mixture, leave in a cool place to stand for several hours. Before grilling shape into flat patties, the size of the palm. Put a piece of cheese in the middle of each. Brush gridiron with oil, grill patties on both sides until nicely brown.

Serve grilled hamburgers with thick yoghurt.

Sjenica is a small town, the center of the Peshter highlands, renowned for their natural beauty and cattle-breeding. The famous Sjenica sheep are raised there and the well-known Sjenica cheese produced.

Bulgaria

LAMB STEAKS WRAPPED UP AND GRILLED — "VESHALITSA"

600 gr lamb from leg
1 lamb double offal membrane
oil
salt
pepper
8—10 paprikas
1 bunch of parsley
2—3 cloves of garlic

Wash meat, wipe, remove thin skins and fat, cut into nice steaks, pound them a little with a mallet and cut each steak in the middle, but not all the way, so as to get the characteristic shape of a coat-hanger (the meaning of the word "veshalica"), add salt and pepper. Cut the offal membrane into squares and wrap up each steak in one of them. Heat gridiron, brush with oil, grill steaks on both sides.

Wash paprikas, wipe and grill. Pour some oil over them and sprinkle with chopped garlic and parsley. Serve with the grilled steaks.

Bulgaria

GRILLED VEAL STEAK — "VESHALITSA"

600 gr veal from leg
salt
1—1,5 dl oil
200 gr onion
2 green paprikas
1/2 bunch of parsley
1 tomato

Wash meat, wipe, remove thin skin, veins and fat, then cut into somewhat thicker steaks, pound them a little with a mallet and cut each steak in the middle, but not all the way, so that it resembles a coat hanger (hence the name in the original, which means "a hanger").

Pour some oil over the steaks, leave them to stand for a while in a cool place. Grill on medium heated gridiron brushed with oil.

Serve on finely chopped onion. Garnish with green paprikas, parsley leaves and slices of tomato.

Pork steaks can be prepared in the same way.

Yugoslavia

MIXED KEBABS

250 gr chicken without bones
200 gr chicken, goose or turkey livers
250 gr turkey without bones
100 gr smoked bacon
50 gr butter
oil for the grill

Wash meat, wipe and cut into nice squares. Thread on to smaller skewers meat, liver and bacon in turn. Grill on medium heated gridiron and turn while grilling.

When done, take kebabs off skewers, arrange over cooked rice and pour heated butter over.

With kebabs serve lettuce, mixed paprika and tomato salad, beetroot salad and others.

Bulgaria

BULGARIAN KEBABS

600 gr ground mixed meat
2 eggs
3 onions
salt
pepper
20 gr breadcrumbs
4 paprikas
150—200 gr mushrooms (button mushrooms and similar)
1—2 dl oil

Mix meat with eggs and finely chopped onion, add salt, pepper and breadcrumbs. Work into a smooth meat mixture and leave to stand in a cool place for 1—2 hours.

Wash paprikas, core and cut into equal squares. Trim mushrooms, leave smaller ones whole and halve them if bigger. Shape meat into smaller balls. Thread on to skewers meat, paprikas and mushrooms in turn. Brush all with oil. Grill on medium heated gridiron about 5—10 minutes on both sides. When done, add more salt and pepper if needed.

Yugoslavia

TURKEY KEBABS

750 gr turkey breast meat
salt
pepper
2 dl oil
6—8 smaller tomatoes
1 bunch of radishes

Wash meat, wipe and cut into equal, slightly thinner pieces, sprinkle with salt and pepper, thread on to small wooden or metal skewers, brush with oil and leave to stand like that until grilling.

Grill kebabs on medium heated gridiron until nicely brown. Grill tomatoes too and arrange them round kebabs. Wash radishes, cut decoratively and put round kebabs, or serve in a separate small bowl.

As accompaniment to turkey kebabs cooked or stewed rice can be served, as well as various kinds of fresh salads.

Albania

KEBABS II

750 gr lamb from shoulder or leg
1 dl olive oil
salt
pepper
sprigs of rosemary

Wash meat, wipe, cut into smaller pieces, sprinkle with salt and pepper and leave to stand like that about 60 minutes. Thread meat on to skewers and in between pieces of meat, put tiny rosemary sprigs. Grill on hotter gridiron (charcoal) about 10 minutes.

Serve straight after grilling, while they are still hot. Onion is usually served with these kebabs, so as to intensify the specific flavour of rosemary.

Turkey

KEBABS WITH YOGHURT

1 bigger onion
salt
750 gr lamb from shoulder
40 gr olive oil
4 slices of bread (preferably rye)
40 gr butter
500 gr tomatoes
1/2 l drinking yoghurt

Peel onion and chop finely, salt a little. Wash meat, wipe and cut into bigger cubes. Put onion into a thick gauze and squeeze. Put meat into a deeper pan, pour onion juice and oil over it, cover and leave in a cool place to stand for 60 minutes.

Remove crust from bread slices, cut into bigger cubes, pour melted butter over and bake in the oven preheated to 175 °C. Drain meat cubes, brush skewers

with oil, thread meat on to them but not too tightly. Prepare gridiron, grill kebabs 10—15 minutes and turn several times.

Wash tomatoes, peel and cut finely, cook slowly in butter until quite tender. Mix yoghurt and add some salt.

Arrange baked croûtons on a big plate, place kebabs over them, put cooked tomato between them and pour yoghurt over the whole arrangement.

Roumania

"SHISH" KEBABS OR KEBABS FROM ARAD

750 gr lamb from shoulder

For marinade:
40 gr oil

1 tablespoon lemon juice
salt
2 cloves of garlic
pepper
hot red paprika pepper
4 smaller onions
4 harder tomatoes
2 big paprikas

Wash meat, wipe and cut into equal cubes.

For the marinade mix oil, lemon juice, salt, crushed garlic, pepper and red paprika pepper. Mix all well.

Put meat into a deeper pan, pour

marinade over, cover and keep in a cool place about 3 hours, turning it at times.

Peel onion and cut into slices. Wash tomatoes, wipe, remove stalk ends and quarter. Wash paprikas, core and cut into equal pieces.

Take meat out of marinade, drain and wipe a little. Thread meat and vegetables on to skewers in turn, brush with marinade.

Grill on gridiron or spit broil in the well heated oven for about 15—20 minutes.

With kebabs serve lettuce with paprikas, tomatoes and cucumbers, cooked rice or brown bread.

If you are fond of grilled food, you have probably ordered and enjoyed the "shish kebabs" in some restaurant, not knowing that it is a Roumanian dish which originated in Arad, the Roumanian industrial and commercial center. Nevertheless, it is only a variation of the authentic Arabic kebabs.

Turkey

GRILLED "SHISH"

1 lamb liver
1 lamb heart
2 lamb kidneys
1 lamb double offal membrane
salt
pepper
1 dl oil
2 dl milk

Wash liver, wipe and cut into small pieces of equal size. Cut kidneys, wash well in cold water and leave to stand in milk about 1 hour. Then drain and cut into smaller pieces. Cut heart into bigger pieces. Cut smaller part of the offal membrane into small squares.

Fix one end of the bigger part of the offal membrane to one side of the spit. Then thread on to it pieces of liver, offal membrane, kidneys and heart in turn. When the spit is full, wrap it up with the free part of the offal membrane. Wrap it up well, as membrane prevents pluck from burning and makes it juicier.

Grill "shish" on medium heated gridiron. When the offal membrane is brown, the pluck inside should be done. Take off heat, sprinkle with salt and pepper.

Instead of wrapping the spit up in a big piece of offal membrane, each piece of pluck could be wrapped up separately in smaller pieces.

"Shish" in Turkish means a coffee roaster in the shape of a cylinder. As threaded pieces of meat or pluck on to the spit wrapped up in the offal membrane, also acquire a cylindrical shape, such kind of kebabs is called — shish.

Greece

GREEK KEBABS

750 gr boneless lamb
1 courgette
2 paprikas (green and red)
1 aubergine

For marinade:
1 dl olive (or other) oil
2 dl white wine
2 cloves of garlic
1 onion
2 bayleaves
1 teaspoon rosemary leaves
salt
pepper

Wash meat, wipe and cut into cubes. Mix well oil, wine, chopped garlic and onion, bayleaf and rosemary, salt and pepper.

Put meat into a deeper pan, pour the prepared marinade over, leave in a cool place (refrigerator) to stand for several hours (3—5). Wash vegetables, wipe and cut into cubes. Intersperse meat with vegetables when threading on to skewers, brush with marinade and grill on medium heated gridiron, turning them at times.

When done, serve with chopped spring onions, tomatoes, paprikas and other fresh vegetables.

Turkey

MUTTON KEBABS

750 gr mutton from leg
salt
pepper
juice of several onions
2—3 dl drinking yoghurt

Wash meat, wipe and cut into bigger cubes, add salt and pepper, pour onion juice over (chop or grind onion and press through thick sieve or gauze). Leave in a cool place to stand about 30—60 minutes. Thread meat on to skewers, grill on medium heated charcoal and turn until grilled and of nice light brown colour.

Take meat off skewers, arrange on a corresponding plate and pour yoghurt over.

With kebabs stewed rice is usually served, seasoned with saffron.

Yugoslavia

HAIDUK KEBABS

(for 6—8 persons)

500 gr pork
500 gr mutton
500 gr veal
salt
pepper

2—3 teaspoons hot red paprika pepper
oil for brushing
maize flour to roll in
500 gr onion
3—4 cloves of garlic
250—300 gr tomatoes

Wash meat, wipe and cut into cubes, sprinkle with salt, pepper and hot red paprika pepper, mix well and leave to stand in a cool place for 1—2 hours.

Thread meat on to skewers (various kinds in turn). Heat gridiron, brush with oil and grill kebabs. Turn while grilling and brush with oil as needed. When meat is half done, roll kebabs in maize flour, grill again. Grilled meat must have a crust of flour. Peel onion and chop finely, crush garlic well, wash tomatoes, remove stalk ends and cut into smaller cubes. Mix all well (shake in a covered pan).

Take kebabs of the skewers, put over prepared onion with tomatoes and serve at once.

Turkey

"SHASHI KEBASSI"

500 gr mutton from leg
2 onions
juice of 1 lemon
salt, pepper
1 dl oil
2 dl sour cream
50—100 gr browned almonds

Wash meat, wipe and cut into bigger cubes. Chop onion finely. Put meat into a deeper pan, sprinkle with chopped onion, pour lemon juice over, add pepper. Leave to stand like that for 2—3 hours. While in this marinade, mix several times.

Thread pieces of meat on to metal or wooden skewers (without onion), grill, turning often, on medium heated gridiron. While grilling brush with oil from marinade, as needed.

Pour sour cream over grilled kebabs and sprinkle with slivers of browned almonds.

Turkey

TURKISH KEBABS

750 gr mutton or chicken
salt
pepper
2 onions
100 gr mutton suet, butter or oil

Wash meat, wipe and cut into cubes, add salt and pepper. Peel onion, cut into cubes or slices. Thread on to skewers (wooden or metal) meat and onion in turn. Brush all with melted suet (butter or oil), grill on medium heated gridiron until nicely brown.

Serve grilled kebabs with rice, seasoned with saffron.

Garnish with paprikas and tomatoes.

Greece

"SOUVLAKYA"

600 gr leaner pork or lamb from leg
1 dl olive oil
1/2 dl white wine
3 tablespoons lemon juice
pepper
salt
1 teaspoon fresh marjoram
1 teaspoon fresh thyme
1 bayleaf
1/2—1 dl oil for brushing

Wash meat, wipe and cut into about 4 cm thick cubes, then put into a deeper pan.

Mix well olive oil, wine, salt, pepper and spice herbs, pour over meat, cover, put into the refrigerator to stand about 12 hours and mix occasionally.

Take out marinaded meat, drain well (preferably on absorbant paper), thread on to wooden or metal skewers and grill on heated gridiron about 20 minutes. Turn while grilling.

With these kebabs serve cooked rice with fresh spice herbs (parsley, dill etc.) and boiled carrots poured over with olive oil.

Turkey

"SHASHLIK"

500 gr boneless lamb
2 dl olive oil
2 tablespoons chopped parsley
a few fresh mint leaves or 1 teaspoon dried mint
salt, pepper

Wash meat, wipe and cut into bigger cubes. Mix well oil, parsley, mint, salt and pepper.

Put meat into a deeper pan, pour the marinade over, leave in a cool place (refrigerator) to stand for 2—3 hours. Drain, thread on to smaller skewers and grill on medium heated gridiron. While grilling brush with oil from marinade. Arrange grilled kebabs over cooked rice. Serve with fresh vegetables (paprikas, spring onions, tomatoes).

Yugoslavia

KEBABS FROM PAZIN

800 gr turkey livers
1 dl oil
250—300 gr smoked bacon
dried basil leaves
rosemary or oregano
salt, pepper
2—2,5 dl oil

Wash livers, wipe and cut into bigger cubes. Heat oil, fry livers shortly, add salt and pepper, sprinkle with crushed basil, rosemary or oregano. Cut bacon into thinner rashers, wrap pieces of liver in them and thread on to skewers. Grill on medium heated gridiron until liver is tender and bacon brown and crisp.

Serve kebabs at once. Add to them spring onions, radishes, tomatoes, paprikas, or some salad.

Pazin is a town in the middle of Istria. Among other things it is well-known for its turkey-breeding farms, so it is not surprising that various specialties made of turkey meat can be found in the small inns, known as "konobas", in the pleasant surroundings of Pazin.

Turkey

GRILLED STEAKS — "TCHULBASTIYA"

500 gr beef (top round steak or fillet)
1—1,5 dl oil
salt
pepper
250—300 gr onion
1—2 fresh paprikas

Wash meat, wipe and remove thin skins and veins. Cut into steaks about 1—2 cm thick, place into a deeper pan and pour oil over. Leave to stand at least 2 and not more than 8 hours.

Heat gridiron well before grilling, then put on meat. Turn once while grilling. Grill for 7—10 minutes, depending on whether raw or well done steaks are wanted.

When done, sprinkle with chopped onion and paprikas cut into pieces. With "tchulbastiyas" boiled and peeled potatoes poured over with butter are usually served.

In Turkey "tchulbastiya" was originally only grilled beef, but now it is prepared with veal, and in other Balkan countries with pork.

Bulgaria

GRILLED MEATBALLS

400 gr mixed ground meat (or ground young beef)
1 onion
1 tablespoon chopped parsley
1 egg
salt
pepper
1 tablespoon breadcrumbs
1 dl oil

For sauce:
4 dl drinking yoghurt
2 cloves of garlic
salt
ground red paprika
a few mint leaves

Put meat into a deeper bowl, add finely chopped onion, chopped parsley, egg, salt, pepper, breadcrumbs and 1 dl cold water. Work into a smooth meat mixture and leave to stand for a while in a cool place. Shape into 4—6 meatballs (flat), pour oil over. Grill on medium heated gridiron, turn them until nicely brown.

In the meantime prepare the sauce: beat well yoghurt, finely chopped garlic, salt, ground paprika and mint leaves. Pour this sauce over grilled meatballs. Serve with fresh brown or rye bread and with paprikas and tomatoes.

Roumania

GRILLED CUTLETS WITH CHEESE

6—8 bigger cutlets (lamb, veal)
1 dl oil
300—350 gr fresh cow cheese in crumbs
2 cloves of garlic
salt
ground red paprika

Wash cutlets, wipe and remove bones. Place pieces of meat in a deeper pan, pour oil over, leave to stand in a cool place for 1—2 hours.

Crush cheese well or pass through a sieve, add crushed or finely chopped garlic, salt, ground paprika. Mix all well.

Drain meat from oil, grill on medium heated gridiron. Turn while grilling and brush with oil as needed. When cutlets are done, cover them with a layer of cheese and leave on the grill until the cheese begins to melt.

Serve at once with spring onions, radishes, paprikas or tomatoes.

Roumania

GRILLED LAMB BREAST (à la gratar)

1,5 kg lamb breast
2 onions
3—4 cloves of garlic
salt
1,5 dl oil
250 gr marinaded beetroot (see page 215)
100 gr pickled onions
100 gr marinaded unripe tomatoes (see page 214)
1 small hot pepper

Wash meat and cook. Cool and remove bones, then cut into bigger cubes. Cut onion and garlic. Rub pieces of meat well with onion and garlic, salt, pass through oil, grill on heated gridiron and turn while grilling.

Arrange grilled pieces on a plate, garnish with marinaded vegetables and serve at once.

Greece

GREEK BEEFSTEAK

600 gr beef
salt
pepper
1 teaspoon oregano
1/2 dl oil

For sauce:
4 tablespoons oil
2 cloves of garlic
3 tablespoons chopped parsley
750 gr peeled tomatoes
1 teaspoon sugar
some crushed dried basil

Wash meat, wipe, cut into smaller pieces and grind. Add salt, pepper, oregano and oil. Work into a smooth meat mixture. Leave to stand in a cool place about 1 hour.

In the meantime prepare the sauce: heat oil, add chopped garlic, fry it shortly, add parsley, fry together about 3 minutes, then add peeled tomatoes cut into smaller pieces, salt, sugar and some basil. Cook slowly at low heat until tomato is tender and the sauce thick.

Shape meat into small patties, grill on rather hot gridiron. When done, arrange "steaks" on a plate, pour tomato sauce over and surround with cooked rice.

Greece

GRILLED LAMB CUTLETS

900 gr — 1 kg lamb cutlets
1 dl olive oil
juice of 1 lemon
1 teaspoon oregano
salt
pepper
slices of lemon
1 bunch of parsley

Wash meat and wipe well. Mix oil, lemon juice and oregano. Put meat into a deeper pan, pour marinade over and leave to stand about 3 hours. Turn occasionally.

Heat grill, arrange cutlets on it, turn and brush with marinade while grilling. When done, sprinkle with salt and pepper and garnish with lemon slices and parsley leaves.

With these cutlets, fried potatoes are usually served and some fresh vegetables or lettuce, tomato salad and other salads.

Greece

GRILLED BEEFSTEAK

2 onions
4 tablespoons oil
3 tablespoons vinegar
2 tablespoons ketchup
1/2 teaspoon Worcestershire sauce
1 teaspoon keen mustard
2 cloves of garlic
some oregano
salt

1/2 bunch of parsley
600 gr beefsteak
1 dl oil for the grill and brushing

Peel onion and chop finely. Put chopped onion into a deeper pan, pour in oil, vinegar, ketchup, Worcestershire sauce and mustard, mix all well. Crush garlic or chop finely, add oregano, salt and chopped parsley, mix and add to the onion mixture. Mix all once again.

Cut beefsteak into nice pieces of about 150 gr each and plunge them into the prepared marinade. Cover and keep in a cool place for at least 60 minutes. Take out before grilling, wipe with absorbent paper. Heat gridiron, brush with oil, grill from 5 to 10 minutes, depending on how thick the steaks are. Turn while grilling and brush with oil as needed.

Serve beefsteaks with grilled tomatoes. Well cooled marinade is also a very good accompaniment.

Turkey

GRILLED MUTTON MEATBALLS — "SHISH KÖFTE"

600 gr boneless mutton (from leg or shoulder)
80 gr (2 smaller) onions
2 cloves of garlic
1 egg
salt
pepper
1/2 teaspoon marjoram
2 tablespoons chopped parsley
20 gr (2 tablespoons) oil for brushing
1/2 teaspoon crushed sage (optional)

Wash meat, wipe and cut into bigger cubes.

Peel onion and cut crudely. Peel garlic. Grind meat, onion and garlic. In a deeper bowl mix well ground meat with onion and garlic, egg, salt, pepper, marjoram and parsley. Shape into small balls with wet hands. Spread tin foil over gridiron. Roll meatballs in oil, grill on well heated gridiron about 10 minutes, turning them all the time.

As accompaniment serve onion cut into small cubes or thin slices, drinking yoghurt and fresh homemade bread.

If some crushed sage is added to the meat mixture, specific flavour is obtained.

Yugoslavia

PIGS' BRAINS WRAPPED UP AND GRILLED

4 pigs' brains
1—2 tablespoons vinegar
1 pigs' double offal membrane
3 onions
1 tomato
oil for the grill, pepper

Put brains into warm water with some salt and vinegar, leave to stand for several minutes, then remove thin skins and veins. Cook brains in salted water with some vinegar, drain, add salt and pepper. Cut pigs' offal membrane into four squares, wrap up brains in them. Heat gridiron, brush with oil, put brains over and grill on all sides. Brains are done when the offal membrane has melted and browned.

Serve over chopped onion and garnish with tomato or paprika slices.

Yugoslavia

GRILLED WHITE KIDNEYS

500 gr young bull's "white kidneys" (sex glands)
salt
2 tablespoons vinegar
1 dl oil for brushing, pepper

Leave "white kidneys" to stand in cold water about 1 hour, then wash.

Slowly bring salted water with vinegar to the boil, plunge "kidneys" in, simmer for 5 minutes, take out, run cold water over, carefully remove thin skin, so that "kidneys" remain whole. Drain them, cut into rounds (not too thin), salt and put on heated gridiron brushed with oil. Grill on medium heated gridiron for about 5—10 minutes and turn while grilling.

When done, add salt and pepper as needed. Serve with fresh vegetables such as spring onions, radishes, tomatoes, paprikas or with some salad (cucumber salad, lettuce and others).

Roumania

ROUMANIAN BEEFSTEAK

600 gr beef fillet
1—1,5 dl oil
salt, pepper
hot red paprika pepper
100—150 gr smoked bacon

Wash meat, wipe, cut into steaks, pound a little with a mallet and pour oil over. Leave them to stand about 60 minutes.

Grill on well heated gridiron for 3—5 minutes. Cut bacon into thinner rashers and grill separately.

When steaks are grilled, sprinkle with hot paprika pepper. Put two rashers of bacon over each beefsteak.

With beefsteak servc spring onions, chopped onion or fresh paprikas.

Yugoslavia

LAMB KIDNEYS WITH BACON

500—600 gr lamb kidneys
20 gr flour
100 gr melted butter (or 1 dl oil)
100 gr smoked bacon
juice of 1 lemon
salt, pepper

Wash kidneys, wipe and cut into nice slices. Leave for 30—40 minutes in cold water, then drain, wipe, roll in flour, pour over with melted butter and grill on medium heated and oiled gridiron. Turn while grilling. Although they must not be grilled for too long, kindeys should have a nice brown colour when done.

Cut bacon into rashers, grill on gridiron together with kidneys. Arrange slices of kidney and bacon rashers in turn on a serving plate. Pour melted butter over and drip with lemon juice. As accompaniment boiled and peeled potatoes can be served, seasoned with butter and chopped parsley.

Yugoslavia

BALKAN BEEFSTEAK

200 gr beef
200 gr pork
200 gr mutton
pepper
marjoram
1/4 rind of unsprayed lemon
salt
oil (about 1/2 dl)
4—5 eggs

Wash meat, wipe, cut into bigger pieces and grind. Add plenty of pepper (so that the steaks are hot), marjoram, grated lemon rind, salt, oil and 1 egg. Work into a smooth meat mixture and leave to stand in a cool place at least 1 hour.

Take about 150 gr of meat mixture at a time, shape into small round breads, press the upper part with the bottom of a water glass to make a hollow in the middle. Grill on gridiron brushed with oil. When nearly done, put a raw egg yolk into the hollow of each steak and grill on until meat and eggs are quite done.

These "steaks" are usually served with baked potatoes, spring onions, fresh tomatoes and toast.

Bulgaria

GRILLED CALVES' KIDNEYS

500—600 gr calves' kidneys
2—3 dl milk
1 dl oil
70 gr butter to pour over
salt
pepper

Accompaniment:
50—100 gr butter or margarine
1/2 bunch of parsley
juice of 1 lemon
1 teaspoon mustard

Cut kidneys lengthways, wash, remove veins but leave some fat on. Plunge them into milk and leave to stand in it for at least 1—2 hours. Then drain, pour oil over, leave to stand again about 30 minutes. Heat gridiron, brush with oil, put kidneys over and grill at medium heat. Turn and pour over with melted butter while grilling.

Mix well butter (margarine), add finely chopped parsley, lemon juice, mustard, salt and pepper. Shape into a small ball and keep in the refrigerator until serving. Serve with grilled kidneys.

Sheep kidneys are prepared in the same way.

Yugoslavia

GRILLED PIGS' LIVER

800 gr liver
1 dl oil
4 cloves of garlic
salt
pepper
1 dl red wine or juice of 1 lemon

Wash liver, wipe, cut into nice slices, place into a bowl and pour oil over. Leave to stand like that at least 20—30 minutes. Brush gridiron with oil, put over slices of liver and grill, turning them, about 4—5 minutes.

When liver is done, arrange it on a long plate, pour over red wine in which garlic and pepper have been cooked shortly, sprinkle with salt.

Wine can be substituted by lemon juice, but both are important for the flavour of liver.

Yugoslavia

CALVES' LIVER SERBIAN WAY

800 gr calves' liver
2 dl oil
salt
pepper
4—6 fresh paprikas

Wash liver, wipe and cut into nice slices. Pour oil over, leave to stand like that about 30—40 minutes. Wash paprikas, wipe, dip into oil and grill together with liver.

When liver is done, sprinkle with salt and pepper and serve with grilled paprikas.

With liver serve stewed rice, mashed potatoes, cooked potatoes mixed with fried onion, and some salad (lettuce, cucumber, cabbage etc.).

Yugoslavia

KEBAB FROM NISH

(for 5 persons)

1 kg pork from leg
1 kg onion
2 green paprikas
pepper
salt
1/2 teaspoon red paprika pepper
1 dl warm water

Wash meat, wipe and cut into bigger cubes. Add salt, pepper and red paprika pepper. Peel onion, core paprikas, wash, dice and add to meat. Mix all, leave to stand in a cool place about 1—2 hours.

Thread meat (without paprikas and onion) on to skewers, brush with oil and grill until brown. Put grilled kebabs into the pan with onion and paprikas, pour in some warm water. Simmer at medium heat until onion and paprikas are tender.

Serve warm without waiting.

Yugoslavia

HADZIYA (PILGRIM) KEBAB

(for 5 persons)

1 kg boneless lamb
150 gr butterfat (oil or butter)
500 gr onion
300 gr paprikas
300 gr tomatoes
1/2 gr parsley
pepper
1 teaspoon ground cinnamon
salt
1/2—3/4 l bone stock or soup from meat cube

Wash meat, wipe and cut into bigger strips. Heat butterfat or oil, add meat, fry on all sides to get nicely golden-brown. Then take out meat, add finely sliced onion into the same fat, cook slowly until tender, add meat, cook together. Wash and core paprikas and cut into bigger strips, add them to meat and onion, mix and cook on. Wash tomatoes, peel and cut into big strips, then add to half cooked meat. Also add chopped parsley, pepper, cinnamon and salt. Pour in warm soup (or water), cover and simmer, and towards the end put into the oven preheated to 200°C to bake a little and brown.

Turkey

MUTTON KEBAB

600 gr fatty mutton
40 gr oil
2—3 onions
1 bunch of parsley
salt
pepper

Wash meat, wipe and cut into bigger chunks. Heat oil, add meat, fry on all sides to brown, take out. Add peeled and finely chopped onion, cook slowly until soft and brown, then add meat, salt, pepper, chopped parsley, pour in some warm water, cover and simmer until meat is quite tender. Serve at once with rice and fresh salads.

Turkey

KEBAB

800 gr meat (mutton, young beef, beef or lamb)
2 bigger onions
1 bigger carrot
1 parsley root
1—2 dl warm water
2—3 cloves of garlic
40 gr tomato purée (from tube or can)
100 gr butterfat (oil or butter)
salt
pepper
1 teaspoon red paprika pepper

Wash meat, wipe and cut into chunks. Peel onion and chop finely; scrape carrot and parsley and grate crudely; peel garlic and crush.

Heat butterfat or oil, add meat, fry it well on all sides, then add onion, carrot, parsley, mix, pouring in warm water at times and cook slowly until slightly tender. Pour in diluted tomato, add garlic, salt and pepper. Mix all, add more water if needed, cover and simmer. Stir while cooking at times and add some

more water. When all is tender, add red paprika pepper. When done, kebab should be succulent, i. e. it must have a lot of juice.

"Kebab" (Arabic word), "tchevap" in Serbo-Croat, means "meat cut into chunks, cooked, or rather, stewed, with plenty of sauce".

Yugoslavia

"MUTCHKA-LITSA" WITH LIVER

400 gr calves' liver
400 gr pigs' liver
2 dl oil
2 onions
2 paprikas
50 gr butter (margarine)
salt, pepper

Wash livers, wipe, cut into nice slices, pour oil over and leave to stand for at least 45 minutes.

In the meantime peel onion, core paprikas and cut into smaller pieces. Heat butter, add onion and paprikas, cook slowly, add salt and pepper.

Arrange liver on heated gridiron. Grill and turn around until tender, salt and put over the stewed vegetables.

Roumania

HAIDUK KEBAB IN FOIL

600—750 gr boneless pork
6—7 onions
4 green paprikas
1 bunch of parsley
salt, pepper

Wash meat, wipe and cut into slightly smaller cubes. Peel onion, wash and chop finely. Wash paprikas, deseed, cut into cubes. Chop parsley finely. Add salt and pepper to meat, onion, paprikas and parsley, mix all well.

Grease a tin foil, big enough and with shiny side inside, with oil, turn in the prepared meat with vegetables, wrap foil up well, so that juice can not leak out.

Heat the oven to 200—250 °C and bake about 60 minutes.

Dish kebab out of the foil and serve.

KEBABS, MUTCHKALITSAS KRZATMAS, PIRYANS

Turkey

"KESHKEK"

(for 5 persons)

1 kg meat without bones (lamb, mutton, turkey, chicken)
500 gr wheat grains (white)
salt
50 gr unripe butterfat or butter
2 l hot water

Pick over wheat, wash, pour in hot water. When water cools, drain and dry a little. When dried, pound with a pestle so as to remove outer skins more easily, then wash and cook until tender.

Cut meat into pieces, barely cover with cold water and cook until tender and falling off bones. Strain cooked meat, remove bones. Put meat back into soup, add cooked and drained wheat, add salt. Cook together stirring occasionally, until the soup reduces and a homogenous mixture of wheat and cooked meat remains.

Before serving, melted butterfat or butter can be poured over it.

Thick yoghurt can be served with this dish.

"Keshkek" in Persian means a soft and well cooked meat mash. So the name reveals the origin of the dish, which came via Turkey to the south-eastern parts of Yugoslavia.

In winter it can be prepared in greater quantities, kept in a cool place, taken when needed and warmed before serving.

Greece

"PAPAZ" — KEBAB

600 gr young beef or beef (part below shoulder)
500 gr onion
2—3 cloves of garlic
2—3 cloves
1/2 sachet of ground cinnamon
salt
pepper
2—3 dl warm water
1 dl oil
1—2 tablespoons vinegar
1 teaspoon red paprika pepper

Wash meet, wipe and cut into cubes (the size of sugar lumps). Peel onion and garlic, chop together, add ground cloves, cinnamon, salt and pepper. Mix all.

Put some oil into a bigger fireproof dish or pan, put in meat, sprinkle with mixed spices, pour oil over. Leave to stand in a cool place for several hours (or overnight). Then add some warm water and simmer covered, shaking and adding water at times.

When all is tender, add red paprika pepper diluted with water and vinegar and cook together for a short while.

Serve kebab with plenty of juice from stewing.

"Papaz" — kebab is a word of Arabic origin taken over into Greek.

Yugoslavia

VINEYARD KEBAB

(for 5 persons)

1 kg boneless pork
500 gr onion
salt
pepper
1—1,5 dl oil

Wash meat, wipe and cut into squares 5 × 5 cm and about 2 cm thick. Peel onion and slice finely. Put onion into a bigger pan, add salt and pepper, add meat and shake well so that onion and meat mix properly. Leave to stand in a cool place for at least 2—3 hours.

In the meantime prepare the grill. Remove onion from meat, thread meat on to longer skewers, brush with oil, grill on medium heated gridiron, turn at times. When done, mix with onion, cover pan, shake well and serve straight away.

This kebab is most often prepared with pork, but it can also be prepared with beef and mutton.

For beef kebab take meat from beefsteak, and for mutton kebab from leg of mutton. For either of these thin rashers of bacon should be put in between chunks of meat.

Vineyard kebab is usually prepared in wine growing parts of Yugoslavia at the time of grape picking, so the quantity of meat depends on the number of people ("pickers").

Turkey

KEBAB WITH AUBERGINES

500 gr smaller aubergines
salt
3 onions
2 cloves of garlic
2 tomatoes
750 gr lamb from leg
40 gr butter
30 gr sunflower oil
pepper
1/2 l bone stock or soup from meat cube

Wash aubergines, remove stalks, cut into cubes, salt and mix. Leave them to stand at least 30 minutes, then rinse with cold water and drain.

Peel onion and chop crudely, crush garlic. Wash tomatoes, peel and cut into small pieces.

Wash meat, wipe and cut into bigger cubes. Mix butter and oil in the frying pan, add drained aubergines, fry to brown a little, take out of the pan and put on a plate. Fry meat in the same fat to become light brown, then take it out. Put onion in the same fat, cook it a little, add tomatoes, cook together about 5 minutes, add garlic. Put meat in a bigger pan, add onion with tomato and garlic. Add salt and pepper, pour in soup, cover and simmer together about 40 minutes, then add aubergines and stew for another 25—30 minutes.

Yugoslavia

"MUTCHKA-LITSA" FROM LESKOVAC

650 gr pork
2 onions
1 dl oil
salt
pepper
2 hot paprikas
4 tomatoes
1/2 bunch of parsley

Wash meat, wipe and cut into smaller chunks, dip in oil and thread on to skewers. Grill on heated gridiron on both sides. When done, sprinkle with salt and pepper.

Chop onion finely, cook slowly in heated oil until slightly soft, add paprikas cut into strips and peeled tomatoes cut into smaller pieces. Cook slowly together for a while, add chopped parsley. When tender, take meat off the skewers, add it to vegetables and stew together for another 5 minutes.

Yugoslavia

"MUTCHKA-LITSA" FROM SHARPLANINA (mountain in Macedonia)

650 gr mutton from leg
1 dl oil
5 onions
4 cloves of garlic
1 green paprika
1 tablespoon vinegar
salt
pepper

Wash meat, wipe and cut into smaller cubes, pour oil over and leave to stand in a cool place for a while.

Peel onion, core paprika and cut into small cubes, peel garlic and crush well. Mix all, add salt, pepper and vinegar.

Thread meat on to skewers. Grill on heated gridiron, turning often. When the meat is done, take it off the skewers, put over the prepared onion with paprika, shake well and serve at once.

Bulgaria

SHEPHERD "MUTCHKA-LITSA" (grilled meat with stewed vegetables)

300 gr pork
300 gr lamb
200 gr mushrooms (ceps, button mushrooms)
1,5 dl oil
salt
pepper
2 onions
3 paprikas
3 tomatoes
2 tablespoons hot paprika pepper

Wash meat, wipe and cut into smaller cubes. Trim mushrooms, cut into halves or if small, leave whole. Thread meat and mushrooms on to skewers, brush with oil and grill on heated gridiron, turning them at times. When done, sprinkle with salt and pepper. Peel onion, chop rather finely, core paprikas and cut into cubes, cut tomatoes into slices. Cook slowly in heated oil until tender, add salt and pepper, sprinkle with hot paprika pepper. Take meat and mushrooms off the skewers, mix with stewed vegetables. Serve warm without waiting.

Turkey

"KRZATMA" WITH PEAS

800 gr—1 kg mutton or lamb from ribs
100 gr butterfat (butter or oil)
1 smaller onion
1 carrot
2 cloves of garlic
20 gr (1 tablespoon) tomato purée
1 teaspoon red paprika pepper
500 gr fresh, shelled peas
2—3 dl warm water
salt

Wash meat, salt and cut into bigger chunks. Heat butterfat, add cut meat.

Fry on all sides to brown, then take out. Add chopped onion into the same fat, then thinner rounds of carrot, cook a little to soften, then add chopped garlic, tomato and red paprika pepper. Cook together shortly, put back fried meat, add washed peas, pour in water, add salt. Simmer until meat and vegetables are soft. While cooking shake the pan at times, add some more water if needed.

"Krzatma" in Turkish means kebab from lamb or other meat (from ribs) with vegetables. Depending on the kind of meat there are various kinds of krzatmas: lamb, mutton, veal, young beef and chicken. Various vegetables are added, so there are krzatmas with string beans, white beans, peas, fresh cabbage, potatoes (most of all new ones) etc.

Turkey

CHICKEN "PIRYAN"

1 slightly bigger chicken
150 gr butterfat (butter or oil)
1 aubergine
150 gr onion
3 fresh paprikas
2 tomatoes
2—3 dl warm water

500 gr potatoes
1/2 bunch of parsley
some ginger

Wash meat, wipe and cut into pieces. Heat butterfat (100 gr), put chicken in, fry on all sides to brown. Peel aubergine, cut into cubes, salt and leave to stand for 30 minutes, then rinse and drain.

Heat the rest of butterfat in another pan, add finely chopped onion and strips of paprikas, cook slowly until onion is slightly soft, add drained aubergines and mix. Arrange meat over vegetables, cook a little, then add washed, peeled and finely cut tomatoes, pour in warm water, cover and stew at medium heat.

When meat is half cooked, add peeled potatoes cut into slices, pour in some more warm water if needed and cook on until meat and vegetables are quite tender.

When "piryan" is cooked, add chopped parsley and ginger.

The word "piryan" has the origin in the Persian word "biryan" which means cook something together (in this case meat and vegetables), or rather stew in fat.

Yugoslavia

FISH KEBAB

(for 6 persons)

1,5 kg freshwater fish (trout or similar, with not so many bones)
salt
1 dl oil
200 gr onion
1—2 carrots
1 parsley root
1/2 celery root
1 smaller parsnip
3—5 dl warm water
juice of 1 lemon or 2 tablespoons wine vinegar
peppercorns

Clean fish, wash, cut into pieces and salt. Leave in a cool place to stand for at least 30 minutes.

In the meantime peel onion, chop it finely. Scrape carrots, parsley, celery and parsnip, wash and grate crudely.

Heat oil, add onion, cook slowly until soft, then add prepared greens. Cook together until slightly tender.

Put half of the onion and vegetables in a bigger pan (or flameproof casserole), arrange pieces of fish over, then put the rest of onion and vegetables, add a few peppercorns and barely cover with warm water. Simmer until fish and vegetables are tender. Shake the pan occasionally and add more water if needed. Before serving add lemon juice or vinegar.

Evdiya Tchelebiya, author of travel books from the 17th century, writes that fish kebab "is prepared by people from the whole city of Sarajevo at the spring of the river Bosna, who fish trout and enjoy themselves eating and drinking".

Turkey

"TCHERVISH"

500 gr meat (lamb, mutton, young beef or chicken)
1 bunch of root vegetables
300 gr wheat flour
1 egg
1 dl milk (or water)
100 gr butterfat (butter or oil)
2 cloves of garlic
2 tablespoons vinegar or lemon juice
40 gr unripened butterfat or kaymak

Wash meat and cut it into bigger pieces. Put up to cook 1—1,5 l water. When it boils, add meat, scraped or peeled roots (1 carrot, 1 parsley root, some celery root, 1/4 kohlrabi, half onion). Simmer until the meat is tender.

In the meantime prepare the "tirit": sift flour, add the egg, milk (or water), rub flour until everything turns into crumbs (tirit). Heat butterfat, add crumbs and fry until brown.

When meat is cooked, take it out, cool a little, then chop. Strain soup. Arrange meat in a pan or a bigger fireproof dish, sprinkle with crumbs (tirit), barely cover with soup, add crushed garlic and vinegar. Cover and simmer until crumbs absorb liquid and get soft.

Before serving pour heated unripened butterfat or melted kaymak over the "tchervish".

Yugoslavia

"PIRYAN" WITH STRING BEANS

1 kg string beans
1 kg mutton (from ribs or loin)
50 gr oil
1 smaller onion
salt
20 gr rice
1—2 tomatoes
2—3 dl soup from meat cube
20 gr butterfat or butter

Wash string beans, remove tops and tails and strings, if any, cut into bigger pieces.

Wash meat, wipe, cut into pieces, pour in soup from meat cube and simmer.

Heat oil, add chopped onion, cook slowly for a while, add string beans, cook slowly together, add meat with soup, salt, and simmer together at medium heat.

When meat and string beans are nearly tender, add picked over and washed rice and peeled tomatoes cut into smaller pieces. Pour in some more soup as needed and stew on until all is tender.

Pour some heated butterfat or butter over "piryan" before serving.

Turkey

LAMB "KRZATMA" WITH POTATOES

1 kg young lamb (ribs, breast)
100 gr butterfat (butter or oil)
salt
1 onion
1 bigger carrot
1 teaspoon red paprika pepper
2 fresh tomatoes or 1 tablespoon tomato purée
2—3 dl warm water of soup from meat cube
500 gr new potatoes
2 cloves of garlic
pepper ground from mill

Wash meat, wipe and cut it into pieces. Heat butterfat, put in meat, fry it on all sides to brown, take out. Add finely chopped onion to the same fat as well as the crudely grated carrot. Cook slowly until slightly tender, add red paprika pepper, peeled and sliced tomatoes (or diluted tomato purée). Cook together for 5—10 minutes, put back meat, peeled and halved new potatoes and garlic in cloves. Add salt, pour in warm water or soup, shake the pan, cover and simmer until all is tender.

Before serving add pepper freshly ground from mill.

CHOPPED UP MEAT

Greece

LAMB GOULASH GREEK WAY

(for 5—6 persons)

1 kg lamb
salt
pepper
1/2 teaspoon powdered cinnamon
juice of 1 lemon
40 gr butter
4—5 dl tomato juice
1/2 bunch of chopped parsley
1—2 dl warm water

Wash meat, wipe, cut into bigger chunks, salt, sprinkle with pepper and cinnamon, pour in lemon juice, cover and leave to stand 10—15 minutes. Then take out meat and drain. Heat butter, add meat, fry on all sides to get nicely brown, add tomato, lemon juice in which the meat was and chopped parsley. Cover and simmer until the meat is tender. Shake the pan at times while simmering and add warm water as needed.

Bulgaria

HAIDUK STEW

750 gr lamb
80 gr lard or 1 dl oil
2—3 onions
200 gr tomatoes
1 tablespoon flour
2—3 dl warm water
2 teaspoons red paprika pepper
peppercorns
2—3 cloves of garlic
500 gr potatoes
150 gr fresh mushrooms
1/2 bunch of parsley
1/2 dl oil

Wash meat, wipe and cut into smaller cubes. Heat oil or lard, add finely chopped onion, cook a little to soften. Then add meat, cook slowly together about 15 minutes, add half of tomatoes, peeled and cut into smaller pieces. Cook to reduce, then dredge with flour, fry a little, add red paprika pepper, pour in some cold, then warm water, add salt, a few peppercorns and chopped garlic. Turn all into a earthenware dish and bake in the oven preheated to 175—200°C until meat is quite tender.

Peel potatoes, dice. Trim mushrooms, wash and slice, cook in some oil.

When meat is done, add potatoes and mushrooms, pour in more water if needed. Towards the end of baking, arrange the rest of tomatoes cut into rounds over the stew, put back into the oven for a short while.

Sprinkle with chopped parsley in the end.

Turkey

MUTTON GOULASH

500 gr boneless mutton
50 gr oil
500 gr onion
3 cloves of garlic
salt
3—4 dl warm water
3 tablespoons tomato purée (from tube)
2 tablespoons red paprika pepper
1 teaspoon caraway seeds
1 teaspoon marjoram
1/4 l sour cream

Wash meat, wipe and cut into bigger chunks.

Heat oil, add meat, fry on all sides to brown nicely. Chop finely onion and garlic, add to meat, cook slowly together. Then pour in 1 dl warm water, stir and cook on slowly. Mix tomato, red paprika pepper, caraway and marjoram, pour in some warm water, add to the meat, pour in the rest of water, cover and simmer about 60 minutes.

Add sour cream mixed with some red paprika pepper just before serving.

Serve very warm, like all the dishes with mutton. With mutton goulash serve boiled potatoes, noodles or cooked rice.

Yugoslavia

VEAL PÖRKÖLT

500—750 gr veal (of leg)
40 gr lard
3—4 onions
2 teaspoons red paprika pepper
20—30 gr flour
1,5 dl warm water
salt
2 dl sour cream

Wash meat, wipe and cut into smaller cubes. Heat lard, add finely chopped onion, cook slowly until tender and beginning to colour, sprinkle with red paprika pepper, add meat, salt and simmer covered in its own juice, then pour in some water at times until meat is quite tender. Mix flour with some cold water, add to the meat, stir, pour in some warm water, cook together for another 10 minutes. Blend in sour cream in the end.

With pörkölt serve pasta, potato dumplings or mashed potatoes.

Turkey

LAMB GOULASH WITH PISTACHIOS

600 gr boneless lamb
4 smaller onions
2—3 cloves of garlic
salt
50 gr (5 tablespoons) olive oil
1/4 l soup from meat cube
50 gr pistachios
10 gr butter
50 gr raisins
150 gr rice
1/2 l warm water
60 gr tomato purée (3 tablespoons)
a pinch of saffron
1/2 bunch of dill
salt
pepper
1/2 bunch of parsley

Wash meat and wipe. Remove suet, cut it into small cubes and melt.

In the meantime cut meat into bigger cubes. Peel onion and garlic, chop onion finely, crush garlic.

Take out cracklings obtained when melting suet, add oil to the fat, heat, cook onion in it shortly, add meat and garlic, pour in warm soup, cover and simmer about 30—40 minutes.

Fry pistachios in heated butter. Remove stems from raisins, pour over with hot water, leave to stand about 5 minutes, then drain. Wash rice and drain. Add pistachios, raisins and rice to meat, add warm water, blend in tomato purée and saffron, add salt and pepper and chopped dill. Cook slowly together another 25—30 minutes.

Serve very warm, sprinkled with chopped parsley.

As accompaniment serve paprika salad, fresh cabbage salad, mixed salad and others.

Bulgaria

KEBABS-STEW

750 gr lamb (tender)
1 onion
1 aubergine
2 tomatoes
2 small hot peppers
40 gr flour
pepper
1 tablespoon tomato purée
red paprika pepper
1 dl white wine
3—5 dl hot water
1/2 teaspoon thyme
1/2 bunch of parsley
salt
1 dl oil

Wash meat, wipe, cut into smaller chunks, thread on metal skewers and intersperse with small slices of onion, aubergine, tomatoes and small hot pepper. Sprinkle all with salt and pepper and roll in flour. Fry in heated oil. Take skewers out and in the same oil mix tomato purée, red paprika pepper, white wine and hot water. Cook for 5—10 minutes.

Take kebabs off the skewers, put into an earthenware or fireproof dish, pour wine sauce over them, sprinkle with thyme and pepper and bake in the oven preheated to 200°C. While baking pour in some warm water as needed. In the end sprinkle with chopped parsley.

With this stew serve fried new potatoes, boiled rice, tomato and paprika salad, lettuce and the like.

Greece

"PRASSATO"

(for 6 persons)

1 kg lamb from shoulder
1 onion
50 gr oil
salt, pepper
1 l warm water
1,5 kg leeks
2 eggs
juice of 1 lemon

Wash meat, wipe a little and cut into equal-sized chunks. Cut onion into thin slices, fry it in heated oil until soft and slightly brown, add meat, salt and pepper and mix. Barely cover with warm water. Cook slowly uncovered. Wash leeks, cut into pieces, add them to half cooked meat and simmer on until all is cooked.

Beat eggs well and pour in lemon juice gradually mixing all the time. Pour this mixture slowly into meat and leeks, stirring constantly, stir until it thickens, but it must not boil any more.

The juice must be neither too thin nor too thick, so pay attention while stewing meat and leeks.

Bulgaria

MUTTON WITH HORSERADISH

2 l water
600 gr mutton
1 onion
1 carrot
1/2 celery root
1 leek
1 parsnip
1 bayleaf
2—3 cloves (optional)
100 gr horseradish
50 gr apple
salt
1 tablespoon of vinegar and 1 of oil

Wash meat and put up to cook in hot water. When it boils, add onion dry fried on top the stove, scraped root vegetables, bayleaf, cloves and salt. Simmer at medium heat. Leave meat to stand for a while in the soup.

Scrape horseradish, grate, peel apple, grate and add to the horseradish, add some vinegar, a bit of soup, some oil and salt. Mix all well. If desired, some sugar can be added to the sauce.

Take meat out of the soup, cut into nice pieces, arrange on a plate and pour horseradish sauce over it.

Arrange cooked vegetables from the soup around the meat.

Serve with boiled potatoes, stewed cabbage or string beans etc.

Greece

BEEF WITH CHESTNUTS

500 gr chestnuts
2 onions
750 gr boneless beef
40 gr butter
1,2 l bone stock or soup from meat cube
salt
white pepper

Cut chestnuts crossways, cook until shells burst, them remove shells. Peel onion and chop finely. Wash meat, wipe and cut into bigger chunks. Heat oil in a bigger pot, add onion, cook slowly until soft and beginning to colour. Add meat, fry it on all sides, pour in warm soup, add salt and pepper, cover and simmer until the meat is tender. Towards the end add shelled chestnuts, cook together with meat, but take care that chestnuts do not get overcooked.

With beef prepared this way Brussels sprouts are usually served in Greece. Brussels sprouts can be replaced with boiled kale, cabbage, cauliflower. Any of these vegetables is just cooked in salted water and melted butter or heated oil poured over it.

Greece

"STIFATO" — VEAL GOULASH GREEK WAY

(for 6 persons)

1,25 kg boneless veal
1 dl olive oil
salt
pepper
1 medium-sized onion
4 dl tomato juice
1/2 dl wine vinegar

1 dl red wine
1 bayleaf
4—5 dl warm water
900 gr pearl onions
1 l hot water
2 cloves of garlic
1 dl melted butter
1/2 bunch of parsley

Wash meat, wipe and cut into bigger cubes. Heat oil (preferably in a pan with double bottom), add meat, fry until brown. Take it out, put on a warm plate, put finely chopped onion into the same oil, cook slowly until tender, put meat back, pour in tomato juice, vinegar, wine, add bayleaf. Pour over with warm water, add salt and pepper and simmer until meat is tender. In the meantime pour hot water over unpeeled tiny onions, leave them to cool in that water, drain, peel and make a cross with a knife at each bottom end, so that onions would not burst while being cooked.

Heat butter in a pan, add onions, finely chopped garlic, fry a little, add about 2 dl water, salt, cover and simmer until tender. Add chopped parsley to soft onions and slowly turn into meat, shake a little and cook together at low heat about 20 minutes, until juice reduces partly and onions get quite tender.

Yugoslavia

GOULASH FROM VOJVODINA

(for 5 persons)

750 gr—1 kg beef
100 gr smoked bacon
4—5 onions
1 tablespoon red paprika pepper
1/2 teaspoon hot red paprika pepper
2—3 cloves of garlic
2—3 tomatoes
2 dl white wine
1 dl warm water
salt,
pepper

Wash meat, wipe and cut into bigger chunks. Cut bacon into smaller cubes, melt it, remove cracklings and in rendered fat cook chopped onions slowly until soft and beginning to colour. Put in meat, cook together until slightly tender, then add chopped garlic, washed, peeled and chopped tomatoes, salt, pepper, white wine and some warm water. Shake all well, cover and simmer until the meat is tender.

With this goulash serve cooked pasta, polenta or boiled potatoes. Peeled and sliced potatoes can be added to the goulash itself after adding wine and water, and stewed together.

Greece

"PASHTITSADA" FROM CORFU

900 gr lean young beef
1 dl olive oil
450 gr onion
2—3 cloves of garlic
salt
pepper
900 gr ripe tomatoes
1 dl white wine
1 tablespoon vinegar
1 cinnamon bark (optional)
1 bayleaf
450 gr macaroni
50 gr butter
100 gr grated cheese (kachkaval, Trappist or similar)

Wash meat, wipe, cut into bigger cubes, fry in heated oil to brown, add finely chopped onion, cook slowly to get slightly tender, then add peeled and chopped tomatoes, wine, vinegar, cinnamon, bayleaf. Add some water, cover and simmer

until meat is tender and the juice thick.

Cook macaroni in salted water, drain when cooked, rinse with cold water and drain well. Bring butter to the boil, pour over macaroni, turn the "pashtitsada" over them, sprinkle all with grated cheese and serve right away.

Roumania

PORK GOULASH WITH POLENTA

1,5 kg pork
100 gr oil (10 tablespoons)
500 gr onion
salt
1 tablespoon red paprika pepper
1 teaspoon thyme
1—2 dl white wine
1 dl sour cream

Wash meat, wipe and cut into bigger cubes. Heat oil, add finely chopped onion, cook slowly until slightly soft. Add meat, salt, red paprika pepper, thyme. Pour in wine and stew covered in the oven heated to 175 °C. Shake occasionally and add some warm water as needed.

Serve goulash with sour cream and polenta.

Turkey

LAMB GOULASH WITH APPLE

500 gr boneless lamb (from shoulder)
3 onions
2 cloves of garlic
30 gr oil
1 bayleaf
salt
pepper
1 apple
1 dl soup from meat cube
2—2,5 dl drinking yoghurt
1 tablespoon flour

Wash meat, wipe and cut into bigger cubes. Peel and chop onion and garlic. Heat oil, add meat, fry until nicely brown, add onion and garlic, cook at low

heat about 5—10 minutes. Add bayleaf, salt and pepper. Peel the apple, remove pips, cut into small cubes, add it to the meat, add more pepper, pour in hot soup, cover and simmer until the meat is tender.

Beat yoghurt, add a spoonful of flour, blend into the stew, stir and cook shortly (10—15 minutes).

Serve with cooked rice sprinkled with parsley and with some salad (lettuce, fresh cabbage, mixed salad and the like).

Greece

PORK WITH CELERY

(for 5—6 persons)

1,250 gr pork from leg
100 gr butter
1 onion
2 smaller carrots
salt
pepper
1 l hot water
1 kg celery root
2 tablespoons flour
2 egg yolks
1—2 lemons
1/2 bunch of parsley

Wash meat, wipe and cut into bigger pieces. Put about 70 gr butter into a bigger pot, heat, add finely chopped onion, scraped carrot cut into rounds, cook slowly until slightly tender, add meat, salt and pepper, then pour in hot water. Cover and simmer about 90 minutes.

Peel celery, wash and cut into thicker slices. Wash and chop tiny leaves which are usually to be found on the roots. Blanch slices of celery about 5 minutes, then drain and add to meat, which should be nearly cooked, together with chopped leaves. Cook for another 30—35 minutes.

Mix the rest of butter, egg yolks and flour into a smooth batter, then pour in soup from the pot gradually, stirring all the time. Beat over steam and add lemon juice bit by bit until the mixture is

smooth and rather thick. Add some more soup from the pot, stirring, and then pour the mixture into meat and celery, mix well but do not cook any more. Sprinkle with chopped parsley and serve without waiting.

GROUND MEAT

Albania

MUTTON MEATBALLS

80 gr white bread
1 dl lukewarm water
500 gr mutton
3 cloves of garlic
2 eggs
1/2 teaspoon cinnamon
mutton suet or oil for frying

Soak a slice of bread in some lukewarm water, leave to soften, then drain. Grind meat. Chop garlic finely. Mix bread, meat, garlic, eggs, salt and cinnamon. Work into a smooth meat mixture. Leave to stand 1—2 hours in a cool place.

Shape meat into long cork-shaped rissols (like tchevapchitchi). Fry in heated oil or suet.

With these meatballs serve some salad or cooked vegetables (kale, leeks, cabbage).

Greece

MEATBALLS — "TCHUFTE"

450 gr ground young beef or veal
1 egg
70 gr breadcrumbs
1 dl water
2 onions of medium size
20 gr butter
salt, pepper
1 tablespoon vinegar
1 teaspoon oregano
1 tablespoon chopped parsley or 1—2 fresh mint leaves
40—50 gr flour
2 dl olive or other oil

Add egg, breadcrumbs and water to ground meat. Chop onion finely and cook slowly in heated butter until soft and beginning to colour. Cool it a little and add to the meat, add salt, pepper, vinegar, oregano, chopped parsley or mint. Mix all well, cover and leave to stand in a cool place (refrigerator) about 1 hour. Shape into smaller balls, roll them in flour. Heat oil, fry meatballs until brown.

With meatballs serve mashed potatoes, baked or fried potatoes and some fresh-tasting salad (lettuce, fresh cabbage, mixed and others).

"Tchufte" is a word of Parsian origin. In Persian it means "meat cakes with juice".

Turkey

BEEF MEATBALLS

600 gr beef
100 gr white bread or 1 bun
2 eggs
2 smaller onions
2 tablespoons chopped parsley
salt
pepper
150 gr butter for frying meatballs
1/2 to 3/4 bone stock or soup from meat cube
30 gr flour
1 dl cold water
1 egg
juice of 1 lemon
1 teaspoon red paprika pepper
some salt

Wash meat, wipe, cut into smaller pieces and grind. Pour lukewarm water over bread, leave to soften. Chop onion finely. Add drained bread, finely chopped onion, chopped parsley, salt and pepper to ground meat. Work well into a meat mixture. Leave to stand in a cool place 30—60 minutes. Shape into smaller balls and fry in heated butter. When fried, place in a deeper pan, pour over with soup from meat cube, or bone stock. Simmer.

Mix flour in cold water, add red paprika pepper, add to the meatballs, shake the pan, add some more soup or warm water if needed and cook on for another 10 minutes. Beat well the egg yolk, add lemon juice gradually, blend into the sauce with meatballs, shake, but do not cook any more.

Yugoslavia

MEATBALLS FROM BOSNIA

100 gr rice
2—3 dl water or soup from meat cube (or bone stock)
600 gr ground meat (lamb, veal)
1 smaller onion
salt
pepper
1 coked carrot
50 gr flour
2 eggs
2—3 dl oil for frying

Pick over rice, wash, add water or soup, simmer until rice is cooked.

Wash meat, wipe, grind, add finely chopped onion, rice, salt, pepper and diced carrot. Work into a meat mixture, leave in a cool place to stand for a while, then shape into small flat patties, roll in flour, dip in well beaten eggs and fry in heated oil. Turn while frying to brown on both sides.

With meatballs serve some fresh--tasting salad.

Albania

MEATBALLS WITH POTATO

2 boiled potatoes
250 gr ground young beef
1 egg
2 tablespoons chopped walnuts
2 tablespoons raisins
1 tablespoon crushed thyme or rosemary
salt
pepper
2 dl oil for frying

Peel potatoes, mash or purée, add ground meat, eggs, walnuts, cleaned raisins soaked in lukewarm water, salt and pepper. Work into a mixture. Leave to stand for 1—2 hours in a cool place.

Shape into small balls, fry in heated oil until brown.

With these meatballs serve boiled vegetables with oil poured over (cauliflower, potatoes, carrots and others).

Bulgaria

MEATBALLS WITH KAYMAK

750 gr young beef or lamb
1 onion
1 clove of garlic
salt
2 teaspoons red paprika pepper (hot if desired)
40 gr flour
2—3 eggs
2 dl oil for frying

Wash meat, wipe and grind, add finely chopped onion, snipped garlic, salt and half of red paprika pepper. Mix all well, leave to stand in a cool place for at least 1 hour.

Shape meat mixture into small balls, roll them in flour, then dip in beaten eggs, fry in heated oil until brown.

Melt kaymak a little, put half in a fireproof dish, sprinkle with some red paprika pepper, place meatballs over, shake, pour the rest of kaymak over, bake in the oven preset at 200°C until nicely brown.

Greece

MEATBALLS WITH SAUCE

500 gr ground young beef or veal
1—2 eggs
75 gr breadcrumbs
1 dl water
2 onions
30 gr butter
salt
pepper
1 tablespoon vinegar
1 teaspoon oregano
1 tablespoon chopped parsley or fresh mint
40—50 gr flour
3 dl olive or other oil for frying

For sauce:
oil left over form frying
30 gr flour
3 dl water or soup from meat cube
1 dl dry white wine
1 teaspoon tomato purée (from tube)
vinegar to taste
2—3 cloves of garlic
1 bayleaf
salt
pepper
a few rosemary leaves

Add eggs, breadcrumbs and water to ground meat. Chop onion finely and cook slowly in heated butter until soft and slightly brown. Then cool and add to meat, add salt, pepper, vinegar, oregano, chopped parsley or mint. Mix all well. Leave covered to stand in the refrigerator about 1 hour. Then shape into smaller balls, roll in flour and fry in heated oil until brown.

For the sauce strain oil left over from frying meatballs. Heat, add flour, fry until slightly brown, pour in about 1 dl cold water, then soup or warm water, white wine, tomato purée diluted with some water, vinegar to taste, sliced garlic, bayleaf, salt, pepper and rosemary. Simmer, stirring often, about 10—15 minutes.

Arrange meatballs on a deeper plate, pour the sauce over and serve warm or cold.

Turkey

PASHA-MEATBALLS

120 gr rice
600 gr mixed young beef and veal or lamb
juice of 1 lemon
pepper
salt
2 eggs
50 gr flour
2—3 dl oil for frying
1 teaspoon red paprika pepper
2 dl sour cream or thick yoghurt

Pick over rice, wash and cook in slightly salted water. When soft, drain. Wash meat, wipe, cut and grind. Mix with rice, add lemon juice, salt and pepper. Mix all well, leave to stand in a cool place for 30—60 minutes.

Beat eggs, add flour, beat into smooth, thick batter.

Shape rounded flat meat cakes from meat mixture, dip them in egg batter and fry in heated oil. Strain oil left over from frying, add some red paprika pepper to it, pour in some water, cook for

a while. Place meatballs on a corresponding plate, pour the sauce and sour cream over.

Another sauce can be made for "Pasha-meatballs": 2 onions finely chopped mixed with 2 tomatoes cut into smaller pieces, 1 tablespoon of flour, 2 dl soup from meat cube. Cook all slowly and when tender, pass trough a sieve and salt.

Roumania

GREEN MEATBALLS

200 gr beef
600 gr fatty pork
2—3 onions
40 gr oil or lard
1 egg
salt
pepper
1 bunch of dill
1 bunch of parsley
100 gr spinach
butter or oil for frying

For sauce:
200 gr mayonnaise
2 cloves of garlic
mustard to taste
red paprika pepper
juice of 1 lemon or vinegar

Cut meat into smaller pieces and grind. Chop onion finely and cook slowly in heated oil until soft. Cool, add to ground meat, add salt, pepper and 1 egg. Work into a meat mixture. Leave to stand for a while in a cool place.

Wash dill, parsley and spinach, remove stalks, wipe in a clean cloth and chop all finely.

Shape small balls out of meat mixture the size of walnuts, roll them in chopped vegetables and fry in heated butter or oil.

Mix mayonnaise with finely chopped or crushed garlic, mustard, red paprika

pepper and lemon juice. This has to be a savoury sauce.

Arrange meatballs on a plate, garnish with dill and parsley leaves. Serve the sauce separately.

Roumania

GREEN MEATBALLS IN SAUCE

For sauce:
1 bunch of root vegetables (carrot, parsley root, 1/2 celery root, parsnip)
1 onion
100 gr smoked bacon
20 gr (2 tablespoons) oil
20 gr flour
1/2 l bone stock or soup from meat cube
1 bayleaf
1/2 teaspoon thyme
1 dl sour cream
1 tablespoon tomato purée (from tube)
1/2 dl white wine

For meatballs:
600 gr beef
300 gr pork
1 onion
10 gr butter
1—2 eggs
salt, pepper
50 gr spinach
1 tablespoon chopped parsley
1 tablespoon snipped dill
1 tablespoon shallots (or spring onion leaves)
100 gr butter or margarine for frying meatballs

Scrape root vegetables. Chop onion finely. Cut bacon into cubes. Mix oil and cubes of bacon, heat until bacon melts, add onion and cook slowly to soften a little. Then add crudely grated root vegetables, cook together until slightly brown. Dredge all with flour, stir and fry flour a little, pour in a glass of cold water, then the soup, add bayleaf, thyme and tomato purée. Simmer until vegetables are tender.

Clean spinach, wash, boil, drain and chop finely.

Wash meat, cut into cubes and grind, add finely chopped onion cooked in some butter, eggs, salt and pepper. Work into a smooth meat mixture, leave in a cool place to stand about 60 minutes. In the meantime pass sauce through a sieve, pour in white wine, leave in a warm place.

Mix spinach with chopped spices. Shape meat into small balls, roll them carefully in spinach and spice greens. Heat butter, fry meatballs at low heat so that butter does not overheat. Dip fried meatballs into sauce and simmer together about 5 minutes. Add sour cream to sauce before serving.

With these meatballs serve mashed potatoes, cooked rice, pasta.

Greece

LAMB MEATBALLS — "KEFTAIDAKIYA"

(for 8—10 persons)

1 kg lamb (or young beef)
2 onions
3 cloves of garlic
salt
pepper
1/2 bunch of dill
1/2 teaspoon thyme
2 slices of white bread
1 dl white wine
1 egg
flour
1—2 dl oil for frying
1 bigger lemon

Wash meat, wipe, cut into smaller pieces and grind. Chop onion and garlic finely, snip dill. Crush thyme. Pour wine over bread, then drain.

Add onion, garlic, salt, pepper, spices, bread and egg to meat, mix all well, work into a smooth meat mixture, leave to stand for a while.

Shape into small balls (the size of a walnut), roll in flour and fry in oil until nicely brown. Arrange fried meatballs on a bigger plate, garnish with dill, serve with slices of lemon. For easier serving, each meatball can be covered with a slice of lemon and a tiny sprig of dill and stuck with a toothpick, especially if served as an appetiser ("meze").

Yugoslavia

CUTLETS WITH POTATOES FROM BATCHKA

200—250 gr cooked or roast meat (left-over cooked or roast meat)
2—4 potatoes (peeled and boiled — 200—250 gr)
1 dl milk
salt
pepper
1/2 bunch of parsley
2 eggs
50 gr flour
100 gr breadcrumbs
about 2 dl oil for frying

Grind cooked or roast meat. Peel potatoes, boil, drain (use water for thick soup), mash, add hot milk, mix well until smooth and fluffy. Cool a little, mix with meat, add salt, pepper, chopped parsley and 1 egg.

Work into a smooth mixture, leave to stand a little, then shape into long "cutlets", roll in flour, then dip into beaten egg and finaly roll in breadcrumbs. Fry in heated oil on both sides until brown.

With these "cutlets" serve lettuce, beetroot salad, mixed salad, cucumber salad with drinking or thick yoghurt or some sauce (tomato, mushroom, or sour cream with horseradish).

Bulgaria

BREADED MEATBALLS

1/2 dl water or milk
500 gr ground young beef or mixed meat
1 onion
1 tablespoon chopped parsley
salt
pepper
2 eggs
100 gr breadcrumbs
2—3 dl oil for frying
50 gr butter for pouring over

Add finely chopped onion (or onion juice) to ground meat, water or milk, parsley, salt and pepper. Work into a smooth meat mixture, leave to stand in a cool place about 1 hour.

Shape rounded flat meat patties (1 cm thick) out of the meat mixture. Beat eggs well. Dip meatballs into beaten eggs, then coat with breadcrumbs. Fry in heated oil until nicely brown on both sides. Pour melted butter over them before serving.

With meatballs serve stewed vegetables (peas, string beans and others), potato salad, bean salad, mixed salad and the like.

Greece

MEATBALLS IN LEMON SAUCE

500 gr ground beef
1 onion
50 gr rice
2 tablespoons tomato purée (from tube)
1 tablespoon chopped parsley
2 eggs
salt
pepper
1 l bone stock or soup from meat cube

For sauce:
4 eggs
1/2 dl warm water or soup
juice of 1 lemon
salt

Add finely chopped onion to meat, as well as picked over and washed rice, tomato, parsley, eggs, salt and pepper. Work into a smooth meat mixture. Leave to stand for 1 hour in a cool place.

Shape into small balls. Heat soup and when it starts to boil slowly, dip in meatballs. Simmer for about 30 minutes.

Prepare the sauce in the meantime: beat eggs well, add warm water, whip over steam until thick, add lemon juice gradually, stirring all the time.

Take cooked meatballs out of the soup, drain, put into a dish and pour the sauce over.

With meatballs serve mashed potatoes or cooked pasta.

Turkey

VENISON PATTIES

150 gr butterfat
600 gr venison from leg
100 gr onion
salt
1 teaspoon red paprika pepper
1 egg
pepper
200 gr butterfat for frying

Wash venison, pour melted butterfat over and leave to stand about 24 hours. Then take meat out of butterfat (remove pieces off meat) mince (do not grind), salt, add finely chopped onion, pepper, egg. Mix all well and shape into small patties. Fry in heated butterfat (only in butterfat, as it takes over the flavour of game) until brown, arrange on a serving plate. Add red paprika pepper to butterfat and pour it over patties.

Albania

MEATBALLS ON ONION

1 onion
10 gr oil
500 gr ground young beef or mixed meat
1/2 bunch of parsley
1 bun or 100 gr bread
1 egg
salt
pepper
1 teaspoon red paprika pepper
4 onions
1,5 dl oil
3 tomatoes
2 dl soup from meat cube or bone stock
breadcrumbs as needed

Chop onion finely, cook a little in heated oil to soften, cool and add to ground meat. Chop parsley finely, put bun in water to soften, then drain and add to meat together with parsley. Add egg, salt and pepper. Work into a smooth meat mixture. Leave to stand in a cool place about 30—60 minutes.

In the meantime peel (4) onions, cut into thin slices, cook slowly in heated oil until soft and brown, sprinkle with red paprika pepper. Shape meat into smaller balls, roll in breadcrumbs. Turn

cooked onion into a fireproof dish or casserole. Arrange meatballs over it. Wash tomatoes, cut into rounds and place over meatballs. Pour soup from cube or bone stock over. Put into the oven preset at 175°C and bake until the liquid evaporates.

Serve with mashed potatoes, rice with parsley or the like.

Bulgaria

BALKAN MEATBALLS

500 gr ground mutton
1 bun, soaked and well drained (or the same quantity of bread)
pepper
2 eggs
2 cloves of garlic
1 teaspoon crushed mint leaves
oil for frying

Mix meat, bun, pepper, finely chopped or crushed garlic, mint and eggs and work well into a meat mixture. Leave it to stand for a while, then shape into smaller balls and fry on all sides in heated oil for about 15 minutes.

Arrange meatballs over lettuce leaves. Serve with the Balkan sauce.

Prepare the Balkan sauce in the following way:

2 fleshy red paprikas
1 fresh or pickled small hot pepper
2 onions
1—2 cloves of garlic
100—150 gr mayonnaise
pepper

Wash paprikas and the small hot pepper, remove seeds and cut into small cubes. Peel onion and chop finely. Crush and press garlic with some salt. Mix all with mayonnaise, add salt and pepper.

Lamb and mutton are the kinds of meat most often used in almost all the Balkan cuisines. As for vegetables, it is paprikas, aubergines, onion and garlic. The last two give the mayonnaise the specific "Balkan" flavour.

Turkey

MEATBALLS FROM IZMIR

500 gr lamb
100 gr white bread
1 dl lukewarm water or milk
juice of 2 onions
1 egg
salt
pepper
30 gr flour
2—3 dl oil for frying

For sauce:
750 gr fresh tomatoes
20 gr flour
juice of 1 lemon
salt
sugar

Wash meat, wipe, cut into smaller pieces and grind. Soak bread in lukewarm water (or milk), then drain. Peel onion, chop and squeeze. Mix ground meat with bread, onion juice, egg, salt and pepper. Work into a smooth meat mixture, leave in a cool place for about 1 hour.

In the meantime prepare the sauce: wash tomatoes, cut into smaller pieces, cook, then pass through a sieve, add salt, lemon juice and sugar to taste. Simmer.

Shape meat into small balls or sausages, roll in flour and fry in heated oil. When fried, dip into tomato sauce. Cook slowly together for a while.

With these meatballs serve mashed potatoes or cooked rice sprinkled with chopped parsley.

Bulgaria

COOKED-FRIED MEATBALLS

750 gr young mutton
1 onion
10 gr (1 tablespoon) oil
salt
1/2 bunch of parsley
1—1,5 l hot salted water
100 gr rice
4 eggs
100 gr breadcrumbs
2 dl oil for frying

Wash meat, cut into bigger pieces and grind. Wash rice, drain. Peel onion, chop finely, cook a little in heated oil, cool. Chop parsley finely. Mix meat with onion, parsley, add 1 egg, salt, rice. Work into a smooth meat mixture. Leave to stand in a cool place for 30—60 minutes.

Shape meat into smaller balls, plunge into the pot with heated salted water, cook at very low heat until rice is tender. When cooked, drain, dip into beaten eggs, coat with breadcrumbs and fry in heated oil until brown.

If served warm, add tomato sauce, mushroom sauce, gherkin sauce or the like, or some salad.

Yugoslavia

BALKAN MEAT PUDDING

600 gr young beef or lamb
3 onions
40 gr oil, salt
1 teaspoon red paprika pepper
1/2 bunch of parsley
150 gr rice
3 eggs
3/4 — 1 l milk
oil for the baking pan
4 dl thick yoghurt

Wash meat, wipe, cut and grind. Peel onion and chop finely. Wash and chop parsley. Pick over rice, wash and cook shortly, then drain.

Heat oil, add chopped parsley, cook slowly a little, add meat, cook together about 20 minutes. Add salt, pepper, drained rice, red paprika pepper, mix all. Whisk whites of egg stiffly, blend slowly into meat and rice, add parsley. Beat egg yolks well with milk.

Grease a fireproof dish or baking pan with oil, turn in the prepared mixture, level, pour beaten egg yolks and milk over. Preheat oven to 175—200°C, bake for about 40—50 minutes until nicely brown.

Serve thick yoghurt with this "pudding". It can be served as a warm appetiser or as the main dish with some cooked or stewed vegetable, lettuce, mixed salad, cucumbers and the like.

Roumania

MEAT LOAF

3 eggs
2 gherkins
100 gr white bread
1 dl milk
75 gr smoked bacon
750 gr mixed ground meat (or young beef)
40 gr flour
1,5 dl oil or lard
1 tablespoon mustard
1/2 bunch of parsley
some thyme
2 dl sour cream

Hard boil two eggs, shell and chop finely. Dice gherkins. Pour milk over bread to soften, then drain. Cut bacon into small cubes. Mix ground meat a little, add bread, eggs, gherkins, bacon, chopped parsley, some thyme, 1 egg, salt, mustard and pepper. Work into a smooth meat mixture. Leave in a cool place to stand about 30 minutes. Dust board with flour, turn the mixture on to it, shape into a nice loaf. Grease a baking pan or a fireproof dish, put the loaf in, pour heated oil over, bake in the oven preheated to 175—200°C. While baking, baste with juice to which some warm water can be added as needed. Towards

the end, pour whipped sour cream over, put back into the oven to brown. The loaf can be served warm or cold. If warm, serve with it stewed vegetables (carrots, string beans, new peas) or some salad (potato, cucumber, mixed).

If cold (as appetiser) serve with it sour cream sauce with horseradish, or some other savoury sauce.

Bulgaria

GROUND MEAT WITH YOGHURT

(for 6—8 persons)

1 dl oil or 75 gr lard
1 onion
1 kg ground beef
salt
pepper
1 tablespoon ground hot pepper
1 tablespoon chopped parsley
2 tablespoons tomato from tube
1 kg potatoes
3 eggs
1 tablespoon flour
3 dl drinking yoghurt

Peel onion, chop finely, cook slowly in heated oil or lard until soft, add meat, salt, pepper, ground paprika, parsley and tomato. Cook together about 30—40 minutes.

In the meantime peel potatoes, wash, cut into cubes, add to the meat, mix and cook together about 10 minutes.

Grease a fireproof dish or casserole, turn in meat with potatoes, pour some oil over as needed. Heat oven to 175—200°C, bake for about 30—40 minutes.

Beat eggs well, add flour and yoghurt, mix all well, pour over meat, put back into the oven until a nice brown crust is formed.

Serve with lettuce, beetroot salad with horseradish, mixed salad or with fresh vegetables (paprikas, tomatoes, cucumbers).

Yugoslavia

DUMPLINGS FROM DOLENSKA

250 gr beef or young beef from leg
250 gr veal from shoulder
250 gr pork from neck
100 gr white bread or 1 bun
1 dl milk or water
1 onion
2 cloves of garlic
2 eggs
salt
pepper
10 gr flour

Pancake batter:
1 egg
150 gr flour
1,5 dl milk
2,5 dl oil for frying

Wash meat and cut it into smaller pieces. Pour milk over bread, leave to soften, then drain and grind together with meat. Add finely chopped onion and garlic, egg yolks, salt and pepper. Work into a smooth meat mixture. Leave in a cool place to stand for 30—60 minutes. Shape into smaller balls (dumplings), roll in flour.

Prepare the batter: beat egg well, add flour and milk in turn, beating constantly. The batter must not have lumps.

Dip meatballs one by one into the pancake batter and fry in heated oil.

With the dumplings serve potato salad, bean salad with endive, young peas salad with sour cream and other more filling salads.

Bulgaria

GROUND MEAT ROLL

For roll:
600 gr mixed meat (young beef and pork)
100 gr white bread (1 slice)
1 dl milk or water
1 onion
1 tablespoon oil
1 tablespoon chopped parsley
salt
pepper
1 bigger or 2 smaller eggs
1 dl oil for baking

For filling:
75—100 gr smoked bacon
100 gr carrots
50 gr celery
1 tablespoon chopped parsley
1/2 tablespoon snipped dill
1/2 dl white wine
1 hard boiled egg
50 gr breadcrumbs
30 gr kachkaval or similar hard cheese

Wash meat, wipe, cut into smaller pieces and grind. Pour water or milk over bread, leave to soften, then drain. Chop onion finely, cook a little in some oil, cool and add to meat. Then add drained bread, parsley, salt, pepper and egg. Work into a smooth meat mixture, leave in a cool place to stand for 60 minutes.

In the meantime, scrape carrots and celery and dice. Cut bacon into smaller cubes, melt it in a frying pan, add vegetables, cook slowly until tender, salt, add chopped parsley and dill. Chop hard boiled eggs finely.

Sprinkle a bigger cloth with breadcrumbs, shape the meat mixture into a square 2 cm thick upon it. Place vegetables over the meat, then chopped hard boiled eggs over the vegetables and roll up. Grease a baking pan with oil, put the roll in, pour heated oil over and bake in the oven preset at 200 °C. Towards the end sprinkle the roll with grated cheese, put back into the oven until brown and the cheese melts. Add some flour to the juice from baking, mix flour in wine first, cook shortly, pour over the roll or serve separately. Cut roll into nice rounds.

If served warm add mashed potatoes, baked potatoes and some salad.

With cold roll, which can also be an appetiser, serve some savoury cold sauce or pickled vegetables.

Bulgaria

GROUND MEAT STEAKS WITH CHEESE

1 bun or 100 gr white bread
2 dl water
500—600 gr mixed ground meat
1 onion
1/2 bunch of parsley
100 gr younger kachkaval
2 eggs
salt
pepper
1 teaspoon red paprika pepper
1—2 dl oil for frying
2 bigger tomatoes
8 thin slices of younger kachkaval or similar cheese

Pour water over bun or bread, soften, then drain. Put meat into a deeper dish, add bun or bread. Peel onion, chop finely; wash parsley and chop finely; cut cheese into small cubes. Add onion, parsley, cheese, eggs, salt, pepper and red paprika pepper to meat. Mix all well. Leave to stand for a while in a cool place. Shape meat mixture into 8 smaller patties.

Heat oil, put prepared patties in, fry quickly on both sides, then cook on both sides about 8 minutes. Pour some of the oil from frying into a fireproof dish.

Wash tomatoes, peel, remove stalk ends, cut into rounds, place over patties, cover each with a thinner slice of cheese. Heat oven to 225 °C, bake patties until the cheese melts. With the "steaks" serve boiled potatoes and lettuce, or rice with butter and parsley, beetroot salad with horseradish or others.

CUTLETS AND STEAKS

Greece

LAMB BUTCHER'S WAY (Lamb baked with tomatoes)

900 gr — 1 kg lamb cutlets
salt
pepper ground from mill
500 gr fresh peeled tomatoes or canned ("pelati")
1 dl olive oil
1 lemon
1 dl oil

Wash cutlets, wipe, add salt and pepper, place into a greased baking pan or dish for baking meat, brush with oil and lemon juice, cover with tomatoes. Heat oven to 175 °C and bake about 90 minutes, basking meat occasionally.

Serve with cooked rice, some stewed vegetable of fresh salad.

Turkey

VEAL CUTLETS WITH YOGHURT

4 veal cutlets of 150 gr each
4 cloves of garlic
salt
40 gr oil (4 tablespoons)
some dried rosemary
pepper
juice of 1 lemon
1/2 dl drinking yoghurt
1 bunch of parsley
1 orange

Wash cutlets and wipe. Mix garlic with salt and crush. In a deeper bowl mix garlic, oil, rosemary, pepper and lemon juice. Spread this mixture over the cutlets, put them into a dish and leave in a cool place about 3 hours.

Heat the rest of oil, put in cutlets and fry about 5 minutes on each side, take out and leave in a warm place.

Mix the juice from frying with drinking yoghurt, add salt and pepper as needed, add half of the chopped parsley, keep in a warm place. Peel orange, cut into rounds, remove pips. Arrange cutlets on a deeper serving plate, garnish with orange rounds, pour sauce over them and sprinkle with chopped parsley. Serve right away.

With the cutlets serve cooked rice, vegetables of the season and lettuce.

Yugoslavia

BAKED PORK CHOPS

(for 6—8 persons)

1,5 kg pork chops in one piece
1 pork double offal membrane
salt
2—3 cloves of garlic
1 lemon
1 bayleaf
pepper
several sage leaves (optional)

Wash meat and the carcass membrane, wipe and salt. Chop garlic finely, add some grated lemon rind, bayleaf, a few sage leaves (optional) and pepper. Mix all well and brush the whole piece of meat with this mixture. Spread the offal membrane, place meat on it, fold all sides and wrap it well. Pour some water into an earthenware dish — djuvetch or a bigger fireproof dish, put meat in and bake for 1,5 to 2 hours in the oven preheated to 175—200°C. While baking often add some water and baste meat with the juice. When all is nicely brown, take out of the dish, cool a little and cut into nice pieces (chops). Arrange them on a warmed plate and pour over with the juice from the baking dish (extra juice can be served separately).

With the chops serve baked potatoes, mashed potatoes, boiled rice with parsley, stewed cabbage and pickles from turshiya (ghirkins, paprikas or mixed salad).

Pork prepared this way is usually associated with late fall and early winter, when in all parts of Yugoslavia meat is being prepared for winter and when on the day when hogs are slaughtered, friends, relatives and acquaintances are invited to lunch or dinner.

Greece

COOKED LAMB SHINS

(for 6 persons)

1,5—2 kg lamb shins
1 onion
1 carrot
1 sprig of celery
salt
5—6 peppercorns
1 bayleaf
2 tablespoons maize flour
3 eggs
juice of 2 lemons
1/2 bunch of parsley

Clean shins, wash, place in a deep enough pan, pour in 1,5 l water and simmer about 60—90 minutes. When it boils, add peeled onion, carrot, celery, salt, peppercorns and bayleaf. Cover and simmer until meat separates from the bones. Pass cooked vegetables through a sieve. Remove meat from bones, add it to vegetable sauce. Mix maize flour with cold water, pour into the sauce and cook slowly about 10 minutes, stirring all the time. Draw aside.

Separate eggs, add about 1,5 dl of sauce to egg yolks, stirring, add lemon juice. Then add this, stirring, to meat and sauce and simmer until the sauce is thick. It must not be cooked any more, as egg yolks would turn into lumbs which make sauce unattractive. Sprinkle with chopped parsley in the end.

Bulgaria

MUTTON IN YOGHURT

1 kg mutton without bones
salt
50 gr ground poppy seed
1/2—3/4 l drinking yoghurt
1 sprig coriander
4 cloves of garlic
1/2 teaspoon cinnamon
2—3 cloves
250 gr onion
juice of 1 lemon
1 dl oil

Wash meat, wipe, cut into bigger pieces, salt, arrange in a deeper dish, pour over with drinking yoghurt, leave to stand about 20—30 minutes. Then put up to cook and simmer until tender. In the meantime crush coriander, garlic, cloves, add cinnemon and poppy seed. Heat oil, add finely chopped onion, cook slowly to soften, add all the spices, simmer together with onion about 10 minutes. Add all to meat, stew at medium heat until the meat is quite tender, mix in lemon juice and serve warm, with rice and some vegetable of the season.

Greece

LEG OF LAMB IN PARCHMENT

750 gr leg of lamb
3 cloves of garlic
1 lemon
4 tablespoons freshly chopped parsley and dill
1 tablespoon mustard
1 teaspoon ground pepper
1/2 teaspoon allspice
salt
1 tablespoon edible starch
1 teaspoon dried mint

Peel garlic and cut into strips. Grate some lemon rind, then cut lemon into rounds. Mix chopped parsley and dill with mustard, pepper, lemon rind, allspice and salt.

Wash meat and wipe well. Pierce holes in it with a sharp knife, fill them with prepared mixture of spices and cork with garlic. Spread a bigger piece of parchment (tin foil will also do), brush with oil, place the prepared leg on it, arrange lemon rounds over, wrap up, put into another ungreased piece of parchment (if foil is used, one is enough).

Preheat oven to 200°C and bake for

about 90 minutes. When done, unwrap parchment carefully, put meat in a warm place. Mix juice from the pan with some water, heat, add starch dissolved in some cold water, cook about 5 minutes, add mint.

Cut meat into nice slices, pour sauce over. Serve with some salad (lettuce, beetroot, shredded cabbage and others).

Roumania

STEAKS IN MUSHROOM SAUCE

(for 6 persons)

750 gr pork steaks cut from leg (6 steaks)
salt
pepper
40 gr flour
6 paprikas
1 dl oil
3 cloves of garlic
250 gr tomatoes
300 gr fresh mushrooms (button mushrooms, ceps or similar)
1—2 dl warm water

Wash meat, wipe, cut into nice steaks, pound them a little with a mallet, sprinkle with salt and pepper and leave for a while. Wash paprikas, wipe and dry fry, skin and cut into strips, add salt and pepper.

Heat oil, add chopped garlic, fry it a little, put in prepared steaks, fry on both sides to brown, take out and put in a warm place. Put peeled and chopped tomatoes into the same oil, cook until tender, then add trimmed and thinly sliced mushrooms, simmer until all is tender.

Put meat back into the vegetables, add some warm water if needed, simmer together until tender. Take out meat, place in a warmed deeper dish, pour sauce over, arrange stripped paprikas on top.

Serve with mashed potatoes, cooked rice etc.

Bulgaria

LAMB WITH YOGHURT

1/2 young lamb or one whole leg of lamb
salt
pepper, 2 dl oil
3/4 l sheep thick yoghurt
4 eggs
1 teaspoon red paprika pepper
1—2 dl warm water

Wash meat and wipe. Mix salt and pepper and rub meat with them, pour oil or melted lard over, put into a baking pan or an earthenware dish, pour in some water. Bake in the oven preheated to 175—200°C. While baking baste with juice and add warm water at times if needed.

When meat is tender and nicely brown, take it out and pour over with the following: beat well thick yoghurt with egg yolks, add salt, pepper, red paprika pepper and stiffly whisked whites of eggs. Mix all slowly, pour oven the meat, put back into the oven and bake until the sauce is thick and brown. Serve in the dish in which it was baked, and cut into pieces when at the table. Each piece is poured over with the yoghurt sauce on the plate.

Yugoslavia

ROAST SUCKLING PIG

(for a bigger company)

1 suckling pig of 5—7 kg
salt
oil or lard for brushing over
1 bottle ale
100 gr smoked bacon
1 big walnut in shell

Wash pig well, drain and wipe with a clean cloth. Rub well with salt only the inside, turn the pig to its back, leave to stand that way for at least 1 hour. The mouth should be open with a walnut put in, because the head bakes more easily that way. If the pig is smaller, put a beer bottle inside the carcass (greased first with oil or lard). If the pig is bigger, a bottle of 1 liter is needed. Truss the carcass opening with fine string.

Four oiled small wooden bars should be put crossways in the baking pan about 5 cm broad and long enough to go to the edges of the pan. Their purpose is to make the pig "kneel" and not touch the baking pan. Brush wiped pig with oil or lard, put into the oven preheated to 175°C. While baking, brush with bacon dipped in ale at times. Oiled sachets made of tin foil should be put over the ears, as they tend to burn. Roast at medium heat for 3—4 hours, depending on the size of the pig. When it is done, a cut should be made behind the head (on the neck) and the pig left in the oven for 5—10 more minutes. Take out of the oven, cool a little, then cut off the head, remove string and take out the bottle. Cut the pig with a sharp knife, or with meat scissors, into two halves, and then into nice smaller pieces.

Serve warm or cold with various kinds of salads.

Albania

VEAL ESCALOPS ALBANIAN WAY

6—8 veal escalopes
salt
pepper
2 tablespoons flour
100 gr butter or
1 dl oil
2 dl white wine
1/2 teaspoon rosemary leaves

Wash meat, wipe well, sprinkle with salt and pepper. Roll in flour and fry in heated butter or oil. When fried, place them in a fireproof dish or a corresponding frying pan, pour the juice left from frying over them, pour in wine, add rosemary. Cook slowly at low heat until the meat is tender. Serve in the same dish.

With these escalopes serve cooked rice or potatoes, or some mixed vegetables.

Turkey

STUFFED ROAST LAMB

(for 10 persons)

1 young lamb for roasting
250—300 gr rice
lamb offal
(liver, kidneys, heart, lungs)
1 bunch of root vegetables
1 bunch of parsley
1 sprig of celery
salt
pepper
1 lamb double offal membrane
1—2 dl oil
1—2 dl warm water

Wash lamb well, wipe and rub with salt. Leave to stand for a while. Wash lamb offal, cook with scraped roots. When soft, drain them and cut into smaller strips or pieces. Take out vegetables, also cut and mix with offal. Pick over rice, wash and boil a little, add to offal. Fry all in some heated oil, add salt, pepper, finely chopped parsley and celery leaf. Mix well, ladle in some of the offal soup. Spread out lamb offal membrane, arrange the filling and roll up. Insert the stuffing prepared this way into the lamb caracass, pour in some soup and truss with fine string or thread, or join with toothpicks. Grease a bigger tepsiya with oil, place in the lamb, brush with oil. Bake in the oven preheated to 175—200°C. Baste often while baking, and add some warm water as needed.

A young kid is prepared in the same way. Instead of rice, crumbled pogatcha or dough dry fried on top the stove can be used in the stuffing.

Greece

LAMB PEASANTS' WAY

(for 6 persons)

6 bigger lamb cutlets or (6 nice escalopes from leg)
2 dl melted butter (or oil)
450 gr canned peas
12 small new potatoes
6 peeled tomatoes
6 thinner (rectangular) slices of kachkaval or similar cheese
6 thinner layers of dough for the pie
piece of parchment (or tin foil)
1/2 dl oil
1/2 bunch of parsley
salt
pepper

Wash cutlets, wipe. Heat 3 tablespoons butter, add cutlets in and half fry them.

Drain canned peas. Peel potatoes, wash and wipe, fry in 2—3 tablespoons of butter, take out. Cook tomatoes in the same butter.

Brush dough layers with butter, fold each over and brush with butter again. On each dough layer place 1 cutlet, 1—2 spoonfuls of peas, 2 potatoes, 1 tomato. Cover all with a slice of cheese, add salt, pepper and some chopped parsley. Fold like a small parcel, place in a greased baking pan, sprinkle each roll with some butter. Cover the pan with parchment or tin foil. Heat oven to 175°C and bake about 1 hour.

Yugoslavia

BALKAN STEAKS

For tomato sauce:
500 gr tomatoes
2 onions (80 gr)
2 cloves of garlic
50 gr (5 tablespoons) oil
salt, pepper
a pinch of oregano

For rice:
200 gr rice
1 l water
salt

For steaks:
4 veal steaks of 150 gr each
salt
pepper
1—2 teaspoons mild red paprika pepper
30 gr butter or oil
oil or butter for greasing
60—75 gr grated cheese (kachkaval, Parmesan or similar)
20 gr butter

Wash tomatoes, remove stalk ends and cut into rounds. Chop finely onion and garlic. Heat oil, add onion, cook shortly, then add garlic and tomatoes. Cook in its own juice about 5 minutes, add salt, pepper, oregano. Simmer for about 20—25 minutes. Pass through a sieve, return to the same pan and cook until the sauce is rather thick.

Wash rice and drain. Simmer in slightly salted water about 10 minutes.

Wash meat, wipe, rub well with salt, pepper and read paprika pepper. Heat butter or oil, fry steaks about 5 minutes on both sides.

Grease a fireproof dish with butter or oil, turn in half of the rice, put half of the sauce over it, place 2 steaks on top and sprinkle with half the grated cheese. Repeat with the rest, so that the last layer is meat. Cut thin slices of butter over it. Heat oven to 220°C and bake about 30 minutes. Serve with lettuce, cucumber salad etc.

POULTRY

Turkey

FRIED CHICKENS

2 poussins of 800 gr each
salt
2 teaspoons red paprika pepper
1 teaspoon pepper

For marinade:
20 gr (2 tablespoons) oil
40 gr (4 tablespoons) sour cream
15 gr (2 tablespoons) lemon juice
1 tablespoon coriander
1 teaspoon cardamom
1/2—3/4 l oil for frying

Wash chickens inside and outside well, drain and wipe. Joint into 8—10 nice pieces. Mix salt, red paprika pepper and pepper (in a plate), roll pieces of chicken in the mixture, arrange them in some rather shallow dish. Beat well oil, sour cream and lemon juice, pour over chicken, sprinkle with coriander and cardamom. Leave to stand like that about 30—40 minutes. Turn now and then.

Take out of marinade, drain well. Heat oil, put pieces of chicken in and fry on both sides about 15 minutes. Arrange fried pieces on a warmed plate.

With fried chickens serve cooked rice with parsley and lettuce, stewed vegetables (carrot, peas or mixed) and cucumber salad or the like.

Greece

CHICKEN WITH OLIVES

1 bigger chicken for roasting
50 gr butter
30 gr flour
4—5 dl warm water
salt
pepper
1/2 bunch of parsley
1/2 teaspoons thyme
1 bayleaf
200 gr olives without stones

Wash chicken, wipe, salt well inside and outside. Heat butter. Put chicken in a greased baking pan, pour butter over it. Heat oven to 175—200°C and bake the chicken, basting it often. When done and nicely brown on all sides, take it out and leave in a warm place.

Melt butter, add flour, fry until slightly brown, pour in some cold, then some warm water, cook a little, add chopped parsley, thyme and bayleaf. Simmer for about 5—10 minutes, add olives, mix.

Joint chicken into 6—8 nice pieces, arrange on a deeper plate, pour sauce with olives over them.

With chicken serve rice with parsley, pasta, salad.

Yugoslavia

"TIPSY" CHICKEN

1 spring chicken of about 1 kg
100—150 gr smoked bacon
1 dl white wine
1—2 dl sour cream
salt
1—2 dl warm water

Wash chicken in and out, wipe and joint into nice pieces. Line the bottom of a deeper (preferably fireproof) dish with thin rashers of smoked bacon. Place pieces of salted chicken over, skin downwards, cook slowly at low heat. When the bottom part is brown, turn round, pour white wine over and continue cooking slowly. Add some warm water if needed. Towards the end, just before serving, pour over sour cream, cook on for a short while.

Arrange chicken in a dish, pour the juice it was cooked in over the meat.

Serve with pasta (macaroni, noodles) or with mashed potatoes. "Tipsy" chicken is a specialty from Vojvodina, but is more and more often prepared in other parts of Yugoslavia too.

Turkey

CHICKEN WITH PAPRIKAS

1 spring chicken for roasting of about 1,25 kg
50 gr butter or margarine
60 gr (6 tablespoons) oil
pepper
salt
2—3 dl warm water
5 bigger red and green paprikas
2 bigger cloves of garlic
1 bayleaf
1/2 teaspoon thyme
1 tablespoon red paprika pepper
2 dl sour cream

Wash chicken, wipe and salt. Heat butter or margarine, put the chicken into the greased baking pan, pour over with heated butter (or margarine). Bake in the oven preheated to 200°C, baste while baking and add some warm water to the juice at times.

Wash paprikas, seed and core, cut into equal strips. Blanch shortly (3—4 minutes). Peel garlic and chop finely. Heat oil, add paprikas, garlic, bayleaf, thyme and pepper. Simmer covered for about 20 minutes.

When done, take the chicken out of the pan, pour the juice out. Add to it red

paprika pepper mixed with some water, as well as the sour cream. Cook shortly.

Joint roast chicken into nice pieces. Arrange on a deeper plate and put paprikas over them. Serve the sauce separately. Best accompaniment is cooked or stewed rice with parsley.

Bulgaria

CHICKEN WITH RICE

(for 5—6 persons)

1 roaster (about 1,5—1,75 kg)
salt, pepper
1—2 dl warm water
150 gr butter (margarine or oil)
100 gr skinned almonds
300 gr rice
1/2—3/4 l chicken giblets soup
1/2 bunch of parsley

Separate wings, neck, legs, gizzard, heart and liver and cook in slightly salted water. Rub chicken in and out with salt and pepper, brush with butter (50 gr). Bake in the oven preheated to

175—200 °C. While baking baste with the juice from time to time, adding some warm water to it. Take roast chicken out of the pan. Heat the rest of butter, add almonds, fry, stirring, until lightly brown, add picked over and washed rice, fry it shortly, barely cover with giblets soup, add juice from baking, cover and broil in the oven heated to 175 °C until tender and the liquid evaporates. Check at times whether some more warm water or soup should be added.

Joint chicken into nice pieces, arrange them on a long plate, put rice balls around.

Serve with some salad (lettuce, mixed, beetroot with horseradish and others).

Yugoslavia

CHICKEN IN KAYMAK

1 spring chicken (of about 1,5 kg)
salt
50 gr butter (lard or oil)
1—2 dl warm water
200 gr younger kaymak, 1 dl sour cream
2—3 cloves of garlic
lemon juice (optional)

Wash chicken, wipe and salt well in and out. Grease a bigger and deeper pan with oil, put in the prepared chicken, pour heated butter or oil over it. Fry on all sides until nicely browned. Pour in warm water, cover and stew in the juice. While stewing baste occasionally and add more water as needed. When cooked, joint into 6—8 pieces.

Heat kaymak in a fireproof or other dish, mixed first with sour cream, melt it, add some juice from the pan in which the chicken was cooked, salt as needed, add finely chopped or crushed garlic and lemon juice. Dip pieces of chicken into this sauce, pour the sauce over each piece with a spoon, cook shortly together.

With this chicken serve some boiled vegetable (cauliflower, potatoes, young peas) or some pasta.

Greece

CHICKEN FROM CRETE

1 spring chicken of 1—1,25 kg

For brine:
4 cloves of garlic
salt
40 gr olive oil (4 tablespoons)
1 tablespoon lemon juice
1 teaspoon crushed rosemary
1 small head of lettuce

Wash chicken well in and out, wipe.

Peel garlic and crush well with salt, add oil and lemon juice, mix all well. Brush chicken with this mixture inside and outside, then leave to stand in a cool place for 30—40 minutes.

In the meantime prepare the oven spit and heat the oven to 175 °C. Spit roast the chicken in the oven about 60 minutes. Baste from time to time with the prepared brine. Towards the end sprinkle with rosemary.

Wash lettuce, drain, arrange on a plate and put jointed chicken over it.

On the island of Crete the peasants roast chicken on the spit over charcoal or dry grapevine twigs. But marinaded chicken spit roasted in the oven is also delicious.

Roumania

CHICKEN IN CREAM

(for 5 persons)

1 spring chicken of about 1,5 kg
1 bunch of root vegetables
peppercorns
30 gr flour
salt
pepper
1 teaspoon red paprika pepper (hot if desired)
3—4 dl double cream
30 gr butter or oil

Wash chicken, joint into 4—6 pieces, barely cover with salted water. Bring to the boil, add roots (carrot, parsley root, celery, kohlrabi) and a few peppercorns. Simmer until tender. Take out and strain soup.

Pass soup vegetables through a sieve. Heat butter, add flour, fry to brown a little, add red paprika pepper, pour in some cold water, then about 4—5 dl soup, add puréed vegetables, simmer for about 10 minutes, add salt and pepper to taste. Arrange pieces of chicken on a deeper plate. Whip double cream, add some red paprika pepper. Add about 1 dl of cream to vegetable sauce, mix and pour over the chicken. Serve the rest of cream separately with the chicken.

As accompaniment serve rice, pasta or some stewed vegetable of the season.

Greece

CHICKEN WITH AUBERGINES AND PAPRIKAS

(for 5—6 persons)

1 bigger spring chicken (about 1,5 kg)
salt
50 gr lard
2—3 smaller aubergines
2—3 paprikas
1 kg potatoes
1 dl sour cream

Wash chicken, drain well, rub with salt in and out. Place the chicken in a greased bigger earthenware casserole, pour heated lard over it. Wash aubergines, cut into rounds, salt, leave to stand about 30 minutes, rinse with cold water, drain and arrange at one end of the casserole. Put washed, cored paprikas cut into rounds at the opposite end. Heat oven to 175—200°C, put in chicken with vegetables and bake. While baking, baste often and turn the chicken round to brown on all sides.

When chicken is nearly tender, arrange round it peeled potatoes cut into slices, put back into the oven and bake on. Towards the end, when chicken and potatoes are baked, pour sour cream over them, leave in the oven for a short while to brown.

Serve in the same casserole with some fresh-tasting salad (lettuce, tomatoes and the like).

Bulgaria

CHICKEN WITH SWEETCORN

(for 5 persons)

1 spring chicken for roasting of about 1,25 kg
40 gr oil or butter
salt
pepper
400 gr cooked sweetcorn (or canned)

For sauce:
30 gr (3 tablespoons) oil or melted butter
30 gr (2 tablespoons) flour
1/8 l milk
1/8 l sour cream
2 eggs
some nutmeg
30 gr breadcrumbs
20 gr butter (margarine)

Wash chicken well, wipe and joint.

Heat oil or butter (in a fireproof dish preferably), add pieces of chicken. Fry on all sides to get nicely brown, add salt and pepper, add sweetcorn and the liquid (4—5 tablespoons) from cooking or canning, draw aside.

Heat oil or butter for the sauce, add flour, fry, stirring, until lightly brown, add cold milk, simmer about 5 minutes. Whip sour cream with egg yolks, salt, pepper and nutmeg, add to the sauce, but do not cook it any more. Whisk whites of egg stiffly, stir slowly into the sauce. Pour the sauce over the chicken and sweetcorn, sprinkle with breadcrumbs and cover with thin slices of butter or margarine. Heat the oven to 200°C, bake for about 45 minutes.

With the chicken serve boiled Brussels sprouts, cauliflower or mashed potatoes.

Roumania

CHICKEN WITH MUSHROOMS

1 spring chicken of about 1 kg
salt, pepper
50 gr butter or margarine
1 dl warm water
2 dl sour cream
2 egg yolks

For mushrooms:
50 gr butter
200—250 gr fresh mushrooms (button mushrooms, ceps or similar)
pepper
1/2 bunch of parsley

Wash chicken, wipe, sprinkle with salt and pepper in and out, brush with softened butter (or margarine), put into a greased baking pan. Bake in the oven preheated to 200°C about 60 minutes. While baking, add some warm water at times and baste.

When done, pour the juice out and put chicken in a warm place. Strain juice, add egg yolks mixed with sour cream, beat over steam until thick, add salt and pepper as needed.

Heat butter, add trimmed mushrooms, washed and thinly sliced, cook slowly. When cooked, add salt, pepper and chopped parsley.

Joint chicken, arrange on a bigger plate, surround with stewed mushrooms. Serve the sauce separately.

Albania

HEN WITH COURGETTES AND AUBERGINES

(for 6—7 persons)

1 bigger hen — boiler (1,5—1,8 kg)
100 gr butterfat (oil or margarine)
4 onions
2 cloves of garlic
200 gr smoked pork
2 tablespoons finely chopped parsley
1/2 teaspoon thyme
1 bayleaf
4 tomatoes
3 paprikas
salt
pepper
1 dl red wine
1—2 dl warm water
4 courgettes
4 aubergines
1 dl oil

Wash hen, wipe, cut into nice pieces. Heat butterfat, add meat, fry to brown, then add finely chopped onion and garlic, smoked pork cut into cubes, parsley, thyme, bayleaf, washed and peeled tomatoes cut into smaller pieces, washed and cored paprikas cut into strips. Add

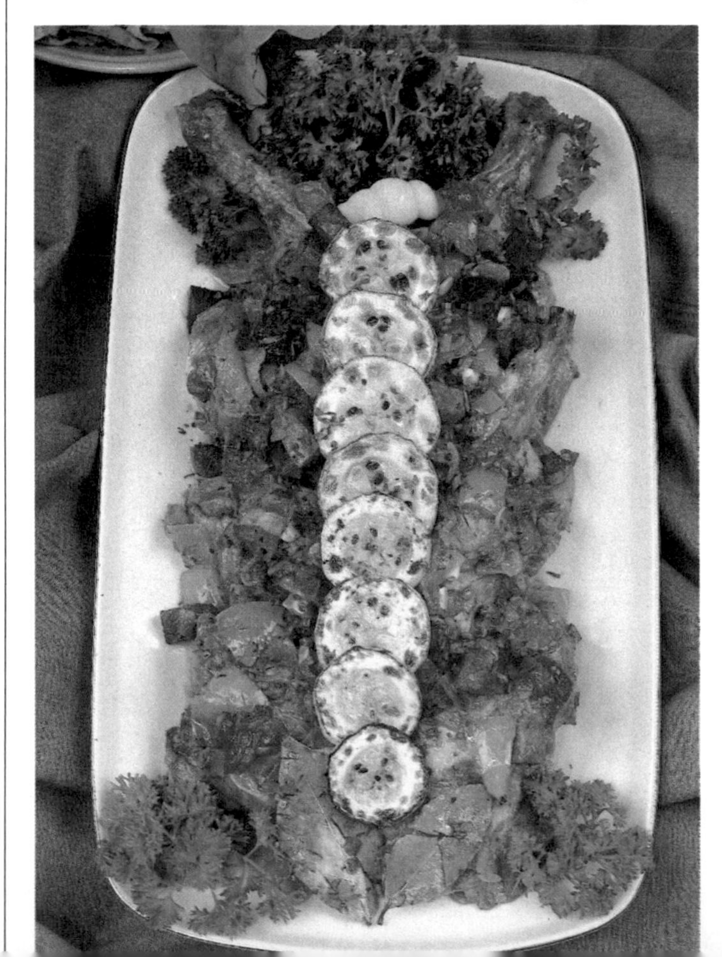

salt and pepper and cook slowly about 10 minutes, add wine and warm water as needed.

Cover and simmer.

In the meantime peel aubergines, cut into rounds, salt, leave to stand about 30 minutes, then rinse with cold water and wipe. Peel courgettes, cut into rounds, salt. Fry aubergines and courgettes in oil, add to hen meat and vegetables, simmer covered until meat is quite tender.

When cooked, sprinkle with chopped parsley and serve warm.

Roumania

DUCK WITH MUSHROOMS

(for 5 persons)

50 gr lard or oil
3 onions
100 gr fresh mushrooms (button mushrooms, ceps or similar)
1 young duck of about 1,25 kg
1 dl white wine
2—4 dl soup from meat cube
1 tablespoon tomato purée
salt
pepper
3 gherkins

Heat lard or oil, add finely chopped onion. Cook at low heat until soft, then add trimmed, washed and sliced mushrooms, cook slowly together.

Wash duck, wipe, cut into nice pieces (4—6), salt, add to onion and mushrooms. Cook together for a while, then pour in wine, soup from meat cube and diluted tomato purée, add salt, pepper and diced gherkins. Shake well, cover and simmer until meat is tender.

When the duck is cooked, the sauce can be thickened with a spoonful of flour mixed with some cold water, then cooked for 10 more minutes.

Arrange duck on a serving plate, pour some sauce (gravy) over and serve the rest separately. Best accompaniments are mashed potatoes, rice with parsley or pasta.

Turkey

TURKISH STUFFED CHICKEN

(for 5—6 persons)

1 spring chicken of about 1,25—1,5 kg

For stuffing:
25 gr raisins
50 gr pistachios, 10 gr butter
125 gr rice, salt
white pepper
1/2 teaspoon ground cinnamon
1/2 teaspoon ground clove, 3/8 l water
1—1,5 dl soup from meat cube
50 gr (5 tablespoons) oil

Wash chicken, drain and wipe. Put aside liver and heart. Pour hot water over raisins, leave to stand 5 minutes, then drain. Pour hot water over pistachios too, leave to stand 5 minutes, then peel, dry a little and chop a bit more crudely.

Wash liver and heart, wipe, cut into small pieces. Heat butter, add giblets, fry about 2 minutes, stirring all the time. Pick over rice, wash and drain well. Put raisins, pistachios, rice and spices into a pot, add giblets, pour in water, mix and cook shortly, then leave at very low heat for rice to swell.

Rub chicken with salt in and out, stuff with the prepared mixture, truss or stick with toothpicks. Heat oil in a bigger casserole, put in the chicken, fry it on all sides first to brown, then pour in soup from meat cube, cover and stew until tender.

When done, remove thread or toothpicks, joint it nicely and serve warm with tomato salad, paprika salad, cucumber salad or others.

Chicken stuffed this way can also be spit or oven roasted. In that case, before stuffing, keep it for a while in the marinade of olive oil, lemon juice and crushed garlic.

Albania

CHICKEN WITH WALNUTS

1 chicken
salt, pepper
50 gr oil
500 gr walnuts
40 gr butter
20 gr flour
2 cloves of garlic

Pluck and draw chicken, wash, wipe, rub with salt and pepper. Grease a fireproof dish with oil, put in chicken, pour the rest of oil over. Bake in the oven preheated to 175 °C basting occasionally. Add some more water as needed.

Grind walnuts. Heat butter, add flour, fry it a little, pour in some cold water, then the juice from baking, walnuts and crushed garlic. Cook together about 5 minutes.

Cut chicken into nice pieces, pour the sauce over and cook shortly until the sauce thickens. Serve at once with rice and some fresh-tasting salad.

Bulgaria

CHICKEN WITH DOUGH PELLETS

(for 4—6 persons)

1 spring chicken of about 1—1,5 kg
2 l hot water
1 bunch of root vegetables
salt, 1 dl oil
1 onion
2 fresh big paprikas
1 teaspoon ground dried red paprika
250 gr flour
3 eggs
2—3 tablespoons milk
50 gr butter
2 dl thick yoghurt or sour cream

Wash chicken, joint, pour hot water over it and bring to the boil. Then add cleaned roots and salt. Simmer until meat is nearly tender. Strain soup and keep meat in a warm place.

Sift flour, make a well in the center, add 2 eggs, salt and some milk. Knead into a harder dough, leave to stand for about 10—15 minutes, then grate it and dry a little.

Heat oil, add finely chopped onion, cook slowly a little, then add cored fresh paprikas cut into strips, ground paprika and salt. Cook slowly until all is tender and the liquid reduces. Add dough pellets, fry a little, then pour in chicken soup. Stew all about 15—20 minutes. Grease a fireproof dish or an enamelled casserole with oil, turn in dough pellets with vegetables, place cooked meat on top, pour melted butter over, add more soup if needed. Bake in the oven preheated to 175—200 °C. Towards the end pour over with 1 egg beaten with sour cream, bake on until nicely brown and tender.

Serve with some salad.

Roumania

CHICKEN WITH APRICOTS

(for 4—6 persons)

1 bigger chicken or hen (1—1,5 kg)
1 dl oil
1 onion
20 gr flour
1/2 l warm water
10 gr edible starch
500 gr apricots
1 teaspoon sugar
salt
pepper (white if possible)

Wash chicken, wipe and cut into 4—6 pieces. Heat oil in a bigger pan, add meat, fry on all sides to brown, then take out. Add finely chopped onion to the same oil, cook slowly until soft and light brown. Add flour, fry it a little stirring all the time, add a glass of cold water, then warm water. Add starch diluted with cold water, put in washed and halved apricots (without stones), add sugar and salt. Simmer for a while, add fried chicken meat, cover, stew at low heat until tender.

Cooked rice with butter is usually served with this dish.

Yugoslavia

DUCK WITH CABBAGE

300 gr onion
60 gr (6 tablespoons) oil
salt
1 smaller duck (about 1,25 kg)
1/2 l soup from meat cube
1 tablespoon red paprika pepper
1 head (about 1,5 kg) of fresh cabbage
pepper

Chop onion finely, put into heated oil, cook slowly until soft and slightly brown.

Wash duck, wipe and cut into nice pieces, salt, add to onion, cook slowly together, add some warm soup from meat cube, cover and simmer until soup evaporates. Then add red paprika pepper, mix, pour in enough soup from cube to cover all, simmer until the meat is tender.

Remove any discoloured leaves of cabbage, wash, pour over with hot water, leave in it about 10 minutes, then drain, cool and quarter. Grease a fireproof dish or an earthenware casserole with lard, turn in cabbage, then duck meat over it. Pour the juice from stewing over it and bake in the oven preset at 200 °C for about 60 minutes.

With duck prepared this way serve boiled potatoes sprinkled with parsley.

Yugoslavia

CHICKEN STEW WITH SAUCE

(for 5—6 persons)

For stew:
4 onions
50 gr lard or oil
some red paprika pepper
1 chicken (of medium size)
salt
1—2 dl warm water

For sauce:
3 eggs
1/2 dl sour cream (about 5 tablespoons)
30 gr flour (3 levelled tablespoons)

Chop onion finely and cook slowly in heated oil or lard until brown and soft, sprinkle with red paprika pepper, then add jointed chicken, salt, stew covered in its own juice about 25 minutes, then pour in water gradually until meat is tender.

Place chicken pieces in a fireproof dish together with the juice, level it and pour the following sauce over:

beat well egg yolks and sour cream. Whisk whites of egg stiffly and add slowly to egg yolks and cream, stirring constantly, then blend in flour. Mix all carefully and pour over the stew. Bake in the oven preset at 200 °C until nicely brown.

Serve in the same dish with some fresh-tasting salad.

Turkey

CHICKEN PUDDING

1 poussin of about 800 gr
salt
pepper
1 teaspoon red paprika pepper
50 gr oil
75 gr raisins
3 dl hot water
8 thinner slices of white bread
50 gr butter or margarine
2 oranges
6 tomatoes
50 gr chopped almonds
1 tablespoon edible starch (or flour)
2 eggs
3 dl milk
2—3 cloves of garlic

Wash chicken, wipe, joint into nice pieces, rub with salt, pepper and red paprika pepper. Heat oil in a frying pan, add meat, fry on all sides until golden-brown, then cover and stew about 30 minutes. Turn at times while stewing.

In the meantime clean raisins, scald with hot water and leave to stand about 10 minutes to swell, then drain.

Remove crust from slices of bread, fry in heated butter to brown a little. Peel oranges, remove white underskin, cut into thinner rounds. Wash tomatoes, remove stalk ends, peel and cut into rounds.

Remove bones from stewed chicken.

Grease a fireproof casserole with oil, line with slices of bread, place over pieces of chicken, sprinkle with half the almonds, place over orange rounds, sprinkle with the rest of almonds, cover with tomato rounds.

Beat well starch or flour with some cold milk, pour in the rest of milk, add well beaten eggs, finely chopped garlic, salt and pepper. Pour this mixture over the chicken pudding, cover and broil in the oven preset at 200°C for 50—60 minutes. After 40 minutes take off lid and bake until brown. Serve warm.

Yugoslavia

ROAST TURKEY AND SAUERKRAUT

(for 6—8 persons)

1 young turkey
salt
juice of 1 lemon
100 gr lard
1 onion
1,5 kg shredded pickled cabbage
2 dl warm water
2 cloves of garlic
1 bayleaf
1 teaspoon red paprika pepper
pepper

Wash turkey and wipe well, rub with salt, spray with lemon juice, brush with lard and leave to stand for several hours in a cool place. Then place in a deeper baking pan (or a special casserole for baking meat) pour in about 2—3 dl water.

Bake in the oven preheated to 175—200 °C. While baking, often baste with juice. If the turkey is rather fat, prick with a fork when baking, so that extra fat can come out more easily.

If sauerkraut is too sour, rinse it shortly with cold water and drain well. Heat lard, add finely chopped onion, cook slowly to soften, add pickled cabbage, pour in warm water, mix and cook covered. Stir occasionally. When cabbage is half cooked, add finely chopped garlic, bayleaf, red paprika pepper and pepper.

When turkey is nearly done, take it out, put in a warm place. Pour out extra fat from the pan, turn in stewed cabbage, level, place the turkey over it. Bake on together until tender and the cabbage light brown.

Carve the turkey into nice pieces. Put sauerkraut in the middle of the serving plate and arrange pieces of turkey around. Extra sauerkraut can be served separately.

Roast turkey and sauerkraut ("podvarak") is the specialty of traditional Serbian cuisine, particularly in the vicinity of the city of Svetozarevo in Serbia, where turkeys well — known for the quality of their meat are bred.

Yugoslavia

GOOSE IN CREAM SAUCE

1 young goose
100—150 gr smoked bacon
50 gr lard or oil
1 bayleaf
a few rosemary leaves
juice of 1 bigger lemon
2—3 dl sour cream
30 gr flour, salt

Wash goose well, drip and wipe, rub with salt, sprinkle with lemon juice, insert into it small chunks of bacon or wrap it in rashers of bacon. (Several small apples and chopped bacon can be put into the carcass.)

Put the prepared goose into a corresponding dish. It is best to use the special deep casserole with a lid for broiling bigger pieces of meat or poultry. Pour into it half of the lard or oil mixed with water, add bayleaf and rosemary. Bake in the oven preheated to 175—200 °C. While baking baste often and abundantly with juice, adding some water as needed.

Take the roast goose out of the casserole, leave in a warm place. Strain juice from baking.

In the rest of lard fry flour, pour in some cold water, then the strained juice, simmer for 10—15 minutes, add sour cream and lemon juice, mix well.

Cut goose into nice pieces, arrange on a long, deeper plate, pour the sauce over. Serve the rest of sauce separately.

With goose prepared this way various kinds of pasta are most often served.

Bulgaria

DUCK WITH SAUERKRAUT

(for 5—6 persons)

1 young fattened duck with giblets
100 gr rice
100 gr chopped walnuts
pepper
1/2 teasoon ground hot pepper
1 teaspoon dried marjoram
salt
2 onions
100 gr lard
1—2 dl warm water
1 kg pickled cabbage (shredded)
2 teaspoons mild red paprika pepper

Wash duck, draw and wipe well. Cut giblets into finer strips. Wash rice, cook shortly, drain, mix giblets, walnuts, pepper, hot paprika, marjoram and salt. Mix all well. Rub duck with salt and pepper, put the prepared stuffing into the carcass, truss the opening with clean white thread. Put the duck into an earthenware dish, pour half (50 gr) of melted lard over, add some warm water and bake in the oven preheated to 175—200 °C. While baking baste duck at times with juice.

In the meantime chop onion finely, heat lard, cook onion slowly until brown, add finely shredded pickled cabbage, red paprika pepper. Cook at medium heat until tender.

When the duck is done, take it out of the dish and turn in pickled cabbage. Put the duck over the cabbage, breast downwards first, then turn round. Bake until the duck is nicely browned and tender. While baking baste with juice as needed.

When done, cut into nice pieces, arrange on a bigger plate. Put some sauerkraut around and serve the greater part separately.

OFFAL DISHES

Yugoslavia

LIVER BALLS

600 gr liver (pigs' or calves')
2 medium-sized potatoes
2 onions
4 tablespoons oil
1—2 cloves of garlic
1/2 bunch of parsley
2 eggs
150—200 gr breadcrumbs
salt
pepper
2—3 dl oil for frying

Wash liver, wipe. Peel potatoes and cut into bigger cubes. Mix liver and potatoes and grind. Chop onion finely, fry in heated oil until soft. Cool a little, add to ground liver and potatoes, add chopped parsley, crushed and squeezed garlic, salt, pepper and about 50 gr breadcrumbs. Mix all, leave to stand in a cool place, and then make balls, roll them in breadcrumbs and fry in heated oil until brown.

With these balls serve stewed peas, new beans, carrots in butter, lettuce, tomato salad and others.

Roumania

STUFFED LAMB OFFAL

(for 6 persons)

1 lamb liver
1 lamb lights (lungs)
1 lamb heart
1 lamb spleen
1 cleaned lamb entrails
2 bayleaves
8—10 peppercorns
500 gr onion
1—2 dl warm water
1—1,5 dl oil
salt
pepper
1 teaspoon red paprika pepper
1 bunch of parsley
3 eggs
1 lamb double offal membrane
2 dl milk
(or sour cream)
1/2 l thick yoghurt

Wash offal well, barely cover with cold water and heat. When it boils, add bayleaf and peppercorns. Simmer until tender. Drain cooked offal, cool a little and mince. Peel onion and chop finely. Heat oil, add onion, cook slowly until soft, add minced offal, cook on together, add warm water as needed, salt, pepper, red paprika pepper and chopped parsley. Grease a fireproof dish and line with the offal membrane, turn in the prepared mixture, cover it with the ends of the membrane and pour in well beaten eggs with milk.

Heat oven to 200 °C, bake until nicely brown. Serve with sheep thick yoghurt as an appetiser, or as main dish with some salad.

Greece

STEWED LAMB LIVER

750 gr lamb (or calves') liver
1/2—1 dl olive (or other) oil
salt
pepper
juice of 1 lemon
2 teaspoons chopped fresh basil or fresh marjoram
1/2 bunch of parsley

Wash liver, wipe, remove all veins and cut into bigger cubes (abour 3 cm). Heat oil in a frying pan, add liver, fry at higher heat on all sides, add salt and pepper, drip in lemon juice, sprinkle with basil, cover and cook slowly for another 5—10 minutes, stirring occasionally. Wash parsley, drain and chop finely, then sprinkle the liver with it. With liver prepared this way peasant salad (see page 220) is usually served, or lettuce, cucumber salad, mixed salad and others.

Roumania

LIVER WITH SOUR CREAM

600—750 gr pigs' liver
3 onions
1 dl oil
40 gr flour
0,5—1 dl warm water
2 dl sour cream
1 teaspoon mustard
salt
pepper

Wash liver, wipe a little and cut into thin slices. Peel onion, chop finely, cook slowly in heated oil until soft and beginning to colour, add salt.

Roll liver in flour and fry over onion, add some warm water, add mustard and cook slowly about 10—20 minutes. In the

end add sour cream, some more salt if needed, shake the pan and cook together for another 5 minutes.

With liver prepared this way serve mashed potatoes or cooked rice and some fresh vegetables (paprikas, tomatoes, radishes, spring onions).

Roumania

LIVER WITH SHEEP CHEESE

600—750 gr pigs' liver
1 l hot water
2 onions
1 dl oil
salt
pepper
4 eggs
250—300 gr sheep cheese
1/2 bunch of parsley

Wash liver, put up to cook in hot water and boil about 20 minutes. When done, drain, cool a little and cut into smaller cubes. Heat oil, add finely chopped onion, cook slowly until soft and brown, add liver, cook on together about 5 minutes, add salt and pepper, sprinkle with crushed cheese and pour beaten eggs over. Cook at very low heat without stirring. Before serving sprinkle with chopped parsley.

Serve with lettuce, shredded cabbage, mixed salad and others.

Greece

MARINADED LIVER

750 gr calves' liver
50—60 gr flour
pepper (white if possible)
1/2 olive or other oil
1 dl warm water
3 dl tomato juice
1 sprig of rosemary
1 bayleaf
1 teaspoon sugar
1/2 dl red wine
2 cloves of garlic
2 tablespoons chopped parsley

Wash liver, wipe, remove harder veins, cut into steaks about 1 cm thick. Mix flour with salt and pepper, roll liver in it. Heat oil, fry liver on both sides, take out of oil and leave in a warm place. Add the rest of flour to heated oil, fry to brown a little, add some cold, then some warm water. Pour in tomato, add rosemary, bayleaf, some sugar, red wine. Cook at low heat, add crushed or chopped garlic, stir and cook on for a while, remove rosemary and bayleaf. Arrange liver on a somewhat deeper long serving plate, pour the sauce over and sprinkle with chopped parsley.

It can be served both warm and cold.

Roumania

GOOSE LIVER WITH ONION

3 onions
20 gr butter or margarine
800 gr goose livers, 20 gr flour
50 gr butter (margarine or oil)
salt

Peel onion, slice thinnly, heat butter or margarine, add onion and fry until slightly brown.

Wash liver, wipe well, remove veins, roll in flour and fry in heated butter (margarine or oil) both sides about 3—4 minutes. When fried, salt, arrange in a corresponding dish and cover with slices of fried onion.

Slices of bread can be fried in the same butter and served with the liver.

As accompaniment serve lettuce or cucumber salad with drinking yoghurt. If this is to be the main dish, then serve baked potatoes with it.

Bulgaria

STEWED OFFAL — "PENDJEVISH"

750 gr—1 kg lamb offal (liver, lungs, spleen, entrails)
2—2,5 l water
2 dl oil
500 gr onion
500 gr big paprikas
500 gr tomatoes
salt
pepper
1 teaspoon red paprika pepper
1 bayleaf
peppercorns

Wash offal, pour over with cold water and cook, add bayleaf and peppercorns if desired. When cooked, cut into pieces. Heat oil, add finely sliced onion, cook slowly to soften a bit, then add cored paprikas cut into strips and cook together shortly. Mix in minced offal, add peeled and chopped tomatoes. Add salt, pepper, red paprika pepper, mix, add some water if needed and stew at medium heat until tender.

Roumania

TRIPES WITH BACON

600—750 gr tripes
100 gr smoked bacon
30 gr oil
3 cloves of garlic
1 bunch of parsley
salt
pepper
3 eggs
50—100 gr grated ripened sheep cheese in slices

Wash tripes well and cook. When tender, cool and cut into strips. Cut bacon into smaller cubes, mix with oil and fry to brown, add chopped parsley. Cook slowly at low heat, add tripes, salt, pepper, finely chopped or crushed garlic, pour in some water (1—2 dl) and simmer covered for 10—15 minutes. Beat eggs well, add 2 tablespoons of cheese. Take tripes off heat, mix in eggs with cheese, taking care that no lumps form. Sprinkle with the rest of cheese. Tripes can be served like this or baked in the oven preset at 200—250 °C for 10 minutes.

Polenta can be served with tripes.

Yugoslavia

BAKED TRIPES

600—750 gr tripes
2—3 l water
5—6 peppercorns
2 cloves of garlic
1 smaller onion
1 bayleaf

For sauce:
1 dl oil
2 onions
5—6 cloves of garlic
2 carrots
a few basil leaves
a few thyme leaves
750 gr—1 kg tomatoes
2 dl white wine
salt
pepper
100 gr grated hard cheese (ripe kachkaval, Trappist or similar)

Wash tripes, leave for 1—2 hours in cold water, then cook in water to which peeled onion and garlic, peppercorns and bayleaf have been added. When cooked, strain and cut into strips.

Heat oil, add finely chopped onion, cook slowly to soften, then add carrot rounds, cook together for a while, add chopped garlic, chopped basil and thyme leaves, peeled tomatoes cut into small pieces, mix, stew together for 10—15 minutes at medium heat. Then add tripes, pour in white wine, add salt and pepper and stew together until all is tender.

When cooked, turn into an earthenware or fireproof casserole, sprinkle with grated cheese and bake in the oven preheated to 200 °C. Serve warm with mashed potatoes.

Bulgaria

CALVES' TONGUE IN VEGETABLE SAUCE

750 gr tongue (about 3 pieces)
salt
peppercorns
1 bayleaf
1 dl oil or 70 gr lard
2 onions
3—4 paprikas
1/2 bunch of parsley
2 cloves of garlic
250 gr tomatoes
1 tablespoon flour
salt
1 dl sour cream or thick yoghurt

Leave tongues to stand in cold water about 2 hours, take them out, rub with salt, leave to stand again. Put up to cook 2 l of cold water, bring to the boil, add peppercorns and bayleaf, plunge in the washed tongues and simmer until tender. Take cooked tongues out of water, peel (remove skin), cut into rounds. Heat oil, add finely chopped onion, cook slowly to soften, add cored and washed paprikas cut into strips, cook on for about 10—15 minutes. Then add crushed or finely chopped garlic, washed tomatoes cut into smaller pieces, cook together, pour in some water in which the tongues were cooked as needed. When vegetables are soft, sprinkle with flour, mix, fry a little, pour in soup from cooking tongues and put in slices of tongue. Cook shortly together at low heat. Add salt to taste, add chopped parsley and sour cream, stir slowly or shake.

Serve with cooked potatoes or cooked rice.

Yugoslavia

TRIPES AND ENTRAILS FROM SKOPLJE

1 lamb entrails
1 tripes
salt
2—2,5 dl oil
2 bayleaves
1 teaspoon red paprika pepper
2—3 cloves of garlic
2—2,5 dl warm water

Wash entrails well (turn inside out and rinse). Wash tripes well also and leave to stand in salted water 1—2 hours. A few pieces of onion can be added to water if desired. Drain offal well, cut into smaller pieces and mix. Grease an earthenware casserole with oil, turn in the prepared tripes and entrails, add salt as needed, add crushed bayleaf and red paprika pepper, pour oil over, add some warm water. Bake in the oven preset at 175°C, pouring in some warm water at times. Baste while baking.

When all is tender, add chopped garlic, mix, add more oil if needed, and bake on for a short time.

This speciality can be served both as the main dish and as an appetiser with young vegetables (spring onions, tomatoes, paprikas, radishes).

Yugoslavia

BRAINS DALMATIAN WAY

600 gr pigs' brains
4 tablespoons vinegar
2 l warm water
2 onions
2—4 cloves of garlic
1 dl olive (or other) oil
500 gr tomatoes
1 teaspoon oregano
1,5 white wine
4—5 tablespoons flour
1/2 bunch of parsley
pepper
salt
2 dl oil for frying

Wash brains in warm water to which 2 spoons of vinegar have been added. Carefully remove veins and the thin skin. Heat 1—1,5 l water, add salt and 2 tablespoons of vinegar, plunge in brains, boil shortly, strain, cool and cut into nice pieces.

Heat oil, add finely chopped onion, cook slowly a little, add crushed or chopped garlic, peeled tomatoes cut into cubes, pour in wine, add oregano, cook at low heat until tomatoes are tender.

Sprinkle brains with salt and pepper, roll in flour, fry in heated oil until brown on both sides. Arrange brains on a long serving plate, sprinkle with chopped parsley and pour wine sauce over.

Serve with boiled potatoes or with Swiss chard with potatoes, poured over with olive oil.

Turkey

"DOLMADZIK"

600 gr sheep's liver
2 onions
20 gr oil or butterfat
1/2 bunch of parsley
1 tablespoon chopped celery leaves
100 gr flour
2—3 eggs
2—3 tablespoons breadcrumbs (as needed)
2—3 dl oil for frying
salt

Wash liver, cook for a short while, wipe and mince finely. Chop onion finely, fry in some oil to soften, cool, add liver, salt, chopped parsley and celery, 1 egg. Mix well, add breadcrumbs as needed. Form little cakes on the board dusted with flour, dip them in beaten egg and fry in heated oil until brown.

Serve with bean salad, potato salad, mixed salad.

("Dolmadzik" is a word of Turkish origin and means "coated cakes" of minced sheep's liver.)

Roumania

OFFAL LOAF — "TOKATURA"

250 gr calves' or lamb liver
1/2 calf's heart
1/2 lights (lungs)
2—2,5 l water
salt
some marjoram
40 gr oil
2 onions
2 potatoes
2 eggs
pepper
2—3 tablespoons breadcrumbs
2—3 tablespoons flour
100 gr smoked bacon
oil for frying

Wash offal, pour water over, add salt and marjoram (or bayleaf instead). Simmer about 60 minutes. When cooked, strain, cool a little and grind. Heat oil, add finely chopped onion, cook slowly until soft and beginning to colour. Mix ground liver and fried onion, add peeled and finely grated potatoes, add salt, pepper, beaten eggs and breadcrumbs. Work all into a homogenous mixture and leave to stand in a cool place for 30—60 minutes.

Form into a loaf with the help of

flour, put into a baking pan greased with oil, pour some oil over, cover with rashers of bacon and bake in the oven preheated to 175 °C. While baking baste with the juice from the pan, and add some oil mixed with water if necessary.

Serve warm with some vegetables (kale, cabbage or others) or with bean salad, potato salad and the like.

Yugoslavia

CALVES' HEART IN SAUCE

750 gr hearts
1 bunch of root vegetables
150 gr streaky smoked bacon
1 dl oil (olive or other)
1 onion
a few rosemary leaves
1/2 teaspoon thyme
1—2 bayleaves
1,5 dl white wine
1 bunch of parsley
salt
pepper
40 gr butter

Wash hearts, remove veins, put in a pot with cold water, heat. When it boils, add cleaned roots, salt. Simmer until tender (about 90 minutes). Then cool and cut into strips. Cut smoked bacon into cubes, fry in oil to brown, take out. Put hearts into the same oil, fry to get nicely brown, take out. Put finely chopped onion into the same oil, cook slowly until soft, add rosemary, thyme, bayleaf, 1/2 bunch of chopped parsley, vegetables cut into small cubes, pour in wine, add salt and pepper. Cook slowly together about 5 minutes, then add hearts and bacon, mix slowly, add soup from cooking hearts if needed, simmer covered about 10—20 minutes. When done, pour heated butter over and sprinkle with the rest of chopped parsley.

With hearts prepared this way serve polenta, cooked potatoes or rice.

Yugoslavia

PIGS' OR LAMB LIGHTS (lungs)

1 bunch of root vegetables
750 gr—1 kg pigs' or lamb lungs
1/2 dl oil or 50 gr lard
100 gr streaky bacon
1 onion
2 cloves of garlic
1/2 bunch of parsley
1/2 teaspoon marjoram
a few rosemary leaves
30 gr flour
soup from cooking lungs or from meat cube
salt
ground pepper
8—10 peppercorns
2 bayleaves

Cook lungs in water to which cleaned roots, peppercorns and bayleaf have been added. When cooked, cut into strips. Cut bacon into cubes, put it into oil, fry to brown, add finely chopped onion, cook slowly to soften, add chopped garlic, chopped parsley, marjoram, rosemary. Cook together another 5 minutes, then add lungs, pour in soup, add salt, pepper, bayleaf. Simmer 10—20 more minutes.

With lungs prepared this way serve bread dumplings or potato croquettes.

This dish is most often to be found on the menus in Slovenia and other western parts of Yugoslavia.

Roumania

SOUR-FLAVOURED KIDNEYS

750 gr calves' or pigs' kidneys
2 dl milk
50 gr lard
2 onions
2 tablespoons flour
pepper
salt
1/2 l warm water or soup from meat cube
2 tablespoons vinegar
1/2—1 dl sour cream

Clean kidneys, wash and leave in milk diluted with some water to stand for about 2 hours. Then drain and cut into thin slices. Heat lard, add finely chopped onion, cook slowly to soften, add kidneys rolled in flour, fry a little together with onion, pour in water or soup, add pepper. Stew for about 10 minutes, add vinegar, mix, then blend in sour cream, salt and some sugar if desired.

With kidneys serve cooked rice, boiled potatoes mixed with fried onion and the like.

Turkey

CALVES' TONGUE WITH ALMONDS AND GRAPES

2 calves' tongues
50 gr almonds
200 gr berries of white grapes
2 cloves
10—15 gr sugar
1 lemon
1/2—1 dl oil
15 gr flour
salt

Wash tongues and leave to stand in enough cold water for 1—2 hours. Then cook in salted water until tender. Then peel (take off skin), cover with a clean cloth and press with something heavy to remain flat.

Dip almonds into hot water, cook shortly and peel, sliver lengthways and stick into the tongues.

Heat oil, add sugar, fry until brown, add some water in which tongues were cooked (about 4 dl), add washed grapes, juice and some rind (not sprayed) of 1 lemon, cloves. Simmer for about 10 minutes, taking care that grapes remain whole. Towards the end add flour mixed with some cold water, cook shortly, put in tongues, turn heat down to minimum so that it does not boil any more. The tongues should be left to stand in the sauce for some time to absorb its flavour. Then take the tongues out, cut into nice slices, arrange on a corresponding plate and pour the sauce over.

Serve with cooked or stewed rice.

Roumania

BRAINS SALAD

4 pigs' brains
2 tablespoons vinegar
2 carrots
2 potatoes
1/2 head of cauliflower

To pour over:
juice of 1 lemon
2 tablespoons mustard
1 dl oil
salt
pepper
a few lettuce leaves

Wash brains well, remove veins and the thin skin. Cook in salted water with vinegar. When cooked, strain, cool and cut into small pieces.

Scrape carrots, cook and cut into small cubes. Cook unpeeled potatoes, drain, peel and cut into cubes. Cook cauliflower and break into sprigs.

Mix well lemon juice, oil, mustard, salt and pepper until thick. Mix brains with vegetables, pour the prepared mixture over, mix slowly, leave to stand in a cool place about 1 hour. Arrange washed and wiped lettuce leaves on the serving plate and put over them the salad made into a cone.

Serve with toast.

Roumania

CHICKEN HEARTS WITH VEGETABLES AND MUSHROOMS

600 gr chicken hearts
1/2—1 dl oil or 50 gr lard
1 onion
1—2 carrots
1/2 celery root
500 gr potatoes
250 gr fresh mushrooms (button mushrooms or ceps)
1 teaspoon red paprika pepper
1 tablespoon flour
1—2 dl warm water
1/2 bunch of parsley
salt

Wash hearts, drain and halve. Heat oil, add chopped onion, cook it a little, add crudely grated carrots, celery, cook slowly to soften, put in chicken hearts, washed trimmed and sliced mushrooms. Simmer covered and add some warm water as needed. When all is half cooked, add peeled potatoes cut into cubes, salt, red paprika pepper mixed with a spoonful of flour and with cold water, add some more warm water, cook slowly together until hearts and potatoes are tender.

In the end add chopped parsley.

GAME

Greece

RABBIT WITH ONION

(for 6—10 persons)

1 wild rabbit
3—4 tablespoons vinegar

For: marinade:
1 onion
1 carrot
3 dl red wine
1 bayleaf
peppercorns
a few rosemary leaves
1 sprig of celery
1/2 dl wine vinegar

For sauce:
1 dl olive oil
50 gr butter
1 onion
2 cloves of garlic
500 gr pickled onions
4 dl tomato juice
salt
pepper

Joint skinned rabbit into 4—6 parts, wash well in water with vinegar in it, drain and place into a bigger, deeper pan.

Peel onion and chop crudely, scrape carrot and cut into rounds, pour in wine, add bayleaf, pepper, rosemary, celery and vinegar. Mix all, pour over the rabbit, cover and leave to stand in a cool place for 2—3 days. Turn the rabbit occasionally and pour over with marinade so that all the meat is covered.

Take the rabbit out of marinade, drain and wipe. Mix oil and butter, heat in a bigger frying pan, put in pieces of rabbit, fry them to get a bit brown, take out, cook chopped onion and garlic in the same fat until tender, add pickled onions, cook slowly together about 15 minutes.

Boil marinade about 10 minutes, pass through a sieve. Put pieces of rabbit in a corresponding dish, pour over it cooked onion, marinade, tomato, salt and pepper, cover and bake in the oven at 175—200°C until the meat is tender and the sauce thick. Serve with rice or potato croquettes.

Greece

WILD DUCK IN WINE SAUCE

1 wild duck
3 tablespoons vinegar
1/2 or 1 small whole apple
1 celery root
40 gr butter
1 dl olive oil
salt
pepper
1 medium-sized onion
1 clove of garlic
1/2 bunch of parsley
2 dl white wine
2 dl bone stock or soup from cube
juice of 1 orange

Pour hot water over the duck, pluck it, then draw. Wash in a lot of water to which a few spoonfuls of vinegar have been added. Put apple and celery root in the carcass, to offset the smell of fish the duck had fed on.

Heat butter (20 gr) mixed with oil (1/2 dl) in a deeper pan, put duck in and fry it until nicely brown on all sides, add salt, pepper, pour in several spoonfuls of soup or warm water, cover and simmer about 30 minutes. Take duck out, quarter it, remove celery and apple.

Cook slowly finely chopped onion and garlic in a bigger frying pan in the rest of oil and butter until tender, add snipped parsley, put in the four pieces of duck,

pour in wine, cook to reduce wine a little, pour in stock and orange juice, cover and stew at medium heat until the meat is tender and the sauce thick. When done, cut the duck into smaller pieces and pour the sauce over them.

As accompaniment serve rice or potato croquettes.

Roumania

RABBIT WITH OLIVES

(for 6—10 persons)

1 rabbit
salt
pepper
5 onions
50 gr olive or other oil
3—4 dl white wine
2 bayleaves
1/2 teaspoon thyme
100 gr black olives
20 gr flour

Joint skinned rabbit, rub with salt and pepper. Peel onion, chop finely, cook slowly in heated oil until slightly soft, add pieces of meat, cook shortly together, pour in wine, add bayleaf, thyme (some rosemary if desired) and halved olives without stones. Cover and stew until the meat is tender. Pour in some warm water occasionally if needed.

As accompaniment serve polenta, rice or boiled potatoes.

Roumania

VENISON HAUNCH IN SOUR CREAM

1 kg venison haunch
3—4 rashers smoked bacon
salt
pepper
3—4 bilberries (juniper berries)
40 gr (4 tablespoons) oil
1 onion
2 dl red wine
1 dl sour cream

Remove veins from venison, salt, insert strips of bacon into it. Put meat into a greased earthware dish — djuvetch, pour over oil and bake in the oven preheated to about 200°C. Baste with juice while baking. After 15 minutes cover meat with chopped onion, add some red wine, bake on and baste occasionally.

Just before the end of baking pour sour cream over the meat, take it out, leave in a warm place, then cut into nice pieces. Strain juice from baking, boil shortly and pour over venison.

As accompaniment serve rice, some pasta or croquettes.

Greece

PARTRIDGES IN WINE SAUCE

(for 2 persons)

2 plucked and drawn partridges
1 tablespoon salt
1 teaspoon pepper
50 gr butter
1/4 l dry red wine
juice of 1 lemon
1 piece lemon rind
2 dl bone stock or soup from cube (as needed)
salt
white pepper

Wash partridges well, wipe and half. Mix salt and pepper. Rub well the inner parts of the four halves with this mixture. Heat butter in a bigger frying pan, put in partridge halves and fry them until brown. Take them out and leave in a warm place. Add some red wine to the juice in the pan, boil, pour in the rest of the wine, add lemon juice and rind, put partridges back into the frying pan, cover and stew at medium heat about 40—50 minutes. Pour in some soup occasionally and some more wine if needed. When partridges are tender, take them out, put on a warmed serving plate and pour over with sauce from the frying pan.

Cooked rice and cooked Brussels sprouts with olive oil are usually served with partridges in Greece.

Yugoslavia

PHEASANT IN CABBAGE LEAVES

1 pheasant
salt
150—200 gr smoked bacon
40 gr lard
1 head of cabbage
2 dl white wine

Pluck and draw pheasant, wash well and drain, then wipe and salt. Chop bacon and put it into the carcass. Put some lard into an earthenware or other corresponding dish, place the pheasant in it, put into the oven preheated to 175 °C and bake until slightly brown.

Take leaves off the cabbage head, wash, pour over with hot water and leave to stand 5—10 minutes. Take pheasant out of the oven, wrap up in cabbage leaves, tie up with stronger white thread. Put back into the oven and bake, basting it often. Pour some white wine into the juice occasionally. When the bird is done, remove thread and cabbage leaves. Cut into nice pieces (like a chicken).

Arrange cabbage leaves on a plate, place over them pieces of pheasant so that it looks like a whole bird. Serve boiled potatoes or croquettes with it. Pheasant can be served also wrapped up in a cabbage leaf.

Yugoslavia

BAKED PARTRIDGES

(for 2—3 persons)

2—3 partridges
salt
150 gr smoked bacon
500 gr young grapevine leaves (not sprayed)
40 gr butter
1—2 dl warm water
100 gr kaymak or sour cream

Carefully pluck and draw partridges, wash well, drain, wipe and salt. Cut bacon into thinner rashers. Wrap partridges in rashers of bacon, tie up with white thread. Put washed, slightly withered grapevine leaves into the carcasses. Heat butter in a pan, place partridges in and

fry until brown on all sides. Pour in some warm water at times, stew, covered, until tender. When the partridges are done, put kaymak (or sour cream) into a pan and cook shortly, then remove grapevine leaves and rashers of bacon from the partridges.

Cut partridges into nice pieces, place on a serving plate, garnish with rashers of bacon and pour over with sauce, or serve it separately.

Bulgaria

RABBIT BACK SHEPHERD'S WAY

1 rabbit back
150 gr smoked bacon
20 gr (2 tablespoons) oil
2—3 dl white wine
1/2 bunch of parsley
salt
pepper

Trim away any pieces of skin from rabbit back, with a sharp knife insert thicker strips of bacon into meat, add salt and pepper. Put meat into an earthenware dish — djuvetch or a fireproof dish greased with oil, pour over it heated oil, add some wine. Bake in the oven preheated to 175—200°C. While baking add wine and some water occasionally. When done, take out meat, cut it into nice pieces, pour over with the juice from the baking dish, sprinkle with parsley.

Baked (jacket) potatoes are usually served with rabbit prepared this way.

FISH AND SHELLFISH

In the Balkan countries fish have been used as food a great deal for a very long time, which is only natural because all those countries have many rivers and are surrounded by seas, while Yugoslavia and Roumania also have lakes rich with fish. The most popular way of preparing fish, especially sea fish, is grilling them. No culinary skill is necessary for it, just the ability to make good charcoal fire. But in case you have no grill or charcoal, the oven of the stove can be a very good substitute. There are, however, more complicated Balkan fish specialties, some of which have a very long tradition and date back to the times when customs or religious reasons dictated when and on which days or holidays fish was to be eaten instead of meat. Today fish is cheaper than meat and its nutritive properties so great, that fish is warmly recommended.

Roumania

CARP WITH OLIVES

(for 4—5 persons)

1—1,5 kg carp
juice of 1 lemon
salt
3—4 cloves of garlic
1/2 bunch of parsley
pepper
1/2 teaspoon thyme
a few rosemary leaves
2 carrots
2 tomatoes
2 dl olive oil
100 gr olives

Clean carp, wash, wipe, drip with lemon juice, then salt and cut gashes in several places.

Chop finely garlic and parsley, crush thyme and rosemary, add pepper and salt, mix, add 2—3 tablespoons of oil. Put part of this mixture into the gashes and the rest inside the fish. Put the prepared carp into a fireproof dish or casserole greased with oil. Clean carrots, grate finely; wash tomatoes, peel and cut, remove stones from olives and halve them. Heat about 1/2 dl oil, add carrot, cook a little, add tomato and olives, add some salt, cook slowly until all slightly tender. Place cooked vegetables and olives over the fish and bake in the oven preset at 175°C until quite tender. While baking baste with juice and add water if needed.

With carp serve boiled potatoes poured over with some oil and sprinkled with chopped parsley.

Albania

FISH ON POTATOES

500 gr potatoes
1—1,5 dl oil
1 kg freshwater fish (carp, perch and others)
salt
pepper
250 gr tomatoes
3—4 dl white wine
4 cloves of garlic
1—2 dl warm water

Peel potatoes, wash and cut into rounds. Grease a fireproof dish with oil. Put in a layer of potatoes, add salt and pepper, arrange cleaned, washed fish cut into pieces, add salt and pepper again. Cover with peeled tomatoes cut into rounds, salt, sprinkle with chopped garlic. Pour over with white wine and oil. Bake in the oven preheated to 175°C about 40 minutes. Add some warm water while baking, as needed.

Roumania

CARP WITH RED WINE

(for 4—5 persons)

1 carp of 1—1,5 kg
40 gr butter or oil
1 onion
3 paprikas
1 lemon
2 tablespoons chopped parsley
salt
2—3 dl red wine

Heat butter or oil, add finely chopped onion, cook it a little to soften, add cored paprikas cut into strips, cook on until tender.

Clean fish, wash well, wipe, sprinkle with lemon juice, rub with salt and parsley inside and outside.

Grease a fireproof dish, put in fish, cover with stewed onion and paprikas. Bake in the oven preheated to 175°C. While baking, baste with juice to which wine is gradually added. Bake until nicely brown.

Serve in the same dish. As an accompaniment serve mashed or boiled potatoes.

Roumania

CARP WITH WHITE WINE

(for 4—5 persons)

1—1,5 kg carp
500—600 gr onion
2 dl oil
salt
pepper
2 bayleaves
2 tablespoons flour
3—4 dl white wine
1 lemon
parsley

Remove scales from fish, draw, wash well, wipe, salt and cut gashes on both sides.

Heat oil, add peeled onion cut into thin slices, add pepper, bayleaf, cook slowly until soft and light brown.

Roll carp in flour, fry on both sides in heated oil. Put it into an enamelled djuvetch, cover with cooked onion, pour wine over and bake in the oven preset at 175°C about 30—40 minutes. When done, take it out carefully, place on a long plate and put in a warm place.

Pass sauce through a sieve, add some water as needed, cook shortly and pour over the fish.

Garnish with lemon rounds and parsley leaves.

Serve with cooked rice sprinkled with chopped parsley.

Greece

CATFISH WITH SOUR CREAM

1 kg catfish
1 lemon
salt
1 dl oil
500 gr onion
50 gr prunes
20 gr raisins

For pouring over:
2 dl sour cream
10 gr flour
1/2 teaspoon red paprika pepper
juice of 1 lemon

Clean fish, wash, wipe and cut into slightly thicker pieces. Drip with lemon juice, salt, cover and leave in a cool place to stand about 30 minutes.

Heat oil, add finely chopped onion, cook slowly to soften, then salt, mix, turn into a fireproof dish or casserole, arrange evenly to cover the bottom. Put slightly soaked prunes and washed raisins over onion. Arrange pieces of fish over.

Blend sour cream with flour, red paprika pepper and lemon juice, beat well, pour over fish. Bake in the oven preheated to 175—200°C until tender and brown.

Serve in the same dish. As accompaniment serve some salad.

Yugoslavia

CARP ON ONION FROM VRANJE

1 carp of about 1,5 kg
1 kg onion
1—1,5 dl oil
200 gr rice
5—6 dl warm water
pepper
salt
1 (levelled) teaspoon dried thyme

Cut onion into slices, cook slowly in heated oil. Add to it picked over, washed

and drained rice, cook until it becomes glassy, barely cover with warm water, add thyme, salt and pepper, mix.

Clean carp, wash, cut gashes (but not very deep) on both sides 3—5 cm apart. Place carp thus prepared on rice, brush it with oil, sprinkle with salt and pepper. Put into the oven preheated to 150—170 °C and bake until all is tender and the fish has a crisp brown crust (about 1 hour or more).

In the vicinity of the town of Vranje carp used to be prepared only on Christmas Eve and St. Nicholas day. Today, however, it is prepared independently of these dates, as fish is more and more being used instead of meat and the original ritual character of some dishes has considerably lost in importance.

Turkey

GRILLED CARP

(for 5—6 persons)

1,2—1,5 kg carp fillets
salt
pepper
1 dl olive oil

For marinade:
juice of 2 lemons
1 onion
2 cloves of garlic
a few rosemary leaves
1/2 teaspoon thyme
a pinch of oregano
a pinch of sage

a small piece of lemon rind
1 bayleaf

For stewed vegetables:
1 dl olive oil
1 onion
1 leek
150 gr carrots
150 gr celery root
50 gr tomato purée (from tube)
1/2 l red wine
1 kg fresh tomatoes

For the marinade mix lemon juice with finely chopped onion and garlic, rosemary, thyme, oregano, sage, ground lemon rind and crushed bayleaf.

Clean carp, wash, wipe, cut into fillets. Sprinkle fillets with salt and pepper, then pour the marinade over and leave to stand about 1 hour.

In the meantime fry finely chopped onion in olive oil, then add leek, carrots and celery root cut into thinner strips, salt and pepper and continue to stew about 10 minutes. Add tomato purée diluted with water, pour in red wine and stew until wine nearly evaporates. Towards the end add washed, peeled tomatoes, cut into strips, and stew for another 10—15 minutes.

Drain marinaded fillets, cut into smaller pieces, pass through olive oil and grill quickly.

Serve at once with stewed vegetables and homemade bread or pogatcha.

Yugoslavia

TROUT IN KAYMAK

1 trout of 1,5 kg or 2 or 3 smaller
1 lemon
salt
200 gr kaymak
50 gr white or maize flour
1 small garlic
1 dl wine vinegar

Clean fish, wash well, wipe, cut into bigger pieces, sprinkle with lemon juice and salt. Leave to stand like that about 30—40 minutes. Roll fish in flour, put into the frying pan in which kaymak has been melted (about 150 gr). Fry at low heat.

In the meantime peel garlic, crush well with salt and chop, add wine vinegar and mix.

When fish is fried nicely on both sides, take it out and place in a warmed dish. Each layer should be poured over with the mixture of vinegar and garlic, and then pour the rest of kaymak over the whole dish.

Bulgaria

CATFISH BAKED WITH TOMATOES

1 lemon
1 kg catfish
salt
30—40 gr flour
1—2 dl oil
500—800 gr tomatoes
30 gr butter
30 gr kachkaval
2 tablespoons chopped parsley
1 dl warm water

Clean fish, wash, cut into bigger pieces, drip with lemon juice, salt. Leave to stand for a while, then roll in flour and fry in heated oil, take out.

Wash tomatoes, peel, cut into halves, remove seed, cook a little in the same oil and salt. Put pieces of fish in a greased fireproof dish or casserole, then put tomato over, add some warm water, sprinkle with chopped parsley and grated cheese. Heat oven to 200°C, bake until brown.

With fish serve boiled potatoes or cooked rice sprinkled with plenty of parsley.

Other kinds of fish can be prepared in the same way.

Bulgaria

CARP BULGARIAN WAY

(for 6 persons)

1 carp of about 2 kg
150—200 gr olives without stones
1 dl olive oil
juice of 1 lemon
1 lemon
2 cloves of garlic
1 bunch of parsley
2 onions
2 tomatoes, 2 carrots
1—2 dl warm water

Clean carp, wash well and drain. Chop olives rather finely, add a tablespoon of oil, 2 tablespoons of lemon juice, chopped parsley and garlic. Salt fish in and out, drip with lemon juice and sprinkle with pepper. Fill the inside with the prepared olives.

Grease a fireproof dish or casserole with oil. Peel onion and carrots and cut into thin slices. Wash tomatoes, peel and cut into rounds. Also cut washed lemon into rounds. Add salt and pepper to vegetables and lemon, mix and turn into the bottom of the fireproof dish. Place carp over, pour heated oil over and put into the oven preheated to 200°C, so that the fish gets nicely brown in the first 10—15 minutes. Then turn heat down to 175°C and bake slowly until all is tender. Baste while baking and add more warm water if needed. Serve in the same dish.

Bulgaria

FISH "PLAKA"

750 gr—1 kg freshwater fish
500 gr onion
1,5 dl oil
100 gr carrots
100 gr celery
450 gr tomatoes
20 gr flour
salt
pepper
1 bayleaf
2—3 cloves of garlic
1 lemon
20 gr breadcrumbs
1 teaspoon red paprika pepper
1 teaspoon sugar
1/2 bunch of parsley
1/2 l warm water

Clean fish, wash, wipe, drip with lemon juice, salt. Peel onion, cut into thinner slices. Heat oil (1 dl), add onion, cook a little, then add cleaned and grated carrots and celery. Cook slowly together until slightly tender. Wash about 300 gr tomatoes, peel and cut finely, add to half-cooked onion, cook on until all is tender. Sprinkle vegetables with flour, fry it a little, add red paprika pepper, pour in some cold, then some warm water, add salt, pepper, bayleaf, chopped garlic and parsley. Simmer about 10 minutes.

Grease a fireproof dish or casserole with oil, turn in the prepared vegetables, put fish over, cover with the rest of tomatoes cut into rounds. Drip each round with some oil, sprinkle with breadcrumbs and sugar. Bake in the oven preset at 200°C until all is brown. Serve cold.

Turkey

FISH IN OLIVE OIL

1 grey mullet of about 1 kg
2 bigger onions
2 paprikas
2 cloves of garlic
500 gr tomatoes
1 bunch of parsley
1 dl olive oil

3 tablespoons tomato purée (from the tube)
salt
pepper
10—12 black olives
2—3 dl warm water (as needed)

Clean fish and wash well, drain and wipe. Peel onion and cut into thin slices or rounds. Core paprikas and cut into strips; chop finely or crush garlic; wash tomatoes, peel and cut into rounds; chop parsley finely.

Heat oil, add fish, fry a little on all sides, then take out. Cook onion slowly in the same oil until soft and slightly brown, add paprikas, cook on until tender. Then add garlic. Arrange tomato over cooked onion and paprikas. Mix tomato purée with 2 dl water, pour it in, add salt and pepper. Simmer together for 10 more minutes. Put fried fish into the sauce. Barely cover with warm water. Simmer for another 10—15 minutes. Halve olives, remove stones. Put fish on a deeper, long plate, pour the sauce over, sprinkle with olives.

Serve cold.

Bulgaria

TURBOT WITH PARSLEY SAUCE

750—1 kg turbot
1 lemon
salt
1 dl oil
30 gr flour
2 bunches of parsley
1/2 teaspoon red paprika pepper
pepper, salt
1/2 l warm water

Clean fish, wash, wipe a little, drip with lemon juice, salt and leave to stand for a while.

Heat half of the oil, add flour, fry it a little, add red paprika pepper and finely chopped parsley, add some cold water, then the warm water, add salt and pepper and simmer for about 10 minutes.

Grease well a fireproof dish or casserole, put fish in, pour parsley sauce over, bake in the oven preheated to 200 °C until brown. Before serving drip with lemon juice or serve lemon slices separately.

Serve with mashed potatoes or stewed vegetables.

Greece

FISH STEW FROM CORFU — "BURTETO"

(for 5 persons)

juice of 1 lemon
1,5 kg sea fish for cooking
1 dl olive oil
3 dl water
250 gr onion
1 teaspoon red paprika pepper
some hot paprika
salt
pepper

Mix oil and water, add salt, pepper, red paprika pepper and hot paprika. Peel onion, cut into thin slices, plunge into the prepared mixture of water and spices. Simer until onion is tender. Clean fish, wash, wipe and drip with lemon juice. Leave to stand for a while. Put it into the liquid and simmer for about 15—20 minutes.

Yugoslavia

FISH STEW FISHERMEN WAY — "BRODET"

750 gr—1 kg blue sea fish (sardelle, mackerel, tunny, sprats)
300—400 gr onion
500 gr tomatoes
4 cloves of garlic
1/2 bunch of parsley and 1/2 bunch of celery leaves
salt
pepper
2—3 tablespoons wine vinegar
2 dl oil
water as needed

Clean fish, wash and drain. Chop onion finely. Put onion into a bigger pot, place pieces of prepared fish over, add salt and pepper. Put washed tomatoes cut into rounds over the fish. Sprinkle all with chopped garlic, crudely chopped parsley and celery, pour in oil and vinegar and barely cover with water. Shake "brodet" occasionally, but do not stir. When all is tender, draw aside and cool a little.

With this fish stew serve polenta.

Albania

RED MULLETS WITH VEGETABLES

(for 6 persons)

6 smaller red mullets
40 gr flour
salt
2,5—3 dl oil
juice of 1 lemon
pepper
1 bunch of parsley
2 cloves of garlic
1 onion
500 gr tomatoes
500 gr courgettes
500 gr aubergines
3 dl white wine

Clean fish, wash, wipe well, roll in flour and fry in heated oil (about 2 dl). When fried, drip them with lemon juice, add salt, pepper and chopped parsley (1/2 bunch).

Peel courgettes, cut into cubes; peel aubergines, cut into cubes, salt and leave to stand about 30 minutes, then rinse with cold water and drain. Cook slowly courgettes and aubergines in heated oil, add salt, pepper and chopped parsley (1/2 bunch).

Rub a fireproof dish with cut garlic, grease with oil (left over from cooking), place in fried fish, sprinkle with chopped onion. Cover with peeled tomatoes, cut into rounds, then with cooked courgettes and aubergines. Bake in the oven preheated to 175 °C about 30—35 minutes. Pour wine over at times, while baking.

Yugoslavia

SARDELLE BAKED IN JUICE

1 kg sardelle
2 dl oil
juice of 1 lemon
1/2 bunch of parsley
4 cloves of garlic
1—2 tablespoons breadcrumbs (if needed)

Clean fish well, cut heads off, wash well and wipe (with a clean cloth). Grease a casserole or a fireproof dish with oil and put fish into it side by side.

Put oil into a deeper bowl, add lemon juice, chopped parsley, chopped garlic, salt and pepper. Beat all until thick, then pour over the fish. Preheat oven to 175 °C and bake about 45—50 minutes.

Sardelle prepared this way can be served warm or kept in the refrigerator for several days.

If there is too much juice when baking, 1—2 tablespoons of breadcrumbs can be added to the fish.

Greece

BAKED FILLETS

1 kg fillets of hake
juice of 1 lemon
salt
pepper
1,5 dl olive oil
6 onions
2—3 cloves of garlic
2 tablespoons of chopped parsley
500 gr tomatoes
2 lemons

Wash fish fillets, drain, wipe, drip with lemon juice, add salt and pepper. Grease a fireproof dish a little with oil, put in the fillets. Cook slowly chopped onion, garlic and parsley in oil. Then add 3 peeled and cut tomatoes. Cook together about 5 minutes, add about 1 dl water, simmer for a short while.

Pour this sauce over the fillets, cover all with rounds of peeled tomatoes and lemons. Heat oven to 175°C, bake for about 45—50 minutes, that is until all is brown.

Albania

RED MULLETS WITH TOMATOES

(for 6 persons)

6 smaller red mullets
salt
30—40 gr flour
1 dl oil
500 gr tomatoes
pepper
2 cloves of garlic
1/2 bunch of parsley
50 gr kachkaval or similar cheese
20 gr breadcrumbs

Clean fish, wash, wipe and salt. Leave them to stand for a while, then roll in flour and fry in heated oil.

Wash tomatoes, remove seed, cut into slices cook slowly in some oil left over from frying fish, add salt, pepper, chopped garlic and parsley.

Grease a fireproof dish a little, put in half of the tomato, place mullets on top, pour the rest of tomato over, sprinkle with breadcrumbs and grated cheese. Bake in the oven preheated to 200°C about 40 minutes.

With fish serve cooked rice with parsley or boiled potatoes.

Greece

BAKED FISH FROM THE ISLAND OF SPETSE

(for 5—6 persons)

juice of 1 lemon
1,5 kg sea fish
salt
pepper
500 gr fresh or canned peeled tomatoes ("pelati")
1 dl white wine
2 dl olive oil
2 cloves of garlic
1/2 bunch of parsley
some breadcrumbs

Clean fish, wash, wipe, drip with lemon juice, add salt and pepper, then put into a greased fireproof dish or casserole.

Mix tomatoes, wine, oil, crushed or chopped garlic, chopped parsley. Simmer for about 15—20 minutes.

Pour this mixture over the prepared fish, sprinkle with breadcrumbs and bake in the oven preheated to 175—200°C uncovered, for about 40 minutes, until brown.

Yugoslavia

COD ISTRIA WAY

300—400 gr dried cod
3 dl oil (olive or other)
salt
pepper
4 cloves of garlic
1/2 bunch of parsley

Soak cod in cold water (preferably overnight). Barely cover with cold water and put up to cook. When it boils, turn to low heat and simmer until tender. Take out cooked cod carefully and place on a clean cloth. Remove skin and bones. Put fish into a bowl, add salt, pepper, finely chopped garlic, plenty of oil and some water from cooking the cod. Cover bowl and shake thoroughly until a white mixture is obtained, similar to mashed potatoes.

It could also be mixed with a wooden mixing spoon. In that case pour in half of the oil and add the rest gradually while mixing. Salt is also added while mixing. Garlic and parsley could be fried in some oil (but they must not change colour) and served separately, so that the dish remains white.

Serve with polenta, cooked sorrel or pasta.

Yugoslavia

HERRINGS BALKAN WAY

8 fresh herrings
1 lemon
25 gr grated cheese (kachkaval, Parmesan or similar)
50 gr flour
1 tablespoon mild red paprika pepper
1 clove of garlic
2 onions
1 paprika
salt
pepper
2—3 dl oil for frying
2—3 tomatoes

Pour lemon juice over cleaned herrings. Mix cheese with flour, red paprika pepper and chopped parsley. Peel onion and cut into rounds. Wash paprikas, core and cut into strips.

Salt and pepper herrings, roll in the mixture of flour and cheese. Heat oil, fry fish on both sides for 4—5 minutes. Take them out, drain and keep in a warm place.

Wash tomatoes and halve. Dip the cut side into the mixture of flour and cheese and fry each side in the oil from frying fish for 2 minutes. Also fry paprikas and onion quickly to soften. Arrange fish on a plate and garnish with vegetables.

With fish prepared this way serve potato salad or lettuce and boiled potatoes with parsley.

Greece

AEGEAN SQUIDS

800 gr — 1 kg squids
salt
350 gr tomatoes
1 bunch of parsley
2 cloves of garlic
1 dl olive oil
1 dl white wine
pepper
juice of 1 lemon

Clean squids, pluck out head and arms, remove the transparent bone, the inside and the black parts. Cut arms up to the eyes. Wash body and arms well, rub with salt, then rinse with cold water,

drain and cut into rounds. Wash tomatoes, peel and cut into small pieces. Chop parsley finely, crush garlic well. Heat oil, fry squids, add parsley, tomato and wine, cover and simmer for about 30—40 minutes. Season with salt, pepper and lemon juice.

Greece

STUFFED SQUIDS

700—750 gr squids
1 bigger onion
1,5 dl olive oil
50—70 gr rice
4 tablespoons pistachios
4 tablespoons red currants
1/2 bunch of parsley
salt
1,5 dl white wine
3 dl tomato juice

Clean squids, cut off heads, remove little bags with the black stuff, the transparent middle bone and the inside. Rub heads, arms and bodies with salt. Wash several times.

Chop onion finely. Heat about 3/4 dl oil, add onion, cook slowly until soft. Pick over rice, wash, cook and add to softened onion. Add pistachios, red currants, chopped parsley, salt and pepper. Mix all well. Fill the squids' bodies with this stuffing. Do not fill too tightly, as rice will swell. Truss the openings.

Heat the rest of oil in a bigger pan or frying pan, put in the stuffed squids, heads and arms, fry them, arrange in a fireproof dish, pour in wine, warmed tomato juice and salt as needed. Simmer at medium heat or bake in the oven preset at 175 °C about 90 minutes, that is until squids are tender, and the juice thick. Serve warm or cold.

Albania

MUSSEL SALAD

(for 4—6 persons)

3 kg mussels with shells on
3/4 l water
2 onions
3—4 cloves of garlic
1/2 celery root
2 bayleaves
1 teaspoon thyme
1 smaller rosemary sprig
salt
pepper
1 bigger lemon
100 gr mayonnaise
olives to garnish

Bring water to the boil, add peeled and chopped onion and garlic, chopped celery and herbs and simmer about 30—40 minutes. Wash mussels well, put into cooked marinade, keep on low heat until mussels open, take them out, remove shells and cool.

Drain marinade, add lemon juice and salt and pepper as needed. Mix mayonnaise a little and slowly pour in the cooled marinade, stirring constantly. Pour this over cooled mussels, shake well and leave to stand in a cool place. Garnish with black olives.

Albania

CRAYFISH STEW — "BRODET"

1 kg cooked crayfish
500 gr potatoes
1—1,5 dl oil (olive oil preferably)
salt, pepper
1 bunch of parsley
1/2—1 dl wine vinegar

Take shells off cooked crayfish and cut meat into pieces if necessary. Peel potatoes, wash and cut into rounds. Grease a fireproof dish a little, put in potatoes, add salt and pepper, cover with crayfish meat, add salt and pepper again, pour oil over, sprinkle with chopped parsley. Pour over with the rest of oil and with wine vinegar, so that all is covered. Simmer for about 30—40 minutes.

Greece

OCTOPUS IN SAUCE

(for 5—6 persons)

1 octopus of about 1,6 kg
2 dl olive oil
2 cloves of garlic
450 gr onion
1 dl red wine
175 gr peeled tomatoes (fresh or canned)
pepper (no salt)

Clean octopus and wash. Put into a pan without water, cover and stew at medium heat for about 10 minutes, then drain and take off skin. Cut it into small pieces.

Heat oil in a pan, add finely chopped onion, cook a little to soften, add chopped garlic. Put in pieces of octopus, cook quickly at greater heat (for several minutes), pour in wine, turn heat down, cook slowly. When wine has nearly evaporated, turn in tomatoes cut into pieces, add pepper. Cover and simmer until quite tender and the sauce thickens. It takes about 2 hours.

Yugoslavia

STEWED MUSSELS

1,5 kg long mussels
1 dl oil
150 gr onion
20 gr garlic (2 cloves)
1 bunch of parsley
2 fresh tomatoes
40 gr breadcrumbs
pepper
1 dl white wine
salt

Heat oil, add finely chopped onion and garlic, chopped parsley, tomatoes washed and cut into small cubes, cook

slowly until all is nearly soft, then add breadcrumbs and pepper.

Wash mussels well, put over the stewed vegetable, stew until mussels open up, then add wine and cook together for about 5 minutes.

Turn into a deeper dish and serve with fresh brown or rye bread.

4

SALADS AND SAUCES

Sauces are not used a great deal in the Balkan cuisine, with the exception of several kinds of tomato sauce and the well-known avgholemono (eggs and lemon sauce), without which it is hard to imagine Greek cooking. There are relatively few dishes in this cookery book with which a specific sauce should be served, but the well-known rule is that warm dishes call for warm sauces, while with cold ones cold sauces should be served. Perhaps the most characteristic feature of the Balkan sauces is that there is always a lot of onion and garlic in them, as well as various aromatic herbs (parsley, celery, dill, bayleaf, rosemary, thyme, oregano etc.). Béchamel sauce has come into use lately and has been taken over from the West, but it is most often used as the sauce to pour over the dish when half-baked and then to brown in the oven, or instead of the usual browned flour with red paprika pepper, and not as a sauce to be served with the dish separately.

Salads are a favourite accompaniment to the main course. They are prepared from nearly all kinds of vegetables, frequently with onion or garlic added, and sometimes sprinkled with cow or sheep cheese (in slices). It is hard to imagine lunch, especially in summer time, without a big bowl of mixed salad. Particular favourites are ayvars and pindzurs, which are true Balkan specialities. It is true that to prepare them takes some more time than is the case with other salads, but they are usually made in greater quantities, because unlike fresh salads these cooked or stewed salads can be kept in a cool place for several days. Pickled, marinaded vegetables can also be prepared to be used several times, but they are more often eaten when there are no fresh summer vegetables. For making potato, bean or beetroot salads, which are considered to be winter salads, nearly every country has its own recipe, though there is no essential difference between them. Whether beetroot salad, for example, is going to be prepared with or without horseradish, with or without caraway seeds, is more a question of personal taste than that of recipes.

Roumania

COLOURFUL CABBAGE SALAD

(for 6—8 persons)

1 small head of white cabbage
1 small head of red cabbage
1 bigger carrot
1 small onion
salt
pepper
1 dl oil
vinegar to taste

Separate cabbage leaves, wash, drain, remove thicker leaf ribs. Put several together at a time, rool up and cut into fine strips. Scrape carrot and grate finely. Chop onion finely. Mix vegetables, add salt and pepper. Mix oil and vinegar together, pour over the vegetables and mix. Keep covered until serving.

Cabbage salad is an excellent accompaniment to potato, courgette or aubergine moussakas, as well as to roast or fried meat, egg dishes and the like.

The old habit to salt cabbage and leave it to stand for a long time should be abandoned, as important mineral substances and vitamins in cabbage are destroyed that way. Cabbage salad should always be kept covered, because oxygen from air quickly destroys vitamin C which cabbage contains to a great extent.

Bulgaria

CUCUMBER AND CHEESE SALAD — "LUKOVITSA"

500—750 gr cucumbers
1 onion
250 gr young cow or sheep cheese in slices
salt
2,5 dl sour cream

Wash cucumbers, peel and dice. Peel onion, wash and chop finely. Crush cheese a little, add to the cucumbers and

onion, salt, pour over with whipped sour cream, mix all well.

This kind of salad is usually served with squash pie, cornbread or maize flour pie.

Greece

MARINADED ONION I

500 gr peeled small onions (or bigger button onions)
2 dl white wine
2 dl water
1 dl olive (or plain) oil
juice of 1 lemon
2 bayleaves
peppercorns
salt

Heat wine, water, oil and lemon juice. Bring to the boil, add prepared small onions, bayleaves, peppercorns and salt. Simmer until onions are glassy, then take aside and cool in the solution in which they were cooked. Take cooled onions out, put into a salad bowl, pour over with some marinade.

Serve quite cold with grilled dishes, egg or meat dishes etc.

Bulgaria

MARINADED COURGETTES

600—750 gr young courgettes
25 gr flour
about 2 dl oil for frying and cooking
1 small onion
4 cloves of garlic
a few sage leaves
2 glasses wine vinegar (or even better, vinegar with aromatic herbs)
salt

Wash courgettes, wipe, then cut lengthways into equal slices, roll in flour and fry in heated oil until nicely brown on both sides. Arrange fried courgettes in a deeper dish.

Peel onion, chop finely and cook slowly in heated oil (1 dl) until tender and beginning to colour, then add crushed or snipped garlic, sage leaves, wine vinegar and salt. Cook together for 5—10 minutes, cool a little and pour over the courgettes. Leave to stand for at least 24 hours before use.

Serve cold with meat or fish dishes instead of salad.

Greese

MARINADED ONION II

1 kg button onions
120 gr tomato purée (from tube)
1 dl olive oil
juice of 1 lemon
salt
peppercorns
thyme
1—2 bayleaves
1/2 bunch of parsley
1 sprig celery
2—3 cloves

Plunge unpeeled button onions into boiling water, blanch (cook for 2—3 minutes), take out, drain and peel carefully so that they remain whole.

In a separate bowl mix puréed tomato, oil, lemon juice and aromatic spices. Mix all well, turn in peeled onions, simmer for about 30 minutes, add salt to taste, turn into a china or earthenware bowl and cool. Serve rather cooled as an accompaniment to roast meat, cooked ham, egg, offal or cheese dishes etc.

If marinaded onions are put into a jar, covered tightly and kept in a cool place, they can be used even after a few days.

Yugoslavia

MARINADED UNRIPE TOMATOES

2 kg smaller green tomatoes
1 l wine vinegar
1/2 l water
30—35 gr salt
40—50 gr sugar
5—6 peppercorns
2 smaller onions
50 gr mustard seeds
1 horseradish root

Wash tomatoes, drain, prick with a toothpick, scald with hot, slightly salted water, leave in it to cool. Then drain and arrange in previously throughly washed and dried jars.

Mix vinegar and water for the marinade, add salt, sugar, peppercorns, peeled onion, mustard seeds or dill seeds. Cook for 5—10 minutes, pour hot over arranged tomatoes, press down with horseradish root, cover and leave to cool. When quite cold, tie the jars up with cellophane and leave in a cool place.

Serve as salad with various roast or fried meats, baked vegetables, moussakas and the like, or use to garnish appetisers and dishes.

Greece

MARINADED ARTICHOKES

8—10 quite small green artichokes
2 dl white wine
2 dl water
1 dl olive or other oil
1 lemon
salt
peppercorns
1 bayleaf
some salt

Trim artichokes, discard sharp tops and "hay", wash. Mix wine, water, olive oil, lemon juice, peppercorns, bayleaf and salt, cook about 5 minutes, then plunge in artichokes. Simmer until tender, then set aside and leave artichokes to cool in the marinade. Keep in the refrigerator until serving, as artichokes prepared this way are served quite cold.

Before serving, take artichokes out of marinade, strain part of it and pour over arranged artichokes.

Serve with roast meat, fish, egg dishes, grilled dishes etc.

Roumania

MARINADED BEETROOT

2 kg beetroots, medium, if possible even-sized
1,5 l wine vinegar
7,5 dl water
60 gr salt
80 gr sugar
10—15 peppercorns
carraway seeds (optional)
1 horseradish root
1 onion
1 bayleaf
several cloves

Wash beetroots, cook in slightly salted water until tender, which means about 2 hours in an ordinary pot, or 30—40 minutes in a pressure cooker. Beetroots can also be baked, which is advisable, as they lose least of their substances that way. Wrap them in a tin foil and bake in the oven (180°C) about 90 minutes.

Run cold water over beetroots, peel and cut into equally thick rounds with a special undulate knife. Arrange in washed and dried jars or an earthenware pot. Place pieces of horseradish in between the rows of beetroot. A small onion can be put in the middle, with several cloves stuck into it.

Yugoslavia

SPRING ONION AND CHEESE SALAD — "SATRITSA"

1—2 bunches of spring onion (depending on the size)
salt
pepper
1/2 bunch of parsley
2,5 dl sour cream or thick yoghurt
200—250 gr young white cow cheese

Trim spring onions, wash, drain, cut rather finely and salt. Crumble cheese into small pieces, mix with onions, pour over with sour cream or thick yoghurt, mix, add more salt if needed, add pepper and sprinkle with chopped parsley.

This kind of salad is served with various dishes with eggs, maize flour, baked (jacket) potatoes etc., but it can also be served as an appetiser, "meze", with plum brandy or other strong drinks.

Bulgaria

CUCUMBER AND THICK YOGHURT SALAD — "TARATOR"

2 cloves of garlic
50—75 gr shelled walnuts
2—3 tablespoons oil
1/2 l thick yoghurt
350—500 gr cucumbers
1/2 bunch of dill
salt

Clean garlic, crush well, add crushed or finely chopped walnuts, oil, whipped thick yoghurt, peeled and cubed cucumbers, chopped dill and salt. If the mixture is too thick, some water can be added.

"Tarator" salad can also be prepared with lettuce. In that case instead of cucumbers, use chopped lettuce leaves.

If the tarator is prepared so that it is more watery it can be served as cold soup in summer months.

As salad, it is served with roast and fried meat or fish dishes, offal, baked or fried potatoes etc.

Yugoslavia

HOME MADE PICKLES — "TURSHIYA" Winter salad with mixed vegetables

1 kg cucumbers (smaller)
1 kg unripe green tomatoes
1 kg cauliflower
1 kg carrots
3 bunches of radishes
1/2 kg button onions
2 bigger celery roots
1 kg pointed paprikas
5 bayleaves
1 sachet peppercorns
salt

2 horseradish roots
3—4 small hot peppers

For brine:
2 l water
125 gr salt
60 gr concentrated vinegar
half a sachet of wine-stopper (substance for checking fermentation)

Remove stalks and leaves from vegetables, wash and arrange in clean, dry jars. Fill in hollows with smaller vegetables. In between put peppercorns, horseradish, bayleaves and small hot pepper to taste. Vegetables can be put whole, or cut into pieces.

Brine to pour over: boil water and salt, cool and add wine-stopper and vinegar essence. Pour over vegetables and leave to stand for 24 hours without covering the jars. Then pour the brine out and pour into the jars again. Cover jars with celophane.

When preparing bigger quantities, this salad can be put into plastic barrels. It can also be prepared separately according to the kinds of vegetables, if the individual taste of a vegetable is to be preserved.

Bulgaria

BAKED PAPRIKAS WITH THICK YOGHURT

(for 6 persons)

1 kg paprikas (fleshy red long ones)
1/2 dl oil
2,5—3 dl thick yoghurt
1—2 cloves of garlic
1 bunch of parsley
salt

Wash paprikas, wipe, dry fry on top the stove, place in a deeper dish, sprinkle with cold water and leave to stand for a while. Then peel them, cut lengthways, put in a bowl or on a salad plate, sprinkle with salt and pour over with oil.

Whip well thick yoghurt, add finely chopped or crushed garlic and snipped parsley, mix well. Pour over arranged paprikas. Leave for a while in a cool place, then serve as an accompaniment to baked egg dishes, baked potatoes, grills, offal dishes and the like.

Bulgaria

OKRA SALAD

500 gr young okras
1 lemon
1/2—1 dl oil
salt
pepper
1 tablespoonful chopped parsley
2 harder tomatoes

Trim okras, wash and cook in salted water. When tender, drain and cool.

Mix lemon juice and oil, add salt and pepper. Mix well to get a thicker mixture. Pour over okras arranged in a bowl, sprinkle with chopped parsley. Wash tomatoes, remove stalk ends and cut into nice slices, then garnish the salad with them.

Okras are used in preparing various Balkan specialties. Only young fruits are picked, before the seeds are formed and the tissue becomes hard and coarse.

Bulgaria

KOHLRABI SALAD

(for 6—8 persons)

500 gr young kohlrabi
200 gr apples (2 apples)
150 gr cucumbers
1—2 paprikas
1—2 tablespoons grated horseradish
1/2 bunch of dill
1/2 dl oil
3 tablespoons vinegar
1 dl sour cream
salt

Peel kohlrabi and apples, grate crudely. Peel cucumbers (if young and not sprayed with insecticide, just wash), cut into cubes or rounds. Wash paprikas, remove seed, cut into strips or cubes. Mix vegetables, add horseradish and chopped dill. Mix well oil, vinegar, salt and sour cream, pour over the vegetables, mix all and leave in a cool place, so that marinade and vegetables blend well.

Serve as an accompaniment to breaded and roast meat.

Yugoslavia

"PINDZUR" SALAD

(for 10 persons)

1 kg big paprikas or fleshy long ones
500 gr unripened tomatoes
500 gr aubergines
2—2,5 dl oil
salt
3—4 cloves of garlic

Wash paprikas, wipe and dry fry on top the stove. Bake green tomatoes and aubergines in the oven. When all the vegetables are baked, peel them, chop and put into a pan, add salt, then pour in oil gradually, stirring all the time and fry at low heat until the mixture is well blended and the given quantity of oil mixed in. Add chopped or crushed garlic, mix. Shape a ball or a cone in the salad bowl and cool well.

Serve with grilled meat, warm cornbread, pogatcha and the like.

"Pindzur" is prepared in several variations, depending on local tradition and on personal taste.

Bulgaria

GROUND UNRIPENED TOMATOES — "AYVAR"

1 kg green tomatoes
50 gr walnuts
2 cloves of garlic
1/2 dl oil
2—3 tablespoons vinegar
1 bunch of parsley
1 small onion
50 gr olives
salt

Bake tomatoes shortly or blanche to soften, then remove skin and grind. Add finely chopped walnuts to ground tomatoes, then crushed garlic, oil, finely chopped parsley, vinegar and salt. Mix all well, turn into a bowl and garnish with onion rounds and olives. Serve rather cool.

This salad is called "ayvar", as it looks like the ayvar salad made of ground paprikas and aubergines. It is served as as accompaniment to roast or fried fish, roast meat, grilled meat, but is also a very good spread for toast, lepinyas and pogatcha.

Bulgaria

GREEN "AYVAR"

(for 6—8 persons)

1 kg aubergines (young and medium-sized)
250—300 gr fleshy paprikas
150 gr tomatoes
1 smaller onion
1/2 dl oil
2 cloves of garlic
2—3 tablespoons vinegar
1 bunch of parsley
salt
olives and tomato slices for garnishing

Wash aubergines, wipe and grill quickly or dry fry on top the very heated stove. This is done so that the "meat" of aubergines would not grow dark with longer baking. Peel them while still warm, add baked and skinned paprikas (without seed), peeled and chopped tomatoes, peeled and chopped onion. Grind all in the meat grinder. To the mixture obtained, add oil, crushed garlic, vinegar, chopped parsley and salt. Mix all well. Turn into a salad bowl and garnish with olives and tomato rounds or slices.

"Ayvar" is served as an accompaniment to roast, fried or grilled meat, fried (breaded) vegetables, but can also be used as stuffing for vegetables (tomatoes, cucumbers, paprikas) or as spread for bread or sandwiches.

Baked paprikas and fresh tomatoes can be replaced by finely chopped walnuts.

Greece

COOKED SALAD

1,5 dl oil
500 gr onion
1 kg aubergines
2 big paprikas
1 bunch of parsley
salt
pepper

Heat oil, add peeled and finely chopped onion, cook slowly until tender. Wash aubergines, remove stalks, cut into cubes, salt, leave to stand for about 30 minutes, then rinse, drain and add to half cooked onion. Then add cored paprikas cut into strips. Add pepper and pour in 1—1,5 dl water. Simmer stirring occasionally until the mixture is rather thick.

Aubergines prepared this way can be served as warm or cold salad with various roasts and grilled specialties.

While preparing it, special attention should be paid to cooking, that is it should be cooked very slowly at medium heat, as greater heat and quick cooking do not give the salad of desired quality.

Yugoslavia

SERBIAN "AYVAR"

(for 6—8 persons)

4 aubergines
8—12 paprikas (big yellow or fleshy red long ones)
1 onion
1 dl oil
2 cloves of garlic
1—1,5 dl oil
1 tablespoon lemon juice or 2 spoonfuls of vinegar
salt
pepper

Wash aubergines, drain, put into the heated oven (175 °C) and bake, then peel while still warm. Wash paprikas, wipe and dry fry on top the stove, then put into a deeper dish, sprinkle with cold water, cover and leave to cool. Skin cooled paprikas and remove seed. Grind paprikas and aubergines together.

Peel onion, chop finely, cook slowly in heated oil until quite soft. Towards the end add cleaned and crushed garlic, cook shortly together, set aside, add ground paprikas and aubergines and mix. Turn all into a deeper dish and drip in oil slowly, stirring all the time. When all the oil is used, add lemon juice or vinegar, salt, pepper and mix well. Put into a bowl, shape nicely, sprinkle with more pepper if desired and pour over with some more oil.

"Ayvar" is the favourite salad prepared in all parts of Yugoslavia. It is often preserved for winter. In that case it is prepared in the same way but without adding onion and garlic, and ground aubergines and paprikas are fried for a longer time in oil. Ayvar is put into small clean jars, pressed tightly so that there are no air bubbles in them, and the jars covered with cellophane or parchment.

It is served with grilled meat, bean dishes etc.

Greece

PEASANTS' SALAD

1 cucumber (bigger)
2—3 tomatoes
1 onion
2 small hot peppers
1/2 olive oil

2 tablespoons vinegar (white)
salt
pepper
200 gr sheep cheese in slices
50 gr olives
1/2 bunch of parsley or 1/2 teaspoon crushed dried marjoram

Wash cucumber well and cut into cubes unpeeled. Wash tomatoes, also cut into smaller cubes. Peel onion, wash and cut into thin rounds, wash hot peppers and cut into small rounds. Mix vegetables.

Mix well olive oil, vinegar, salt and pepper to get a thick mixture. Pour over vegetables, mix slowly. Sprinkle all with cheese cut into cubes, then with chopped parsley.

Greek salad will certainly be a pleasant "culinary souvenir" of the holiday in the homeland of the Hellenes.

Roumania

GIPSY SALAD

1 young sweetcorn cob
3 bigger paprikas
2 tomatoes
1 onion
1—2 cloves of garlic
2—3 tablespoons oil
1 tablespoon vinegar
salt

Cook maize cob, then husk. Wash paprikas, scoop out seed and cut into strips. Peel tomatoes and cut into smaller cubes. Peel and chop onion and garlic. Mix all.

Mix well oil, vinegar and salt and pour over the vegetables, mix and leave to stand for a short while in a cool place. Serve as an accompaniment to some egg dish, roast meat or fish, or to grilled meat.

Yugoslavia

"SHOPSKA" SALAD

1 onion
500 gr tomatoes
150—200 gr ripened cow or sheep cheese in slices
1/2 dl oil
1 small hot pepper
1 cucumber, salt

Peel onion and chop finely. Wash tomatoes, peel, cut into rounds or slices, mix onion and tomatoes, pour over with oil, salt and add peeled cucumber cut into cubes. Mix all slowly, sprinkle with grated or crumbled cheese and with small pepper cut into rounds.

This delicious salad is a frequent accompaniment to maize flour dishes (cornbread, green vegetables pie), to baked or cooked potatoes, French toast, tchevapchitchi (grilled cork-schaped ground meat, a Serbian specialty) and the like.

Roumania

AUBERGINE "AYVAR"

4—5 aubergines
1,5 dl oil
juice of 1 lemon
salt
pepper
1—2 harder tomatoes

Wash aubergines, wipe and bake. When tender and the skins dark, cool them and peel, then chop finely or grind. Stirring constantly add oil bit by bit until a well blended mixture is obtained. Add lemon juice, salt and pepper. Mix all well. Turn on to a plate, garnish with tomato slices and keep in the refrigerator until serving.

Serve with meat dishes, cold roasts or as bread spread.

Greece

AUBERGINE SALAD

(for 6 persons)

3—4 aubergines
1 smaller onion
1 bigger tomato
1 dl olive or plain oil
vinegar to taste (2—3 tablespoons)
salt
pepper
100 gr black olives
2 small peppers

Wash aubergines, wipe, put in a baking pan and bake at medium heat (175°C) until tender. Aubergine skins should get dark so that the salad could have the taste of smoke. Peel while still hot. Chop peeled aubergines finely, then add finely chopped onion, crushed garlic, peeled and chopped tomato, oil, vinegar, salt and pepper, stirring constantly. Mix all well into a homogeneous mixture.

Shape salad into a cone or a ball on a plate or in a bowl and garnish with olives and small pepper rounds.

Serve as an accompaniment to roast and fried meat and grilled fish.

Albania

BAKED PAPRIKAS AND TOMATO SALAD

(for 8 persons)

8 green or yellow paprikas
1 kg bigger and harder tomatoes
1 onion
1—1,5 dl oil
1/2 bunch of parsley and 1/2 bunch of celery leaves
salt
pepper

Wash paprikas, wipe and dry fry on top the stove, sprinkle with some cold water, cover and leave to stand for a while, then skin, remove seed and cut into strips. Plunge tomatoes shortly into hot, then into cold water, peel and cut into rounds. Peel onion, wash and cut into thin rounds. Wash parsley and celery leaves, wipe and chop finely. Mix all vegetables, add salt and pepper, mix carefully but well.

During the season of tomatoes and paprikas this salad is often prepared not only in Albania, but also in many parts of Bulgaria and Yugoslavia.

It is usually served with grilled meat, egg dishes, beans etc.

Roumania

BEETROOT SALAD

(for 8 persons)

1 kg medium-sized beetroots
1 smaller horseradish root (or a few spoonfuls of canned one)
1 level teaspoon caraway seeds
salt
1/2—2 dl oil
1—2 tablespoons lemon juice or wine (or fruit) vinegar

Wash beetroots, cook in slightly salted water, or even better, bake in the preheated oven. When cooked or baked, cool, peel, then cut into rounds or grate crudely. Add scraped and finely grated horseradish, salt, some caraway seeds, oil, lemon juice or vinegar. Mix carefully not to break beetroot too much. Leave for a while in a cool place.

Beetroot salad is usually served with roast or fried meat, fish, various moussakas etc.

In can be prepared from fresh beetroot, which is advisable as beetroot has not only nutritive but also preventive qualities. If the salad is prepared with raw beetroot, only very young ones should be used, and sour cream and lemon juice are suggested for marinade to offset the pungent taste of raw beetroot.

Beetroot is used rather a lot in the Balkan diet. Older people remember that it used to be sold and eaten in the streets, like boiled or grilled sweetcorn.

Greece

MARINADED MUSHROOMS

500 gr mushrooms (button mushrooms and similar)
2 dl wine
2 dl water
1 dl olive oil
juice of 1/2 lemon
2 bayleaves
6—10 peppercorns
salt

Wash mushrooms, trim and cut into thicker slices or pieces. Mix wine, water, oil, lemon juice and spices. Bring to the boil, then add prepared mushrooms. Cook at medium heat 10—20 minutes, then leave to cool in the same solution. When cooled, take out, put into a salad bowl, pour over with some marinade and put into the refrigerator.

Serve cooled with grilled dishes (offal, tchevapchitchi etc.).

Turkey

TURKISH SALAD

200 gr fresh white cabbage
200 gr carrots
200 gr white turnips
1 l water
salt
12 stuffed green olives
1 bunch of parsley
1 bunch od dill
1 bigger orange
1 lemon
1 smaller onion

For marinade:
1 clove of garlic
60 gr olive (or plain) oil
3 tablespoons lemon juice
1 teaspoon sugar
white pepper
100 gr riper goat cheese

Remove any discoloured leaves from cabbage, wash, wipe, then shred (or grate). Peel carrots and turnips, wash and grate crudely. Heat water, add salt. When it boils, plunge prepared vegetables, leave to boil 1—2 minutes, then drain well.

Cut olives into rounds. Wash parsley and dill and wipe (with absorbent paper). Chop parsley finely and snip dill (with kitchen scissors). Mix drained vegetables with olives, parsley and dill. Prepare the marinade in the following way: crush garlic well, add salt, some sugar, oil, lemon juice and pepper. Pour this marinade over the vegetables, mix well and put on a bigger plate or into a bowl.

Peel orange and lemon (remove white underskin), cut into thinner rounds. Garnish salad with these rounds. Put rounds of onion over them. Leave to stand in the refrigerator at least 30 minutes. Before serving sprinkle with crumbled goat cheese.

Serve with grilled dishes or with rusks as light supper (adding maybe some hard boiled eggs).

Greece

BAKED POTATOES SALAD

(for 6 persons)

1 kg potatoes (preferably the "pink" variety)
3 dl oil
1/2 dl wine vinegar
2 cloves of garlic
salt
pepper

Wash potatoes, wipe, put into the oven preheated to 175°C and bake. Peel baked potatoes and while still warm, pass through a potato press one by one or mash them in a deeper bowl. Add oil bit by bit while still warm, stirring all the time, then turn on to a plate or into a bowl, add vinegar, crushed garlic, salt, pepper and mix well. Decorate it a little with a spoon.

Serve as warm or cold salad with egg dishes (omelet, scrambled eggs, fried eggs sunny-side up), quickly baked offal (liver, kidneys, brains), stewed or roast meat or fish.

Turkey

BEAN SALAD I

250 gr beans (brown or similar)
1,5 l water
1 smaller onion

For marinade:
60 gr (6 tablespoons) olive or plain oil
3 tablespoons lemon juice
salt
pepper ground from mill
4 smaller tomatoes
50 gr green olives (without stones)
2 hard boiled eggs

Pick over beans, wash, pour over with cold water and leave to swell overnight, then cook in the same water and add peeled onion. When tender, drain and put into a deeper bowl. Remove onion.

For the marinade: mix well oil, lemon juice, salt and pepper. Pour over still warm beans, leave to cool about 30—40 minutes. Wash tomatoes, peel, remove stalk ends, cut into slices, remove seed. Halve olives. Shell eggs and also slice. Add tomatoes, olives and egg slices to the beans, mix carefully and leave to stand for at least 40—60 minutes.

Serve as an accompaniment to baked meat dishes or grills. Canned beans can also be used for this salad, which should only be rinsed and drained. In that case the salad can be prepared quickly.

Bulgaria

BEAN SALAD II

250 gr beans (preferably white)
1 leek
1—2 cloves of garlic
1/2 dl oil
1 teaspoon mustard
salt
pepper
2 tablespoons vinegar

Pick over beans, wash and cook in slightly salted water. When tender, drain and cool a little. Trim leek, wash and cut into rounds. Chop garlic finely or crush. Add leek and garlic to cooled beans and add some salt.

Mix oil, mustard, salt, pepper and vinegar thickly. Pour over beans, pour in some water in which beans were cooked, if necessary.

Serve with egg dishes (omelet, scrambled eggs, hard boiled eggs), with grilled offal and others.

Roumania

POTATO SALAD WITH APPLES

(for 6—8 persons)

1 kg potatoes
2 sour apples
1 gherkin
1/2 bunch of parsley
150 gr mayonnaise
1 dl sour cream
salt
beetroot rounds for garnishing

Scrub potatoes and boil in their skins. When tender, drain, run cold water over them, peel and cut into smaller cubes. Peel apples and also cut into cubes. Mix apples and potatoes, add some salt, pour over with mayonnaise diluted with sour cream, add ghirkin cut into small cubes and chopped parsley. Mix all and leave to stand for a while. Before serving garnish with beetroot rounds.

Serve with egg dishes, roast and fried meat, roast and fried fish.

Yugoslavia

POTATO SALAD FROM VOJVODINA

(for 6—8 persons)

1 kg potatoes
salt
pepper
1/2 dl oil
2 tablespoons vinegar
1 celery root
2 egg yolks
3 tablespoons oil
1 teaspoon mustard
juice of 1/2 lemon
3 dl sour cream
tomato or paprika for garnishing

Scrub potatoes and boil in their skins. When cooked, drain, peel and cool a little, then cut into rounds, salt a little, add oil, vinegar, pepper, mix all well and leave to stand for a while. Wash celery, scrape and grate finely, add to the potatoes and mix.

Beat egg yolks, add oil bit by bit, stirring constantly, add salt, mustard and lemon juice and make a homogenous mixture, blend in sour cream in the end, slowly. Pour over potatoes, mix carefully. Form a cone or a ball in a salad bowl. Garnish with tomato slices or red paprika rounds.

Serve salad with egg dishes, roast or fried fish, meat and offal.

Albania

ALBANIAN SALAD

250 gr boiled potatoes
250 gr paprikas (big fleshy ones)
500 gr harder tomatoes
2 smaller onions
1 bunch of parsley
1 bunch of dill
50 gr raisins
2—3 dl sour cream or drinking yoghurt
30 gr (3 tablespoons) oil
salt
pepper

Wash paprikas, scoop out seed; wash and peel tomatoes; peel potatoes. Cut all into nice small cubes, add finely chopped onion, washed wiped and finely chopped parsley and dill, washed and cleaned raisins. Mix all well, add salt and pepper.

Mix well sour cream and oil, pour over vegetables. Once again mix slowly but well. Leave to stand for a while.

Serve salad as an accompaniment to roast and fried meat, fish, offal, various kinds of moussaka.

Bulgaria

LEEK SALAD

500 gr leeks
200—250 gr potatoes
1 smaller celery root
1/2 dl oil
2—3 tablespoons vinegar
salt
pepper

Trim leeks, wash well, cut into smaller pieces, cook in slightly salted water, drain. Peel potatoes, wash, boil in salted water, cut into rounds. Wash celery, scrape and grate finely. Mix carefully leeks, potatoes and celery and add pepper. Mix well oil and vinegar to get a thick mixture. Add salt if needed. Pour over mixed vegetables and stir. Leave to stand until quite cold. Serve as an

accompaniment to meat, fish, offal and egg dishes. Water in which potatoes and leeks were cooked can be used to prepare some thick soup, as it contains important mineral substances.

Roumania

TOMATO SAUCE I

750 gr ripe tomatoes
2 teaspoons salt
1 teaspoon sugar
30 gr butter or margarine (3 spoons melted)
1 tablespoon flour
pepper
several leaves of fresh or dried basil (optional)

Wash tomatoes, remove stalk ends, cut into slices, add salt and sugar and cook about 15 minutes, until tender.

Pass through a sieve and cook for another 15—20 minutes, until thick. Mix butter and flour, add to the sauce. Simmer together for 5 more minutes, stirring constantly. Towards the end add pepper and basil leaves.

Bulgaria

BALKAN SAUCE

2 red fleshy paprikas
1 fresh or pickled small hot pepper
2 onions
1—2 cloves of garlic
100—150 gr mayonnaise
pepper
salt

Wash paprikas and the hot pepper, remove seeds and chop finely. Peel onion and also chop. Crush garlic with some salt and pass through a press. Mix all with mayonnaise, add salt and pepper.

Roumania

ONION SAUCE

30—40 gr lard
10 gr sugar
2—3 onions
30 gr flour
salt
1—2 tablespoons vinegar
1/2 dl sour cream
2—3 dl warm water (or stock)

Heat lard, add sugar, fry until brown, add finely chopped onion, cook slowly until tender and light brown. Dust with flour, mix until flour is fried and slightly brown, add some cold water first and then some warm water (or strained stock), add salt and vinegar to taste. Simmer for a few more minutes. The sauce can be passed through a sieve in the end, and is seasoned with sour cream before serving.

It is served as an accompaniment to cooked warm beef, young beef, chicken or any other meat.

Yugoslavia

SOUR CHERRY SAUCE

40 gr lard or oil
30 gr flour
250 gr sour cherries (without stones)
1/2—3/4 l bone or meat stock
1 teaspoon sugar
salt
1/2—1 dl sour cream

Heat lard or oil, add flour, fry it until brown. Add sour cherries, cook slowly together until the cherries are soft, pour in strained stock (or warm water), cook together, add salt and sugar to taste. Season with sour cream before serving.

Serve with warm cooked meat (beef, young beef, chicken).

Bulgaria

HORSERADISH SAUCE WITH BEETROOT

250 gr horseradish
125 gr beetroot
1 dl vinegar
1/4 l water
salt
1 teaspoon sugar

Scrape horseradish, wash and grate finely, pour over with hot water, cover and leave to cool that way. Wash beetroot, peel and also grate finely, add to cooled horseradish, pour in vinegar, add salt and sugar. Mix all well.

This sauce is most often served with aspic, roast meat (especially pork), and with cooked vegetables (cauliflower, leeks, potatoes).

Yugoslavia

HORSERADISH SAUCE WITH BEANS

250 gr beans
1 dl oil
1 dl wine vinegar
1 horseradish root
salt
pepper

Cook beans, drain when soft and pass through a sieve. Add oil, vinegar, salt and pepper and mix. Scrape horseradish, wash and grate finely, add to the beans. Mix all, add water in which beans were cooked as necessary.

The sause is served with various kinds of roast meat and fish, with offal and egg dishes.

This sauce is most often to be found on the menus of Slovenian cuisine.

Turkey

AUBERGINE SAUCE

2 ripe aubergines (of medium size)
1 onion
1/2 dl oil
juice of 1/2 lemon
1 teaspoon honey
salt
pepper

Peel aubergines, cut into cubes, add salt, leave to stand for a while, then rinse and drain. Peel onion and chop finely. Heat 3 spoonfuls of oil, add onion, cook it a little, then add aubergines, pour in some water and simmer covered until tender. Then pass through a sieve, add the rest of oil, lemon juice, honey, salt and pepper. Mix all well (preferably with a mixer).

Serve sauce very cold with roast or fried fish.

Greece

TOMATO SAUCE II

1/2 cup olive (or plain) oil
2—3 cloves of garlic
1 bunch of parsley
500 gr peeled ripe potatoes
salt
sugar
pepper
some dried basil

Heat oil, add snipped or crushed garlic and chopped parsley. Cook slowly about 5 minutes.

Cut tomatoes into smaller pieces (remove seeds), add them to garlic and parsley, add salt, pepper sugar and basil. Simmer at very low heat until thick and until tomato is tender.

Serve with cooked meat, cooked pasta or cooked potatoes.

Bulgaria

BULGARIAN SAUCE

100 gr mayonnaise
7 tablespoons condensed milk (or sour cream)
2—3 tablespoons tomato purée (from tube or can)
hot red paprika pepper
salt
50 gr cooked celery

Mix well mayonnaise, milk (or sour cream), tomato, salt and hot red paprika pepper. Drain well cooked celery, dice and mix into the prepared sauce. Until serving the sauce should be kept in a cool place.

It is served with all kinds of cold meat dishes.

Greece

EGG SAUCE — "AVGHOLEMONO"

3 eggs
juice of 1 bigger lemon
2—2,5 dl hot stock
or soup from cube

Beat well eggs (or only egg yolks), add lemon juice gradually, stir all the time and pour in hot soup bit by bit.

The sauce prepared this way is added as seasoning to thick soups, or to roast meat or stewed meat gravy. When "avgholemono" is added to some dish, it should be stirred constantly and cooked at very low heat until it begins to thicken. The dish must not boil, however, as eggs would start to curdle, forming small lumps (which do not change the taste but are not nice to see).

In the traditional Greek cuisine this sauce is the final accompaniment to many dishes.

Yugoslavia

DILL SAUCE

20 gr lard or oil
20 gr flour
1 bunch of dill
juice of 1/2 lemon
1/2 dl sour cream
about 1/2 l warm water

Heat lard or oil, add flour, fry a little until slightly brown, pour in 2—3 tablespoons of cold water, add chopped dill, pour in the necessary quantity of warm water, add salt and lemon juice. Cook together for 5—10 minutes at low heat. Serve with warm cooked meat.

Sauce with sorrel, either cultivated or growing wild,can be prepared in the same way.

Bulgaria

HORSERADISH SAUCE WITH KAYMAK

250 gr horseradish
350 gr young kaymak
salt
1 teaspoon sugar

Scrape horseradish, wash and grate finely. Whip kaymak well, add horseradish, salt and sugar.Mix all well, then leave in a cool place. Serve with cold cooked meat, aspic with meat, stuffed eggs and the like.

If kaymak is not to be found, sour cream can be used instead.

5

SWEETS

The Balkan cuisine abounds in various rich cakes, tortes and different sweets, as this region had for centuries been under the direct influence of the Orient — the cradle of sweetmeats. At the time of the Ottoman rule, the sweets were probably the only "sweet consolation" to the conquered people, and when the Osmanlis left, the sweets and cakes remained. Then the influences of the West began to be felt more and more, resulting in imaginative combinations of sugar, flour, eggs, walnuts, almonds, fresh fruit, cream, butter and the unavoidable oriental spices.

In choosing dessert for a meal the only thing to bear in mind is what precedes it as the main course. If it is a filling dish, than the sweet must be light and digestible, preferably with fruit. Conversely, if the main dish is light, then the sweet can be richer and contain walnuts, various creams, sugar syrup and the like. A great variety of pies and baklavas with sugar syrup are still the main characteristic of the Balkan sweets, but the way of preparing them has changed a great deal. There are not many people any more who make the thin layers of dough for the pie or puff pastry themselves, when they can be bought in the shops as industrial products and are of very good quality. This means saving a lot of time and effort and specialties are prepared "in no time", with no great skill needed.

Turkey

APPLES STUFFED WITH NUTS – "TUFAHIYE"

1/2 l water
500 gr sugar
1 sachet vanilla sugar
500—700 gr apples ("delicious" or some other kind that remain whole in cooking)

For filling:
150 gr sugar
100 gr walnuts
50 gr almonds
lemon rind
2,5 dl double cream
cherries and some whipped cream for garnishing

Mix water, sugar and vanilla, then heat. Wash apples, peel and core carefully (with a sharp teaspoon or knife for peeling potatoes). When the water boils, plunge apples in and simmer for about 10 minutes (watch out that they do not "fall apart"!), take them out, drain and leave to cool (in a sieve or strainer). Mix sugar, ground walnuts and almons, grated lemon rind and slightly beaten cream. Stuff cooled apples with this filling. Arrange on a serving plate and garnish each apple with some whipped cream and cherries (sour cherries, strawberries etc.). Althoough "tufahiye" are considered to be a Turkish sweet, they are of Arabic origin, as their name denotes. Namely, "tufahiya" is an Arabic word for apple.

Turkey

"HALVAH"

250 gr butter
250 gr white flour

For syrup:
250 gr sugar
1/2 l water
vanilla-bean or vanilla sugar

Melt butter and heat, add flour and stir constantly as it must not burn. Mix until it is brown and does not stick to the spoon any more.

Prepare syrup as follows: pour water over sugar, add vanilla, cook for about 5—10 minutes. Pour hot syrup over browned flour and mix quickly until the "halvah" is thick.

When ready, take out with a tablespoon and arrange on a plate, sprinkle with powdered sugar mixed with vanilla or some other spice (cinnamon etc.).

Browned flour can be taken off heat,quickly poured over with syrup, covered and left to stay for a few hours, then mixed on heat, the spoonfuls of it arranged on the plate and sprinkled with powdered sugar.

Greece

SEMOLINA "HALVAH"

50 gr butter
50 gr skinned almonds
1 cup semolina

For pouring over:
2 cups sugar
3 cups water
100 gr butter
2 sachets vanilla sugar
powdered sugar with vanilla for dusting

Melt butter, heat, add almonds (chopped) and semolina, fry, stirring, until yellow.

Mix water, sugar and butter, add vanilla sugar. Bring to the boil.

Pour in this mixture into semolina

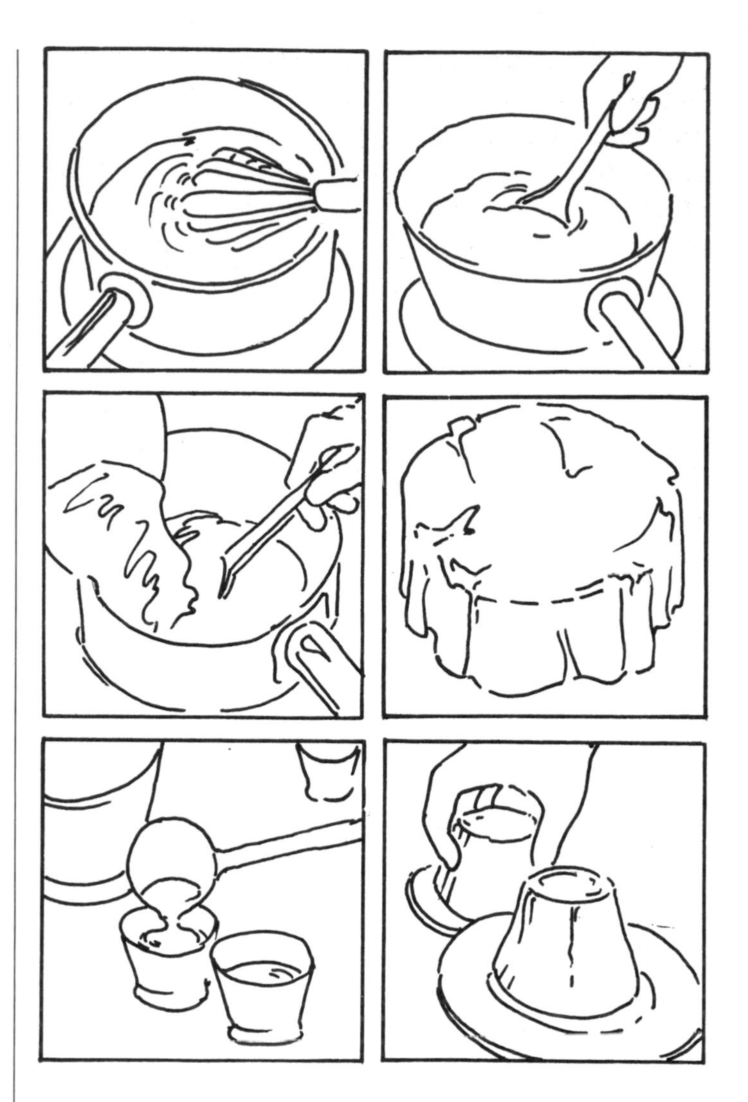

and almonds gradually, stirring all the time. When semolina has thickened, cover with a clean cloth, then with a lid and leave to cool.

Rinse smaller (tea or coffee) cups with cold water, fill them with "halvah", press well, then turn out on to a glass plate nad dust with powdered sugar mixed with vanilla.

Turkey

YELLOW "HALVAH"

250 gr sugar
250 gr hazelnuts
5 egg yolks
200 gr sugar
1 sachet of vanilla sugar
1 cup strong black coffee
200—250 gr butter or margarine

Fry sugar until it melts and becomes brown (caramel). Then add baked and shelled hazelnuts, fry shortly together, toss the mixture on a moistened tin plate or board, cool and grind or pound. Beat egg yolks and sugar until foamy, add vanilla sugar and black coffee. Mix over steam until thick, then cool, add to butter beaten well first, blend in ground hazelnuts with caramel.

This kind of "halvah" is most often used as filling for wafers or for cakes.

Turkey

NOUGAT — WHITE "HALVAH"

4 eggs
250 gr sugar
100 gr honey
200 gr chopped walnuts

Beat egg whites stiffly, add sugar, then beat together until sugar melts and the foam is stiff and glossy. Heat honey a little and add it to beaten egg whites. Put the dish with this mixture over a bigger one in which water is boiling. Beat over steam until the mixture is smooth and stiff. Draw aside, add chopped walnuts and mix. Halve one wafer. Put the prepared mixture on one half of wafer, spead it and level with a moistened knife, then cover with the other half of wafer, press with a heavier object until cool. Cut "halvah" the following day into bars or rhombs.

Albania

SWEET JELLY — "SUDZUK"

1 l water
300 gr flour
150 gr sugar
juice of 1 lemon

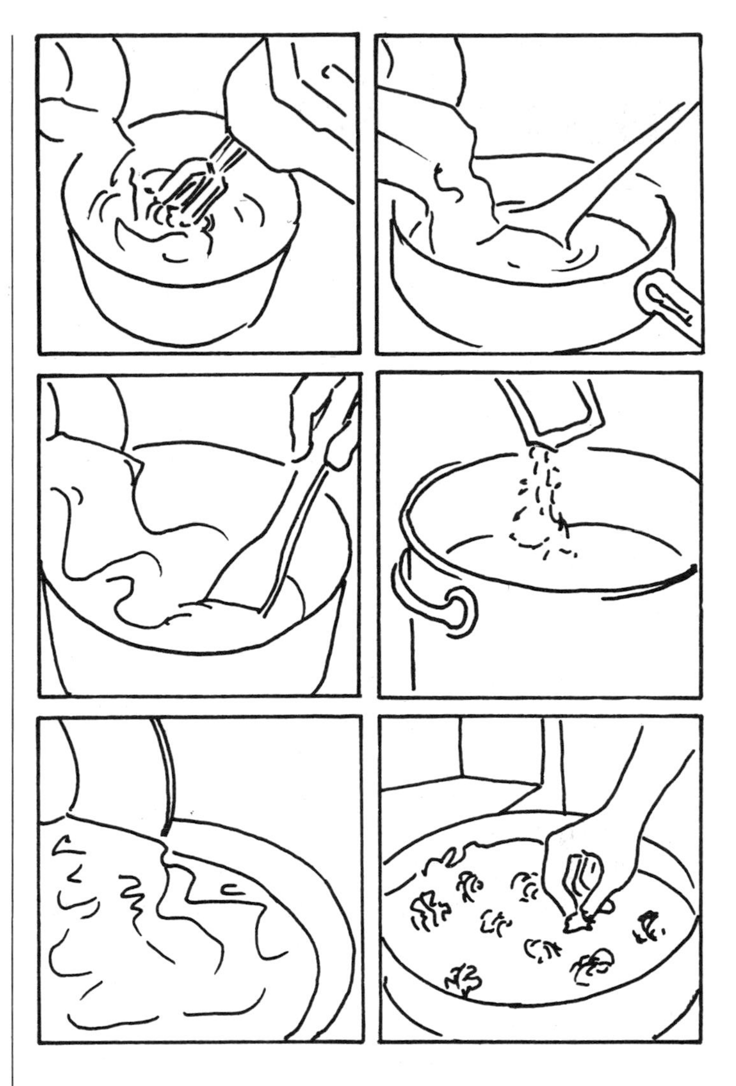

40 gr edible starch
2 dl water
2 sachets vanilla sugar
150 gr shelled walnuts

Take some water from the given quantity and mix well with flour until the mixture is smooth, without lumps. Add sugar and lemon juice to the rest of water. Bring to the boil, then blend in the flour mixture and simmer stirring constantly, so that it does not stick to the pan. Dissolve starch in cold water, blend it into the flour when it is only half cooked. Simmer on, stirring all the time, until it thickens. Add vanilla sugar in the end.

Rinse a cake tin with cold water, turn the mixture into it, sprinkle with chopped walnuts, level with a moistened knife and leave to cool.

When cold cut into squares.

This "sudzuk" is prepared in exactly the same way in Turkey and in the south-eastern parts of Yugoslavia.

Yugoslavia

WHEAT WITH WALNUTS

500 gr white wheat grains
2 l water
500 gr ground walnuts
500 gr powdered sugar
2 sachets vanilla sugar or 1 dried vanilla-bean

Pick over wheat, wash well, leave to stand in water for several hours (or overnight), then drain. Put up to cook in 2 l water, bring to the boil, turn heat down and simmer until tender. While cooking, shake the pot occasionally and add some more lukewarm water as needed. When cooked, drain, rinse well, drain again, then spread on a clean cloth to dry completely. Grind twice in a meat grinder. Add ground walnuts, powdered sugar and vanilla sugar (or scraped vanilla from

vanilla-bean) to the ground wheat. Use hands to mix throughly. Put on a glass plate, shape into a ball or cone, sprinkle with ground walnuts, then dust with powdered sugar mixed with vanilla. If desired garnish with raisins.

Whipped cream can be served separately with wheat. Wheat used to be prepared this way only for family feasts (family patron saint's day) and was served to each guest on coming into the house. Now it is often prepared as a favourite sweet in Serbia, Macedonia and some parts of Bosnia.

Turkey

CAKE WITH SYRUP – "RAHVANIYA"

For batter:
6 eggs
100 gr sugar
70 gr flour
butter for greasing

For syrup:
300 gr flour
3 dl water

Beat eggs and sugar well until smooth and foamy. Add flour gradually, stirring slowly all the time.

Grease a cake tin with butter or oil, turn in the prepared batter. Heat oven to 175 °C and bake until nicely brown. In the meantime prepare syrup: pour water over sugar and simmer for 10 minutes until syrup is of medium thickness. Cut baked "rahvaniya" into squares or rhombs while still warm and pour syrup over it.

Serve cold.

Yugoslavia

BELGRADE SWEET WITH APPLES OR PEARS

1 kg slightly sour apples or aromatic pears
2 dl white wine
40 gr sugar
thinly cut lemon rind

For cream:
6 egg yolks
75 gr sugar
20 gr flour or edible starch
3/4 l milk

For meringue topping:
6 egg whites
80 gr powdered sugar
50 gr minced walnuts or almonds

Peel apples or pears, remove pips and cut into thinner rounds. Pour wine over, add sugar and lemon rind and cook in heated oven for about 15—20 minutes.

In the meantime prepare cream: beat egg yolks and sugar until foamy, add flour or starch, slowly pour in heated milk and stir all the time. Mix over steam until the cream is thick, then cool. Blend cold cream with cooled apples or pears. Turn into a fireproof dish.

Beat egg whites adding powdered sugar gradually until stiff. Cover apples with stiff meringue, then sprinkle with minced walnuts or almonds. Keep in the oven preset at 200°C only for 2—5 minutes for the topping to brown a little. Cool well and keep in the refrigerator until serving.

Bulgaria

APPLE "MOUSSAKA"

1 kg bigger and slightly sour apples
2—3 tablespoons sugar
1 lemon
2 eggs
200 gr breadcrumbs
1—2 dl oil for frying
butter for greasing

For filling:
1 l milk
150 gr ground walnuts
150 gr raisins
1 l sachet vanilla sugar

For pouring over:
2 dl double cream or milk
1 egg yolk
20 gr sugar
powdered sugar with vanilla

Wash apples, peel and cut into rounds about 1 cm thick. Sprinkle with

sugar and drip with lemon juice, then leave to stand for a while.

Beat eggs well, then dip each apple round in eggs, roll in breadcrumbs, fry in well heated oil and drain.

For filling, bring milk to the boil,

draw aside, add ground walnuts, raisins and vanilla sugar. Mix well, then cool a little. Put a layer of fried apples in a greased tepsiya or cake tin, cover with filling, repeat until all has been used, finish with apples.

Beat well egg yolks and sugar, blend in double cream or milk, mix well. Pour over the sweet "moussaka". Bake for about 20—25 minutes in the oven preheated to 200°C. Turn carefully out of the tin or tepsiya, cool a little, then dust with powdered sugar mixed with vanilla.

Turkey

SOFT WALNUT CAKE–"ULUTMA"

6 eggs
75 gr sugar
200 gr walnuts
200 gr semolina
75 gr raisins
lemon rind
butter and flour for the tin

For syrup:
500 gr sugar
2 dl water
1 lemon
1 vanilla-bean or 1 sachet vanilla sugar

Beat egg yolks and sugar until foamy, add ground walnuts, semolina and raisins. Beat egg whites stiffly, blend them slowly into egg yolks.

Grease a cake tin with butter, dust with flour, turn in the prepared mixture, level and bake in the oven preheated to 175°C. When baked, cut into bigger squares and then diagonally into triangles. Pour syrup over while the cake is warm, cover and leave to stand until syrup is absorbed.

For syrup: pour water over sugar, bring to the boil, add vanilla and lemon juice and simmer for a further 5—10 minutes.

Turkey

CAKES WITH SYRUP FROM ISTANBUL – "TATLIYE"

1,1/4 l milk
2 sachets vanilla sugar
400 gr semolina
100 gr butterfat (butter or margarine)
80 gr sugar, 8 eggs
butter for greasing

For syrup:
1 kg sugar
1/2 l water
vanilla-bean or 1 sachet vanilla sugar
1 lemon

Heat milk, add vanilla. Bring to the boil and cook semolina in it slowly, stirring constantly. When semolina is thick, draw aside and cool.

Beat butterfat and sugar until foamy, add eggs one by one, then blend in cooled semolina. Mix well into a smooth mixture. Grease a cake tin with butter or butterfat. Shape the mixture into small round cakes, press a little in the middle and put into the baking tin. Heat oven to 200°C and bake until nicely brown.

For syrup, pour water over sugar, cook at medium heat, add vanilla, lemon juice and a few lemon rounds. Simmer until thick, that is until dripping from the mixing spoon like honey.

When "tatliye" are done, pour warm syrup over them in the tin, and leave to absorb syrup and cool.

Turkey

SOFT CAKE — "SEVDIDZAN"

200 gr sugar
4 eggs
200 gr melted butter
lemon rind
150 gr semolina
50 gr flour
1 dl double cream
butter for greasing

For syrup:
250 gr sugar
1 dl water
1 vanilla-bean or 1 sachet vanilla sugar

Beat sugar and egg yolks until foamy, add melted butter gradually, stirring all the time, add grated lemon rind and double cream. Beat egg whites stiffly. Mix semolina and flour. Add flour and beaten egg whites in turn to egg yolks, stirring slowly.

Grease a cake tin with butter, dust with flour, turn in the prepared batter and level it. Preheat oven to 175°C and bake for about 25—30 minutes.

Pour water over sugar, add vanilla, cook about 5 minutes. Pour this syrup over the cake when done, then put back into the oven for a short while.

When slightly cooled cut into squares.

This cake is often prepared in other Balkan countries, too.

Bulgaria

DRY WALNUT PIE

500 gr thin layers of dough for the pie
400—500 gr ground walnuts
100—150 gr raisins
250 gr sugar
1 sachet vanilla sugar
oil for sprinkling dough layers and for greasing

For syrup:
400—450 gr sugar
1 dl water
1 vanilla-bean or 1 sachet vanilla sugar
1 lemon

Grease a cake tin and place 2—3 dough layers in, sprinkle with oil. Mix walnuts, raisins and vanilla sugar. Spread some of the mixture over the dough layers, then again place a couple of dough layers sprinkled with oil, then walnuts. Repeat until all the dough layers and walnuts have been used and finish with 2—3 sprinkled dough layers. Before baking, cut the pie in the tin into small squares.

Bake in the oven preheated to 200°C until nicely brown.

In the meantime prepare syrup: pour water over sugar, add vanilla and lemon cut into rounds. Simmer for about 20 minutes until the syrup is nearly thick.

Pour hot syrup over baked pie, put back into the lukewarm oven and leave for a further 15—20 minutes to absorb the syrup. When cooled turn the pie on to a plate and leave to stand for 1—2 days until completely dry. If it is kept in a dry and cool place it can be used up to 10 days.

Turkey

SWEET FRITTERS — "MAFISHI"

250 gr flour
3 egg yolks
1 tablespoon sugar
1 tablespoon sour cream
lemon rind
1 tablespoon rum
lard or oil for frying
powdered sugar for dusting

Add egg yolks, sugar, sour cream, finely grated lemon rind and rum to sifted flour. Mix with a knife or fork first, then with hands until the dough is smooth and rather thick.

Shape into a ball and leave to stand covered about 15—20 minutes. Then roll out into a dough layer a bit thicker then for noodles. Cut with a cutter into squares, triangles or strips (which can be

interwoven) and fry in heated oil until brown. Drain on absorbent paper, then dust with powdered sugar. Serve either warm or cold.

After frying, "mafishi" can also be poured over with sugar syrup and sprinkled with grated walnuts.

"Mafishi" are well-known and prepared nearly all over the Balkans and their origin is not Turkish in fact, but Arabic. In Arabic "mafish" means something that disappears, and this fritter melts — disappears — as soon as it is put into the mouth.

Greece

WALNUT CAKE FROM ATHENS

350—400 gr walnuts
4 eggs
60 gr butter, 150 gr sugar
1 teaspoon cinnamon
350—400 gr flour
1 teaspoon baking powder

For syrup:
180 gr sugar
1/4 l water
1 small glass cognac

Chop walnuts crudely and put aside two tablespoons for sprinkling. Separate eggs and beat egg whites stiffly. Mix sugar and butter into a smooth mixture, add egg yolks one by one and cinnamon, mixing all the time. Add flour gradually and slowly, mixed with baking powder, then add walnuts. When all is mixed, carefully fold beaten egg whites. Turn into a greased cake tin, sprinkle with walnuts put aside before and bake in the oven preheated to 175°C for 30—40 minutes.

For syrup, cook water and sugar until thick. Then add cognac. When the cake is nearly quite cooled in the oven, pour hot syrup over. When cold, cut into squares or rhombs, arrange on a big plate and serve.

Turkey

TURKISH CAKE WITH NUTS

1 package frozen puff pastry
flour for dusting

For filling:
125 gr raisins
250 gr ground hazelnuts or almonds
100 gr powdered sugar
4 teaspoons rose water
100 gr butter

For syrup:
1/4 l water
100 gr sugar
75 gr honey

Thaw out puff pastry. Dust board with flour, roll out pastry into 5 pieces the size of an oblong tin (about 30 cm long). Clean raisins, pour hot water over, drain and wipe with a clean cloth. Then mix with hazelnuts or almonds and powdered sugar. Line the cake tin with tin foil, rinse with cold water. Put in a layer of pastry, spread one quarter of the prepared filling and sprinkle with rose water and melted butter. Repeat until all the pastry and filling has been used. Sprinkle the top layer of pastry with melted butter.

Heat oven to 200 °C, bake for about 35 minutes. Take the cake out of the tin carefully and cool.

Mix water and sugar, heat and cook for 5 minutes, add honey and cook together for a further 3—5 minutes.

Cut cake into squares but only half way down, then pour in 2/3 of syrup and cool. Cut cake all the way down and pour in the rest of the syrup. Leave to absorb syrup and serve cold.

Yugoslavia

FIG ROLL

500 gr dried figs
125 gr sugar

125 gr walnuts
1 vanilla-bean or 1 sachet vanilla sugar

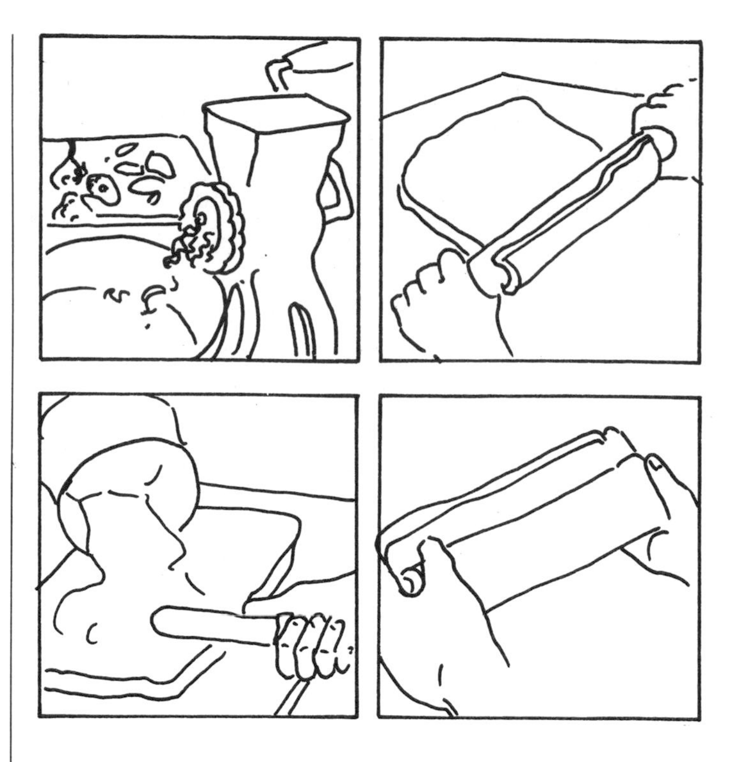

For filling:
250 gr almonds or walnuts
125 gr sugar
1—2 tablespoons water
1 lemon

Wash figs and remove stems, then grind. Brown walnuts a little and grind together with sugar. Then mix all and grind once again together. Sprinkle the board with sugar and spread the nut and fig mixture into an oblong about 1 cm thick.

Prepare the filling as follows: brown almons (or walnuts) a little and grind. Pour water over sugar, add lemon juice, cook until the syrup is thick, add almonds, mix well and cool.

Spread the cooled mixture over figs and roll up firmly. Cut into rounds about 1 cm thick.

Instead of figs, prunes or dates can be used.

Turkey

TURKISH DELIGHT — "RATLUK"

1 kg sugar in cubes
3/4 l water

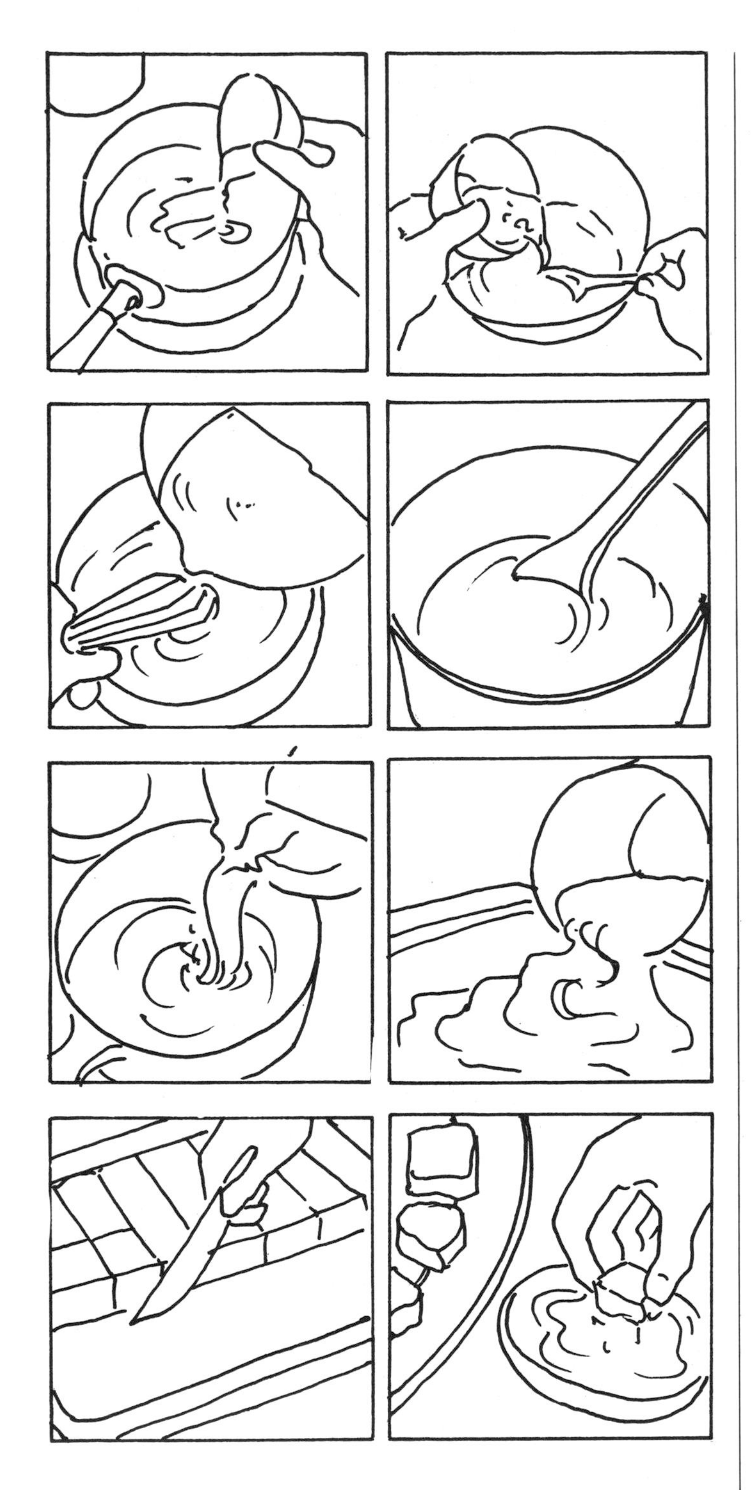

juice of 1/2 lemon
rose extract
150 gr edible starch
1 l cold water
125 gr skinned chopped almonds
mixture of powdered sugar and starch for dusting
almond or plain oil for greasing the pan

Heat sugar, water and half of the lemon juice and simmer it for about 15 minutes, until the syrup is as thick as honey. Pour cold water into the starch and make a smooth mixture without lumps. When the syrup is thick enough, draw it aside, stir into it the dissolved starch (with a wire-whisker), heat it again stirring all the time (with a clean mixing spoon without any smell) and cook until the mixture falls off the spoon. In the end add the rest of lemon juice, a few drops of rose extract and almonds, then mix well.

Grease an enamelled baking pan well with almond or plain oil, then pour out extra oil. Turn the warm mixture in, levelling it evenly with a knife. It should be about 3—4 cm thick. Leave it in a cool place to harden.

When cold, cut it into cubes 2 × 4 cm big and roll each cube in the mixture of powdered sugar and starch. Keep in a covered box in a dry place.

"Ratluk" is served on small glass plates,as a rule with a glass of cold water or cold mineral water and usually together with black coffee.

Like many other sweetmeats in the Balkans, "ratluk" is of Arabic or Persian origin. It came to the peninsula with the Turkish invasion and found a new "home" there in the course of the centuries-long Turkish rule in these parts.

Turkey

TURKISH NUT PIE — "BAKLAVA"

20—30 thin layers of dough for the pie
200 gr butter for sprinkling dough layers and greasing

For filling:
300 gr ground walnuts
300 gr ground almonds

For syrup:
600 gr sugar
2—3 dl water
1 vanilla-bean or 1 sachet vanilla sugar

Grease tepsiya with butter, place in two dough layers, sprinkle each with melted butter. Sprinkle every second layer of dough with mixed walnuts and almonds. Repeat until all has been used, then cut into equal squares. Each square can be cut diagonally to get triangles.

Pour some melted butter over each piece obtained by cutting. Preheat the oven to 200°C and bake for about 40—50 minutes. Towards the end reduce heat to 150°C.

In the meantime prepare syrup: pour water over sugar, add vanilla. Cook until syrup is so thick that it drips from the mixing spoon like honey.

Cool baked "baklava" a little, pour warm syrup over and leave to stand until all the syrup is absorbed.

Greece

GREEK WALNUT PIE — "BAKLAVA"

2 packets frozen puff pastry
250 gr butter

For filling:
500 gr shelled walnuts
80—100 gr breadcrums
100 gr sugar
1 teaspoon powdered cinnamon
1/2 teaspoon ground cloves

For syrup:
200 gr sugar
2,5 dl water
5 tablespoons honey
juice and rind of 1 lemon

Thaw out puff pastry, melt butter. Grease a cake tin about 25 × 30 cm big and about 8 cm deep with melted butter.

Grind walnuts, mix with breadcrumbs, sugar and spices.

Roll out puff pastry into about 20 layers the size of the tin. Put 5 layers into the tin, sprinkle each with butter. Spread filling over, cover with 2 sprinkled layers of pastry, repeat until all the layers and filling have been used. Finish with a few sprinkled layers of pastry.

Bake "baklava" for about 45—60 minutes in the oven preheated to 190°C and after 40 minutes reduce heat to 150°C.

For syrup, cook sugar with water, honey, lemon juice and thinly cut lemon rind for about 10 minutes.

When baked, pour hot syrup over "baklava", leave to cool.

Cut into nice squares.

Roumania

BISCUIT "BAKLAVA"

6 eggs
45 gr semolina
20 gr flour
rind of 1/2 lemon

100 gr raisins
150—200 gr ground walnuts
50 gr semolina
butter or oil for greasing

For syrup:
375—400 gr sugar
2,5 dl water
juice and rind of 1 lemon
vanilla-bean or vanilla sugar

Separate eggs. Beat egg yolks, add 30 gr semolina, mix well. Beat whites of eggs stiffly and add them, and flour, to egg yolks in turn. Divide the mixture into two parts. Add cleaned raisins washed and wiped to one part, together with ground walnuts and ground lemon rind. Grease a cake tin with butter or oil, turn in this part of the mixture. Add two more tablespoons of semolina to the other part, mix slowly. Then spread this part over the one in the tin, level and bake in the oven preheated to 175 °C for 25—30 minutes.

In the meantime prepare syrup: pour water over sugar, add thin strips of lemon rind and vanilla. Cook until the syrup is so thick that it drips from the spoon like honey. In the end add lemon juice.

When "baklava" is done, cut it into squares and pour slightly cooled syrup over.

Turkey

DATE-SHAPED CAKES — "URMASHITSE"

500 gr butter (or butterfat)
2 eggs
200 gr (1 cup) thick yoghurt
750 gr—1 kg flour
butter for greasing
flour for dusting

For syrup:
750 gr sugar
3—4 dl water
1 vanilla-bean or 1 sachet vanilla sugar
juice of 1 lemon

Mix butter until foamy, add 1 whole egg and 1 egg yolk, mix well, then add thick yoghurt and flour. Work into a smooth dough.

Dust grater with flour. Take with hand pieces of dough the size of a walnut, press them against the grater, flatten and shape like dates. Grease a cake tin or tepsiya, dust with flour, put cakes in. Bake about 25 minutes in the oven preset at 200 °C, until brown.

In the meantime pour water over sugar, add vanilla, cook at medium heat for 10—15 minutes. When cooked, add

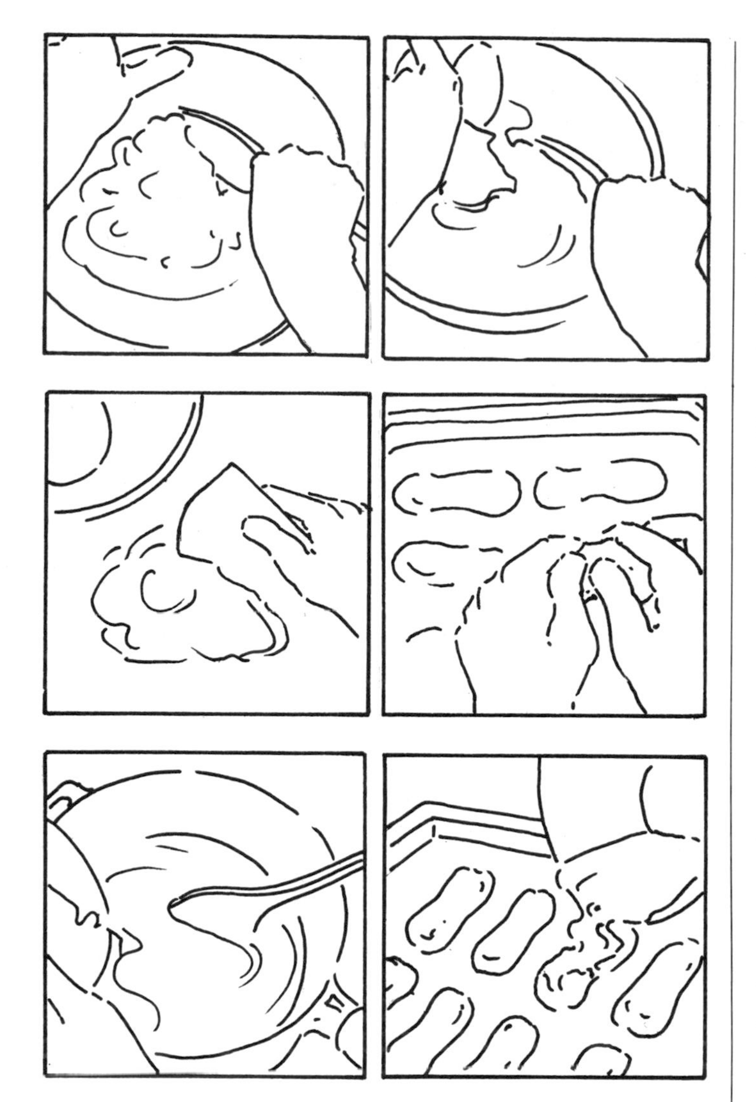

lemon juice. Take the cakes out of the oven, pour hot syrup over them and leave in the tin until all the syrup is absorbed.

The name of this cake, too, is of Arabic origin. "Urma" in Arabic is date. That is why the same cake is called slightly differently in various Balkan countries, depending on the pronunciation of the word for date.

Turkey

FRIED CAKES — "DILBER DUDAGI"

500 gr flour
1/2 l water
150 gr sugar
50 gr butter
3 eggs
a pinch of salt
1—2 dl oil for frying
sugar to roll in
100 gr mixed walnuts, almonds and pistachios
flour for dusting the board

Mix flour with water in a pan, add sugar and stirring constantly bring to the boil. Add butter, mix firmly with a wooden mixing spoon and cook at medium heat until the batter is thick. Draw aside and cool. Then mix in eggs one by one stirring well every time. Add salt. Toss on to the board dredged with flour and knead until quite smooth.

Take bits of dough slightly bigger then walnuts, shape into round flat cakes, then fold each up to look like "lips". Fry in heated oil to brown nicely.

Drain fried cakes on absorbent paper, then roll in sugar and sprinkle with the mixture of chopped walnuts, almonds and pistachios.

"Dilber dudagi" in the original means "sweetheart's lips". That should mean that the cakes are as sweet as the dear one's lips and so they are given that shape.

Bulgaria

SWEET WITH NOODLES AND SYRUP — "KADAIF"

200 gr butter
500—550 gr fine, very thin noodles
200—300 gr walnuts or almonds
100 gr raisins

For syrup:
700 gr sugar, 1 l water
1 vanilla-bean or 1 sachet vanilla sugar
1 lemon

Grease a cake tin or corresponding fireproof dish with butter, put in a layer of noodles, sprinkle with melted butter, then with finely chopped walnuts (or almonds) and raisins, repeat until all has been used and finish with noodles sprinkled with butter.

For syrup, pour water over sugar, add vanilla and lemon cut into thin rounds. Cook at medium heat for about 5 minutes.

Bake in the oven preheated to 200°C. After about 25 minutes, when half baked, pour syrup over and put back into the oven to bake on (for a further 15 minutes).

When done, leave it to stand for one day, as it will be tastier that way. Before serving cut into squares, arrange on a big plate and garnish with lemon rounds from the syrup.

Noodles for the "kadaif" can be prepared at home. For about 600 gr noodles take about 3 egg yolks, 1 whole egg and 750 gr flour. Work into a thick dough, roll out into a very thin layer, leave to dry for a while, then cut into very thin strips.

Turkey

ROSE-SHAPED PIE — "DJUL-PITA"

500 gr ready-made layers of dough for the pie
150 gr butter or oil

For filling:
100 gr edible starch
1/2 l milk
150 gr sugar
200 gr ground walnuts

For syrup:
500 gr sugar
3 dl water
1 vanilla-bean or 2 sachets vanilla sugar
several lemon rounds

Dissolve starch in some cold milk. Bring the rest of milk to the boil, cook dissolved starch in it, mix until thick, add sugar, mix and cool. When cold, add ground walnuts.

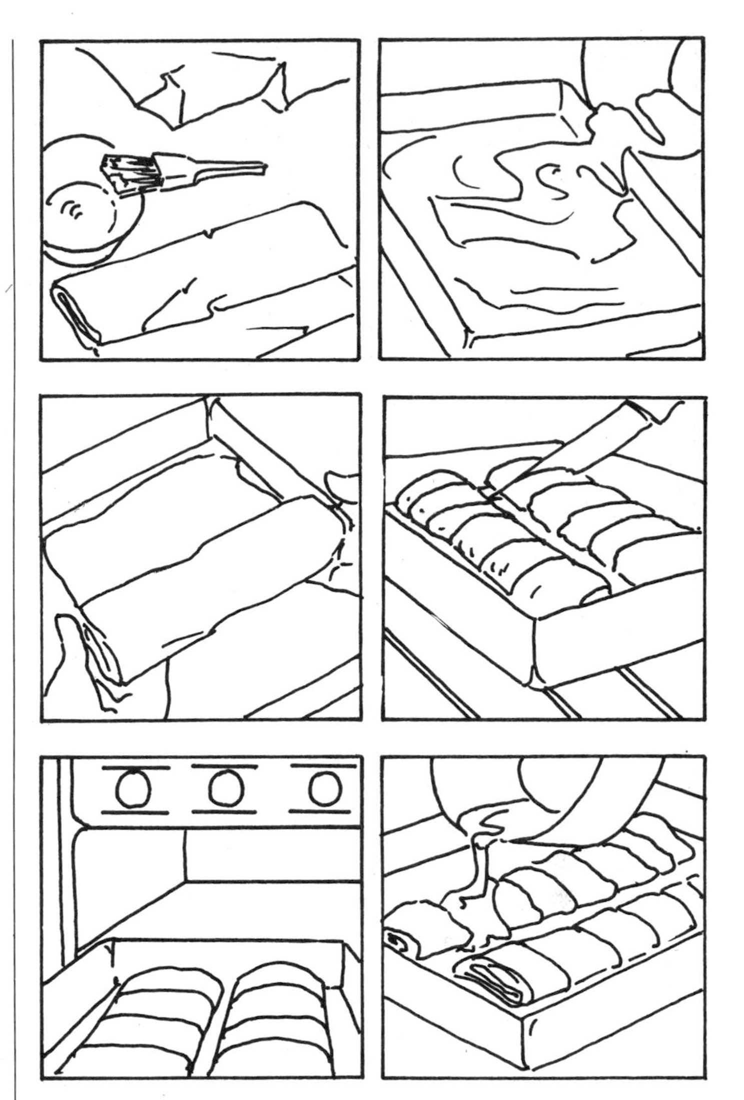

Put 4 layers of dough one on top of the other, sprinkling each with melted butter or oil. Place filling along one end of the dough layers and roll up firmly starting from that end.

Cut the roll thus obtained into pieces about 3 cm long with a sharp knife. Arrange them in a greased cake tin to stand upright, with one cut side on the tin.

Bake in the oven preheated to 200—250°C for about 25 minutes, until nicely brown.

In the meantime mix water, sugar and vanilla, heat, add lemon rounds, bring to the boil and simmer for a further 10—15 minutes.

Pour warm syrup over the baked "djul-pita". Keep in a warm place until all the syrup is absorbed, then arrange on a serving plate. "Djul" in Turkish means rose. As these cakes resemble roses in bloom, they have been given this nice name.

Bulgaria

FRIED CAKES IN SYRUP — "TULUMBE"

For dough:
1/2 l water
2 dl oil
1/2 kg flour
2 sachets vanilla sugar or 1 vanilla-bean
1/2 lemon
5—6 eggs
oil for frying

For syrup:
700 gr sugar
1 l water
juice of 1 lemon

Heat water and add oil. Bring to the boil, add vanilla and blend in flour, mixing all the time. Simmer until the mixture is smooth, slightly "sticking" to the bottom of the pan. Cool a little, then add eggs one by one. After adding each egg, work well and leave to stand for a while every time.

When ready, put the dough into the confectioner's pipe with a broader star-like nozzle. Heat oil. When hot enough, press out pieces of dough about 5—7 cm long. Fry on all sides until nicely brown.

Cook sugar, water and lemon juice for 10—15 minutes, then cool. Pour cooled syrup over warm cakes.

Roumania

CHEESE CAKES

1 package frozen puff pastry
250—300 gr soft, unsalted cheese
2 egg yolks
50 gr sugar
some salt
1 egg for brushing over

Thaw out puff pastry, roll out with a pin and cut into bigger sqaures.

Beat egg yolks and sugar until foamy, add cheese passed through a sieve or crushed well, salt. Mix all well. Place some filling over each square of puff pastry, joining the ends of the pastry together. Beat the egg well and brush the cakes with it. Rinse a cake tin with cold water, place the cakes in and bake in the oven preheated to 250°C until nicely brown.

Do not open the oven for the first 15 minutes of baking.

When done, the cakes can be sprinkled with powdered sugar.

Yugoslavia

SOUR CHERRY PIE FROM VOJVODINA

500 gr ready-made layers of dough for the pie
100 gr ground walnuts or breadcrumbs
1 dl oil or melted butter for sprinkling
1 kg sour cherries (or 1 package frozen sour cherries)
300 gr sugar
2 sachets vanilla sugar
3 egg yolks
1 dl double cream
powdered sugar for dusting
oil or butter for greasing

Wash sour cherries, drain and remove stones. If frozen, thaw out. Leave them in a sieve or strainer so as not to be too juicy.

Take 3 dough layers at a time, sprinkle each with oil or butter. Sprinkle the third with some ground walnuts or breadcrumbs. Mix sour cherries and sugar, put

some over the dough layers, sprinkle with vanilla sugar, roll up and place in a greased cake tin.

Repeat until all the dough layers and cherries have been used. Bake for 30—40 minutes in the oven preheated to 170°C until slightly brown.

If wanted, the pies can be brushed with well beaten egg yolks and cream, when the pies are half-baked. In that case turn the heat up towards the end, to brown nicely.

Albania

SQUASH PIE

500—700 gr peeled pumpkin or ripe squash
500—600 gr ready-made layers of dough for the pie
3 eggs
50 gr oil
40—50 gr sugar
1 sachet vanilla sugar
1 teaspoon cinnamon
100 gr oil for sprinkling
powdered sugar mixed with vanilla for dusting

Grate peeled pumpkin crudely. Heat oil, add pumpkin and sugar, cook slowly until tender. Then add cinnamon and vanilla. Beat egg yolks until foamy, add cooled pumpkin, then slowly blend in stiffly beaten egg whites.

Put 3—4 dough layers sprinkled with warm oil in a cake tin.

Cover with some pumpkin filling. Repeat until all the dough layers and filling have been used. Sprinkle the last layer of dough with some more oil. Bake in the oven preheated to 175°C for 45—50 minutes.

Cool a little and dust with powdered sugar mixed with vanilla. Cut into squares.

Yugoslavia

SHORTCRUST PIE WITH CREAM

750 gr flour
375 gr butter or margarine
200 gr sugar
4 egg yolks
1 whole egg
lemon rind
a pinch of salt
butter for greasing

For filling:
2,5 kg apples
200 gr sugar
100 gr raisins
1 dl water

For cream:
4 eggs
1/2 l milk
120 gr flour
125 gr sugar
powdered sugar for dusting

Sift flour, add thinly cut butter of margarine, egg yolks, 1 whole egg, ground lemon rind, a pinch of salt. Knead quickly into a smooth dough. Leave to stand for a while in a cool place.

Peel apples, cut into slices, mix with sugar, add some water (or white wine), cook slowly until soft. Then add cleaned and washed raisins, mix well.

Roll out dough the size of the cake tin, grease tin, place the dough in and half bake in the oven preheated to 200 °C (about 10—15 minutes).

In the meantime beat egg yolks and sugar, add flour mixed in milk. Beat over steam until the cream is thick. Beat whites of eggs stiffly, blend into the warm cream.

Spread cooked apples over the half-baked dough, then pour in cream. Dust with powdered sugar and put back into the oven with heat turned down (about 170 °C) and bake for a further 30 minutes.

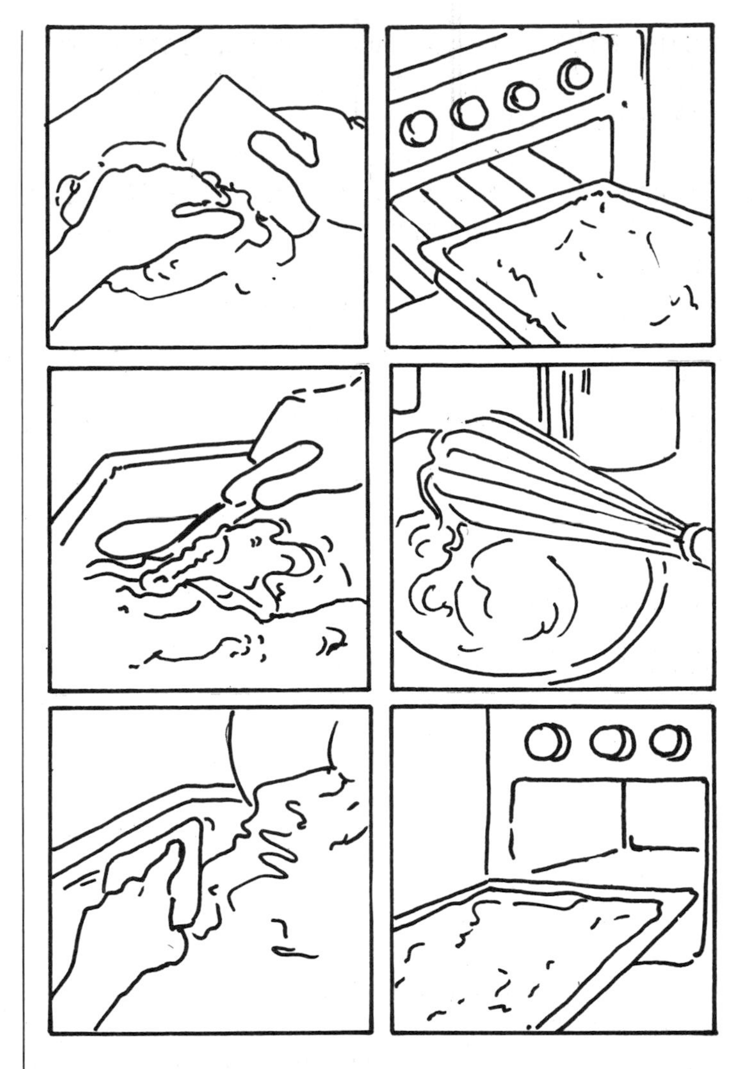

Yugoslavia

QUINCE-PIE FROM LESKOVAC

For dough:
250 gr flour
150 gr butter or margarine
50 gr sugar
2 egg yolks
ground rind of 1 lemon
2 tablespoons rum
1/2 teaspoon salt

For filling:
200—250 gr quince jam
5 egg whites
200 gr sugar
juice of 1 lemon

Sift flour, add thinly cut butter or margarine, sugar, egg yolks, lemon rind, rum and some salt. Knead quickly into a smooth dough. Leave to stand for a while in a cool place. Rinse a cake tin (a round one would also do) with cold water, spread the dough in it and bake in the oven preheated to 200 °C for about 25—30 minutes, until nicely brown.

When done, cool in the same tin. Mix well quince jam and spread it over the dough. Beat whites of eggs stiffly, add sugar and lemon juice, spread over the jam and bake at low heat until slightly brown and until the dough absorbs the jam.

The city of Leskovac is well-known for vegetables of very good quality (especially paprikas), but little is known that the region also produces best quality quinces, classified in world literature as quinces of exceptional kind.

Yugoslavia

PUMPKIN PIE

500 gr ready-made layers of dough for the pie
1 kg peeled pumpkin
4—5 tablespoons oil or melted butter
3 eggs
6 tablespoons sugar
2 sachets vanilla sugar
1 dl oil for sprinkling and greasing
powdered sugar for dusting

Grate pumpkin crudely, cook slowly in oil or butter until the liquid evaporates and the pumpkin is tender. Cool, then add egg yolks one by one, sugar and vanilla sugar and stiffly beaten egg whites in the end.

Take 2—3 dough layers, sprinkle each with oil, put some pumpkin filling over and roll up. Repeat until all the dough layers and filling have been used. Arrange rolls side by side in a greased cake tin. Sprinkle with some more heated oil. Bake for about 30 minutes in the oven preheated to 200°C until brown. When done, cut into pieces and dust with powdered sugar.

Serve warm.

Greece

CHEESE PIE — "MELOPITA"

350 gr flour
a pinch of salt
1 teaspoon baking powder
150 gr butter

For filling:
700 gr unsalted green cow cheese
150 gr sugar
250 gr honey
4—5 eggs
2 teaspoons cinnamon

Sift flour together with baking powder, add salt and knead into a smooth dough with beaten butter. Shape into a ball, dust with flour and leave to stand in the refrigerator for at least 1 hour.

In the meantime prepare filling: mix cheese well with sugar and 1 teaspoon of cinnamon. Add honey, mix further until smooth. Add eggs one by one mixing all the time to get nice and creamy.

Roll out the dough into a round slightly bigger then the bottom of the tepsiya. Rinse tepsiya with cold water and line with dough. Shape a "wreath" of dough round the edge. Turn the filling in and level. Bake for about 45 minutes in the oven preheated to 150°C. Then turn heat up and bake for a further 15 minutes. Cool the pie in the oven (open oven a bit), then sprinkle with the rest of cinnamon. Cut into slices.

Instead of making dough, "melopita" can be made with frozen puff pastry.

Yugoslavia

SHORTCRUST PIE WITH WALNUTS

For dough:
300 gr flour
200 gr butter or margarine
75 gr sugar
2 tablespoons double cream
1 tablespoon rum
ground lemon rind

For filling:
4 eggs
160 gr sugar
lemon rind
1/2 teaspoon cinnamon
200 gr walnuts
1 egg for brushing dough
powdered sugar for dusting

Add thin slices of butter or margarine to sifted flour, then add sugar, cream, rum and ground lemon rind. Quickly knead into a smooth dough and leave to stand for a while in a cool place. Divide into two parts and roll out both on the board dusted with flour into two layers the size of the cake tin. For filling, beat egg yolks and sugar until foamy, add ground lemon rind, powdered cinnamon and ground walnuts, mix well. Beat whites of eggs stiffly and blend them into the above mixture.

Put one layer of dough into the tin. Spread filling over, level and cover with the other layer. Brush with beaten egg. Bake in the oven preheated to 200°C for about 40—50 minutes.

When done, dust with powdered sugar and cut into squares.

Roumania

CHOCOLATE AND WALNUT CAKE — "DIOSH PITA"

For dough:
6 eggs
180 gr sugar
1 bar of chocolate
120 gr flour
butter or oil for greasing

For filling:
150 gr walnuts
1/2 dl milk
120 gr butter (or margarine)
150 gr sugar
2 tablespoons rum
powdered sugar for dusting

Beat egg yolks and sugar until foamy, add finely grated chocolate. Beat whites of eggs stiffly. Add flour and egg whites to egg yolks in turn, stirring slowly. Grease a cake tin with butter or oil, turn in the prepared mixture, level it. Heat oven to 175°C and bake for about 30—35 minutes. When done, take out of the tin and cool.

Pick over walnuts, brown a little and grind, then pour over with hot milk. Beat butter well, add sugar, beat together until smooth and creamy, add walnuts, mix and add rum.

Cut baked dough into two equal parts lengthways. Spread filling over one layer, cover it with the other layer, dust with powdered sugar and cut into squares.

It is better to prepare this cake a day earlier, as it gets softer and easier to cut, and lookes nicer.

Bulgaria

SWEET MUSH WITH SEMOLINA

2,5 dl milk
2,5 dl water
50 gr sugar
50 gr butter
60 gr semolina
50 gr chopped walnuts
1 teaspoon cinnamon
apricot, peach or other fruit compote

Mix milk, water and sugar and bring to the boil. Heat butter, add semolina and walnuts and brown a little. Then pour in boiling milk syrup, stirring constantly. Draw aside and leave to stand covered, until semolina absorbs the syrup. Cool a little and sprinkle with cinnamon. Serve compote with this mush.

When mush is quite cold and hard, it can be cut into squares, poured over with fruit juice and served with compote.

Bulgaria

APPLE PIE

For dough:
250 gr flour
120 gr butter or margarine
70 gr powdered sugar
70 gr ground walnuts or almonds
2 eggs
grated lemon rind
butter for greasing

For filling:
1,5 kg peeled apples, slightly sour
150 gr sugar
1 small glass rum
1 glass white wine
2 dl double cream

Sift flour and add to it butter or margarine cut into thin slices, sugar, ground walnuts, eggs and some lemon rind. Knead quickly into a smooth dough, then leave in a cool place to stand for about 30 minutes. Roll it out and place into a greased cake tin of medium size. Bake in the oven preheated to 200—250 °C for about 30 minutes, i.e. until nicely brown.

Peel apples and cut into smaller pieces, sprinkle with sugar, pour in rum and wine, then cook until tender and mushy. Cool and then spread over the baked and slightly cooled dough. When cold, cover with whipped cream. Cut into medium-size squares.

Yugoslavia

BAKED SEMOLINA PUDDING

5 eggs
5 tablespoons semolina
5 tablespoons sugar
rind of 1/2 lemon
oil for greasing
breadcrumbs for sprinkling
1 l milk
200 gr sugar
1 sachet vanilla sugar
some double cream for garnishing (optional)

Separate eggs. Beat egg whites stiffly, then add spoonful by spoonful of sugar beating all the time (a mixer can be used) until quite stiff and glossy.

Blend in egg yolks one by one, then spoonful by spoonful of semolina and grated lemon rind in the end. Turn into a round cake tin (or corresponding pan) greased and sprinkled with breadcrumbs. Bake in the oven preheated to 175°C for 20—25 minutes (check whether it is baked with a toothpick).

In the meantime boil milk with sugar and vanilla. When the mixture is done, turn it into a deep dish (a compote bowl etc.) and pour hot milk over. Leave it to stand and absorb the milk, then put into the refrigerator. Before serving it can be garnished with whipped cream.

Greece

SEMOLINA CAKE

160 gr flour
3 teaspoons baking powder
6 eggs
120 gr sugar
200 gr butter
100 gr semolina
orange rind and 1 dl orange juice
50 gr chopped almonds
butter for greasing

For syrup:
1 small glass cognac
350 gr sugar
1 dl water

Sift flour, add baking powder. Separate eggs. Beat egg whites stiffly, add half of the sugar bit by bit and beat further until quite stiff and glossy. Cream butter with the rest of sugar, add egg yolks and grated orange rind. Into this mixture blend slowly flour, semolina and beaten egg whites in turn, add orange juice and almonds in the end. Turn the prepared mixture into a big greased cake tin. Bake for about 40—50 minutes in the oven preheated to 180°C until nicely brown. Cool the cake in the tin.

Mix sugar and water, cook for about 5 minutes, cool a little and add cognac. Pour this syrup over the cake. Cool and cut into squares.

Yugoslavia

ROLLED-UP PIE WITH POPPY SEED OR WALNUTS

For yeast dough:
750 gr flour
60 gr fresh yeast
100 gr sugar
2—2,5 dl lukewarm milk
some salt
2 eggs
150 gr butter or margarine

For filling:
350 gr ground poppy seed
1/4 l milk
50 gr semolina
50 gr sugar
1 sachet vanilla sugar
100 gr raisins
1 tablespoon rum
1—2 cloves
100 gr margarine or butter for sprinkling and greasing
flour for dusting
powdered sugar for dusting
1 egg for brushing

Prepare yeast dough as in the recipe on page

Heat milk, cook semolina in it slowly (stirring constantly) for about 5 minutes. Add poppy seed, sugar, scalded and drained raisins and vanilla to hot semolina. Mix all, cool a little, then add rum and ground cloves. Toss raised dough on to the board dredged with flour, divide into two equal parts. Roll out both thinly, sprinkle with melted butter or margarine, spread filling over so that one end of the dough, about 10 cm wide, remains without filling. Roll up starting with the end with filling, so that the end without filling is down. Place into the greased tin and leave to stand about 20 minutes covered with a clean cloth. Heat oven to 200°C. Before baking brush the pies with beaten egg yolk and bake for 40—45 minutes.

Turn out on to a clean wooden board, cover with a clean cloth and leave to cool a little, then dust with powdered sugar. Cut into nice rounds.

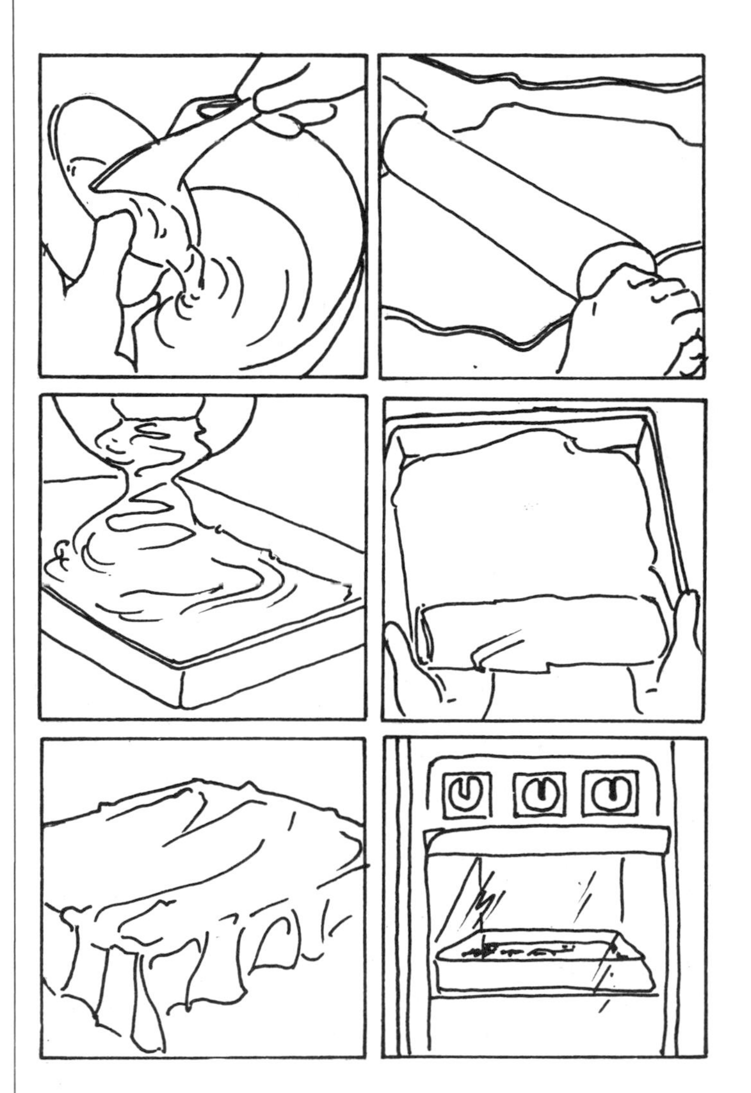

Walnut pie is prepared in the same way. Instead of semolina put a grated, rather sour apple into the filling.

Yugoslavia

CAKES WITH SUET — "SALTCHITCHI"

50 gr yeast
1 teaspoon sugar
3—4 tablespoons lukewarm milk
1 tablespoon flour
2 egg yolks
100 gr sugar
500 gr flour
lemon rind
1 teaspoon salt
1—2 dl lukewarm milk
250 gr pork suet
1 cup apricot jam
powdered sugar for dusting

Crumble yeast, add sugar, lukewarm milk and flour. Mix well and leave in a warm place to rise.

Beat egg yolks and sugar until foamy, add creamed yeast, flour, milk, grated lemon rind and some salt. Work out into a medium hard smooth dough. It is well kneaded when small bubbles appear and when it does not stick to the walls of the dish any more. Sprinkle with some flour and leave in a warm place to stand about 20—30 minutes and rise a little.

In the meantime remove thin skin and veins from pork suet, crush it well or grind in a meat grinder. Roll out dough, spread suet over it evenly, then fold as follows:

fold left third to the right, then right third over it. Do the same with lower and upper thirds. After that leave to stand for about 15 minutes. Repeat this procedure 3—4 times. When rolled out for the last time, cut into squares or triangles. Put some apricot jam on each little piece, then fold into two, or make small rolls and place in ungreased cake tin. Bake in the oven preheated to 175—200 °C until nicely brown. While still warm, dust with powdered sugar and serve.

Roumania

FRITTERS WITH YEAST

25 gr yeast
300 gr flour
1 dl milk
30 gr sugar
2 egg yolks
40 gr butter or margarine
1 tablespoon rum
a pinch of salt
2 dl oil for frying
powdered sugar for dusting
apricot jam or fruit syrup (optional)

Crumble yeast, mix with a teaspoon of sugar and a tablespoon of milk and leave in a warm place to rise.

Sift flour, heat a little, pour in lukewarm milk, add sugar, egg yolks, melted butter or margarine and the creamed yeast. Mix all well and work into a smooth

dough with a mixing spoon until it does not stick any more to the walls of the dish. Dust with flour and leave in a warm place to rise (it is ready for frying when it has doubled in bulk).

Heat oil well, mix the dough lightly. Dip a tablespoon into heated oil, take up spoonfuls of dough and drop into hot oil. Do not put too many at a time so that they can rise and fry evenly. When brown, drain on absorbent paper, arrange on a serving plate and dust with powdered sugar. Serve warm. Apricot (or other) jam or some fruit syrup can be served with fritters.

Greece

GREEK CHRISTMAS CAKES — "MELOMACARONA"

2 dl refined olive (or plain) oil
150 gr sugar
1—1,5 dl orange juice
1 dl cognac
750 gr flour
1—2 teaspoons baking powder

For syrup:
2 dl water
200 gr sugar
200 gr honey
100 gr chopped walnuts
cinnamon to taste

Mix well oil, sugar, orange juice and cognac. Sift flour together with baking powder, add to the oil mixture and work slowly into a smooth dough. Divide dough into pieces the size of an egg, shape into oblongs and roll up into long rolls. Place in an ungreased cake tin and bake for about 30 minutes in the oven preheated to 175°C.

In the meantime bring to the boil water, honey and sugar and cook for 5 minutes. Pour this syrup over baked cakes. Leave to stand for 15 minutes, take out of syrup and arrange on a big serving plate. Sprinkle with chopped walnuts and with cinnamon if desired.

Yugoslavia

ROLLED-UP CHEESE PIE

500 gr thin layers of dough for the pie
750 gr fresh unsalted cow cheese
3 egg yolks
3 tablespoons double cream
50 gr sugar
50—70 gr raisins
lard for sprinkling and greasing
powdered sugar for dusting

Crush cheese well or pass through a sieve, add egg yolks, cream and sugar. Mix all well, add washed raisins, cleaned and wiped. In the end blend in stiffly beaten egg whites.

Place two layers of dough at a time on a clean table cloth, sprinkle each with melted lard, put some filling over one half of the dough layer, roll up and put into a cake tin greased with lard. Sprinkle with melted lard again. Repeat until all the dough layers and filling have been used. Bake in the oven preheated to 175°C until brown.

Cool the pies a little, then dust with powdered sugar which can be mixed with vanilla sugar.

Greece

CAKES WITH WALNUTS AND RAISINS

100 gr butter or margarine
140 gr sugar
4 egg yolks
140 gr ground walnuts
2 bars grated chocolate
60 gr raisins
60 gr flour
a pinch of baking powder
butter or oil for greasing
flour for dusting

Beat well butter or margarine, add sugar, mix together shortly, then add egg yolks one by one mixing all the time. Beat further until smooth and creamy. Add ground walnuts, finely grated chocolate and cleaned raisins, washed and wiped. Sift flour, mix with baking powder. Beat egg whites stiffly. Add flour and beaten egg whites to creamed egg yolks in turn and slowly, stirring continuously.

Grease a narrower long cake tin with butter or oil, dust with flour, turn in the prepared mixture, bake for about 25—30 minutes in the oven preheated to 175°C.

When done, take out of the tin carefully and cool. It can be dusted with powdered sugar or covered with chocolate icing. Prepare the icing as follows: heat over steam until soft 100 gr chocolate with 2 tablespoons of milk. Then add butter, mix and pour over the cake. Cut into squares when the icing gets hard.

Greece

APPLE FRITTERS

2 eggs
1/2 l milk
25 gr fresh yeast
a pinch of salt
40 gr sugar
250—300 gr flour
1 kg apples
lard for frying
powdered sugar with vanilla for dusting

Mix well eggs, milk, crumbled yeast, salt and sugar, add flour. Work well into a smooth, soft batter (slightly thicker then for pancakes), leave to rise.

Peel apples, grate and add to batter, mix and leave again to stand a little.

Heat lard, dip a tablespoon in it, take up bits of dough with apples and fry until brown. When fried, drain on paper, sprinkle with powdered sugar and serve warm.

Yugoslavia

WALNUT TORTE

5 eggs
125 gr sugar
125 gr walnuts
20 gr breadcrumbs
1/2 vanilla-bean or 1 sachet vanilla sugar
butter for greasing
flour for dusting

For filling:
100 gr butter
100 gr sugar
1 coffee cup strong black coffee (or 3 teaspoons Nestlé coffee)
ground walnuts for garnishing

Beat egg yolks and sugar until foamy, add vanilla. Beat egg whites stiffly. Add breadcrumbs, ground walnuts and egg whites in turn to creamed egg yolks. Turn into a greased round cake tin dusted with flour. Bake for 25—30 minutes in the oven preheated to 175°C.

Walnuts can be browned a little before grinding to get a specific pleasant flavour.

For filling, beat butter and sugar, pour in coffee gradually and mix until butter absorbs coffee. Leave in a cool place to harden a little.

Cool baked dough and split into two equally thick parts. Spread filling over one and cover it with the other layer. Cover the whole cake with the rest of filling and sprinkle with ground walnuts.

Roumania

GRANDMA'S TORTE

8 egg whites
250 gr sugar
30 gr flour
250 gr ground hazelnuts or walnuts or almonds
butter for greasing
flour for dusting

For filling:
8 egg yolks
250 gr sugar
150 gr chocolate
250 gr butter or margarine
12—15 whole hazelnuts for garnishing

Beat egg whites into a stiff foam, add sugar gradually and beat until glossy and quite stiff. Add ground haleznuts and then add flour. Grease a deeper pan or a round cake tin and dust with flour. Turn in the prepared mixture and bake for 20—25 minutes in the oven preheated to 150—175°C. When done, turn out carefully and cool.

For filling, beat egg yolks and sugar until foamy, add chocolate softened over steam. Mix all over steam until thick. Draw aside and cool. Mix well butter or margarine and stirring constantly add to it the cooled cream bit by bit, mix and leave in a cool place to harden a little.

Split cooled dough to make 3—4 layers. Spread each layer with cream before putting the next. Then cover the whole cake with cream filling and sprinkle with browned ground or chopped hazelnuts.

Garnish with whole hazelnuts.

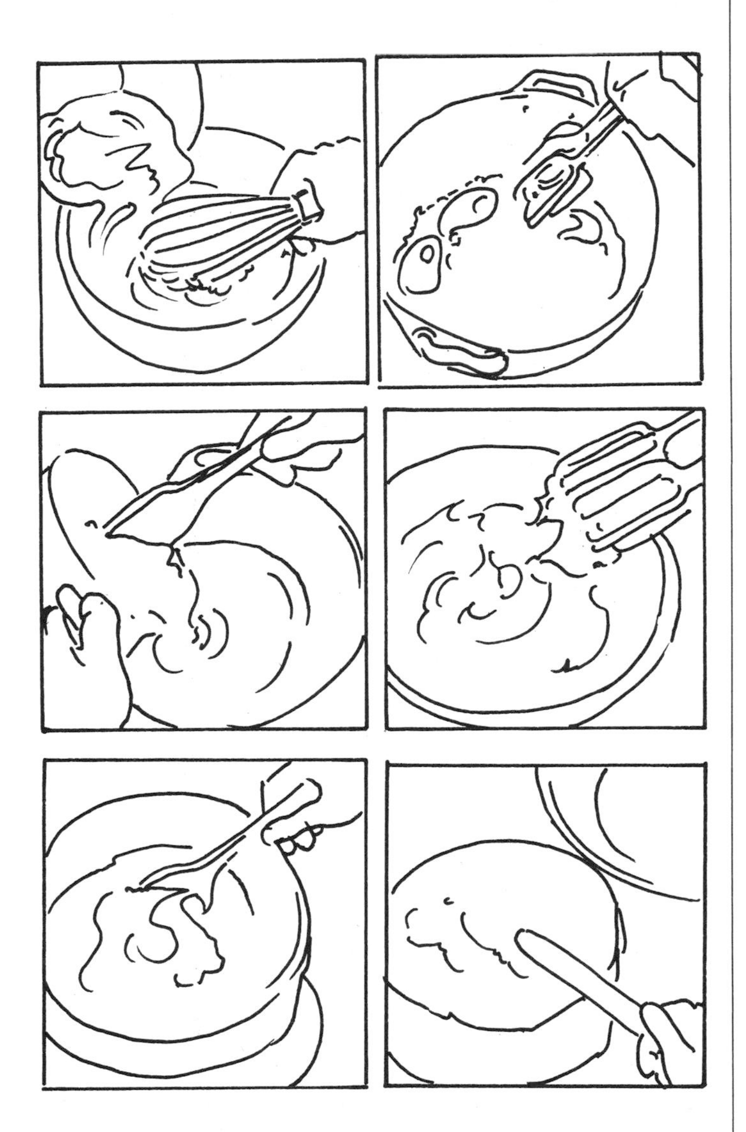

Yugoslavia

PLUM TORTE

For dough:
6 eggs
100 gr sugar
1 sachet vanilla sugar
40 gr breadcrumbs
150 gr ground hazelnuts or walnuts
1 tablespoon rum
butter for greasing
flour for dusting

For filling:
1 kg plums
75—100 gr sugar
1 small piece cinnamon bark
1 clove
1/4 l water
30 gr edible starch
1/4 l double cream
20 gr sugar
3—4 sheets gelatin (or cream hardener)

For garnishing:
1/4 l double cream (or 2 bags whipped cream powder)
1 tablespoon sugar
1 sachet vanilla sugar
100 gr sliced almonds

Beat egg yolks, sugar and vanilla until foamy. Beat egg whites stiffly. Add to egg yolks slowly and in turn, egg whites, breadcrumbs, hazelnuts and rum in the end.

Grease a round cake tin with butter, dust with flour (or breadcrumbs) or line with tin foil and grease a little.

Turn in the prepared mixture. Heat oven to 180—190°C and bake for about 30—35 minutes. When done, cool and split to make two layers.

Wash plums, drain, remove stones and halve. Pour in water, add sugar, cinnamon and clove. Cook covered until plums are tender. Then pour out juice, add starch to it dissolved in cold water, cook shortly, put in plums, mix and cool.

Put aside about 16 cooled plum halves for garnishing. Drain them on a paper napkin. Put the rest of cooled plums over the dough layer. Whip cream slowly, add sugar, soaked and melted gelatin, then mix. Cover plums with this mixture. Put into the refrigerator to stand for about 20 minutes.

In the meantime whip cream for garnishing, add sugar and vanilla. Put the other dough layer over the cooled filling, cover the whole torte with whipped cream, garnish with plum halves and sprinkle the sides with sliced almonds.

Keep in a cool place (refrigerator). Cut into slices before serving.

Yugoslavia

VASA'S TORTE

5 eggs
75 gr sugar
10 gr flour
75 gr ground almonds
oil or margarine for greasing
flour for dusting

For filling:
1/8 l milk
1 tablespoon sugar
200 gr ground walnuts
4 egg yolks
60 gr sugar
juice and rind of 1 orange
3 bars of chocolate
150 gr butter

For topping:
250 gr sugar
2 dl water
6 egg whites
candied fruits or fruit from preserve for garnishing

Beat egg yolks and sugar until foamy. Beat egg whites stiffly. Add almonds, flour and egg whites to egg yolks in turn. Stir slowly.

Grease a cake tin well and dust with flour. Turn in the prepared mixture and bake for 20—25 minutes at 175°C. Cool when done. For filling, bring milk to the boil, add sugar, ground walnuts, cook shortly together stirring all the time, then cool. Mix egg yolks with sugar, add cooled walnuts, juice and grated rind of orange, grated chocolate or melted over steam. Beat butter well separately and blend it into the prepared walnut filling. Cover the cooled dough with this filling.

For topping, pour water over sugar and cook at medium heat until thick as honey. Beat egg whites stiffly and add them bit by bit to sugar syrup, stirring slowly. Mix over steam until smooth, thick and glossy. Draw aside and continue mixing until cool. Cover the filling with cold topping and level with a moistened knife. One part of it can be put into the confectioner's tube to garnish the whole torte with. Then garnish with candied fruits or fruit from preserve. Keep in refrigerator until serving.

Greece

ORIENTAL CAKES — "KOURABIETHES"

500 gr flour
1 teaspoon baking powder
250 gr butter
100 gr sugar
1 teaspoon gin (rum or similar brandy)
1 sachet vanilla sugar
1 egg yolk
some rose water
powdered sugar for dusting
1 sachet cloves for garnishing
butter for greasing
flour for dusting

Sift flour with baking powder. Cream butter with sugar, add rum, vanilla and egg yolk, mix. Add flour gradually, mixing all the time. Toss dough on to a board and knead into a smooth mixture. If too hard, add some more rum or one more egg yolk. Shape into a long sausage about 4 cm in diameter and cut into rounds about 1 cm thick with a sharp knife. Arrange in a greased and floured big cake tin. Press a clove into the middle of each cake. Bake for 20—30 minutes in the oven preheated to 150—175 °C. They must not get dark, but quite light brown. When still warm dust with powdered sugar. These cakes ("gurabiye" in Serbo-Croat) can remain fresh for 2—3 weeks.

This is probably the oldest Balkan cake recipe which has been preserved up to the present times. As the usual Christmas cakes they were mentioned at the end of the 4th Century by Ivan Chrysostom, born in Antioch and the patriarch of Constantinople at that time. Due to later converting of the Balkan nations, the recipe had probably spread from Byzantium to the whole peninsula.

Bulgaria

PLUM CAKE

700 gr plums
125 gr butter
125 gr sugar
1 sachet vanilla sugar
2 eggs
175 gr flour
1 teaspoon baking powder
100 gr ground almonds
butter for greasing
50 gr fried chopped almonds for sprinkling

Wash plums, drain, remove stones and halve.

Beat well butter, sugar and vanilla, add eggs one by one. Sift flour and mix with baking powder, blend in beaten butter, add ground almonds and mix.

Grease a round cake tin or pan (about 24 cm in diameter) with butter, turn in the prepared mixture. Arrange plum halves over with cut sides downwards, like fish scales.

Heat oven to 180 °C and bake for about 70 minutes. When done, take out, sprinkle with chopped almonds and with some sugar, if desired. Cut into slices when cold.

6

WINE

Wine has always had a special place not only in human diet, but also in human cultural history. Ever since ancient, mythological times its power to elate man, to bestow on him gaiety and the gift of speaking, made it in the eyes of men a "drink of gods". The poems of ancient poets were dedicated to it and one whole kind of poetry is from its very beginnings called "poems on wine" or anacreontic poetry, after the poet who was delighted with wine and its properties. People liked to peep into the world of the "divine drink", into the cellers of the old god Bacchus, whose face among the grapes with a grapevine wreath round his forehead was a frequent subject-matter of Renaissance painting. Poets were convinced that wine gave them inspiration, the ever mysterious creative fire. To them bread and wine were of the same importance, bread being essential for the power of the body and wine for the exultation of the spirit and for warm-hearted friendship. Poets and artistic Bohemians have always been apt to partake of "wine and fire", the two vital things stolen from Olympic immortality, without which we can hardly do even today and which, in moderate quantities, can only be useful.

The beneficial effect of wine on human body and its influence on the psychological and physical relaxation have been known for a long time and much has been written about it. It is not surprising, therefore, that the great scientist Pasteur said that wine was "the healtiest and the most hygienic of drinks". It should be pointed out, however, that it is no good exaggerating in anything and that good wine, when consumed moderately, if it does not secure for us Olympus and poetic inspiration, will certainly not harm our health and reputation.

Types of wine and their classification according to quality

Wine is a product obtained by fermentation of grape juice — must, or of crushed grapes. According to colour, wines are classified into white, rosé, light red and red wines.

White wines are obtained by fermentation of must rendered after crushing fresh grapes of uncoloured juice. As compared to red wines, white wines are of a considerably lighter taste due to a lower content of extract, more fresh because of their higher acidity and a greater quantity of carbon dioxide in them, and can vary a great deal depending on what sort of grapes they are made from and on which wine district they come from. White wines from southern wine districts are as a rule richer (thicker) in taste, with less acidity and of a slightly darker yellow colour than the wines from northern wine districts.

Rosé wines are made by crushing coloured sorts of grapes and straining the

juice immediately after that process, so that a small quantity of coloured matter goes into the must, which turns into rosé wine after fermentation. Rosé wines differ from white wines only in colour. In taste they are practically identical. These wines are getting more and more popular in recent years.

Light red wines are much darker than rosé, but much lighter than red wines. They have a considerably fuller taste than rosé, but they must not be astringent, i.e. they should not have a great quantity of tannin which has a mouth-puckering effect. Light red wines are made by a short fermentation of crushed grapes, 48 hours at the most, depending on the sort of grapes. After that the liquid part – wine, is separated from the hard part – husks, by way of dripping and straining.

Red wines vary from dark-ruby to dark-red colour, and they have more extract as compared to the above types, which makes them thicker and fuller in taste. Depending on the way of producing them, they are all more or less astringent, due to greater quantities of tannin. Generally speaking, red wines are considerably heavier than the other types. They are made by fermentation of crushed grapes of coloured sorts for at least 5—7 days, after which wine is dripped and the husks strained.

Although several thousand kinds of grapevine are known in the world, only about a hundred different sorts are grown in wine growing countries to obtain grapes for making wine, for using them as fresh fruit or for drying them. Depending on the quality of wine they render, all these sorts are divided into those for getting table wines, and those for getting quality, i.e. high-quality wines. Apart from the sort from which wine is obtained, its quality also depends on ecological conditions in which grapevines are grown, such as climate and soil, as well as on the technology applied in wine making. This is important to point out because a riesling, a white burgundy or a traminac can not be expected to be of light greenish-yellow colour, to have the marked flavour and freshness of their sort, if they are grown in the districts with the typical southern or mediterranean climate. Likewise, from the red wine sorts grown in the northern districts, it is not possible to obtain a red wine which is rich, thick, with plenty of coloured matter and with marked characteristics of the sort.

Table wines differ from quality wines in colour, but most of all in taste and smell. While high-quality white wines are greenish-yellow, olive or light yellow, table wines are of intensive yellow colour which is less appreciated. Table wines often lack acidity and freshness, they are "thinner" or rather emptier, and what is more they have ordinary wine smell, while quality and high-quality wines have the flovour of their sort and after 2—3 years of keeping, develop the typical bouquet – the fine smell that is the result of proper years-long maintaining and keeping of wines of quality.

White, light red and red wines can be of different quality, namely they can be table wines, table wines with geographic origin, quality wines with geographic origin and first-class (famous) wines with geographic origin. As for the quantity of sugar these wines contain, they can be dry, if they have up to 4 g/l sugar, half-dry, with 4—12 g/l sugar, half-sweet, with 12—50 g/l sugar and sweet, with more than 50 g/l sugar. The so-called "still" wines are those in which the pressure of carbon dioxide (CO_2) in bottled wine is less than 0,5 atmospheres. In addition to these "still" wines, there are those which have a greater quantity of carbon dioxide and consequently, a higher pressure in the bottles. They are the so-called sparkling wines which include carbonated wines, pearl wines and champagnes. They differ in quality as a result of the wine-making process, of the quantity of carbon dioxide, i.e. the pressure in the bottle. Their common characteristic is that they all produce the specific bang when opening the bottle, they sparkle when poured into the glass, "pearls" – bubbles of carbon dioxide go up to the surface in the glass, they have a tingling taste and are refreshing. As for the quantity of sugar they contain, sparkling wines, for example champagnes, can be with less then 15 g/l, then extra dry (with 12—20 g/l), dry (with 17—35 g/l), half-dry (33—50 g/l of sugar) etc.

In adition to "still" and sparkling wines, there are the so-called special wines which include the category of "yellow wines" such as tokay, jeres (sherry-wine), then the well-known Sauternes wines in France (Château Chalon) and Rhine and Mosel wines in Germany. They can be dry if the sugar content is 0-4 g/l, half-dry with 4—20 g/l and half-sweet and sweet with more than 20 g/l. These wines are made from slightly dried berries of grapes which turn into the state of raisins, or from berries taken up by the harmless mold (in favourable years), resulting in high sugar content in grape berries. Such berries are used to produce the world-famous dessert wines with high alcohol content (at least 15%) and a considerable sugar content.They are of golden-yellow colour and of specific aroma and smell which is similar to the smell of baked bread crust. In bad years berries do not have enough sugar content to get dessert (sweet) wines from them, so that they are used for making completely fermented (dry) wines, which are also of specific aroma and smell. As they have no sugar, they are recommended as aperitives.

Another category of special wines are the so-called fortified wines such as port, malaga, marsala, madeira, samos etc. They can be extra wines (with 0—6 g/l of sugar), dry (6—40 g/l), half-dry (40—80 g/l) and sweet (with more than 80 g/l of sugar). These wines keep well and are of specific aroma and smell.

Flavoured wines are the third category of special wines which include vermouth (light and dark), bermet, absinth etc. These wines are considered to be aperitive wines, because they are made with different compositions of aromatic and bitter herbs. Their usual alcohol content is about 16% and their sugar content varying.

How much wine should be served and drunk in the course of a meal?

One wine is served if there is only one course served. It can be riesling, rosé or some red wine, depending on the dish. It should be noted that rosé, similar to beer, can be drunk with almost any kind of dish. Two wines, one white and one red, are usually served if there is a smaller number of people (a narrow circle) at a meal, and if there is an appetiser to be served before the main course. Three wines, one white and two red, are served at a more formal lunch or dinner with a greater number of people present. Four to five wines are to be served if it is a festive meal or banquet, two white wines or rosé with the appetiser or fish and two red wines with the roast and cheese. Champagne is served at the end, or some well kept dessert or half-sweet wine.

The quantity of wine recommended to one person as optimal or maximal for one meal is quite relative and depends (apart from the individual factor) on the number and strength of the wines served, on the kind and quantity of food, on the duration of the meal etc. If it is an ordinary dinner, with only one main course served, then it is usually 2,5 to 3 dl per person. At a richer, more festive dinner one person usually consumes 6—8 glasses of wine, i.e. about 7 dl. If several different wines are served, the lighter ones served at the beginning of the meal should be drunk in greater quantities, at the expense of the stronger and heavier ones served towards the end of the meal.

To avoid mistakes in serving drinks in the course of a meal, the following instruction should be useful:

1. The most convenient aperitives are dry sparkling wines, dry (more bitter) vermouths, more bitter absinths, bermets and liqueurs.

2. With appertisers, fresh, dry white wines are served.

3. At the beginning of the meal lighter and younger wines are served, and at the end older wines, rich in extract.

4. Light dishes call for light wines and heavier dishes for heavier wines, white wines always come before the coloured, lighter before the heavy, acid some first, then less acid, then sweet in the end.

5. White wines are served with white meats and coloured with dark ones.

6. Fine dishes call for wines of high quality.

7. With sweets, only sweet or dessert wines are served.

8. Hot, sour-flavoured and piquant dishes are best with fresh dry wines.

9. Some good cognac (wine brandy) or some other fine brandy (apricot, cherry, pear, grape brandy and the like) are recommended for the end of the meal, with black coffee.

10. With soft or melted cheese white, dry wines are served, while with piquant, processed cheese with an aroma heavier red wines go better.

11. Wine should be cooled at the prescribed temperature and for every new wine corresponding glasses are brought, the shape of which depends on the type of wine.

12. Wine is not drunk with pickled salads, sour fruits and sweets made with chocolate.

Albania

Wine growing is located in the coastal parts of the country with Mediterranean climate, then in the river valleys and by the Ohrid and Prespan lakes. Table grapes consumed as fresh fruit or used for drying are produced more in Albania, mostly for religious reasons.

The local wine sorts are debin, vljash, koteks and others.

White and coloured wines from imported, cultivated sorts of high quality are Italien riesling, rkaciteli, white burgundy, aligote, cabernet, merlot, saperavi and barbera. Riesling is produced for export. White wines are generally of southern type.

Red wines intended for export and partly for the home market are cabernet, merlot, shesh and zi and their characteristic is strong colour and fulness of taste. Merlot is of dark red colour, with a full taste and some quantity of unfermented sugar.

Dessert wine malaga is of sweet taste, with a light caramel flavour, dark red in colour.

Aperitives such as fernet, are a kind of bitter with bitter, aromatic herbs added, similar to the Italian fernet bianko or the well-known anderberg. Bitters are drunk before the meal as aperitives, undiluted or freshened with some soda-water.

Digestives are strong drinks of the brandy type which can be drunk with black coffee after the meal such as the Skenderbey wine brandy, extra cognacs and grape brandies (Raki Rushi).

Some wine-growing terms:

vrshtë — vineyard
rush — grapes
verë — wine
e bardhë — white
rozë — rosé
e zezë — red
verë shkumëzuar — sparkling wine

Greece

There are 20 different wine sorts grown in Greece, both local and imported from France. Among the imported ones the best-known are Italian Riesling, Sylvaner, Gamay, Sengiovese, Trebbiano, Carignas, Cabernet Sauvignon, Merlot, Pinot nero and others. Wine growing districts are on Peloponnese, then in Attica, Thessaly, Epirus and on the Ionian and Aegean islands. In about 15 per cent of the total wine growing districts, i.e. on about 15.000 hectares, wines with certified geographic origin are produced.

White wines:

In Montania on Peloponnese, white wines of the local sort moshi filero are made, and white dessert wines of the sort white muscat, in the district of Patras. In Attica and Kanza, white wine of golden-yellow colour is made from the sort savariano. Attica is also the homeland of retsina, the wine made with fir-tree resin added, which together with sealing the wine amphoras with resin, dates back to the times of ancient Greece. Wines produced today by adding resin are not of special quality, but they are aperitive wines which go well with dishes such as mutton or octopus in garlic sauce. In the Zetsa district, white wines of the sort debina are made. On the island of Santorina (Thira) dry and sweet wines of the sort asiriko are made. Sweet white wine of the sort white muscat and dry wine of the sort ahiri are made on the island of Rhodes. Famous liqueur muscat wines from the sort white muscat, dry, half-dry and sweet are made on the island of Samos.

Red wines:

From the local sort agioritika (St. George) dark red wines, dry and sweet, are made in the district of Nemea on Peloponnese, and dark liqueur wines of heavy taste which bear the name of the sort — mavrodafni, in the district of Patras. Wines of the rosé type are produced from the sort rodicis (Patras Cephalonia). Aromatic liqueur wine from the sort laitiko is made on the island of Crete, as well as red wines of fine bouquet from the sorts kotsifaki and mendilaria. In northern Greece (the district of Aminteon) wine of very dark hue with a lot of acidity is made from the sort ksinomavron, which is not of exceptional qualities, except some of the type wines (Santa Laura, Aymetus, Demestica). At Zimnos red liqueur wines, sweet and full are made from the sort limnion, while aromatic and liqueur wines are made from Alexandrian muscat. Full and harmonious red wines from the sort amorgiano are made on the island of Rhodes.

In Greece there are also some wines with a corresponding mark, which are of very good, standard quality and which undergo regular control (Contessa, Himitos, Palinim Castel Danielis, Morea, Santa Marina, Kisamos, Chevalier de Rhodes and others).

Wines in use do not bear the name of the sort they are made from, but mostly the name of the broader district they originate from, or the name of the producer.

Some wine growing terms:

ΠΑΛΑΙΟΝ — PALEON — old
ΕΝΔΙΚΟΣ ΔΙΑΤΙΡΙΜΕΝΟΝ — ENDIKOS DIATIRIMENON — special wine
ΕΠΙΤΡΑΠΕΖΙΟ ΚΡΑΣΙ — EPITRAPEZIO KRASI — table wine
ΟΙΝΟΠΑΡΑΓΩΓΟΣ — INUPARAGOGOS — wine producer
ΟΙΝΟΠΟΙΕΙΟΝ — INOPIION — cellar
ΠΑΡΑΓΩΓΝ ΚΑΙ ΕΜΦΙΑΛΟΣΙΣ — PARAGOGI KE EMFIALOSIS — produced by and bottled
ΟΙΝΟΣ ΛΕΥΚΟΣ — INOS LEFKOS — white wine
ΟΙΝΟΣ ΕΡΥΘΡΟΣ — ΜΑΥΡΟΣ — INOS ERITROS — MAVROS — red wine
ΡΟΖΕ ή ΚΟΚΚΙΝΕΛΙ — ROZE — rosé
ΞΗΡΟΣ — KSIROS — dry wine
ΑΦΡΩΔΕΣ ΚΡΑΣΙ — AFRODES KRASI — sparkling wine
ΣΤΑΦΥΛΙ — grapes
ΓΛΥΚΟ — GLIKO — sweet wine
ΗΜΙΓΛΥΚΟ — IMIGLIKO — half-sweet
ΜΠΟΥΚΑΠΙ — BUKALI — bottle
ΣΥΓΚΟΜΙΔΗ — SIGOMIDI — vintage

Aperitives: vermouth.

Digestives: strong drinks such as ouzo — brandy to which mastic resin has been added and similar to the one produced in Macedonia, then the grape brandy named tsipouro, and the well-known Metaxa brandy.

Bulgaria

In Bulgaria there are over 200.000 hectars of vineyards and the annual wine production is about 3,000.000 hl, of which even 80% is exported. The areas under grapevine are divided into five wine districts in which various sorts of vine are cultivated and various types and qualities of wine made. In the north of Bulgaria south of the Danube, from Vidin all the way to the town of Silistra, the sorts mostly grown are gamza or kadarka, zartchin (prokupac), pamid (plovdina) and dimyat (smederevka). This district is well-known for light and red wines.

The eastern district is along the coast of the Black Sea and is well-known for the white sorts dimyat, rkaciteli, Italian riesling, petaksa (leanjka) and pamid. "Still" and sparkling white wines are produced from the above sorts.

In central Bulgaria wine growing is located round the cities of Karlova and Trnova. Well-known wines from this district are Karlova misket (muscat and aromatic) and the dessert wine Trnova.

South-eastern part of Bulgaria specializes in making coloured wines, red and light red ones, such as the light wine pamid and the darker and fuller wines mavrud and cabernet.

In the district from Kustendil to Melnik, in south-west Bulgaria, white wines of the Italian riesling sort and rkaciteli are made, and in the south red wine melnik, with high alcohol content.

White wines:
Dimyat (smederevka) is white table wine, light and fresh in taste, with a discrete smell of grapes. Misket is white wine known at the market as Karlova misket, with a muscat smell and of dry and soft taste. Vinena (proslava) is table wine obtained from the sort of the same name. Songular misket is a fresh, light and dry wine of discrete muscat smell. Italian riesling is produced as dry, or as more or less sweet in taste.

Red wines:
Dry red wine gamza is a ruby wine of mostly darker colour, of harmonious taste and typical smell of the sort it is made from. In good years the quality of this wine can match the burgundy wines from France. Melnik is very thick wine of dark red colour. It is made by mixing the approximately same quantities of the sort mavrud and alicant bushe. Mavrud is the wine from the sort of the same name, thick, full, of harmonious taste and with high alcohol content. Pamid (plovdina) is wine of the rosé type, light, of light colour and a tender aroma. Among dry red wines the following should be mentioned: mehandziysko (cabernet), meknik, vojevodsko, zagore and trakiya.

Dessert wines:
In Bulgaria about 10—15 per cent of the total quantity produced are the dessert wines (e.g. varna) and the various types of madeira, marsala and malaga, which are known for their specific colour (dark yellow), for their aroma, strength and sweet taste (Madaru, Sozopol, Tchirpin). Out of red dessert wines of the cabernet, sauvignon and merlot types, sliven and haskovo should be mentioned.

Sparkling wines:
Well-known wines of this kind are white iskra, white magura, red magura (muscat), lazur and others.

Aperitives:
Light and dark vermouths are produced in Bulgaria, both sweet (Orpheus,

aglica, vinprom) and bitter (amaro) ones.

Digestives:
Among the strong drinks the ones of the cognac (wine brandy) type should be mentioned: pliska (40%), prslav (42%), pomorje (41%), aheloy (42%) and others.

Some wine-growing terms:

Лозова пръчка — vine
Лозя — vineyard
Бутилирано — bottled
Бяло вино — white wine
Червено вино — red wine
Сухо вино — dry
Сладко вино — sweet
Искрящо вино — sparkling
С остатъчна захар — semi-dry or sweet

Roumania

Climatic conditions for growing wine and table grapes are very favourable, and wine-growing in Roumania can be divided into six districts, which differ in soil and climate and consequently in the character and type of wines. They bear the name of the sort they are made from, of the place or district they come from.

White wines:
The sorts such as feteaska alba (leanjka, white fetjarska), Italian riesling, sauvignon, grey burgundy and green silvanoe, in Transilvania, render light and fresh white wines. From the sort feteasca alba, white muscat and grey burgundy, in Moldavia, sweet white wines are made. Grey and white burgundy, Italian riesling and sauvignon are the sorts grown in Dobrudza, between the Black Sea and the Danube, where the well--known white wine, murfaltar, of amber colour is also produced. From the sorts kreace (Banat riesling) and feteasca, light table wines are made in Banat. In the north west district from the sorts feteasca, grey and white burgundy, ordinary table wines are obtained.

Red wines:
In Transilvania, light and tasty wines of ruby colour are made from the sorts negru moale (kadarka), Babeasca neagra, cabernet sauvignon and merlot. In the south Carpatian district, quality wines caberne sauvignon, merlot, red burgundy and Feteasca negra (red fetjarska, leanjka) are made. In Moldavia, light wines are made from the local red sorts. In the district of Dobrudza merlot and cabernet sauvignon are grown, and in the north-west, local sorts for making rosé and light red wines.

Some wine growing terms:

Vie — vine
Viile — vineyard
Strugure — grapes
Recolta — vintage
Vin superior — quality wine
Vin de masa — table wine
Vin usor — light wine
Imbuteliat — bottled
Vin alb — white wine
Vin rosu — red wine
Vin rose — rosé
Sec — dry
Dulce — sweet
Spumos — sparkling

Sparkling wines, aperitives and digestives:
In Roumania, mostly white wines are produced (80%) and the rest (20%) are coloured wines. As for sugar content they can be up to 4 g/l, dry with 5—15 g/l, half-dry with 16—40 g/l, half-sweet with 41—80 g/l and sweet with more than 80 g/l of sugar. Aromatic wines of the vermouth type are also produced.

The following strong drinks are produced: cognac, i.e. wine brandy with the name of the producer or of the place in which it is made (Zarja, Vasluj, Napoka, Triumf, Ovidia, Datchia, Mlorica, Milkov, Dunarea, Murfaltar). Plum brandy — shljivovitsa is known under the name of Tuica (cujka), and the old plum brandy is called Tuica batrima.

Turkey

Grapevine is wide-spread all over Turkey, but for religious reasons people do not consume wine, so that only 3 per cent of the total production of grapes is used to make wine. There are six wine-growing districts in this country with different climates.

White wines:
In the district by the Black Sea, high quality sorts are grown, such as semiyon and Rhine riesling. In the north, round Istanbul and Tekirdaga, white wines are made, some of which are quality wines (Guzel Marmara — dry and sweet, Marmara Incisi and Beyaz). From the sort semiyon, Trakiya is made.

Red wines:
In central Anadolia the most wide-spread sort is the local, table sort-dimrit, the grapes of which are very aromatic and used for making red wine.

By the Black Sea, in addition to table sorts, some of which are used for making light table wines (e.g. sorta japundzek), the sorts imported from France are also grown, cabernet, merlot, red burgundy and others, from which red wines of very good quality are obtained. Wines in Turkey are mostly type wines and their names indicate the districts they come from (Ankara, Göreme, Trakiya, Sarabi and others). Red wines marked for their quality are Trakiya, Buzbay, Horozkarasi, Kalicik, Izmir etc. Those are dry wines of fine aroma and moderately full, and wines of high quality are Navince, Misket and Vinkol.

Strong drinks:
The well-known aromatic Turkish brandy Yeni Raki is of anise flavour (similar to mastic). Cognac of very good quality is also produced. There is also a number of whiskeys of local production.

Some wine-growing terms:

Asma — vine
Üzüm Bagi — vineyard
Üzüm — grapes
Kaliteli Sarap — quality wine
Beyaz Sarap — white wine
Siyah Sarap — red wine
Kirmizi Sarap — rosé
Sekerrsiz — dry
Sekerli — half-sweet
Normal Sarap — table wine
Sampanya — champagne

Yugoslavia

Ecological conditions (soil and climate) and the variety of grapevines in Yugoslavia are such that it is possible to make a great number of quality and first-class wines.

White wines:
Light Italian riesling, Rhine riesling, green silvanac, sauvignon, traminac, white burgundy and shipon (furmint) are grown in Slovenia and in the valley of the Drava river. From these sorts excellent, quality white wines of very fine aroma are made, of fresh taste and olive colour — dry, half-dry and sweet. Rebula and tokay are made in the highlands round Dobrovo. Traminac, Italian riesling, green silvanac, white burgundy, rizvanac and shipon are made in the northern, continental part of Croatia, and they are mostly dry wines with the exception of traminac which is made as half — sweet and sweet. Along the coast thick southern wines of amber colour are made, such as vugava, marshzina and poship. High-quality sort krstatch is grown in Montenegro. The wine is of light yellow colour, of full and fresh taste and specific aroma. Italian riesling, traminac, muscat otonel, semiyon and sauvignon are the white wines of Vojvodina. They are high-quality wines, greenish, fresh and tasty. In Serbia the dry wine župljanka is made, of full taste and

similar in quality to Italian riesling, then neoplanta (half-dry and half-sweet), and in the district of Smederevo, smederevka, Italian riesling, sauvignon, semiyon and župljanka. In Kosovo, Italian riesling, sauvignon, semiyon, žilavka and smederevka are made. In Macedonia smederevka is made more and more, then belan (white grenash), žilavka and Italian riesling. Those wines are full, light yellow in colour and of moderate acidity.

Coloured wines

In Slovenia, round Kras and Sežana, teran is the well-known quality red wine. In Croatia, rosé and red wines are mostly made from frankovac, of a tender aroma, fresh and tasty, and on the Croatian coast thick red wines of dark-red colour and slightly astingent, such as plavac and babitch. Montenegro is well-known for the vranac, high-quality dry wine of dark-red colour. Merlot is also made there. The local sort blatina is well-known in Bosnia and Herzegovina, which gives a full and fresh wine of dark-red colour and of an aroma which eventually turns into a fine bouquet. In Serbia, going to Svetozarevo, various red wines are made, the best-known of which is prokupac. The others are red burgundy, red gamay, frankovka, merlot, cabernet etc. The rosé types of wine are also produced from prokupac. Red wines of high quality are made in Kosovo, such as red burgundy, red gamay, merlot, cabernet and frankovka, and in Macedonia vranac, prokupac, kratoshiya, refoshko, red gamay, merlot, red burgundy etc., all of which are mostly half-dry or dry wines, tasty and of a fine aroma.

Sparkling wines

These wines are made in Slovenia and Gornja Radgona in the usual way of making champagne wines, naturally sparkling and dry. Sparkling wines of the pearl and champagne types are also made in Serbia.

Strong drinks

Strong drinks are made in Yugoslavia with the help of most modern technological processes and they are traditionally used as aperitives. They are numerous and varied and can be divided into fruit brandies and grape brandies. Of the former, the best-known is shljivovitsa, plum brandy, made strong (40—50%) or soft (about 25%). Very renowned are the plum brandies which have been kept in oak casks for eight and twelve years (e.g. Manastirka, 12 years old, produced by Prokupac, and Takovo, 8 years old, produced by Gornji Milanovac). Juniper berry brandy, klekovatcha, is made in considerable quantities in Serbia. Fruit brandy krushkovatcha is the pear brandy of 40% strength. From apples (jonathan and gold delicious), brandy of the kalvados type is made, of 40% strength. Much smaller quantities of apricot-brandy and cherry-brandy are produced.

Lozovatcha (grape brandy), komovitsa (crushed husks brandy) and vinjak (wine brandy) belong to the other category of brandies made in Yugoslavia. There is a great number of wine brandies of different quality and age. The oldest are those 5—8 years old, of 40% strenght. The above-mentioned brandies are used to make a great number of herb brandies. Very bitter is the lincura brandy, made from the bitter root lincura (Gentiana lutea) and of 52% strength. A great number of herb brandies are neutral or bitter. Mastica is made in Macedonia with the mastic resin, of 40% strength, which is drunk with some water added. Various bitters, vermouths and absinths are also produced (the well-known producer is Istravino from Rijeka).

Some wine-growing terms:

Belo vino — white wine
Crno vino — red wine
Roze — rose
Suvo — dry
Poluslatko — half-sweet
Stono vino — table wine
Penušavo — sparkling

BALCAN COUNTRIES
GERMANY
CZECHOSLOVAKIA
USSR
SWITZERLAND
Zürich
AUSTRIA
Wien
Donau
HUNGARY
Budapest
RUMANIA
București
Danau
YUGOSLAVIA
Beograd
BULGARIA
Sofiya
ALBANIA
Tiranë
ITALIA
Roma
GREECE
Athinai
TURKEY
Ankara
Azovskoye more
Black sea
Adriatic sea
Tyrrhenian sea
Ionian sea
Aegean sea
Mediterranean sea
AFRICA

7

KEY TO UNUSUAL WORDS AND TERMS AND INDEX

AYVAR — *(ajvar)* is the word of Turkish origin for a special kind of salad made of red paprikas and aubergines. Paprikas and aubergines are first baked (in the oven or on top the stove), then peeled and ground or minced. Then they are cooked at low heat, first without oil, and then oil is added. When done, ayvar must be a homogenous mixture easy to spread, to which salt and some stronger vinegar are added towards the end of the frying process. Some chopped garlic can also be added, but it is usually done just before serving. This salad is used as an accompaniment to various meat and offal dishes, as bread spread and as an accompaniment to hot cornbread.
It can also be prepared from unripe tomatoes or from mixed vegetables (paprikas, aubergines, tomatoes, string-beans etc.).

BUREK — (in Turkish, *börek*) is a pie, a bakery product made of thin layers of rolled out dough (kore), with a meat, offal, cheese, vegetable or fruit filling. The dough layers are abundantly sprinkled with oil. In all the Balkan countries burek is sold at the baker's or in specialized burek-shops (burekdzinitse). It is most often eaten for breakfast or as a mid-morning snack.

DJUVETCH — *(djuveč)* is the name both of the pan in which the dish is prepared and of the dish itself. The dish is a vegetable and meat stew, which is baked in the oven and served in the pan in which it is baked — the djuvetch — usually an earthenware or enamelled pan of oval or oblong shape.

DRINKS — in addition to thick or drinking yoghurt, there are other special drinks in the Balkans which are very healthy, refreshing and even curative.
The best known refreshing drink greatly consumed in summer months is:

BOZA — the name is of Persian origin and so is most probably the drink itself. It used to be sold by the boza-sellers (bozadziye) in their shops, on the market counters or in little carts in the streets, with the sellers shouting loudly to attract customers. Today boza is most often produced and sold in pastry shops. Recipe for boza is very simple and it is easily prepared at home, too:

5 l boiled water
200 gr maize flour
10 gr brewery yeast
70—80 gr sugar
10—15 gr browned sugar (caramel)

Dissolve maize flour in some boiled water, then mix it into the whole quantity of boiled water. Simmer for at least two hours. Cool a little and strain through a sieve or gauze. Add crumbled yeast, sugar and caramel to strained boza, mix well and leave in a warm room to stand for about 24 hours, i. e. until small bubles start to appear on the surface. That means that the drink is ready and that it should be put into the refrigerator. Lemon juice or some cold milk can be added to boza before drinking.
The other popular Balkan drink is:

SALEP — consumed most often in winter months, as it is drunk warm. The name is of Arabic origin and so is most probably the drink itself. "Salep" in Arabic means full, fresh crocus bulbs with which this drink is made. The bulbs are washed in cold water, then dipped for a short time into boiling water. After that they are kept to dry in the sun or in a dry, draughty place. Dried bulbs are kept to prepare the drink when needed. Then they are cooked in very sweetened water until a rather thick, sweet liquid of specific flavour is obtained. When served, it is sprinkled with some ground ginger or cinnamon.
At any time of the year or day people in the Balkans drink:
BLACK COFFEE — (kahva, kava, kafa). The name is of Arabic origin so it is certain that the Turks, with whom it came to the Balkans, took it over from the Arabs. Most probably coffee used to be consumed in the Balkan countries even before the 16th century, because cafés existed before the end of that century. It had been recorded that there was a "very nice café" working in Sarajevo in 1591. So the first cafés in Europe were in Bosnia (Yugoslavia) and not in Paris (1671) or in Vienna (1683) as it is usually thought. Coffee was used as medicine at first, with warning that overdoses of it mean poison.
Preparing black coffee used to be a ritual in old times, from roasting it in special metal vessels over open fire, to serving it in small cups without handles called "fildzans". It was prepared exclusively in special small copper pots with tin-covered insides, narrower at the top and with a long handle. These "dzezvas", as they used to be called, are made today of enamelled metal or fireproof glass, but the shape has remained unchanged. Coffee must be very finely ground. It used to be achieved by crushing and pounding it with a mallet in a special vessel called "dibek".
On teaspoonful of ground coffee is put into the coffee pot for each cup of coffee and poured over with the corresponding quantity of boiling water. The pot is put back on the stove to boil. Then it is drawn aside, waiting for the foam to settle, then put back on the hot stove to boil again. It is brought to the boil like this three times. Then 1—2 teaspoons of cold water are poured over and the foam stirred gen tly. A well prepared coffee must have "kaymak" on top, i.e. foam with tiny bubbles. Sugar can be put in when making it, or served separately and each teaspoon of coffee calls for one teaspoon of sugar. In some parts a lump of

sugar is kept in the mouth and unsweetened coffee sipped over it.
Black or Turkish coffee (in Turkey it is called Greek coffee!) is served after meals. It is also served between meals and to guests as a rule. On such occasions coffee is served with Turkish delight, fruit juice or brandy. Drinking coffee used to mean that the visit is over, so that such coffee was given the name "sikter" coffee, because "sikter" in Turkish means "go away".

KACHKAVAL — *(kačkavalj)* is the cheese produced either of sheep milk only, or of a mixture of sheep and cow milk. It is made in all the Balkan countries, manufactured or produced in mountain households. In country households it is still given the traditional shape similar to a shorter thick suasage, while the industrial products are in the shape of wheels, slightly smaller then that of the hard cheese with "eyes" called ementaler. It belongs to the category of hard cheeses with a crust.

KAYMAK — *(kajmak)* is the word of Arabic origin for a dairy dish most often made of cow milk. Kaymak of best quality is produced in the vicinity of Kraljevo, Užice and Tchatchak, the towns in Serbia (Yugoslavia). Milk is boiled and cooled and the skin that forms on top is skimmed off and arranged one by one in special wooden vessels. Each layer of skin is sprinkled with salt. If kaymak is used at once, then it is the so-called young kaymak, and if the full wooden dish is left to stand for 15—20 days at the temperature of 15—20°C, then kaymak ferments and ripens and the so-called old kaymak is obtained. As it is perishable, it should be kept at low temperatures. For the time being it is produced only in the households in the country or in peasants' cooperatives, but the peasants bring it to country fairs and city markets.

LEPINYA — *(lepinja)* is the smaller variety of pogatcha, round, flat, usually home-made bread. Warm lepinyas are usually eaten with kaymak or tchevapchitchi inside. Today they are often served in restaurants instead of bread.

MEZE — see the text on appetisers in the preface. It is served, however, not only before meals or until all the guests assemble, but also between meals, when friends or relatives gather in some restaurant, open-air café or at somebody's home.

OKRA — *(bamija, bamnja* or in Turkish, *bamya)* is fruit of the plant of the same name, which is grown and cultivated mostly in the south-eastern parts of the Balkans. In diet it is used when green and just formed, and it has the shape of a crooked pod with a point at the top, which is cut off after washing. The fruit is covered with tiny hairs, which turn into a rough, hard skin as the fruit ripens. Okra is considered to be of special importance in diet, as it contains some aromatic substances and a great deal of vitamins. One fruit (pod) contains about 18 mg of vitamin C and considerable quantities of provitamin A, and it is also full of organic matter of coagulating quality. Okras are exported to the western European market, especially from Bulgaria.

POGATCHA — *(pogača)* is the name of round, flat bread, usually home-made, prepared for guests or on special festive occasions. Most often it is prepared without yeast, but with baking powder or mineral water instead.

TEPSIYA — *(tepsija)* is the round copper baking pan, usually rather big, in which vegetable or meat dishes, pies or breads are baked in the oven, or in summer taken to the baker's in the neighbourhood. The inside is covered with tin and the outside kept as shiny as possible, as tepsiyas used to hang on the walls of old-fashioned kitchens as decoration and the housewife's pride.

TURSHIYA — *(turšija,* in Turkish, *turšu)* in the name for pickled vegetables or fruit or a combination of vegetables and fruit with aromatic herbs added, or fruits and plants which produce fermentation or contribute to conservation. Turshiya is most often made with paprikas (special pointed kind), then with cucumbers, green tomatoes, carrots, cauliflower, cabbage, courgettes etc. Vegetable is arranged in big glass jars and poured over with the water and salt solution, while for some kinds of vegetables concentrated vinegar is also added. In country households turshiya is still prepared in wooden barrels or similar vessels.
Fruit is also used for turshiya, most often uncultivated apples and pears. The Turkish 17th century chronicler, Evliya Tchelebiya, mentions the turshiya which is made in the Bosnian town of Travnik (Yugoslavia) from a special kind of pears, called "karamut". Good, hard pears are put into a scrubbed wooden barrel, covered with water, then with a linen cloth on top and left to ferment. When pickled, they are used as salad.

INDEX

Page numbers shown in *italics* refer to color illustrations.

ALBANIA

BULGARIA

GREECE

ROUMANIA

TURKEY

YUGOSLAVIA